GLORY DAYS

Bruce Springsteen in the 1980s

GLORY DAYS

Bruce Springsteen in the 1980s

DAVE MARSH

PANTHEON BOOKS · NEW YORK

Library of Congress Cataloging-in-Publication Data

Marsh, Dave.
  Glory days.

  1. Springsteen, Bruce.   2. Rock musicians—
United States—Biography.   I. Title.
ML420.S77M35   1986   784.5'4'00924 [B]   86-42620
ISBN 0-394-54668-7

Produced by Rapid Transcript, a division of March Tenth, Inc.
Composition by Folio Graphics Company, Inc.

Manufactured in the United States of America

For Sasha and Kristen:
Take a good look around. . . .

Once I spent my time playing tough guy scenes
But I was living in a world of childish dreams
Someday these childish dreams must end
To become a man and grow up to dream again
Now I believe in the end
Two hearts are better than one

—"TWO HEARTS"

ACKNOWLEDGMENTS

To begin with, there's Sandra Choron. Sandy served this book from the day I thought it up, first as agent, then as designer and packager. But that's not what she really did; mostly, she did what she has done for the best part of a decade, which is make me believe in myself. Writing is a pretty easy job, compared to some, but when you're in the midst of a difficult and overdue project, it has its own terrors. Because of Sandra Choron, I can tackle those head-on, without looking over my shoulder. In the words of a singer we both love, she "makes my burden a little bit lighter/Makes my life a little bit brighter." If I didn't begin by thanking her, I wouldn't be able to begin at all.

In the spring of 1986, I called Sandy—she was wearing her agent hat—and told her that this book wasn't going to come out that fall. She did not shoot me, for which she deserves undying gratitude. Instead, she listened to what I had to tell her about a still-secret Springsteen project that would alter not only the book's ending but its entire shape. Without knowing exactly what I was talking about, she told me I was right and not to worry. This is not what you pay someone for; this is how you find out that someone is really your friend.

A few days later Sandy and I went to see Wendy Goldwyn, my editor at Pantheon. I told Wendy the same sketchy story.

She didn't throw me out of the twenty-eighth-floor window; she listened, said okay, and asked me to step down the hallway to the office of her boss, Andre Schiffrin, who runs the joint.

I had never met Andre Schiffrin, but he didn't run out into the hallway, break open the fire alarm box, and murder me with the axe that he'd have found there. He listened, and then he said Pantheon would get the book out anyway as quickly as it could after the secret project became a reality.

When I say each of these people is responsible for the existence of *Glory Days*, you see, I'm not kidding.

Bob Oskam deserves some credit, too. His empathetic editing consistently improves hasty writing and half-baked thinking (even if I did crumble some of his grammatical perfection). Thanks, Bob; let's do it again.

I'd also like to thank the following friends, neighbors, colleagues, and general rock and roll riffraff for various forms of assistance: Lee Ballinger, my indispensable partner in *Rock & Roll Confidential*; Frank Barsalona; Barry Bell; Bob Benjamin; Bob Brown; Glen Brunman; Harry Choron; George Cole; Greg Drew; Jim "Sneak Preview" Dunning, for many kinds of confidence building; Ben Eicher; Stanley Fischer; Dave Gahr; Barbara Hall; Karen Hall; John Hammond; Frank Joyce; Wayne King; Andrea Klein; Barbara Landau; Marilyn Laverty; Greil Marcus; Milo Miles; Bob Muller; Steve Perry; Neal Preston; Neil Quateman; Larry Regan; Maggie Renzi; Marta Renzi; Cynthia Rose; Harry Sandler; John Sayles; Toby Scott; Suzy Shaw, Craig Hankin, and the Springstones; Chris Sprowal; Daniel Wolff. (Apologies to Michael Balhaus for nearly decapitating him with that cue ball.) Also Leslie Nolen, Pantheon's steadiest unrecognized hand.

For putting up with my presence, I'd like to thank the E Street Band, who have given me and several million others a thousand and one unforgettable nights at the opera out on the turnpike. These were their glory days, too. And especially Little Steven, at whose feet I have studied soul music of many varieties.

If George Travis didn't exist, somebody would have had to invent a tour director who could work twenty-six-hour days, juggle several dozen egos, face down customs officials without blinking, always make the last flight out, and never complain (although he may sometimes be seen smirking). Travis doesn't do it alone, of course; he heads a crew shaped in the image of that philosophy, and watching them work together throughout the *Born in the U.S.A.* tour was an inspiration. In small ways and large, each of these members of the Springsteen crew went out of their way to help me throughout the tour, and I feel privileged to think of them as friends: Steven DePaul, Bob Thrasher, Lyle Centola, Jim McDuffie, Bruce Jackson, Terry Magovern, Jeff Ravitz, Bob Wein, Max Loubiere, Mike Grizel, Wayne Williams, and Drew Houseworth, with whom I once closed the Philadelphia Spectrum. Without Arthur Rosato, I don't know what I would have done for an ending. Thanks also to Denise Sileci for maintaining her usual air of complete calm, and to Carol Green for making sure everybody was where they were supposed to be.

Personal to Chris Chappel: This was *a lot* more fun than the last trip we went on.

Special thanks to Chuck Plotkin: We ought to do this again sometime in six or seven years.

Jon Landau is a person to whom I owe more things than space allows me to define or a simple thanks can begin to express. Hopefully, some of the rest is embedded in the story itself.

Extra special thanks to my personal Jersey Girl, Barbara Carr, for keeping me (and everybody else) in line. And to Sasha and Kristen Carr, who for the last three years have functioned well in a house where there was often only one parent. Someday, I hope, you'll look back on this and it will all seem funny.

Finally, I thank Bruce Springsteen—for many things, music and conversation included, but most of all for giving me a chance to tell a true story with a happy ending.

INTRODUCTION

"When the legend becomes fact, print the legend, not the fact," says the newspaper editor in John Ford's *The Man Who Shot Liberty Valance*, an aphorism as useful as it is dangerous. But neither Ford nor anyone else tells you what to do when the facts and legend converge.

This book is a sequel to *Born to Run: The Bruce Springsteen Story*, which I wrote in 1979. That was my first book, and I wrote it partly as an attempt to convince people who didn't like rock and roll and/or Bruce Springsteen that both were great and worthy subjects. *Glory Days* is something like the eleventh book that I've written or edited, and though I'm still capable of the occasional harangue, I now understand that they're for the benefit of my own soul as much, or more than, anyone else's. If you find these arguments convincing, thanks; if not, well . . . I do.

I don't mean to imply that *Glory Days* is any more "objective" than *Born to Run*. Even if I believed that objectivity existed, that's a quality this book couldn't possess. Bruce Springsteen is my friend, as is Jon Landau, as are most of the other characters in the tale. Barbara Carr, who plays a role or two herein, is my wife and, now that this book is finally written, we're feeling a hell of a lot friendlier, too.

Having all these relationships didn't make writing this book easier (although I suppose it made it possible). It's much more difficult to sit and think and pry and analyze when you're likely to be sitting next to one of the principals at dinner tomorrow night. *Glory Days* isn't authorized—in fact, I'm sure all the principals disagree with some things in it—but everybody concerned, especially Bruce and Jon, cut me miles of slack. I hope I've done the story and them some justice.

The personal backdrop for everything here is this: In 1974 Jon Landau and I went to see Bruce Springsteen and the E Street Band in a Boston bar. Both of us have seen a lot of music performed in a lot of bars but never with an effect like that. I can remember it now as clearly as I did the next morning—as a complete blur but the most glorious blur I'd ever run into.

What began that night is essentially the subject of *Born to Run: The Bruce Springsteen Story*. That book bottled enough lightning to make the best-seller lists. At the time, nobody had ever done this by writing a book about a rock musician of lesser celebrity than Elvis Presley or the Beatles. I was never under the illusion that the book sold for any reason other than its topic, which left me less surprised than most when the story continued to develop. *Born to Run* was updated in 1981, in the midst of the tour following *The River,* and the story by then had an air of completion, if not finality. But the protagonists continued to stir.

In 1984, a few weeks before *Born in the U.S.A.* was released, I proposed writing a sequel, on the grounds that the new album would create a new story, too different and complex to simply be tacked onto *Born to Run*. What did that mean? Something different then than now. Everybody who heard *Born in the U.S.A.* knew that there were hit singles on it, and that having hits would not only expand Bruce's audience but change it. It seemed to me that how he dealt with those changes and how he'd already dealt with the changes behind *Nebraska* would constitute a story.

But who would have dared to dream that the story would be this good? Certainly, nobody could have expected that Bruce would become quite this famous or that he would more than maintain his equilibrium, continuing to grow in the face of celebrity pressure. After all, hardly anybody else ever has. As for the rest, I didn't even know he was going to get married (which is okay, because neither did he). I'll take credit for being right about one thing, though, because it's the one that matters: This is a great story.

It's been about fifteen years since I first heard a test pressing of *Greetings from Asbury Park, New Jersey*. In that time, rock and roll dreams and dreamers have come and gone, but the music and the story behind it have remained a fascination every single day. As a writer rather than a rock star, I don't have to apologize for sittin' around thinking about it, which is a good thing, since, as numerous great men have said over the years, it's too late to stop now. But then, why would anybody want to?

GLORY DAYS

Bruce Springsteen in the 1980s

PART ONE

ONLY THE LONELY

Only the lonely
Know the way I feel tonight
Only the lonely
Know this feeling ain't right
—ROY ORBISON

1 DANCING IN THE DARK

His mother told him someday you will be a man,
And you will be a leader of a big ol' band
Many people comin' from miles around
To hear you play your music when the sun goes down.
—CHUCK BERRY

In the heart of a city, darkness gathers and a crowd accumulates—fifty, sixty, eighty thousand and more, pulling up in sports cars and jalopies, wearing custom-cut slacks and Levis on their last legs. They file into the stadium, a cross-section of white America, as much like football fans (only younger, more often female) as rock and rollers (but older, better mannered).

This could be any of half-a-hundred American towns in the summers of 1984 and 1985, but as it happens, the place is the Los Angeles Coliseum and the biggest tour in rock and roll history is just a night or two from its end. In the full moon's light, the Coliseum is beautiful, as ancient-looking and hallowed as its name. The air is clear and crisp, as befits the end of September anywhere, and it cools sharply as the night seeps in, so that the fans must huddle while milling for seats, snacks, and souvenirs.

The atmosphere crackles. The crowd knows what it's in for: a four-hour spectacular that is both sheer intoxication and a ritual invocation of the human spirit in the most peculiarly American way. For the first time since Elvis Presley, the king of rock and roll is native-born and, maybe for the first time ever, that crown is worn not lightly but with the full weight of adult awareness. In the

3

crowd almost everybody bounces with anticipation, but there are fewer drunken bleats than you'd expect. Nevertheless, beneath the taped music blaring from the huge stacks of speakers surrounding the stage, a hungry murmur builds.

Backstage, the singer has a few last-minute words with his aides, sneaks a final glance in the mirror, gives his wife a farewell kiss and, for the one hundred sixty-second time in the past eighteen months, steps through the dressing room door ready to rock. In the hallway, his bandmates already await him.

Together they set out for the stage, the singer's motorcycle boots clumping on the concrete. As they move, a few quips and good-luck grins are exchanged with stagehands and buddies, forced jokes working off last-minute nerves. But the band passes only a few individuals on the way, most of whom are hard at work. With each step, the group begins to zero in on each other, converging in a mutual tunnel of concentration.

The sun has dimmed now, sunk beneath the stadium's rim, eclipsing the crowd, which looked so colorful—all reds, whites, and blues—just half an hour before. From above, the audience seems a single primitive organism, waiting to be fused into a single shape and voice and purpose.

The three-story stage has been set up beneath the Coliseum's giant arch, which looms above the stage in the twilight. When they reach it, the band members look at one another, draw a collective deep breath, and descend, their way lit by flashlights held by the crew. They clamber quickly down the concrete stairs, past broad sections of empty seats. They're led blind into the hungry murmur, which builds a bit as those on the fringes of the crowd spot their movement. The house lights go black and the murmur raises its pitch and volume, becomes a scream.

The musicians stride to their places, spread out across the broad stage. Behind them hangs a fifty-foot flag, flat without a flutter, at once an icon of the most deeply fixed symbolism and a blank slate on which the evening's meaning will be inscribed. You could write almost anything here, and for the past eighteen months, everybody from the President of the United States on down has tried. But right now, all that's clear is the ambiguity of the image and the intensity of the figures that it dwarfs.

The singer glances left, right, and behind, nods his head. Mumbling a greeting into the howling face of the mob, he signals his readiness and raises his guitar before him like a sword. An instant later, white hot light smacks him in the face as he snaps off the cadence—"One-two, one-two-three-four." Synthesizers and drums rumble into life.

For a moment he stands, legs splayed, swinging his guitar like a weapon. Then, taking a stride to the microphone and gripping it with his right fist, he begins his tale at the beginning. It starts with a sound sharp and cruel as the first slap on a baby's fanny. The noise that explodes from his mouth could be called a scream or a bellow, but it's really just a bawl:

> Born down in a dead man's town
> First kick I took was when I hit the ground
> You end up like a dog that's been beat too much
> Till you spend half your life just coverin' up

In a sense, Bruce Springsteen has spent half *his* lifetime uncovering those lines, cutting to the core of himself, and in the process unleashing the mighty energy that unites his audience until, by the end of the night, that shapeless mass becomes 80,000 separate but united faces. The power he has accumulated stems straight from the intensity of his conviction that such a feat is possible, and from the incredible assertion of will required to bring it about. It's exactly what has made him, less suddenly than it would seem, the first white American to approach the mystique and popularity of Elvis Presley. It's what presidents and paupers fight over. It's the essence of this story.

■

Who was Bruce Springsteen in the months and years before he became such a visibly fortunate son? Even though it must seem so to noninitiates, he didn't just vanish into a woodshed in the time between his near-disastrous simultaneous appearance on the covers of *Time* and *Newsweek* on October 27, 1975, and the release of *Born in the U.S.A.* on June 4, 1984. Unlike Peter Frampton, the other great rock phenomenon of 1975, Bruce Springsteen was never a burnt-out rock star. To have fallen into

that valley and reclimbed the heights of megastardom Springsteen reached in the mid-Eighties would have surpassed the
recuperative powers of Lazarus. No. Between *Born to Run* and
Born in the U.S.A., Bruce Springsteen occupied himself as one of
the biggest stars in the world—or at least in the world of rock and
roll.

Springsteen survived the hype surrounding *Born to Run*
because the nature of the hype was of two distinct kinds. Most
obviously, there was the enthusiastic hyperbole poured out by
rock critics, disc jockeys, and fans with the zeal of fundamental-
ist converts. This hype was lubricated—but not fueled—by a
$250,000 Columbia Records promotion campaign. The fuel was
provided by Springsteen himself, partly through the excellence of
the *Born to Run* album, but primarily through his three- and four-
hour stage shows—rock and roll marathons that combined the
bluesy bite and drive of rock at its best with a theatrical
production that packed in more tragicomedy than had been seen
since the heyday of James Brown. No performer has ever extended himself further than Springsteen onstage in those years,
risking everything in headlong dives into the audience, revealing
himself with stories of growin' up young and poor in central New
Jersey, continually concocting a series of minor events and
holidays to celebrate as the show concluded in an apex of
mugging and riot. Imagine "The Honeymooners" with amplifiers,
an all-male cast, and a live audience, and you'll know what it was
like at the end of those nights. Imagine reinventing "art rock" as
something that ignored Beethoven's Ninth in favor of Del Shan-
non's "Runaway" and the Ronettes' "Walking in the Rain." All
CBS really had to do was spread the word.

There was also a negative hype at work, driven by naysayers
who saw the very innocence that allowed Springsteen to balance
so precariously between artfulness and slapstick as a kind of
cultivated naïveté, who heard his theatricality as closer to
Howard Keel than Jackie Wilson, who saw his all-American
loser-made-good persona as a backdoor mechanism for returning
rock and roll to the greaseball dummies from which it (presumably) sprang. At the time, there seemed nearly as many critics,
deejays and rock fans devoted to denying Springsteen's greatness

as to celebrating it. "Springsteen needs to learn that operettic pomposity insults the Ronettes and that pseudotragic beautiful-loser fatalism insults us all," wrote critic Robert Christgau, who admired *Born to Run* but despised the mythology on which it was founded.

Corny as it may have seemed to modernist intellectuals, Springsteen's mythos was the very thing that enabled him to recast the rock and roll version of the old American dreams—right down to waving the flag in mourning rather than joy. Within rock's narrow world, this made Springsteen an eccentric icon and provided the leverage for altering the terms on which at least one section of rock and roll was made and understood. But to those for whom Liverpool, London, and San Francisco had completely overshadowed Memphis, Detroit, and Muscle Shoals, the entire exercise must have seemed preposterous. With punk in the process of being born and the British rock bands of the late Sixties and their American imitators stumbling to dinosaur deaths, what Springsteen was about just didn't seem feasible, much less desirable. In fact, Springsteen's effort to tap the abandoned American folk mythology at the core of Elvis Presley and Chuck Berry's version of rock and roll may have seemed like just what Christgau implied it was: a task for the half-bright in alliance with the cynical.

But Springsteen is neither dim nor a hypocrite. "I was a big daydreamer when I was in grammar school. Kids used to tease me, call me dreamer. It's something that got worse as I got older, I think," Springsteen told Kurt Loder in 1984. But in 1975, he didn't feel that way at all. "I looked at *Born to Run* and the things people were saying about it, that it was just a romantic fantasy and all that, and I thought, 'No, this is me. This is my story.' And I really felt good about it," Springsteen said in early 1986. "But later, as time went on, I started to look around and see what other stories there were to tell. And that was really when I started to see the lives of my friends and the people I knew, and they weren't that way at all."

Of course, a big part of Springsteen's own story wasn't that way, either. Born on September 23, 1949, at the height of the postwar baby boom, he grew up in the richest country in the world during the greatest period of material prosperity in human history. Yet the Springsteen family was never economically prosperous; they continually struggled to make ends meet. The Springsteens certainly never knew the depths of poverty so many black musicians experienced as a matter of course, but they were clearly—and through no fault of their own—at the poorer end of the American working class.

After *Born to Run*—and an ensuing lawsuit with his former manager, Mike Appel—Bruce began to work intensively on a follow-up album. It was 1977, and as one result of the lawsuit, his closest adviser was now his manager/producer, Jon Landau. A former rock and film critic, Landau is a deeply introspective and relentlessly analytical person, and he brought out many of the same qualities in Bruce. Those characteristics had always been part of Springsteen's makeup, but they'd been dormant for lack of stimulation and guidance—or worse, had to be hidden because psychological insight and intense analysis were scorned in the working class culture in which Bruce grew up.

The legacy of such passivity is more of the same, generation upon generation, and for a long time Springsteen's analysis of why he'd succeeded where so many, including his own father, had failed boiled down to an almost superstitious belief in hard work and personal conviction. "I believe in the love and the hope and the faith," he sang at the beginning of 1978's *Darkness on the Edge of Town,* the sequel to *Born to Run* and the first album in which he began to portray and assess the living shambles around him. But as the Seventies wore on and more and more men of bright hopes and good intentions were discarded or destroyed, it became obvious that the tragedy of lives such as Doug Spring-steen's weren't the result of individual failure at all.

Springsteen's performance legend grew. *Darkness on the Edge of Town,* like *Born to Run,* sold something more than a million copies, but Springsteen concert tickets sold out of all proportion to his popularity in the record stores or on Top Forty radio. He could sell out 20,000-seat sports arenas faster and more often than artists who sold four or five times as many records. By 1980, when he completed his fifth album, the double-disc *The River,* he was acclaimed as the greatest performer in rock. The stage show had changed somewhat since *Born to Run,* adding scads of new material, but its essential framework remained the same, as did the essential message: Believe in yourself and the world will work better.

With the assistance of his first Top Ten single, "Hungry Heart," *The River* expanded his album audience to 2 million. Yet, at a time when the Bee Gees, the Eagles, and Fleetwood Mac were selling more than 5 million consistently and more than 10 million copies of their biggest hits, Springsteen was basically still reaching only a cult of initiates, and the initiates were largely those who had seen their dreams pay off as well—nonconforming yuppies. To the vast majority of pop music listeners, whose lives were often as bleak as the vistas of his darkest ballads, Springsteen had not begun to speak at all, even though such songs as "The River," "Stolen Car," and "Jackson Cage" at least began to include such figures in his imaginative universe.

"Springsteen's wholeness—the fact that he embodies rock and roll as no one person ever has, except Elvis—springs from his noble-savage persona. Such shocking innocence can't be faked, but it also suggests that Springsteen scarcely exists outside the rock and roll world that created him," wrote critic Stephen Holden in his review of *The River.* "Fifteen years ago, rock and roll music stormed the frontier of contemporary culture, and the major albums of the day addressed the moment. *The River* doesn't—it addresses rock and roll. The product of one thirty-year-old man's incredible exertion and faith, it conjures an American-provincial world of a guy, a girl, and a car hurtling into the night, fleeing time itself."

In one sense, this reflected a brilliant and complete expression of Springsteen's artistic vision. But in another way, it represented the frustration of his talents. Though he had grown immensely as a songwriter and recordmaker, his themes refused to expand. Pump them up as he might, they continued to revolve around the same small center. What Springsteen really hoped to do was call a halt to the flights of which Holden spoke. To do so would require a confrontation with his most cherished beliefs about himself, his music, and the world. Yet it was only after he had faced down his illusions, stared into the blank eyes of his own ruptured dreams, that Springsteen could step forth and speak not just to the world of rock and roll, but to everyone willing to listen.

When he did, the results were tangible in the most extreme sense: 10 million albums sold in the United States; 18 million worldwide; seven Top Ten singles; the highest-grossing, longest-running concert tour in rock history; a quartet of successful videos and the increased visual identification that went with them; community support and political clout; status as a legend not only of rock and roll but of popular culture. But in order to attain that status, Springsteen first had to cross more fields of fire than those who came late to the story or who didn't watch closely as it developed could have imagined.

The first thing he had to do in order to become the embodiment of America that *Born in the U.S.A.* would make him was leave the country.

2 IN ANOTHER LAND

For the ex-colonials, the declaration of an American identity meant the assumption of a mask, and it imposed not only the discipline of national self-consciousness, it gave Americans an ironic awareness of the joke that always lies between appearance and reality, between the discontinuity of social tradition and that sense of the past which clings to the mind.
—RALPH ELLISON, *Change the Joke and Slip the Yoke*

Bruce Springsteen and the E Street Band landed at Frankfurt, West Germany, on April 5, 1981. It was two days before the first show of their first full-scale European tour, but they were already way off schedule.

The tour was originally set to start two weeks earlier, in England. Tickets for shows in Newcastle, Manchester, Brighton, Stafford, and Birmingham, as well as six nights at London's Wembley Arena, the Madison Square Garden of the U.K., sold out in hours. Tickets for April dates on the Continent went equally quickly. Even though Springsteen's only previous European concerts had been a pair of London dates at 3,000-seat Hammersmith Odeon and single shows at theaters in Amsterdam and Stockholm six years previously, the legend of his concert marathons preceded him.

Then on March 12, only days before the first gig, manager Jon Landau got a late-night call from Springsteen. Bruce was sick; he needed rest. Landau immediately rang U.K. promoter Harvey Goldsmith to tell him that the English dates were postponed.

Awakened before the British dawn, Goldsmith first thought Landau must be kidding; finally convinced that the decision was for real, he spent the better part of an hour trying to talk the

11

manager out of it. The next morning, he issued the statement Landau gave him: "Bruce is simply exhausted and suffering from the assorted ailments that can crop up during a grueling tour. While his health is not in serious danger, doing his first full tour of the U.K. without adequate rest would run the risk of later cancellations. Bruce regrets any inconvenience to his U.K. fans." The shows were rescheduled for the last three weeks of May and the first week in June. Rather than beginning in England, Bruce's first full-scale European tour would end there.

"The risk of later cancellations" was no bluff. A few weeks before, on the final leg of his U.S. tour, a cold in Bruce's throat caused the postponement of early February shows in Indianapolis and Lexington, Kentucky. The physical breakdown wasn't surprising: The band had been on the road for five months, since the week before his fifth album, *The River*, was released, with only one two-week break, at New Year's. And once the European tour started, missed shows would have to be cancelled, not just pushed back.

Bruce wasn't willing to risk such a calamity. The memory of his first trip abroad, during the *Born to Run* tour, and of the hype surrounding it, lingered. The hoopla had peaked in London when Bruce arrived for his debut appearance outside North America on November 18, 1975.

Playing by the rules of the more gimmicky, sensationalized British pop star game, CBS had planned to launch a Springsteen frenzy. So they plastered the city with round blue stickers bearing Landau's quote, "I saw rock and roll future and its name is Bruce Springsteen." Landau had written this in 1974, when he was a music critic; his production and management role with Springsteen evolved later. Bruce needed the push then, but by the time of his London appearance, the statement had been so robbed of context (it was originally part of a highly personal 2,000-word article) that its only meaning was an obnoxious assertion of superiority. No one in the Springsteen camp could look upon it any longer without annoyance.

When Bruce arrived at Hammersmith Odeon several hours before showtime, the theater was festooned with posters and flyers reading, "At Last London Is Ready for Bruce Springsteen!"

Suddenly he snapped, roaring through the hall, tearing the offending posters down. He performed in a sullen rage that evening, spending a large portion of the night with his back to the crowd.

Springsteen had never before seemed especially disturbed by his record label's blowout promotions, but his seeming passivity obscured the intensely serious purpose with which he pursued his rock and roll dream. Springsteen believed deeply in the inherent worth and dignity of popular music and in his own responsibility to its traditions, which he was convinced had saved him from a life of frustration and fury. "A businesslike attitude toward that sort of thing is not appropriate," he once said. "I want our band to deliver something that you can't buy. That's the idea behind it."

To those, including many in the media and show business, who believed that cooperation with modern merchandising machinery was inherently corrupting, those sentiments couldn't just be idealistic; they were either hopelessly naïve or rankly opportunistic. In 1975, Springsteen had barely had time to demonstrate that they were neither, just a statement of convictions that he meant to uphold. That he'd been able to maintain such an attitude through the process of making and selling three albums and being acclaimed both "the new Dylan" and "rock and roll future" spoke to his ferocity of will and his ability to reconcile opposites simply by letting things be.

In America, Springsteen was sheltered from some of the contradictions of his career—particularly the tension between his desire for stardom and the anxious populist sentiments of his work—by a devoted following of writers and disc jockeys who had seen his shows and come away gasping. But even in the States in 1975, that network of professional supporters existed only in pockets—the Northeast, Cleveland, Austin, and Phoenix, most notably—and the hype spawned a counter-reaction, which focused on the naked mechanics of CBS salesmanship and proclaimed him a fraud. In Britain, only a few writers had seen Springsteen, and with the notable exception of *Melody Maker*'s Michael Watts, the idea of an American appearing to reclaim the title of champion rock and roller after fifteen years of British dominance of the white pop music scene struck many as beyond the realm of possibility, especially since Bruce's music and image were throwbacks to pre-Beatles American rock and soul music and late Lennonism respectively. Concurrent with the idea that Bruce Springsteen could singlehandedly save rock from its mid-Seventies doldrums, there sprang up the notion that he was the biggest con job of the decade, a pure creation of the CBS Records publicity machinery.

"That bothered me a lot, being perceived as an invention, a ship passing by," he told journalist Kit Rachlis in 1980. "I'd been playing for ten years. I knew where I came from, every inch of the way. I knew what I believed and what I wanted." And at the same time, "there was all the publicity and all the backlash. I felt the thing I wanted most in life—my music—being swept away, and I didn't know if I could do anything about it."

During the U.S. dates of the *Born to Run* tour, Bruce kept calm, rarely asserting his doubts, preferring to withdraw. "I felt I was in my *I Walked with a Zombie* routine," he told Rachlis. Maybe, working on home turf, he was just more certain that the show would get over on its merits. Outside the States, robbed of context and without any clues about what to expect, he couldn't be so sure. The London shows brought him out of a defensive shell, forced him to confront his own doubts about the way his music was being presented and sold.

To Mike Appel, then his manager, Hammersmith felt like the beginning of the end. "Bruce was so mad that night in London. He went really nuts. And I guess I looked just as guilty to him as CBS . . . He wanted that fame and glory, but I guess he wanted it on his own terms," Appel told Robert Hilburn many years later. What Hammersmith really began was Springsteen's insistence on defining those terms—and *that* is the point at which Mike Appel, whose method was the hype, found himself gone despite his complete emotional commitment to Springsteen and his music.

Bruce knew exactly where to lay the blame. "It was nothin' to do with the place. It was me. It was the inside world. It's a hard thing to explain, but I learned a lot about my strengths and weaknesses in those days, especially on that particular night," he said to Rachlis on a night when the 1981 European dates might have been very much on his mind.

Bruce took the European tour, particularly the 1981 British shows, too seriously to play at less than top condition. Back in the States, Springsteen had effectively rubbed out the repercussions of the *Born to Run* hype during the 1978 tour that followed *Darkness on the Edge of Town*, his bitterest, most resolute album. The screaming intensity of those '78 shows are part of rock and roll legend in the same way as Dylan's 1966 shows with the Band, the Rolling Stones' tours of 1969 and 1972, and the Who's *Tommy* tour of 1969: benchmarks of an era.

The tour following the release of *The River* began with great anticipation, because Springsteen hadn't released an album in nearly three years, and hadn't toured in two. His only public performance since the *Darkness* tour had ended on January 1, 1979, was his appearance at a pair of anti-nuclear benefit shows that September. The *No Nukes* record and film, the overwhelmingly adulatory reception he received at those Madison Square Garden shows, and the remarkable kick-ass rock and roll the E Streeters played in an essentially folk-rock setting added to the anticipation. In the States, the five months of touring in late '80 and early '81 built as much demand as they fulfilled. Bruce had graduated from playing 2,000- to 3,000-seat theaters to filling 10,000- to 20,000-seat sports arenas on the *Darkness* tour. After *The River* and his first Top Ten single, "Hungry Heart," and the most ecstatic reviews since the comeback of Elvis Presley, he was capable of selling out multiple dates in each city's arena, something only a few acts in history had achieved.

The legend traveled but it created strange resonances in foreign ears. Almost no one in Europe had ever seen him play. In most countries, his records sold respectably but no better. Furthermore, the entire basis of European—particularly British—pop music had changed after the twin revolutions of disco and punk, while Bruce stuck to rock and roll basics as established by Elvis and Chuck Berry, Dylan, the Stones, and the Beatles. Finally, Springsteen was a quintessentially American artist appearing in Europe at a time of enormous anti-American sentiment created by the U.S. government's recent foreign policy, particularly the insistence on foisting upon such NATO allies as West Germany and Britain missile systems that made those countries the likely front-lines of a so-called "limited nuclear war."

Springsteen would also be playing in halls ranging in size from 3,000 to 10,000 seats—a radical change from the 10,000- to 20,000-seat sports arenas of North America, which just didn't exist in Europe.

Translating this show outside of its American context wasn't something that could entirely be taken for granted. For one thing, Bruce's concerts generally involved a fair amount of story-telling and dialogue with the audience. How would he speak to an audience that for the most part didn't understand English, much less the highly vernacular American he spoke? Yet that aspect of the show was crucial to creating a sense of shared revelation between the musicians and the crowd.

By reputation the Springsteen show was a bigger-than-life extravaganza recapturing that Nirvana Under the Boardwalk created for Bruce (among others) by early Sixties rock and soul songs, in which beauty and dignity, self-respect and love were the basis of all relationships. It was the ideal behind that music, his own wonder at it, and his frustration that so little of it had been realized that made Bruce Springsteen exert himself so strenuously onstage, and it was nothing else and nothing less that kept him on the road. The show's nightly ritual, which built from songs of foreboding to an ecstatic celebration, arose from the belief that by completely absorbing self and audience, player and spectator, in a prolonged ritual, some great, transcendent community would be formed. And if in the next cold dawn this project seemed damned unlikely, if not just preposterous, well then, one was still left with a need to explain exactly *what* that orgiastic experience the night before was all about.

How did he do it? Partly, by working harder than anybody in the house did at his or her day job. After a sound check that lasted anywhere from thirty minutes to a couple of hours, during which Bruce was liable to run through any new song he'd lately written or some obscure oldie that had just caught his fancy, the arena doors were opened and the crowd filed in. Then the E Streeters played for about two hours, the length of a normal headline set. After a twenty-minute break, they came back to do another ninety minutes or so, followed by encores—in effect, a *third* set—that lasted anywhere from thirty to sixty minutes. The show hadn't finished in under three hours in years; many nights, the band was up there for more than four.

They played so long because Bruce still thought of himself as a bar band musician. As he once pointed out, "In the bars, you do five sets and they're like, you know, forty-five minutes. And then as you go along, usually when you first make records, you'll play two or sometimes three shows a night that are maybe an hour long. So [our show is] actually about the same amount of time." He laughed and continued less glibly:

"Mainly I did it because there was a point where just playing the one set didn't seem enough. People came wanting to hear certain favorite songs of theirs which I still liked playing . . . It was just really to allow for more expression. It wasn't a plan to play for a real long time, or it wasn't even a plan to give people their money's worth or whatever. It was just expression. You know, if a fan goes out, it's a whole night out. It's three hours, and he should be much more tired than me when he walks out. 'Cause I do it all the time." He finished, laughing again.

Half hidden between his jokes is the greatest distinction of Springsteen's show: its purpose and the fact that it has one. Springsteen wants to entertain—he can be rock's greatest ham— but he can't quit until he has also inspired.

In the Pentecostal churches whose gospel music spawned so much of rock and roll, the purpose of music is to enhance interaction between congregation and performers. What Springsteen idealized in early rock and roll music were attempts to achieve something similar. (Listen to Sam Cooke's *Live at the Harlem Square Club*, for instance.) But by the late Sixties, the rock ritual had become so empty that the performers' exhortations actually confirmed their distance from the crowd. (Listen to *Woodstock*.) Springsteen seemed a throwback because it was his intention to regain that dialogue with the audience. It was as if he couldn't rest until the distance between artist and onlooker was obliterated.

In 1981 his munitions were mostly drawn from *Born to Run*, *Darkness on the Edge of Town*, and *The River*. Some of his audience missed the more eclectic early material, of which only "Rosalita," which had closed every Springsteen performance since he wrote it in 1973, regularly survived. But the saga of American innocence found and lost contained in his last three records gave Springsteen a musical center in rock and roll and a ready-made dramatic structure. He also drew on a repertoire of rock, folk, and soul classics: Woody Guthrie's "This Land Is Your Land," the Beatles' "Twist and Shout," Arthur Conley's "Sweet Soul Music," John Fogerty's "Who'll Stop the Rain." Together they added up to a sweeping story that felt as if it had a new chapter written every night.

■

Bruce hadn't returned to Europe only to work. He wanted to learn about that part of the world, gain some feeling for its famous cities, internationalize his horizons. Neither he nor the band, personally or professionally, had ever spent any significant amount of time outside of the United States. So the tour was arranged with a leisurely schedule, with days off in each town. That was a luxury—every idle date on tour costs thousands of dollars in hotel and meal fees—but even professionally, the purpose of this junket wasn't just to cash in: It was to build a base in the same way they'd done in the States.

Six months earlier, dining on fried chicken and grilled cheese in an Arizona hotel room while recuperating after yet another of these marathons, Springsteen spoke of what touring gave *him*. He remembered feeling itchy by the end of the prolonged sessions for *The River*, anxious to get back onstage.

"When I was in the studio and wanted to play, it wasn't the way I felt in a physical kind of way, it was what I felt mentally," he said. "I was excited about the record and I wanted to play those songs live. I wanted to get out there and travel around the world with people who were my friends. And see every place and play just as hard as we could play, every place in the world. Just get into things, see things, see what happens. . . . All I knew when I was in the studio, sometimes, was that I felt great that day. And I was wishing I was somewhere strange, playing. I guess that's the thing I love doing the most. And it's the thing that makes me feel most alert and alive."

But hadn't stardom been isolating? The question pushed at Springsteen's entire purpose.

"Usually . . . you can do anything you want to do," he said, speaking hesitantly at first, as if testing to see if the idea would play, then with increasingly passionate conviction. "The idea that you can't walk down the street is in people's minds. You can walk down any street, any time. What you gonna be afraid of, someone coming up to you? In general, it's not that different than it ever was, except you meet people you ordinarily might not meet—you meet some strangers and you talk to 'em for a little while.

"The other night I went out, I went driving—we were in Denver. Got a car and went out, drove all around. Went to the movies by myself, walked in, got my popcorn. This guy comes up to me, real nice guy. He says, 'Listen, you want to sit with me and my sister?' I said, 'All right.' So we watch the movie." He paused and laughed. "It was great, too, because it was that Woody Allen movie [*Stardust Memories*]—the guy's slammin' it to his fans. And I'm sittin' there and this poor kid says, 'Jesus, I don't know what to say to ya. Is this the way it is? Is this how you feel?' I said, 'No. I don't feel like that so much.' And he had the amazing courage to come up to me at the end of the movie and ask if I'd go home and meet his mother and his father. I said, 'What time is it?' It was eleven o'clock, so I said 'Well, okay.'

"So I go home with him; he lives out in some suburb. So we get over to the house and here's his mother and father, laying out on the couch, watching TV and reading the paper. He brings me in and he says, 'Hey, I got Bruce Springsteen here.' And they don't believe him. So he pulls me over and he says, 'This is Bruce Springsteen.' 'Aw, g'wan,' they say. So he runs in his room and brings out an album and he holds it up to my face. And his mother says [breathlessly], 'Ohhh *yeah!*' She starts yelling, 'Yeah,' she starts screaming.

"And for two hours I was in this kid's house, talking with these people; they were really nice, they cooked me up all this food, watermelon, and the guy gave me a ride home a few hours later.

"I felt so good that night. Because here are these strange people I didn't know; they take you in their house, treat you fantastic—and this kid was real nice, they were real nice. That is something that can happen to me that can't happen to most people. And when it does happen, it's fantastic. You get somebody's whole life in three hours. You get their parents, you get their sister, you get their family life, in three hours. And I went back to that hotel and felt really good because I thought, '*Wow* [now he was almost whispering], what a thing to be able to do. What an experience to be able to have, to be able to step into some stranger's life.'

"And that's what I thought about in the studio. I thought about going out and meeting people I don't know. Going to France and Germany and Japan and meeting Japanese people and French people and German people. Meeting them and seeing what they think, and being able to go over there with something. To go over there with a pocketful of ideas or to go over there with just something, to be able to take something over. And boom! To do it!"

So the tour began with freelance visits to Hamburg's notorious Reeperbahn, a squalid district of whorehouses and dives storied now in rock and roll lore (as it has been among sailors for decades) because the Beatles got their start there—carrying especially poignant memories, because it was only weeks after the murder of John Lennon.

For the most part, the band and crew hung together, as travelers will. They were entertained and shown the sights by the local promoters or by the local CBS Records staff, to whom extending such courtesies was the customary way of coping with the arrival of an offshore rock group.

In a way, after so many months of touring the U.S., another round of hotels and airplanes and concert halls must have felt more normal than being home. After a while, as a veteran tour manager once said, you get so you have to look out the window and check the language of the street signs to know which country you're in. The shows themselves become a sort of maze, the band winding from one to another until they finally work their way out and return to homes they barely recall. It's no life for someone who doesn't love it. And it's no life for anyone who isn't traveling with friends. Most rock bands are not, their internal grappling for position reflected even among the road crew.

The E Street Band was a little different for two reasons: First, everyone knew that Bruce alone occupied the tour's top slot, and second, Bruce insisted that the band and crew stay in the same hotels wherever possible and that all parties be held for everyone or no one. Both stipulations reflected wisdom accumulated over a decade of playing clubs for small wages and no glory. One result was that Springsteen had been working with an identical band and much of the same crew since those scuffling days. To call them a family would have been to succumb to an illusion, but there was an aspect of camaraderie and cooperation among the crew that was rare, and it added to the Springsteen legend in professional circles.

"It's funny, I go back a certain amount of time with the same guys. We can think of nights when we were sixteen, playing in this teen club, and we get into all the stuff that's come down in between," Bruce once commented. "It doesn't feel that much different. What happens inside you is very much the same."

In fact, the E Street Band had held together under his leadership much longer than anyone could have expected. The newest member, guitarist Miami Steve Van Zandt, officially joined in 1975, but he and Bruce had been playing together since those teen club days back at the Jersey Shore. So had organist Danny Federici and bassist Garry Tallent. Saxophonist Clarence (Big Man) Clemons had appeared one night out of the mist, entering a Jersey boardwalk club as a gust of wind ripped the door off in his hand. He stuck around to play the King Curtis riffs that were one of the signatures of Bruce's early sound and to serve as Springsteen's most important stage foil. Drummer Max Weinberg and pianist Roy Bittan signed up in 1974. If they couldn't remember clear back to the days of Bruce's search for a record deal, seven years is still a very long time in show business, much less rock and roll.

Nevertheless, it would be hard to think of a more personally diverse group of musicians. They were all the same age, in their early thirties, except for Clarence, who was nearing forty, and they all came from the East Coast. But personal resemblances stopped there. Their dress ranged from Bittan's elegant *couture* to Van Zandt's piratical pop star gear. Their musical tastes spanned the gamut, from Tallent's rockabilly record collecting to the boogie-all-night hard-partying of Clemons. Their offstage personalities went every which way. Weinberg's hotel room had to meet precise standards, and he padded his drums with only a specific brand of paper towels; Federici tended to disappear into his own world between shows. Perhaps they came together with such force onstage because they were pulled in so many directions off it—though even onstage they never achieved any cohesive look.

What they had in common was a belief in Bruce Springsteen's music that led to an unwavering willingness to follow his direction. They earned the right to call him Boss.

■

The previous November, German promoter Fritz Rau had flown to New York to see Bruce's Madison Square Garden shows. Rau, a concert promoter for thirty years, was astonished by what he saw, but the frenzied response of the audience worried him. "Now, don't be upset when everybody just sits there and applauds politely," he continually warned Bruce and the band after their arrival in Europe. "That's what happens here. European audiences are much more reserved than those you're used to. They will be very appreciative but don't expect them to rise up out of their seats cheering."

Bruce hadn't known what to expect in 1975, and like any newcomer to a foreign land, he needed orientation. But there's such a thing as overcompensation. "Bruce must have heard this a hundred times in the three days between when he got to Germany and when he did the first show," Landau remembered. "It got to the level of 'Listen, if they stone you, don't worry about it, that's just the audience, they really love it.' "

Rau's worries were reasonable but ultimately unnecessary. Part of what Bruce had learned from the *Born to Run* tour was the need to distinguish between the audience interaction that he wished to create and his own need for a specific reaction. "The moment you begin to depend on audience reaction, you're doing the wrong thing. You're doin' it wrong, it's a mistake, it's not right. You can't allow yourself, no matter what, to depend on them," he said a few months before leaving for Europe. "I think when you begin to expect a reaction, it's a mistake. You gotta have your thing completely together—boom!—right there with you. When I put that mike out to the crowd, you have a certain faith that somebody's gonna yell somethin' back. Some nights it's louder than other nights, and some nights they do and on some songs they don't. But that's the idea. That's what makes nights special and what makes nights different from other nights."

Whatever the problems were supposed to be, Bruce felt "tremendous confidence in the band and in the music. I felt we had a really good band. We had a point of view, good ideas, good music. I knew what I wanted to say; I knew why we were going over there."

Nevertheless, the E Street Band entered Hamburg's beautiful Congress Center, a modern 4,000-seat concert hall, with the sense that after five years of knowing just what to expect, they were lighting out into unknown territory. And if all this was irrelevant in theory, all the players felt a twinge of contradiction in the quivers of their nerves.

They took the stage just after eight, starting out, as always, with some of Bruce's strongest songs: "Thunder Road," "The Ties That Bind," "Out in the Streets," anthemic rockers that would have brought an American audience to its feet from the first familiar chord. But though the applause after each song was enthusiastic, there was no leaping from the chairs, no rush to the stage or dancing in the aisles. This crowd sat down.

Bruce hadn't changed his set at all. As he would during any show in the States, after twenty minutes of sizing up the audience, Springsteen called for "Tenth Avenue Freeze-out." In America he sang that song (or its alter ego, "Spirit in the Night,") leaning far forward over the crowd until he came to the next-to-last verse. Then he'd slip to his knees and slither over the lip of the stage into the front row, where he'd be eagerly engulfed by the crowd, and sing the rest of his song surrounded by them. It was a terrifying act of complete confidence in his audience, a physical expression of the show's central idea—one-to-one interplay between performer and listeners.

Back home, this had always meant leaping into a crowd already clamoring for contact. In Hamburg, however, the audience still sat in perfect decorum. And when Bruce called for "Tenth Avenue" on this night, nobody in the band or crew really thought he'd make the leap.

"I was watching and wondering to myself," remembered Landau. "The whole move of going out into the crowd seems predicated on the fact that the audience is physically involved, and there's that sharing and that physical interaction and, you know, all the weird things that used to happen: People'd pick him up and put him on their shoulders, people'd give him their seats and he'd stand on somebody's seat and sing that stretch in 'Spirit in the Night.' There's all the interplay and what're you going to do if everybody's just sitting there?

"Of course, he went out in the crowd. And people didn't really get up, but it was great anyway. It was like it was important for him to do it. He was havin' a great time, it seemed to me. He had this look of, 'It's fine. It's just fine. People want to sit down, that's fine. People want to stand up, that's fine. But I'm out here doing my thing.'

"That really broke the ice. Even though they didn't stand up then, he almost was showing them what they could do."

This wasn't just a collision between theory and practice. It was an example of Bruce rising to an occasion and living up to his own best ideas. As Landau put it, "He has that lack of fear about maybe making a fool of yourself. You've got a bunch of people who are all sitting down and you know that they're friendly, but they don't know how to respond to the situation, and you say, 'I'm gonna do it anyway; maybe it'll look silly.' And I'm sure that the idea that it might look silly didn't cross his mind at that moment . . . but to any of us, looking at him, you'd say, 'Jeez, wouldn't I be worried about makin' a fool of myself if I were the person up there at that point.' "

The payoff was bigger and better than the risk. The rest of the set roared by. Roy Bittan began the final number with a quietly beautiful piano introduction based on Ennio Morricone's score for *Once Upon a Time in the West*, the greatest European Western ever made. From within this delicate music, Max Weinberg's drums suddenly erupted in march time and the guitars shot off like cannons and Springsteen leaned into the mike, bearing down hard, shouting the opening lines of "Badlands":

> Lights out tonight, trouble in the heartland
> Got a head-on collision, smashin' in my guts, man

As if on cue, half the crowd exploded from its seats. Onstage, the band looked out at the crowd in amazement, watching as first one person, then another, finally decided to dare it all and rose, until everyone in the house was standing, fists upraised, shouting and dancing. When the song ended and they'd taken their bows and vowed to return for more, the band stepped backstage with tears in every eye.

At the very beginning of the tour, the band had begun playing the first verse and chorus of "Hungry Heart" as an instrumental, then starting over with Bruce's vocal. Then in Chicago, their first stop after "Hungry Heart" hit the Top Ten, the crowd sang the lyrics back to them. Bruce stuck out his mike to encourage them and a ritual was born. It became one of the show's tell-tale moments. Some audiences sang strongly, some faltered; some were off-pitch, some sounded sweet. The point was the adventure itself.

"Hungry Heart" wasn't a hit single in Germany but half an hour into the second set, the crowd was still wild and willing for whatever was to come. When the band hit that rolling riff and Bruce stuck out his mike, the Hamburg fans took the cue and began to sing. But they didn't really know the words. "The verse in that song and the chorus have the same music," said Landau. "So some people were singing the verse, some people were singing the chorus, some people were singing in English, and some people were singing in German. But everybody was singing something, in the spot where you're supposed to sing.

"As I watched him, Bruce seemed to be quite overwhelmed with the moment. I think it was just experiencing the most basic thing of music being something that communicates across borders—and Bruce experiencing the fact that he had the capacity to create work whose ability to communicate was not limited. It was not limited to New Jersey, it was not limited to the East Coast, it wasn't limited to the United States, it was not limited to any country. He was just making music for people. And all different kinds of people are able to understand what he's doing. I think that was the night we all got it. There it was, you could see it. It was just . . . international."

After that, the show ascended into what Landau termed "a phenomenal level of amiable disorder." And as if to seal his victory, Springsteen closed the show by debuting a brand-new number, John Fogerty's "Rockin' All Over the World," as the Hamburgers stood and stomped and roared their approval.

Soaked in sweat, Springsteen came bubbling off the stage. Before he reached his dressing room, Fritz Rau, a dignified gentleman thirty years his senior, came up to him once more, this time wearing a huge smile.

"*What* have you done to my Germans?" he asked.

"Well," said Bruce, "I guess they know how to stand up."

■

The unquestionable triumph of the German shows set the tone of an altogether remarkable European tour. Bruce and the band played some of the finest music of their career, and the audiences proved amazingly responsive. Whatever might have been lost in the translation was instead transformed into a series of unspoken understandings. Bruce never told as many stories as he did to those half-comprehending crowds, and few performers have ever been met with such a fervent combination of respect and delight. The shows in Berlin, Frankfurt, and Zurich were the equal of Hamburg, and the German swing closed with a date in Munich that was almost *too* good-naturedly rowdy.

To Miami Steve, at least, this was no surprise. "Just before we went to Europe, as the American part of the tour ended, we started to focus in on musical things," he said. "A lot of conversation was going on. We just started re-examining.

"We discovered some major things that were going on, and the first time we had a chance to really try them out was on the European tour. Combined with the fact that we were expecting a little coldness from the audience, we tended to play for each other for the first time, I think, in many years. We just tended to pull in a little bit, and consequently we were just . . . great."

Then the band played Paris on Easter weekend, where Bruce began to tinker with the show the same way he would have back in the States, adding new songs, repositioning others, adapting to circumstances and new experiences. He made one significant modification from the start of the tour: Just before singing the evening's first slow song, he requested the audience's quiet attention, a subtle but savvy way of acknowledging that many in the crowd would have trouble keeping up with his highly vernacular English and, equally important, of asserting his control over the proceedings, making sure he could do a concert and not just a flat-out rock and roll show. And from the start, he was rewarded with rapt silence, a stillness so deep in its attention that you could actually hear people listening. European crowds may not have known how to rock out as automatically as Americans, but they listened up far more smartly.

Bruce had previously premiered new songs in the unlikeliest circumstances, but he came up with no originals in Europe. The songs he added to the set were written by others, though often so radically altered that they seemed new. The changes he made were not always solemn. He plugged Arthur Conley's "Sweet Soul Music," a tribute to the giants of soul, into the final encore, a lengthy medley of old rock hits, and added a hilarious interpolated lyric: "Spotlight on my personal self now/Don't I look boss now." The look on his face as he sang those words was both cool and clownish, a shamelessly funny glance at his own stardom.

In Paris he appeared unaccompanied for the first encore, holding an acoustic guitar. He thanked the audience, then serenaded them with a number he'd never before sung publicly, "my favorite Elvis song," the *Blue Hawaii* ballad "Can't Help Falling in Love." As corny as it was haunting, the song was written way out of Bruce's range. His voice cracked and faltered as he sang it, but that only made the moment more poignant, taking what had been an ironic undercurrent in Elvis's version— the song as the ultimate tease of his devotees—and turning it into a bittersweet tribute to the faceless fan.

The next night, he stepped on stage and without preamble debuted his version of another Elvis hit, "Follow That Dream." Springsteen reinvented the song, one of Presley's bits of movie-era jive, keeping just the basic melody and the chorus: "You gotta follow that dream, wherever that dream may lead/You gotta follow that dream, to find the love you need." Springsteen's version was slow, echoing like a haunt until he reached the new verse he'd written for himself.

Now every man has the right to live
The right to the chance
To give what he has to give
The right to fight
For the things he believes
For the things that come to him in dreams
Baby in dreams, baby in dreams

■

In one sense, the recast "Follow That Dream" was simply Bruce's most eloquent tribute to the one artist he idolized. Seeing Elvis first made thirteen-year-old Springsteen want a guitar, and he reveled in the King of Rock and Roll's commanding power, his sexiness, the pure freedom his presence suggested. But more importantly, it was Elvis who first gave Bruce a glimpse of rock and roll as a means of expressing a vision: *"It was like he came along and whispered a dream in everybody's ear and then we dreamed it,"* Bruce once said from the stage.

"Follow That Dream" was also a reflection of Bruce's changing concept of his role as a rock star, of the secret dream *he* wished to breathe into the public ear. As early as his first album, Springsteen had expressed complicated social ideas—listen to "Lost in the Flood," as good a song as was written about Vietnam during the war—and both *Darkness on the Edge of Town* and *The River* are steeped in class-consciousness. But it wasn't until the *No Nukes* concerts that Bruce began to connect his (and his characters') class origins to a more specifically political outlook. Springsteen's tendency was to look at his life and those of his friends and the characters he invented as roles played in an ongoing drama, caught up in processes great and small. It was only after *The River* that he began to understand those processes as the product of something larger than the circumstances of individual lives. Springsteen had to escape the relatively narrow idea that "politics" is something that only happens when you vote or attend a protest rally, in order to reveal the powerful political undercurrents that surged in his songs from the very beginning.

Springsteen is an extremely cautious man, and he'd always been extra careful not to speak out about issues he didn't fully understand. This was an admirable way to avoid becoming "the new Jane Fonda," but it sometimes meant he sold himself short. At *No Nukes,* for example, he was the only artist who didn't make a statement on the issue in the concert program. Rhetorically, this was supposed to mean that he preferred to let his music speak for him, but an unavoidable implication was that he didn't really feel that he knew what he was talking about (and as the unreleased song, "Roulette," proved, that just wasn't true).

So a radical alteration in attitude was apparent when he played Arizona State University on November 5, 1980, the night after Ronald Reagan's wipeout of Jimmy Carter. "I don't know what you thought about what happened last night," Bruce told the crowd. "But I thought it was pretty terrifying." Then he smashed into "Badlands." That was all he said, but it was far more than he'd ever risked before. And while some of the change was just due to current events, Bruce's ability to see Reagan as a bogeyman wasn't all there was to it. Bruce Springsteen himself was changing.

That same Arizona evening, Bruce was given a copy of Joe Klein's *Woody Guthrie: A Life,* the biography of America's best known folk singer. Reading the book over the next few weeks, Bruce became fascinated by Guthrie, an eccentric character whose mingling of personal and political topics had a lot in common with Springsteen's own songwriting, and whose ambiguous relationship to celebrity was not unlike a rock star's.

For Springsteen, Guthrie had been little more than a name. Despite the Dylan comparisons made early in his career, rock and soul were pretty much the only kinds of music Bruce was aware of back then. He knew more about *West Side Story* than folk music; he could tell you succinctly and persuasively why the Dave Clark 5's hits were critically under-rated, but he'd never heard the great bluesman Robert Johnson. Folk and country blues were campus music, and Springsteen had spent only about a hot minute at the local community college before dropping out.

Working with Jon Landau began to change his awareness of where his music came from. Landau grew up around the Boston folk music scene. He'd played bluegrass and rock and roll. He had both a passionate and scholarly knowledge of blues, gospel, country, bluegrass, and R&B, the bedrock on which rock and soul were built. Bruce and Jon's relationship was based on personal as much as professional considerations, even at the outset, and one of the ways in which they'd gotten to know each other was by talking about music—the latest pop hits, old rock and roll they both knew, personal favorites of Jon's, or records Bruce might have read about but never had the chance to hear.

Bruce reacted to such musical encounters as though given a key with which to tap the memories of his ancestors. His songs drew more and more on what he heard there, though not in the sometimes shamelessly overt way he recast old rock songs. For instance, he based "The River" on lines from Hank Williams' "Long Gone Lonesome Blues," although no one had ever guessd it until he mentioned the fact in an interview.

Springsteen was no folkie; his instincts were those of an inheritor, not a preservationist. "My music utilizes things from the past, because that's what the past is for. It's to learn from. It's not to limit you, you shouldn't be limited by it," he said in 1980. "I don't want to make a record like they made in the Fifties or Sixties or Seventies. I want to make a record like today, one that's right now.

"To do that, I go back, back further all the time. Back into Hank Williams, back into Jimmie Rodgers. Because the human thing in those records is just beautiful and awesome. Wow! What inspiration! It's got that beauty and the purity. The same thing with a lot of the great Fifties records, and the early rockabilly . . . Those records are filled with mystery; they're shrouded with mystery. Like these wild men came out from somewhere, and man, they were so *alive*."

Obviously, Bruce Springsteen saw himself as another wild man come out from somewhere that might as well have been nowhere. The myth said that he'd grown up on the New Jersey seashore, in rundown but romantic Asbury Park. The fact was he'd spent the first eighteen years of his life in Freehold, New Jersey (where his first band rehearsed), in a neighborhood called Texas because it was so dominated by immigrants from the southern United States, the kind of people who looked and spoke a little like the singers from the mountains and cottonfields. Texas was on the wrong side of the railroad tracks; it bordered the town's black ghetto. Springsteen's background was East Coast working class prosaic: Irish and Italian, with a smattering of Dutch (whence the surname). But he could identify with the rockabillies because he'd known people like them in his youth: crackers, white trash, folks who hadn't gotten their cut of postwar prosperity.

This background primed Bruce to hear Woody Guthrie, who marched out of the Dust Bowl to take Manhattan by storm, then turned his back and walked away whistling, as a kindred spirit. Bruce was particularly taken by Joe Klein's story of how Guthrie's American anthem, "This Land Is Your Land," was written. Guthrie wrote the song as a furious response to "God Bless America," written by that other great people's balladeer, Irving Berlin. Guthrie made a song of many verses, and he went to his grave immensely troubled that the most radical of his lyrics were forgotten as his finest song was adopted by the very jingoists and false patriots the song meant to attack.

The irony, perhaps, is that Springsteen's interpretation of what the song was about was smack dab in the middle between Woody Guthrie, who wrote as a Marxist disillusioned with the America of fable, and Irving Berlin, who wrote as a man who had seen his every dream fulfilled and in one lifetime moved from the hellish pits of New York's Lower East Side to Beekman Place, the shortest, most exclusive street uptown. What "God Bless America" and "This Land Is Your Land" have in common is that both were written out of certainty. Springsteen didn't see things that clearly. You could almost think he sang "This Land" instead of "God Bless" simply because he preferred the ambiguity of Guthrie's words. He performed the song at the shows he did at Nassau Coliseum at New Year's; more surprisingly, he kept doing the song when he got to Europe.

It's hard to think of a song more indivisibly American than "This Land Is Your Land." Singing it in Europe, given America's role there as a cultural usurper, added a rich additional layer of ambiguity. Better yet, singing the song in places where "this land is your land" is still a principle to fight over, not simply a slogan, wrenched it out of its context as a great folk cliché. "This is an old song about an old dream," Springsteen told his Paris audience. "It's hard to think what to say about this song, because it's sung a whole lot in the States and it's been misinterpreted a whole lot. It was written as a fighting song and it was written, I feel, as a question everybody has to ask themselves about the land they live in, every day."

■

In a sense, asking questions was exactly what the European tour was about for Bruce—exploring a new environment, amazed at the perspectives it opened for him, including the light it shed upon life back home. A simple example suffices: In Gothenburg, Sweden, Roy Bittan's wife, Amy, was forced to undergo an emergency appendectomy. Beyond the worry caused by illness 3,000 miles from home, the surgery was simple and everyone was impressed with what they saw of Sweden's socialized medicine. Although private rooms and telephones weren't available, it was taken for granted that any person's health needs were an immediate priority, regardless of that person's nationality or income. The comparison with America was unavoidable and, in this case, unflattering.

The tour moved on from Paris to Barcelona, in Spain's Catalonia; doubled back to France for shows in Lyons; then went on to Brussels, Rotterdam, Copenhagen, Gothenburg, Oslo, and Stockholm. From Paris to Brussels, Bruce was accompanied by his girlfriend, actress Joyce Hyser, but most of the time, he was on his own, often able to simply get out and wander the streets of towns he'd never imagined seeing. He was recognized only occasionally, and European fans tended to be less aggressive than Americans when they came upon him in person. On the final morning in Lyons, for instance, Bruce went out for a walk and was stopped by a local kid who asked him for the time, which was pretty funny, considering that Bruce fetishistically eschewed watches while the kid himself was wearing one. But then, a new approach to a familiar gambit had to be appreciated.

There were sights to see—from the surrealistic Gaudi architecture of Barcelona to the opening day fireworks of Copenhagen's Tivoli Gardens, which was a long way from the boardwalk in every way—and museums to visit, restaurants that had to be fitted in. But more than anything, the tour gave Bruce exactly the opportunity he wanted: "Going to France and Germany and Japan and meeting Japanese people and French people and German people. Meeting them and seeing what they think, and being able to go over there with something. To go over there with a pocketful of ideas or to go over there with just something, to be able to take something over. And boom! To do it!" He didn't get to Japan on this go-'round but, offstage and on, he otherwise fulfilled that program exactly.

Great stories could be told about almost every show on the tour. In Lyons the show was delayed for a night because of the national elections; President Giscard d'Estaing had preempted the local Palais des Sports to hold his party's election eve rally. The result was that the show was played the next night in a room whose ceiling was filled with red, white, and blue tricolor balloons. But the finest moment of that evening came when Roy Bittan hit the Morricone-based introduction to "Badlands." The crowd *sang along* to that spectral melody, making a beautiful, haunting sound that no one could have predicted, upsetting and enriching the spectacle of the show. (It turned out that the *Once Upon a Time in the West* theme had been a jukebox hit in northern Italy, where about a third of the crowd came from.) In Paris the band played the Palais des Sports, where the audience didn't expect chairs. The audience simply folded them up and stacked them aside, leaving Bruce to play a festival-seating show whether he wanted one or not. In Brussels, which is NATO headquarters, a sizable percentage of the audience was American military personnel, but in the evening's still moments you could hear whispered translations going on in several languages simultaneously.

As in America, there were surprise guests—Flo & Eddie in Brussels, Link Wray in Copenhagen—and Bruce continued to pull new song renditions out of his hat, the wildest being a scarifying slowed-down Credence Clearwater's "Run Through the Jungle" with at least one original verse, which opened the show a couple of nights—the most daredevil move of the tour. Not that he had to go that far. In Barcelona he played "Because the

Night," which Patti Smith had made a massive European hit, and the crowd simply flipped out, began dancing and carousing as though he'd come to liberate them all.

And maybe, not in his own mind so much as in theirs, he had. Rock and roll represents one basic thing around the world— a dream of freedom. In part, the dream is false. By itself, music is not a liberating force and, anyway, the particular kind of freedom of which rock fans often dream is really a kind of license to do what they will, damn the consequences, or worse, the freedom to sit back as fat and sassy consumers who never move a muscle.

But another part of that dream is true—or can be, under the right circumstances. The dream that Elvis Presley whispered into the ear of the world had such long-lasting echoes and repercussions because it was a peculiarly American expression of the fantasies of mobility, liberation, rebellion, and success that are dreamed the world over. Yet Elvis had never played a single show in Europe, and after him the States produced hardly any figures capable of carrying the myth and only one—Bob Dylan—who did. With Dylan in an artistic decline, Bruce's reception picked up a lot of the slack. You could be sure that when he said the words *United States* the cheers would be as loud as when he mentioned whatever town he happened to be playing. So he toured as a symbol of what people loved about America, leaving him immune, at least for the hours onstage, to all the caveats and criticisms.

Back in the States, looking for something to read while on the road, Bruce had picked up a copy of Henry Steele Commager and Allen Nevins' *History of the United States*, a textbook-length paperback that describes U.S. history in pluralist terms. Far from radical, the book nevertheless opened his eyes time and again, reinforcing an interest in the iconography of America that had been quickened by earlier encounters with such novels and films as *The Grapes of Wrath* and *The Searchers*.

Springsteen grew up in a classically anti-intellectual environment, and as far as he could, he played along: When he signed his first record contract, he claimed the only two books he'd read were *The Godfather* and Tony Scaduto's biography of Bob Dylan.

But after Brandeis-educated Jon Landau gave Bruce a couple of pushes in the right direction, the singer responded with the voraciousness of the born autodidact. At the movies, he found himself fascinated with great genre artists, directors like John Ford and Sergio Leone who returned obsessively to the same subject matter, often at the expense of artistic cachet. He seemed to read whatever he'd heard was good.

One of the more fascinating bits of byplay on the European tour took place late one night on a bus ride from Copenhagen to Gothenburg. Bruce and Clarence sat in a dimly lit seat with an atlas spread across their laps, Clemons listening attentively while Springsteen explained the German army's pincer movement in World War II. However unlettered his roots, Bruce responded to art—or even just plain old information skillfully presented—with the enthusiasm of an intellectual, and despite his shyness at moments like *No Nukes,* in private he was becoming more and more confident that he knew a little bit. Simply by exposing him to so much more, Europe was accelerating the reformation of Springsteen from an attitude-is-everything street punk to a mature adult, a transformation that was vital if he was to survive his grapple with stardom and remain a productive, functioning artist.

Reading Commager and Nevins' history book had an immediate onstage payoff. As always, he transferred social information to a personal context, but this time he fused the two perspectives so tightly that it was all but impossible to say where or whether they diverged.

"I grew up in this house where there was never any books or I guess anything that was considered art or anything," he told his Paris audience. "And I remember when I was in school, at the time, the things that they were trying to teach me and the things that later on, when I got older, I missed not knowing . . . when I was fifteen or sixteen, either [there was a problem with] the way that they were tryin' to teach it or I just wasn't interested.

"But when I got older I looked back and I saw that my father, he quit high school and went in the Army and he got married real young and picked up jobs where he could, workin' in a factory, driving a truck. And I look back at my grandfather and he worked at a rug mill in the town that I grew up in. And it seemed like we all had one thing in common and that was that we didn't know enough, we didn't know enough about what was happening to us. Like, I'm thirty-one now and I just started to read the history of the United States." Here he had to pause, for the audience was cheering wildly.

"And the thing about it is, I started to learn about how things got to be the way they are today, how you end up a victim without even knowing it. And how people get old and just die after not having hardly a day's satisfaction or peace of mind in their lives.

"I was lucky, too, because I met this guy, when I was in my middle twenties, who said you should watch this or you should read this. And most people, where I come from, never have someone try and help them in that way.

"So all I'm sayin' is, is try and learn, learn about yourselves, learn about who you are now. And try and make it better for who's gonna be, who's gonna be comin'. Because the real future of rock and roll's only about nine years old today."

He started to say more, but the roaring crowd wouldn't let him. So he just sang "Independence Day," his song about a son laying his father to rest after years of conflict and disruption.

Later, in other shows, he was able to amplify. "I started reading this book, *The History of the United States,* and it seemed that things weren't the way they were meant to be—like the way my old man was living, and his old man, and the life that was waiting for me—that wasn't the original idea," he said one night in England. "But even if you find those things out, it's so hard to change those things. And it wasn't until I started listening to the radio, and I heard something in those singers' voices that said there was more to life than what my old man was doing and the life that I was living. And they held out a promise, and it was a promise that every man has a right to live his life with some decency and some dignity. And it's a promise that gets broken every day, in the most violent way. But it's a promise that never, ever dies, and it's always inside of you."

That was what Bruce brought to his exchanges with the European audiences. What did they give him? He summed it up on the band's last night on the Continent, in Stockholm, before an audience that was just on the friendly side of riotous. (Sweden was probably the country in Europe where Bruce's popularity was greatest.)

"There's a Marvin Gaye and Tammi Terrell song; it's called 'It Takes Two,' " Bruce began, speaking with unusual nervousness. "In the song, Marvin Gaye sings, 'It takes one to dream but it takes two to make a dream come true.' And I guess that's why we're here tonight talking to you and you guys are talking to us.

"Because it's funny, you know, on this tour, since we've been over here, I've learned, I've learned . . . I've learned a lot over here. I've learned the importance of the audience, the importance of you in the show.

"Because we come out and we play, and we play hard and try to tell you about the things that mean a lot to us, and when you respond the way that you have tonight and last night, it's like . . . it's a big, like '*me too,*' you know." Here he paused to laugh one of his short, nervous giggles, and the applause, which had periodically interrupted him, swelled to its fullest.

"It's in a buncha little things. I want you to know that it means a lot to us just how quiet you've been on the slow songs since we've been here. I want to thank you a lot for doing that . . ." He did not continue. Maybe the emotion was too great; perhaps whatever came next just didn't require words. After a moment, he picked up again.

"This song is about two people that once had that kinda connection and for some reason it got broken apart. And it's like a song ain't no good until somebody hears it. By yourself, you can't have an effect. You have to reach out. This is a song about someone who loses that power, which is the most powerful thing in the world—your ability to affect your friends' lives . . ." he hesitated, and then spoke very quickly: "and my life . . . and maybe I can do somethin' for you. So . . . this is called 'Point Blank.' "

The grand piano chords echoed through a starkly still concert hall, swelling over whispering percussion and bass, until the band picked up the song's theme and tempo and Bruce played a guitar obligato before beginning to sing.

"Point Blank" emerged on the '78 tour, marking an emotional and musical transition between *Darkness on the Edge of Town* and

The River. But it was also the last song completed for the new album—Bruce added the central monologue only in the final days of recording.

In Stockholm he nearly rewrote it again. In the process he recreated this story of the ultimate betrayal—of no one so much as the betrayer herself—as something more than a song. It became a dialogue between the saved and the damned. Bruce maintained the tone, containing his voice until near the end. Then, breathing heavily, almost gasping, he began to reinvent not just his method of singing the song, but the lyrics themselves: "We were standin' at the bar, but it was hard to hear because the band was playin' loud and you were shoutin' somethin' in my ear. You pulled my jacket off as the drummer counted four. You grabbed my hand and pulled me out on the floor. At first, we just stood there and we started dancin' slow, and I pulled you tighter and I swore I'd never let you go. Well, I saw you last night down on the avenue. Your face was in the shadows, but I knew that it was you. Because you were standin' in the doorway, just outta the rain, but you didn't answer when I called out your name. You just turned and then looked away, like just another stranger, just waitin' to get blown away—Point Blank! Right between the eyes! Yeah, point blank! Right between the pretty lies, you fell—point blank. Now you been shot straight through the heart. Girl, point blank! You been twisted up 'til you become just another part of it. Well, point blank . . . you're walkin' in the sights. Girl, point blank—whatsa matter? Did you forget how to love? Girl, did you forget how to fight? . . . They caught you in their sights. Girl, point blank! Just one false move, and baby, the lights go out. But you're not even there now, because you don't even care no more. You can't even hear me. You're not even there anymore. Well, point blank. They musta shot you in the head! 'Cause point blank . . ." He whispered: "Looks like they won." Then, in a perfectly even tone: "Bang, bang, baby, you're dead."

∎

They moved on to England, where the language barrier dissolved and others replaced it. And the pressure lurked again, as Bruce and the band headed for London, the one capital of rock and roll they hadn't yet conquered. Despite all the Continental triumphs, until the Wembley shows, their task wasn't complete.

They started out at Newcastle City Hall on May 11, the smallest venue on the tour with the wildest crowd, 2,000 ale-swigging Geordies. Then on to Manchester and Edinburgh, Scotland, for two shows apiece, before moving to a London hotel headquarters and driving out for one night at Stafford's Bingley Hall—which still smelled of livestock exhibitions—and a pair at Brighton's Congress Center, which, in late May, seemed still prepared for the Mods and Rockers riots of twenty years before.

The provincial English shows were mostly uneventful, although in Manchester Bruce debuted a new song, "Bye Bye Johnny" (later retitled "Johnny Bye Bye"), about the death of Elvis Presley. He sang it for the first time, ironically, in a show in which he dedicated "This Land Is Your Land" to reggae king Bob Marley, who had just died in New York City of cancer. (Springsteen had been the opening act for Marley and the Wailers when they made their U.S. debut at Max's Kansas City in 1973.)

"Bye Bye Johnny" wasn't just the product of an obsession with rock stars who died too young, though. It was the result of four years of brooding about the useless way that Elvis Presley allowed his life to decompose. "I think everybody remembers where they were when Elvis died," Bruce said. The memory seemed to exhaust him, an emotion reflected in the music, clocklike block beats setting up a thin wash of synthesizer and guitar.

The story begins with lines from Chuck Berry's "Bye Bye Johnny" that capture the romantic promise of rock and roll stardom, twisted now into a portent of death: "Leaving Memphis with a guitar in his hand/With a one way ticket to the promised land." In the ensuing verses, the whole mythic romance of the Elvis legend is replayed, right down to a beautiful vision of the funeral procession itself. But at the end, the song turns its gaze unflinchingly upon the ugly fact:

> They found him slumped up against the drain
> With a whole lotta nothin' runnin' through his veins
> Now bye bye Johnny, oh, Johnny bye bye
> You didn't have to die, you didn't have to die

In the studio the song would pick up a quicker tempo and a neater arrangement; the released version could almost be an Elvis song. Bruce never let go of the first verse or that last one, but he changed a lot of the other lyrics. The result was a better, more professional song, but it also distanced him from the original's emotion. Not everyone *does* recall where they were when Elvis died, nor did they spend years trying to figure out how the King's death could have happened. It didn't even bother most people in rock and roll, much less the rest of show business, that much. An early, gruesome demise is built into the legend of pop stardom as most of us understand it.

Speaking of Elvis in such universal terms, Bruce Springsteen was revealing both a compulsive fascination with rock's king and his own ambitions and fears. The fascination went back to his childhood. To this child of poverty, Elvis Presley, so obviously the transcendent product of similar everyday misery, loomed like an interstate highway, eight lanes screaming full tilt in both directions *somewhere*. "I remember when I was nine years old and I was sittin' in front of the TV set and my mother had Ed Sullivan on and on came Elvis," Bruce told another audience later that summer. "I remember right from that time, I looked at her and I said, 'I wanna be *just . . . like . . . that.*'

"But I grew up and I didn't want to be just like that no more. Because he was like the biggest dreamer. He was like a big liberator. I remember I was sittin' at home when a friend of mine called and told me that he died, which wasn't that big a surprise at the time because I'd seen him a few months earlier in Philadelphia. I thought a lot about it—how somebody who could've had so much could in the end lose so bad and how dreams don't mean nothin' unless you're strong enough to fight for 'em and make 'em come true. You gotta hold onto yourself."

Never has a performer given advice more clearly meant for himself. In those lines can be felt all of Springsteen's lust for stardom and his terrible desire to have the world know him, and his equally terrible fear of what the consequences of such fame and such knowledge might be. It would be glib and unfair to describe him as the world's greatest Elvis imitator—unless you were willing to include in that category, at one time or another, everyone from James Brown to Bob Dylan, Jackie Wilson to John Lennon. Then you'd have a clearer picture of where Springsteen fit in.

Also in that statement are the things that distinguished Springsteen as a seemingly fearless artist—most obviously, the idea that dreams are what counts and that they're worth holding onto, fighting for. More important, however, is his flat statement about where his path and Elvis's diverged: *"But I grew up and I didn't want to be just like that no more."*

In the time of punk and disco, however, Bruce's music not only seemed to be a throwback; in some important ways it really was one. It could be argued, on the evidence of his rockabilly rhythms and persistent optimism, that he hadn't a radical bone in his body and perhaps far too many conservative ones. Yet in another way, he represented the most radical of all threats to the juvenile hegemony within rock and roll. He represented the idea that performers and audiences *could* grow up, assume adult responsibility, and tackle serious themes, without abandoning rock and roll's kernel of joy.

As a prototypical all-American boy, Bruce Springsteen had learned that might and main and sparks of invention could carry you much farther than rationalists and cynics ever dreamed. His show was the most outstanding example of the efficacy of sheer will in modern popular culture, yet it was the product of more than hard work and more than raw talent, too. His entire career was a triumph of conviction over trendiness and, more important, of content over form, reversing the typical priorities of contemporary artists. His songs lacked disco's mammoth groove and the impudent purity of punk, not because he rejected either form of music (he wrote a song for Donna Summer, loved the Clash) but because Bruce Springsteen, all but alone among post-Beatles pop singers, seemed immune to nihilism. Despair was a familiar companion in his recent songs, but dark portents were always overwhelmed, if not dispelled, by cascading affirmations of the tenet succinctly summarized in "Badlands": "It ain't no sin to be glad you're alive." What he learned from Elvis was the importance of that principle and the potential price of ignoring it.

The London of 1981 was transformed from the city Bruce had visited six years before. The British national economy had disintegrated along with the last vestiges of empire; unemployment rose toward fifteen percent, and many kids left school knowing they'd never in their lifetimes have a steady job. Government policy was to ignore such wasted lives. (In this respect, the political economy of Great Britain was a couple of years ahead of America's.)

Pop music was both an important component of England's foreign trade and one of the few available vehicles for the working class to make any headway in a brutally class-stratified system. In this respect, rock stardom, for all its rebellious and outrageous poses, provided an essential safety valve by creating a veneer of mobility. Having made it, on the other hand, pop stars were absorbed into a sort of aristocracy, an acceptable development during the expansionist Sixties but a traitorous move when the roof fell in.

Thousands of England's disenfranchised young people turned against the star-making machinery. Rock had become flatulent and arty; many of the stars were now pompous, self-impressed buffoons. The spirit of engagement and vitality had disappeared. Punk rock arose as the antidote. From 1976 to 1978, a horde of nasty-tempered tatterdemalion bands spat and shouted their way through brief, ultra-fast, musically primitive records, thrilling declarations of disgust and determination to overturn the rotted corpse of pop and the social structure that created it: The Sex Pistols' "Anarchy in the U.K.," "God Save the Queen," and "Holiday in the Sun"; and the Clash's "I'm So Bored with the U.S.A.," "Complete Control," and "White Man in Hammersmith Palais" were only the best of it.

As music, punk was as exhilarating as anything since Little Richard first hollered "Awopbopaloobop, awopbamboom." As political insurrection, it was doomed. As a means of disrupting the British pop industry and replacing one star system with another, it was brilliantly if accidentally effective.

Punk ideology proclaimed that anyone could become a star; it was replaced by the idea that anything was permissible in pursuit of stardom. Since this was Britain, where every new pop moment must have a name and be accompanied by a fashion fad, those who crawled out from under the rock punk had tipped over became "the new romantics." In the spring of 1981, new romanticism was the current fad in trendy London quarters, where the current fad is everything. No one could define exactly what new romanticism *was*, of course, but in a way, that just made it better, in the grand tradition of "The men don't know but the little girl understands."

As Dave Rimmer wrote in *Like Punk Never Happened*, his excellent study of British pop in punk's wake, "In refusing to be pinned down to any one particular style or sound, new romantic successfully avoided being marketable and thus also avoided becoming The Next Big Thing. It didn't turn into a new center, but it eroded enough of the old one—challenging traditional rock patterns of consumption at least to the extent of shifting attention from live concerts to club life, from weighty LPs to dance-mix 12-inch singles—to leave everyone wondering just what was going on. Once it was clear that the toy soldier look—the frilly shirts and velvet breeches usually associated with the term *new romantic*—was definitely not hip, nor even saleable in the high street, it was suddenly very hard to work out what was.

"Into the uncertain vacuum roared a confusion of sounds and styles. There was a new fad or revival every week. Rockabilly, most notably in the shape of the Stray Cats, enjoyed a brief renaissance. . . . Brief revisits of psychedelia, be-bop and beatnik all failed to stick. As people cast around for the right new sound, anything became grist to the pop mill. Jazz, Latin, northern soul, funk, Euro-disco, African, Indian and Chinese musics were all variously used as ethnic spice to enliven the staples of mainstream pop. In the case of African music, for example, this boiled down to little more than Adam [Ant] and Bow Wow Wow basing their sound round the drums of Burundi. But it all added to the confusion of a restless, rowdy, eclectic and ultimately brilliant year for white pop music. In 1981 there seemed to be only one rule: don't stand still.

"What was happening was a complete dissolution of the traditional British relationship between music, style and subculture. . . . style was now no longer a badge of allegiance. It was simply this week's outfit. Something to wear for a night but hardly something worth getting into a fight over. Fashion, and pop music along with it, seemed suddenly to have lost its old importance."

From the perspective of an insider like Rimmer, the waning of new romanticism and the dawn of eclecticism took place after Steve Strange and Rusty Egan's Valentine's Day 1981 People's Palace event, in which the decadent, androgynous Soho underground centered around clubs like Blitz moved up to the working class residential neighborhoods in North London. Nevertheless, when the E Street Band landed in London near the end of May, there was still sufficient polyphony of weirdness accumulated in the chic shopping streets and being written up in the music papers to make a Saturday tour of King's Road, just 'round the corner from their hotel, a block-by-block adventure.

To trendy London, Bruce's roots rock and soul approach, his lack of pomp and splendor, his eschewing of trappings and fashion must have looked suspicious or too corny for words. Punk hadn't discernibly affected his music, but Bruce was well aware of it, even though in America it was a fringe movement that had little popular effect. Perhaps he seemed anachronistic to London's trendies. If so, he wasn't concerned about it. But all this made the shows he was about to do at crumbling Wembley Arena that much more difficult and that much more crucial. Bruce was glad to be there. He'd learned a tremendous amount just by soaking up the atmosphere walking down King's Road on a Saturday afternoon, where every block brought another jolt of outrageousness and unconventional finery. But his job was still to transmit a much more homespun and unadorned idea of popular music to the 10,000 per night who'd be there to meet him.

■

That first show would finally happen, after the months of delay, on Friday, May 29. Before showtime the band and crew rehearsed, dressed, and ate with no histrionics, but you could feel the nervous tension. Springsteen's principle was that every show counted equally, but there were nights when more chips were on the table than usual, and there was no denying that this was one of them.

Springsteen may have been fearless, but that didn't mean he was unconcerned. In the end, it was still up to him to go out and do the show that needed to be done, the one that made *him* feel right at the end of the night. He'd done it that way in Los Angeles, at the Forum, and he'd gone the same route, after years of resistance, at Madison Square Garden. London was the last crucial capital of rock and roll, and in a way it counted more than everything from Hamburg to Manchester rolled into one. People's choice he may have been—he'd sold out six shows in England's largest and most prestigious arena without having had a hit record there—but in these citadels of the fickle, you never knew. After all, he *was* from New Jersey, the most despised domicile in America.

They reached the stage a half hour late and opened with "Thunder Road." The crowd roared its approval and before the end of the third song, almost everyone was on their feet. But the band didn't know that. Onstage, with the glare of spotlights in their eyes, it's impossible for performers to see more than a couple dozen rows into the crowd. And the band couldn't count on hearing the response accurately, either, since the sound is amplified in strictly one direction.

For just this reason, Springsteen's contract provided that no tickets were to be taken for use by the band, the crew, the promoter, or the record company in the first twenty rows. But somehow, promoter Harvey Goldsmith had missed that stipulation, and the first few rows were packed with music business insiders.

As usual, Bruce dove into the audience during "Tenth Avenue Freeze-out," although this time with more risk than usual— the London town council had threatened to revoke permits for the final three shows if he dared to do anything as dangerous as entering the crowd. (He was greeted so rapturously—even the stiffs down front got up, at least while he was in their neighborhood—that the councilors came to their senses.) What he read there was hard to say—probably not the reticence of Hamburg. This crowd knew just what he was up to, and there was no social sanction preventing them from joining in. But first night crowds in London are a show-me bunch; to get over with this gang, the band really would have to prove it all night.

Thirty minutes into the show, ninety percent of the hall was roaring on its feet, all but saluting. But the band saw only the complacent sitters in front of them. And the band, if not Bruce, seemed taken aback, maybe a little dejected, by that response. They hadn't seen this much resistance since the first set in Germany.

Bruce spoke very little, as if on this night it was especially crucial that his songs speak for him by themselves. He said nothing even when, near the end of the first set, he began a new song. Anyone who didn't know better would have sworn it was an original, and he provided no additional information.

The music surged around a skeletal structure, much like the revamped "Run Through the Jungle," but the lyrics were even more amazing, a cruel and vivid crescendo that built to the point of snapping and ended each verse and chorus with an expostulated "Trapped!" As it turned out, the song had been found on an old Jimmy Cliff cassette that Bruce had purchased in the Amsterdam airport, and about all the E Street arrangement altered was the rhythm, which was flat rock without a hint of reggae.

The idea of debuting a song, much less such a daring one, in the midst of one of the most crucial sets of his career, got even the deadheads down front into it. As the band segued into the powerhouse chords of "Badlands," the whole room once again exploded. Suddenly, there wasn't a sitter in the house. The sight incited the band; you could see them *lift*, kicking up their heels as they rocked to the set's conclusion. They'd cracked London, once and for all.

Before the end, Bruce still found it necessary to apologize, not only for the postponement of the March tour dates but for the 1975 gig at Hammersmith. But the gesture was needless. Tough as the Wembley crowd may have been, it went home convinced.

The tour ended in euphoria, with the final five shows at Wembley and the last two at Birmingham serving as the coming-out party of a band that had no more worlds within rock and roll to conquer. In Birmingham, as if to pass the torch, the Who's great guitarist, Pete Townshend, showed up to play along on "Born to Run."

"That tour was tremendously exciting," Bruce remembered five years later. "We really reached out around the world, and it gave the band tremendous confidence. I can remember coming home in the end and everyone feeling it was one of the best experiences of our whole lives."

3 OPEN ALL NIGHT

T he story that follows was told onstage in 1984. It is almost certainly true. In any event, it summarizes quite tidily the relationship between our hero and his native province, then, now, and forever.

"Now this, this is a song about the Golden Roadway of the East, the New Jersey Turnpike. I used to work up in New York City, so I'd always have to drive home late at night—and my girlfriend lived down farther in southern Jersey.

"I used to kinda like to ride. I'd get out there around three-thirty . . . Just start drivin', put the window down a little bit. I never had too much trouble on the Turnpike, but if you get off at Exit Eight, that's the Freehold exit, you gotta ride through Hightstown down Thirty-three to the shore. Out in Hightstown, these guys don't have nothin' to do but sit around and wait for ya all night long.

"So I's drivin' home one night and I was thinkin' about seein' my girlfriend and thinkin' about raidin' the refrigerator, seein' my girl, makin' a peanut butter and jelly sandwich, and seein' my girl and makin' a ham and cheese sandwich and raidin' the refrigerator and goin' back to the refrigerator—no." He laughs. "And I know I wasn't speedin', but I musta been goin' suspiciously slow. Because all of a sudden I see them red lights, I get pulled over and . . . 'License, registration, please.'

"Now, I didn't have any. See, I always forget my wallet—one of them people always leaves their wallet home. So I give 'im my name and he goes back and sits in the patrol car and he calls me back in about five minutes and kinda looks at me and he says, 'Hey are you . . . are you that rock and roll singer?' So I say, 'Yeah! Yeah, that's me.'

" 'You the guy that wrote that "Born to Run" song?'

"I say, 'Yeah! Yeah, I wrote that one. That's me.'

"He says, 'Yeah, well, you know, I got some of your albums at home. And son, you're in a lotta trouble.'

"So they took me in, impounded my truck. But the weirdest thing about it was I had to go to traffic court. And when you go to traffic court there are generally three pleas that you can plead. One is innocent, which hardly nobody pleads that. The other one is guilty, which not many people plead *that*. But the one that almost everybody pleads is guilty with an explanation. If you sit in traffic court all night, you figure out that the whole world is guilty with an explanation.

"And what that means is that you really did what they said you did but now you got about five minutes to bullshit your way out of it.

"So like, I'm sittin' in there and some guy recognizes me and comes over, and he's one of the people when they sit down they sit so close to you that you gotta like lean away. And he was drunk. He gets up before me, and he was caught doin' sixty on a residential side street. And his explanation was that he was drunk and thought he was on the main highway.

"So anyway, my turn came and I got up and they got a little microphone. You gotta stand there and everybody's lookin' at you and you feel like a complete jerk. I said, 'Well, judge, now let me start at the beginning' . . ." Against a rockabilly beat, he sings long crazy, unpunctuated lines:

> Your eyes get itchy in the wee wee hours sun's just a red ball
> > risin' over them refinery towers
> Radio's jammed up with gospel stations lost souls callin' long
> > distance salvation

Hey Mr. Deejay woncha hear my last prayer hey ho rock 'n
  roll deliver me from nowhere

■

*When I was a kid, I really understood failure. In my family,
you lived deep in its shadow.*

During the midwinter break before leaving for that European
tour, Steve Van Zandt produced an album for Gary "U.S." Bonds,
one of his and Bruce's heroes of the soul era. (For years, Bonds'
greatest hit, "Quarter to Three," served as their final encore.) The
album, *Dedication*, featured four songs written and co-produced
by Bruce including a revamped version of the Cajun classic "Jole
Blon," which Springsteen and Bonds sang as a duet. When
Dedication was released, just about the time that the E Street
contingent landed in Paris, its first single, the Springsteen-
penned "This Little Girl," became a hit, Bonds' first chart record
in nineteen years.

Steve Van Zandt had met Bonds in the mid-Seventies, while
both were touring on the oldies circuit (where Van Zandt was the
Dovells' band leader for a time). When Bonds first met Springsteen the summer before *The River* was released, he had no idea
who Bruce was: "You know, Springsteen, I thought it could have
been an old car . . . or a sandwich or something."

Van Zandt wrote the album's finest number, "Daddy's Come
Home," selected such bold songs as Bob Dylan's "From a Buick
Six" and Jackson Browne's "The Pretender" for Bonds to sing,
arranged and produced everything. Bruce was also involved in a
limited way. Steve and Bruce had worked this way before,
notably on the three albums that Miami produced for Southside
Johnny and the Asbury Jukes, but the Jukes albums never had
more than moderate commercial success. "This Little Girl"
reached thousands who had no idea of that history, and Bruce got
a lot of credit for the Bonds comeback. (No artist had ever spent
so many years off the charts and returned to the Top Twenty.)
Suddenly the Springsteen magic seemed to encompass the ability
to rejuvenate the careers of fallen idols.

Gary Bonds' hit, the triumph in Europe (sparsely covered as
it was in the States) and the lingering memory of the 1980 tour

contributed to an upsurge in Brucemania that reached the band the moment they returned to the States. The key was the tour, which grew in stature as fans and critics looked back. In a sense, Bruce's show was taken for granted while he was doing it; only after he'd been gone awhile and there were other tours to compare it with did it become clear how remarkable it really was.

The tour forged its own context. "Rock and roll is, today, too big for any center. It is so big, in fact, that no single event . . . can be much more than peripheral," critic Greil Marcus wrote around this time. "In one sense, this is salutary and inevitable. The lack of a center means the lack of a conventional definition of what rock and roll is, and that fosters novelty. . . . But this state of affairs is also debilitating and dispiriting. The fact that the most adventurous music of the day seems to have taken up residence in the darker corners of the marketplace contradicts the idea of rock and roll as an aggressively popular culture that tears up boundaries of race, class, geography and (oh yes) music. The belief that the mass audience can be reached and changed has—until now—been the deepest source of the music's magic and power.

"The music does not now provide much evidence that this belief is based on anything like reality. . . . Bands with very broad—or at least very big—audiences continue to exist, of course, but they don't destroy boundaries; they disguise them, purveying music characterized principally by emotional vapidity and social vagueness.

"A concert by Bruce Springsteen offers many thrills, and one is that he performs as if none of the above is true. . . . His show is, among other things, an argument about the nature of rock and roll after twenty-five years. The argument is that rock and roll is a means to fun that can acknowledge the most bitter defeats, that it has a coherent tradition which, when performed, will reveal possibilities of rock and roll the tradition did not previously contain."

Springsteen's confidence in this tradition—not just in its existence, but in the idea that the general principle Marcus describes still worked—was singular at this time. Others operating inside the tradition used it as a crutch, so that it became a substitute for the transaction between artist and audience. Because Springsteen was so internally centered, that problem never arose for him. He poured all his energy and imagination into *what* he wanted and needed to say, not worrying about how. He could do this in part because he was such a naturally gifted rock and roll musician: Songs sprang out of him by the dozen, where they trickled from others, and his music was focused in styles that endured, which allowed him to be oblivious to fashion in ways that almost no other rock performer could afford.

One result was that he made solving the most difficult problem pop performers face look ridiculously easy. But it was never easy for Springsteen, only simple. He was not afraid to show the strain of getting it right when that struck him as appropriate. But it's also true that talking about his faith in tradition misses the mark. ("Having posited a tradition," Marcus commented, "Springsteen acts as if every bit of it is backing him up—rooting for him.") What really distinguished Springsteen was that he had something he wanted desperately to communicate—something he believed counted, that would make a difference in the lives of those who experienced it, including himself. Invest yourself in that way and the world will beat a path to your door.

Yet the contradiction between Springsteen's live appeal and his record sales and radio airplay persisted. "Fade Away," the followup to "Hungry Heart," had stalled at Number Twenty, and there was no third single. *The River* spent four weeks at Number One. It sold about 2 million copies, substantially more than any of Bruce's other albums but not equal to the day's biggest record acts, who sold 5 million or more copies of their biggest hits. While Springsteen was king of the hill at album-oriented radio (AOR), he remained a marginal figure at more-influential Top Forty stations, and it was Top Forty exposure that sold records in multiplatinum quantities.

All of this indicated the ultimate irony of Springsteen's situation: Though he was celebrated and loved as the last true believer in the possibility of speaking meaningfully to a mass audience, he spoke essentially only to a very large cult.

Bruce shunned talk of marketing. His discoverer, the venerable producer and talent scout John Hammond, once commented that Springsteen was the only performer he'd met in forty years in the business who cared nothing about money, which happens to be true, however unbelievable. And his lack of interest in commerce went way beyond money. For most performers, the claim that their work comes first is merely serviceable rhetoric. To Bruce the work was literally the only thing that mattered. When he entertained any discussion of how to sell himself, it was solely as a means of getting people to hear his work.

So other acts selling more records never fazed Springsteen. He was not competing with what anybody else had to say. His concern was always what happened to the people who *did* hear him, not those who didn't, a reflection of the inverted optimism built into the bedrock of his personality at an early age.

"I never got into being discouraged, because I never got into hoping," Bruce once told Robert Hilburn. "When I was a kid, I never got used to expecting success. I got used to failing. Once you do that, the rest is real easy. It took a lot of the pressure off. I just said, 'Hell, I'm a loser. I don't have to worry about anything.' I assumed immediately that nothing was happening.

"But that's not the same as giving up. You keep trying, but you don't count on things. It can be a strength. Because I know some people who sweat out winning so much it kills them. So, in the end, they lose anyway."

Again, Springsteen makes his outlook seem too simple: just a matter of common sense. And in this particular case, he was being disingenuous, since fame and success gave him more than his share of problems. That was obvious even when it came to simple matters. For years he refused to play sports arenas for fear that it would disrupt his rapport with his audience, as though that intimacy were created by physical proximity, not his own passion. The latest wrinkle in concert promotion was "tour merchandise," the selling of t-shirts, programs, buttons, and other souvenirs. For most of the 1980 tour, he held out against providing a significant array of such trinkets, even though his fans were clearly eager for them, and the graphics and programs he did allow were understated and unpretentious to a fault.

For that matter, his lack of hit singles boiled down to a kind of avoidance. "If success was what it was like with *Born to Run*,"

Landau remarked, "Bruce didn't want that. He didn't want to have one song that could be taken out of context and interfere with what he wanted the album to represent."

His records may not have been played on Top Forty radio much, but his songs were staples there. Others picked up on his material and had half a dozen Top Ten hits in the late Seventies and early Eighties. The biggest hits came with songs that could just as easily have fitted into his own albums—the Pointer Sisters' "Fire" and Patti Smith's "Because the Night." Ironically, by eschewing such obvious smashes, Springsteen avoided full contact with the very human mass that his concerts celebrated.

Nevertheless, when he returned from Europe, Springsteen had to change, and not only as a result of what he'd seen and learned there. Whether or not he had any use for celebrity, he'd become a huge star. And the U.S. tour planned for that summer, playing multiple arena dates in the dozen cities where he was already biggest, amounted to a victory lap.

4 WAY BACK HOME

I never will forget those nights
I wonder if it was a dream
Remember how you made me crazy?
Remember how I made you scream
—DON HENLEY, "The Boys of Summer"

Onstage at the Brendan Byrne Arena in New Jersey's Meadowlands sports complex in early July of 1981, Bruce Springsteen was a king returned to a throne. His six-night stand was the arena's maiden event. He'd play to more than 120,000 people, two or three times the capacity of Giants Stadium next door. But even that number was dwarfed by the demand. Tickets for the Jersey shows were sold by mail, and when the first day's orders arrived, Meadowlands general manager Loris Smith reported, there were enough requests for twenty-two shows.

Bruce was more than just New Jersey's favorite son. Requests came from all over the New York metropolitan area. It seemed everyone who had ever lazed away a weekend down at the shore wanted to get in. But the Meadowlands dates were nonetheless a special kind of homecoming. Because the shows would also mark the new arena's inauguration, there was a full complement of political brass squabbling for seats; Springsteen's associates prevailed over the promoters, and the public won that round.

Mostly, the huge attendance reflected a massive outpouring of love by the area's rock and roll fans, teenagers to middle-agers. When Bruce came onstage for the first show on July 2, the

54

greeting was so huge—a long screech and stomp rising and swelling to all but overwhelm the first song, which was, inevitably, "Born to Run," Bruce's first anthem—it almost seemed the new building might not survive.

Not a bad welcome for a kid who had grown up on the wrong side of Freehold, one of the seedier towns in the seediest state in the union. Pretty impressive for a boy who had seemed so weird twelve years before that he was requested to leave Ocean County Community College by his fellow students, all of whom now remembered him fondly. A bitter man would have savored the irony. Bruce Springsteen just played his heart out.

"I just want to say you guys *made* tonight for us," he told the crowd during the encore. "We don't play for anybody better. Anyway, this is something special that we learned for ya." They launched into a rendition of Tom Waits' "Jersey Girl," complete with a new verse written by Bruce, and though he didn't sing Waits' lines about "whores on Eighth Avenue," his own were even harder-boiled. "Go in the bedroom, put your makeup on/We're gonna take that little brat of yours and drop her off at your mom's," he sang to his dream doll. Not altogether dispensing with irony, he immediately thereafter slammed into a song of Steve Van Zandt's, which in its way summed up the occasion perfectly: "I know he's talking about the way I feel/And I don't want to go home."

If anything, the second night's crowd and show were even wilder. The dignitaries had split, making more room for hard-core Springsteen fanatics. These were fans to whom Bruce Springsteen spoke forcefully and almost across the board. His songs illuminated the glory and the tragedy of dead-end lives played out in dead towns; they also seemed to celebrate the ability to rise in the world, to make it. Yuppies in their cups, teenagers with their hopes up, workers down on their luck in an economy gone sour could all listen to the words of "The River"—"Is a dream a lie if it don't come true/Or is it something worse?"—and hear a fragment of their own stories. It may have been that the Yuppies heard what they feared, a story about what they believed had been left behind, and that others heard a tale much more realistic. But everybody heard a story no one else was telling, and they loved the teller as much as the tale.

In this environment, Bruce Springsteen had only two things to fear. One was those ugly green tubes filled with phosphorescent chemicals. Bruce's concert contract banned them from being sold inside the arena, but they found their way in anyhow. When he looked out into the dark, their ghoulish glow was one of the few things he could see, and it was an ugly distraction. "If you've got one of those green things, please give 'em to somebody . . . so they can throw it in the trash," he snapped during the third show, on July 5. In the background, Miami Steve nearly doubled over with laughter; Bruce gave a gruff snort at his own overreaction. "I *hate* those things."

But not as much as he hated firecrackers. There was no show on the Fourth itself, but whatever leftover fireworks existed in New Jersey seemed to have been reserved for Bruce's gig the next night. Bruce had particular reason to understand the danger of setting off cherry bombs in an arena. During the final show of the *Darkness* tour, in Cleveland on New Year's Eve 1978–79, a firecracker tossed on the stage went off in his face and he had to retire for several minutes, reemerging with a bloody bandage over his eye.

It was also annoying, because the fireworks most often went off during his quietest and most serious numbers. Bruce's shows opened with a series of cornerstone rockers, but the middle of the first set was somber, as if he were setting the crowd up for the good times ahead by reminding them of the price that had to be paid, not only that night but every day. On the fifth, he opened with "Thunder Road" and a smoking "Prove It All Night," rollicked through "The Ties That Bind," then pulled the mood back down for "Darkness on the Edge of Town" and "Factory." During the latter, the night's first fireworks went off.

"I'd like to just make one announcement," Bruce said as soon as the song was done. His tone was quiet but stern. "If by any chance you brought any fireworks with you, please don't set 'em off in the hall. Keep 'em in your pocket or throw 'em away. If you see somebody settin' em' off, tell the usher or tell the security guard because I want 'em thrown out. 'Cause you're gonna hurt yourself or hurt somebody that's around ya.

"That's not what 'Independence Day' is about anyway." On

cue, music began, the organ and piano chords that led into the song.

"I remember when I was a little kid, every Fourth of July my mother and father used to take me out to the racetrack in Freehold," Bruce said. "I guess they don't have fireworks no more down there, but they used to have 'em every Fourth of July. And there used to be this cemetery that was right on the outside of the track, and there was this hill called Cemetery Hill, and everybody used to go up there and park and sit up on the hill and watch the skyrockets.

"When I was little I didn't know what it was about. I just knew that on Fourth of July we'd go out there and there were all these fireworks and stuff.

"We just spent a couple of months over in Europe. And I found myself thinkin' of home a lot more than usual, from being away. I'd never been away from the States for so long. And I started to read this book called *History of the United States*. And in it, I found a lot of things that were important to know, because they helped me understand the way that my life was and the way that my life developed. They helped me understand how when I was a kid all I remember was my father worked in a factory, his father worked in a factory . . ." His voice just faded out, as if speaking of a chain too endless to recount.

"And the main reason was that they didn't know enough," he said, echoing his Stockholm rap. "They didn't know enough about themselves, and they didn't know enough about the forces that controlled their lives.

"I started to read this book and the thing that most impressed me was the idealism. It was like when you were a kid and you leave home. You leave home because you believe in yourself or you think you're gonna do somethin'. And because you wanna be different—you wanna be different than your old man was . . ." He stopped, drowned out by cheers, then began again as they died down.

"And that's what happened here. The idea was that there'd be a place for everybody, no matter where you came from, no matter what religion you were or what color you were, you could help make a life that had some decency and some dignity to it.

"But like all ideals, that idea got real corrupted. And as I read through the book and I got up into the Sixties and the Seventies . . . in the Seventies I was in my twenties and I was in my teens in the Sixties, but I felt like I'd been sleepin' all the time through all those years. 'Cause I didn't know what was goin' on; I didn't know what the government that I live under was doing.

"It's important to know about yourself, that's all, and know about the things around you. So, you get a chance, read that book, *History of the United States*. It's good!"

He launched into a memorably tender version of the song, one of his finest and most important, in which a father is laid to rest by a son still struggling to resolve the hopelessness of their lives together. He had performed the song in moods ranging from rage to anguish, he'd recorded it as what sounded like the recessional from a folk mass funeral, but tonight he simply sang it as a gentle confession of incomprehension—two people so close that they were blinded to one another: "There was just no way this house could hold the two of us/I guess that we were just too much of the same kind." After that introduction, the song became, at least for this night, an act of absolution.

In a way, this was the closest Bruce came during the Meadowlands shows to explaining to his audience what had happened in Europe. His efforts at a direct explanation petered out. "It's really somethin.' It's different than New Jersey," he said opening night and stopped to laugh at the ludicrousness of the remark.

The difference seemed to express itself most often when he was unable to control the behavior of his expanded audience, when it lacked those respectful and empathetic qualities that he had found in the overseas crowds. On July fifth, during "Racing in the Street," another firecracker exploded. When the song ended, Bruce spoke in a tone he virtually never used from the stage: cold fury.

"When I was over in Europe"—he broke off, fighting to command himself—"one of the things that I hadn't thought about that much before, that I started to think about, was the importance of the audience at the show." Cheers forced him to pause again; when he began speaking it was in the tone of a parent who had just been given the perfect setup for the lesson to come.

"And I just want to say that I'm proud that everybody's come down to see us. And whoever it is—and there's only one person or two out of, I guess, twenty thousand people here tonight—that has to set off a firework in the middle of a song, the only thing I can . . ."—he paused to rein himself in again—". . . I can say is, you can do me a favor and never come back to one of my shows ever again. Because if you don't . . . if you don't have the respect for yourself, you should at least have respect for the people that are around you. And if you don't have that, you should at least have the guts to do it where I can see you."

For the most part, Bruce's shows were not confrontational occasions. He ripped into the firecracker crowd all through the Meadowlands series because such activities spoiled the creative atmosphere he wanted to create. Springsteen's concerts were a refutation of the idea that rock was anarchic rebellion. If anything, his shows were a masterwork of crowd control, an adventure in pure cooperation, a challenge to chaos. After angrily cursing the final firecracker thrower of the Meadowlands series, on the last night of the stand, Bruce snarled, "Whoever you are, you're no friend of mine." It was the worst epithet he could conceive.

By the same token, politics weren't really the focus of Springsteen's essays in public speaking. His introductions were an art in themselves, a crucial and revealing segment of his performances, but their focus was always on personal revelations of various kinds. His references to Europe, to studying United States history, to the hidden American class system were profoundly *prepolitical*. He had no ideology to sell; in that sense, he was continually groping to coalesce these interests and incidents into a coherent shape that would do nothing so much as explain himself to himself. He was never so naïve as to believe that the good fortune that rained upon him could happen to just anyone. "I wrote this song because I've been lucky—I've got about as much freedom as money can buy in this country," he remarked later that summer. "And it seems like you're never really free until everybody else is." The song that followed was "Jackson

Cage," perhaps the most overtly *psychological* number from *The River*, the story of a woman trapped in her own house by an existence that's too trivialized to make sense.

It was just such moments of revelation that kept the Springsteen cult returning to his shows, night after night, with a thirst that approached greed. One of the few problems associated with the Springsteen tour was ticket-scalping, not because scalping was particularly worse around his shows than those of other superstars, but because his fans were convinced that scalping violated the principles those shows epitomized (without considering that those principles were in direct conflict with a market economy) and because every Springsteen fan was sure that an equitable distribution would never leave him or her out. The fact that concerts are inherently inequitable—that there are only a finite number of seats in the front rows, only a finite number of seats in "good" locations, that playing any sort of facility imposes a limit on the number of people who can enter it—was deemed irrelevant. And the reason for it all was that if you missed one of Bruce's shows, you might really be missing something. It didn't have to be a new song or a new story; it could just be a juxtaposition of images or songs, a matter of tone or inflection.

On this final leg of *The River* tour, though, Bruce's onstage musing acquired an almost compulsive character. You could hear in his anxious breathing that he was probing at parts of himself that were extremely discomfited, dredging up aspects of his life that perhaps did not really want to emerge—certainly, aspects that almost no other performer would have found it necessary or desirable to expose.

A classic example, and one that also shows the process by which the same song and story could have their meanings transformed from night to night, lay in the comments he made before the final "Independence Day" of the Meadowlands shows. Like all such stories, it began in childhood.

"I grew up in this house where nobody ever talked to each other," he began, sounding miserable. "We used to live on the left side of this little three-room house. There was a front room and then the kitchen and two bedrooms and a bathroom upstairs. With everybody livin' that close, it seemed that nobody ever sat down without being angry, tellin' each other what was on their mind. I could never talk to my old man, he could never talk to me, my mother couldn't talk to him . . .

"So I was glad when I finally got old enough and I started to live alone. Then, for about ten years I never saw my folks that much. And just recently, we came back from Europe . . . If you get a chance, you gotta go there because you can't imagine it—it's not what you think it is or what you read in the papers. But we got back and I got a phone call a night or two later that my father had gotten sick. And I went out to California where he was in the hospital there.

"I started thinkin' on the way out about all the things that I always wanted to say to him that I never said and I always figured, well, someday we'll sit down and we'll talk about all this stuff—talk about why it was the way it was when I was young, talk about why he felt the way he did.

"But the years go by and it never comes up. I guess it feels like a dangerous subject or something. But he got sick and I realized that he was gettin' old and that . . . and that if I had somethin' to say to him, I should say it now . . . 'cause family is forever and it's somethin' that . . ." Here he was drowned out by cheers but continued anyway, the audience all but irrelevant. "It's somethin' that don't ever go away, no matter how far you move away from each other or no matter what your feelin's are towards each other. It's just there in your blood all the time, in your blood.

"So if you got folks at home and have been waitin', waitin' to say stuff to 'em, don't waste too much time. 'Cause you'll always regret it." He said the last line in a mumble, so low and muttered that it was doubtful anybody ten feet from the mike heard him, although the listener who mattered most at that moment surely did. The song that night was nothing less than an act of contrition.

■

When the band returned from Europe, they took the rest of June off. While in California with his parents after his father's stroke, Bruce wound up playing two shows, the Survival Sunday anti-nuclear benefit with Jackson Browne and a number of others, and a Gary Bonds gig at San Francisco's Old Waldorf nightclub. Clarence Clemons busied himself—against Bruce's advice, it later developed—preparing to launch a Red Bank rock club, Big Man's West. The others relaxed, but not too much. They'd been on the road for six of the past eight months, but the tour still had a long way to go.

Even before going to Europe, Jon Landau and Springsteen had planned another swing around the States. They'd be playing many of the same towns as in the fall, but with a difference. "The concept was to go back to cities that had been very special in Bruce's career," Landau later explained. "Basically, come in and stay for a while and play a little bit in depth. You know, when you're in the city for more than a day, when you're not just on the bus coming in that day and driving out after the show, you go out, you get a feeling for the place, maybe you drop in on a club. You have a chance to personalize your visit to that particular town."

The result encompassed thirty-five shows in only ten cities. In every city except San Diego, Springsteen played for at least two nights in the city's largest arena. In addition to the six nights at the Meadowlands, he played five shows in Philadelphia and five in Los Angeles. In every town, the issue was not whether he sold out, but how quickly the tickets went. In most places there were enough requests to have played two or three times more shows, even considering that, in a mail-order ticket lottery, many customers apply several times, and in Springsteen's case, just as many were bent on seeing *all* of his performances in their town.

This level of fanaticism was not unprecedented. The Who, the Grateful Dead, the Rolling Stones, Led Zeppelin, and a few other top rock acts had acquired equally devoted followings. What made Springsteen's massive cult surprising was that he did not have the Sixties cachet of those other groups. He was the one concert superstar whose career was entirely post-Woodstock.

More significantly, what each of these groups had in common was that they represented an idea. Superficially, that idea could be almost anything, from the macho 'n' mysticism of Zeppelin to the spaced-out good vibes of the Dead. But underneath it all, each of these bands acted out a form of community, whether with the aristocratic-bohemian arrogance of the Rolling Stones or the familial squabbling of the Who. Each of the central figures of rock history had this in common; even those seemingly monolithic individuals, Elvis Presley and Bob Dylan, acquired much of their force from this idea. In their cases, though, the community was not something they acted out so much as a phenomenon that gathered around them.

In a sense, Bruce Springsteen and the E Street Band had it both ways. In reaching out so intimately to his audience, Bruce conveyed an especially lucid idea of community; by making demands on that audience—demands of stamina, attention and, increasingly after the European tour, responsibility—he became continuously more articulate about the community that he was trying to shape. Bruce played several roles in this sense, alternately acting as good-natured older brother, the most incorrigible and charming juvenile in town, stern parent, generous uncle.

On the other hand, the internal dynamics of the E Street Band represented another form of community, as rock bands always have. In this respect, the polyglot look of the group was even an advantage, for looking from Bittan to Clemons to Van Zandt, one was given the firm impression that no one—at least, no one male—was excluded. (And when Bruce went into the crowd or brought a fan from the front rows on stage to dance with him, women became an important part of the group.)

Bruce's relation to all of this was especially fascinating because he was privately such a loner. He always had been. "In the beginning, my goals were pretty modest," he said. "I wanted to learn to play rhythm guitar, just so I could get in a band—just to be in a band; I didn't want to be the lead singer or I didn't want to be the lead guitarist. I didn't become a lead guitarist until I got thrown out of the first band I was in. I just wanted to play rhythm guitar, just find my spot, kinda stand there in the background, just, you know, just be in the band." Even though being in a band was of such tremendous importance to him, he kept to himself offstage, communicating with the band (except Steve) and crew mostly at the hall. Back at the hotel, he was no party animal. Bruce never took drugs—and that means he never took a single pill for pleasure (he was reluctant to swallow medication) or smoked a single joint of grass. He never smoked cigarettes, for that matter. He drank rarely, and when he did, he got wasted (and silly) fast.

"He's so unlike everything you think a real successful rock star would be," exclaimed pianist Bittan, and after twenty years of observing stars in various stages of dissolution, it was impossible to disagree. Besides, Bruce's abstemiousness made him mysterious and that made him more attractive. His personality was perfectly in synch with times in which Huey Lewis could make a hit of "Hip to Be Square." As the audience weaned on rock grew up, it became ready for a more wholesome and constant kind of rock star, someone who would both act out fantasies and provide a model of values. Maybe for the first time in the history of pop stardom, someone like Bruce could become an idol.

Compared to Mick Jagger, much less Johnny Rotten, Springsteen was conservative. The term seems a bit misleading—despite rock's anarchist propaganda, restraint and caution aren't reactionary tendencies—but it was one Bruce himself accepted, at least when it came to creativity. "Generally, I'm pretty conservative in some ways," he said. "I don't really have a desire to experiment for the sake of experimentation, because mainly what I'm tryin' to do is get an idea across. I'm not really that concerned with style. I wanted our thing to be basically real content-oriented. It's what you're sayin'. So I kinda go from there. I go from like, Is this a good song? Is there a human being in this song? If I sing this song, do you hear a real person's voice? And then, what's their story, what are they sayin'? Is it something that's worth takin' up people's time with?"

One part of punk's legacy was the introduction of modernist (and academic "postmodernist") ideas into pop discourse. "Rock was, after all, a modern form—the expression of dislocated, rootless youth," wrote critic Tom Carson. "Its public images and media masks were of a piece with the technological leaps-into-the-void that made it feasible. We didn't respond to Jagger because he was being himself; we responded because he was acting out ploys and stratagems open to us. We expected the truth from our avatars, but not candor." For Carson, Springsteen (until *Born in the U.S.A.*) "was never an entirely satisfying rock star," and the reason was quite basic: "He thought rock and roll was basically wholesome. It was an alternative, an escape—but not a rebellion, either as a route to forbidden sexual or social fruit, or, by extension, as a rejection of conventional society. To him, rock *redeemed* conventional society." Carson pointed to Springsteen's use of rock to work through his relationship to his parents, and to the friendly but generally unsexual way that women were portrayed in Bruce's songs as examples. Critic Milo Miles neatly summed up the problem Springsteen presented for postpunk partisans: "Granted, *Born to Run* sent a tremor through West Coast soft-rockies and warned that several hundred thousand pop fans were spoiling for an old-fashioned rumble, but at bottom the record proved that the avant-garde of rock and roll was out of the hands of extremists."

In this respect, Springsteen's subordination of form to content is not so much reactionary as anachronistic. Even his repetition of themes and images—his fixation on automobiles and driving metaphors, for instance—was a pragmatic rather than theoretical device. This approach may not have been critically fashionable, but it played perfectly in a pop climate in which a substantial portion of the audience had been deadened by the dictum of change for its own sake.

The summer tour confirmed Bruce's stature—and it did something more. "As a band, I think we were different, and not only just musically," Van Zandt said. "Once you communicate internationally, you feel that, even if it's subconscious. You're never the same." Bruce simply said that when he got back home, "I wasn't really sure what was going on, I just knew something had changed."

If it wasn't obvious to him, it was to others. However great the changes in his audience and in his band, the greatest of all were taking place within Bruce Springsteen. He'd entered the record business as a twenty-one-year-old who had barely earned his high school diploma. It wasn't really until 1974, when he and Jon Landau became friendly, that Springsteen had a chance to develop intellectually. Landau's relationship to Bruce was significant not only because he encouraged the singer to believe that he really was as good as his dreams, but also because in the course of spending time together—at first on the phone, then socially, and finally in the recording studio—Jon exposed his new friend to the very idea of art. Bruce became extremely attentive to classic Hollywood films and began to read classic American literature. By 1981, a rather arty film like John Huston's adaptation of Flannery O'Connor's *Wise Blood* had become as inspiring to Springsteen as the Ronettes and Rolling Stones.

Landau didn't deliberately set out to educate Bruce, but his enthusiasms were infectious. When Bruce complained that he couldn't stand to watch John Ford's *The Grapes of Wrath* on television, Landau simply sat down with him the next time it was on and showed him what he was missing. Landau played an extremely useful role in the process by which Springsteen made records; as manager, Jon translated Bruce's ideas into business-like terms as no less empathetic figure could have done. But if there was a bottom line to their relationship, it was simpler and stranger: Jon Landau was the first person who had ever realized that Bruce Springsteen had not only an amazing talent but was also extremely intelligent. Explaining himself to a Paris audience, Bruce paid tribute to what that meant to him: "I was lucky, too, because I met this guy when I was in my middle twenties who said you should watch this or you should read this. And most people, where I come from, never have someone try and help them in that way."

The prime beneficiary of Bruce's growth wasn't Jon Landau; it was Bruce himself. As he gained a better grasp of himself and his world, Springsteen was able to channel this understanding more and more clearly into his work. When he returned to America, seeing his own country with fresh eyes and confronting an audience that was increasingly huge and anonymous, Bruce began to think about a way of returning some of what he'd been given. In part, this meant money, but just as much, it meant opportunity—the opportunity to have one's story heard and case presented.

Of all the shut-out groups of Americans he knew, Bruce was most moved and intrigued by the plight of the Vietnam veterans. He was no Rambo, and he frankly admitted doing everything he could to avoid being drafted. "I had no real political standpoint whatsoever when I was eighteen. And neither did any of my friends," he said. "The whole draft thing, it was just a pure street thing. You didn't want to go. You didn't want to go because you'd seen other people go and not come back. The first drummer in my first band, the Castiles, enlisted and he came back in his uniform and he was 'Oh here I go, I'm goin' to Vietnam.' Kinda laughin' and joking about it and that was it. He went and he was killed. There were a lotta guys from my neighborhood, guys in bands . . . One of the best singers in the neighborhood, he was drafted and he went and he was missing in action.

"And so it got to be a thing. We didn't even know where Vietnam was when I was eighteen, seventeen. We just knew we didn't want to go and die. It wasn't until probably later in the Seventies that the awareness of the type of war it was, what it meant, the way it felt to be a subversion of all the true American ideals, twisted the country inside out—it wasn't until then that we had any what you would call political awareness about it."

Springsteen was 4-F because of a brain concussion received in a 1968 motorcycle accident in which he also badly injured his leg. Getting out of the draft wasn't that simple though. Springsteen filled out forms crazily, didn't take tests, did his best to get out of serving. But he never forgot how near he'd come.

"When I got on the bus to go take my physical, I thought one thing: *I ain't goin'*. I had tried to go to college, and I didn't really fit in. I went to a real narrow-minded school where people gave me a lot of trouble and I was hounded off the campus—I just looked different and acted different, so I left school. And I remember bein' on that bus, me and a couple of guys in my band, and the rest of the bus was probably sixty, seventy percent black guys from Asbury Park. And I remember thinkin', like, what makes my life, or my friends' lives, more expendable than that of somebody who's goin' to school? It didn't seem right."

By 1981 Springsteen's position on the war hadn't changed and neither had his feelings for those who couldn't escape fighting it. The war had been wrong and worse, and the men and women who fought it had been badly betrayed—not by "lack of national will," but by a government that was eager to use them to carry out pernicious foreign policy objectives and then discarded them without thanks when they returned defeated.

Bruce read *Born on the Fourth of July*, the memoir of Ron

Kovic, a paraplegic vet who had joined the antiwar movement, and was deeply moved, both by Kovic's personal story and by the tragedy that had befallen all the Vietnam veterans.

Largely conscripts, the vets had nonetheless volunteered for combat duty, believing they were fighting for civics class ideals. But when they arrived in the jungle, they found themselves shooting and being shot at only to maintain corrupt regimes both in Saigon and Washington. Returning to national scorn, they found no G.I. Bill. The Veterans Administration, set up to cope with the aging veterans of Korea and World War II, wanted as little as possible to do with these vets who were young, often black or Latin, almost always working-class, and justifiably furious. And if the government's treatment was inept, the public was simply callous. Americans didn't want to know about the vets at all. The war had revealed a massive split in American society, and acknowledging the vets' existence could tear it open again.

Meantime the veterans, who had come from the poorest sections of society in the first place, were visited with all sorts of plagues, from mental exhaustion to drug addiction to the aftereffects of Agent Orange, a defoliant that caused affected soldiers' children to be born with genetic defects. Americans sufficiently well-to-do to afford higher education had been spared military service; in the face of the double digit unemployment of the early Eighties, the poor and poorly trained Vietnam vet was one of the citizens most likely to be found destitute.

Having thought about the veterans, having read about them, and with the memory of his friend, drummer Bart Hanes, still in his mind ("He was one of those guys that was jokin' all the time, always playin' the clown"), Bruce decided that he wanted to help. He asked Jon Landau to locate a Vietnam veterans organization and find out what kind of help might be provided.

Landau, who had of course been antiwar, asked Joe Klein, his former *Rolling Stone* colleague who had written the Woody Guthrie biography. Klein was just beginning research on a book about Vietnam veterans that was eventually published under the title *Payback* in 1985. He told Landau that the organization most worthy of aid was Vietnam Veterans of America.

Landau got in touch with VVA president Bob Muller, a thirty-

six-year-old former Marine Corps first lieutenant who was left
paraplegic after being shot in the spine in 1969 at Con Tien, just
outside the demilitarized zone.

When he returned to the States and was finally released from
a VA hospital (an experience he said was even more depressing
than what he underwent in 'Nam), Muller joined Vietnam Veterans Against the War, the most militant of the veterans groups
within the antiwar movement. After the war ended, VVAW died
out. By 1978 Muller determined to form a more broadly based
group to fight for the rights of Vietnam-era soldiers, which the
American Legion and Veterans of Foreign Wars basically refused
to do. This was the Vietnam Veterans of America.

By 1981, Muller and VVA had gotten precisely nowhere. The
government continued its policy of benign neglect toward the
Vietnam vets, refusing to acknowledge their special problems.
Muller worked unceasingly, and he was effective in getting some
media attention for the veterans. *The Washington Post* wrote
thirty-five editorials in favor of Vietnam vets' rights. Muller was
named one of the fifty "future leaders of America" by *The New
York Times Magazine*. Such establishment credentials gave him
access to every key figure associated with the war, including all
the major policy-makers, and he arranged meetings with everyone from former Secretary of Defense Melvin Laird to former
Time editor Henry Gruenwald. "They all told me to go away," he
said. Although VVA chapters were proliferating, because it was
the *only* game in town for Vietnam vets, Muller couldn't raise
enough money to create a functioning home office or even put out
a regular newsletter.

Rock and roll was probably the last place Muller would have
thought to turn for support. The music's historic association with
the antiwar movement suggested hostility toward the vets. But
when Landau called and invited him to come to the Meadowlands
shows and meet afterwards with Bruce, Muller went eagerly. No
matter what rock musicians thought of Vietnam veterans, most of
the vets were rock fans. He may not have seen the opportunity as
a main chance, but a good time was never against Bobby Muller's
principles.

After Jersey shows, Bruce was inevitably tied up for a couple of hours, first recovering from the rigors of the show, then greeting family and friends. Because Bruce didn't want to place a time limit on his meeting with Muller, Bobby came in last. The wait was worth it for everyone concerned. The two men hit it off immediately, forming a friendship that extends beyond the bounds of politics. They talked for forty-five minutes. "I think Bruce decided right then, five minutes into the conversation, that he was going to hook something up with him," Landau said.

Muller may not have been looking for a main chance, but he was smart enough to grab one when it presented itself. Soon after meeting Bruce, he began pursuing other rock stars. After some discussion, Bruce agreed to do his first show in Los Angeles, on September 20, as a benefit, with all proceeds donated to VVA and several Southern California veterans' aid facilities. Meantime, Muller lined up similar commitments from singer Pat Benatar and country-rocker Charlie Daniels (who was not a vet but had a road crew of veterans). Bruce's show was a guaranteed sell-out, and the others did about as well. In all, nearly a quarter of a million dollars was raised. "Without Bruce and that evening, we would not have made it," Muller has said repeatedly since then. "We would have had to close down." Today VVA operates with a multimillion-dollar annual budget and has a Congressional charter. It is the only recognized, effective national organization for Vietnam veterans. Muller has also become one of the key figures in attempting to rebuild diplomatic relations between the United States and Vietnam.

After the Jersey shows, Bruce and the entire band spent a stifling Saturday night closing out the grand opening of Big Man's West. A couple of days later, the tour proceeded to Philadelphia and ground to a temporary halt. On the first night at the Spectrum, the air-conditioning failed; when the cooling system came back to life for the second show, it was overpowering. By the time the run ended, Bruce's throat was too sore for singing. Shows scheduled for Chicago and Cincinnati's Riverfront Coliseum had to be postponed, flipped to the end of the tour.

After a ten-day layoff, Bruce got back on track with his three-gig stint in Largo, Maryland (between Washington and Baltimore), and the tour charged through Detroit and Denver on its way to the West Coast. The band had never played better. Even a downpour that drenched the crowd and had Bruce playing "Who'll Stop the Rain" to open the show at Denver's outdoor Red Rocks amphitheater couldn't dampen spirits. (Bruce came out and offered either to postpone the show or play on through the rain; he clearly thought it would be a good idea to start all over another night. The crowd voted him down.)

Arriving in Los Angeles, Bruce and Landau's associate, Barbara Carr, spent an entire day at the local veterans' center, meeting with several dozen men and women, a great many of them still suffering from war wounds. Those confined to wheelchairs were the least of it. There were vets who would never leave their hospital gurney tables, and there were men whose bodies were intact but whose minds were in pieces. All of them were coming to the show—so many wanted to attend that tickets were ultimately provided for all the L.A. shows.

At the Los Angeles Sports Arena, tour manager George Travis built a kind of gallery along the side of the stage for the disabled. On the night of the benefit, dozens of paraplegic and quadriplegic vets were ushered into the special section, honored onlookers who served—that night and on those that followed—as a visible reminder of what the occasion was all about.

Visiting the vets center left a deep impression on Bruce. He told Muller that he'd barely slept the night before the benefit, just thinking about what he was going to have to do. "He said he was petrified, that when he walked onstage without the guitar, he felt naked." Muller had his own worries. He'd made speeches for years, but how was he going to get across to 20,000 rock fans screaming for their hero?

At showtime, Bruce walked out, picked up the mike, and began to speak in an unusually nervous tone. At the same time, what he had to say was forceful and considered. He wasn't telling a story or introducing a song; he was making a speech, but he did it with the same combination of straight-from-the-shoulder plainspokenness and artful metaphor he always used.

"Listen. Listen for a second," he said. "Tonight we're here for the men and the women that fought in the Vietnam war. Yesterday I was lucky enough and I met some of these guys. And it was funny, because I'm used to comin' out in front of a lot of people and I realized that I was nervous and I was a little embarrassed about not knowin' what to say to 'em.

"And it's like when you feel like you're walkin' down a dark street at night and out of the corner of your eye you see somebody gettin' hurt or somebody gettin' hit in the dark alley but you keep walkin' on because you think it don't have nothin' to do with you and you just wanna get home.

"Well, Vietnam turned this whole country into that dark street. And unless we're able to walk down those dark alleys and look into the eyes of the men and the women that are down there and the things that happened, we're never gonna be able to get home . . . and then it's only a chance."

He looked out to the restless crowd, over at the vets, and began speaking more loudly, his tone sharpened. "You guys! You guys out there that are eighteen and nineteen years old—it happened once and it can happen again." He broke off momentarily to let the cheers subside.

"So," he sighed, "I guess all I'm sayin' is, You gotta go down there and you gotta look. And we got the easy part, because there's a lotta guys here tonight who had to live it and live it every day. And there's a lotta guys who made it home to America but died and didn't make it here tonight. So what I want to ask you to do is, I wanna ask you to give a few minutes of your attention and listen to a friend of mine, a Vietnam veteran named Bob Muller."

Muller wheeled forward into the spotlight. The crowd may have been eager for the show to start, but he was greeted warmly—after all, he'd just been introduced as Bruce's friend.

"It's very exciting to be here tonight," he said eagerly. "It's a great night for Vietnam veterans. You may have been hearin' about Vietnam veterans and not really understanding what it's all about. Very simply, there was a lotta controversy and there was a lotta pain surrounding the tragedy of Vietnam. Because of that, a lotta people have tried to forget it and pretend that it never happened. That doesn't do much for the families of the fifty-five thousand Americans that were killed in Vietnam. It doesn't do much for the three hundred thousand that were wounded fighting that war.

"But tonight is the first step in ending the silence that has surrounded Vietnam." Cheers stopped him. "It is the beginning of taking all the people that have worked so hard for these years all over the country—people like in L.A., the Shad Meshads, the team leaders from the vet centers, the Center for Veterans Rights, *all* the Vietnam veterans—and it's bringin' us together. And by that, it'll make sure that the programs are enacted, it'll make sure that the lessons are learned and that the Vietnams aren't allowed to happen again." Cheers interrupted.

When Muller spoke again, his voice had risen with excitement. He'd been waiting for this part of what he had to say for weeks; it still seemed too good to be true. He wasn't making a speech anymore. He was celebrating an alliance that could not only help keep his organization alive but would push it much closer to victory.

"The last thing I gotta say: It's a little bit ironic that for the years that we've been tryin', when the businesses haven't come behind us and the political leaders have failed to rally behind us that, when you remember the divisions within our own generation about the war, it ultimately turns out to be the very symbol of our generation—rock and roll!—that brings us together. And it is rock and roll that is going to provide the healing process that everybody needs."

Now Muller was shouting like a Top Forty deejay: "So let's not talk about it, let's get down to it, let's rock and roll it!"

Quickly, the E Street Band took its place and Bruce strode to the mike. Counting it off quickly, they hit John Fogerty's "Who'll Stop the Rain," a song probably written about Woodstock but adopted by Vietnam veterans as their anthem. At least two members of the group played the song that night with tears in their eyes. Bruce told Muller afterward that when he counted off the song, his emotions were at such a pitch that he felt as if he'd already played an entire show.

The music simply exploded off the stage, a contained but frenzied pounding that surged with all the complicated emotions the war still evoked. And out front, Bruce Springsteen's voice, crackling with mourning and fury against the almost elegant chords. They sailed out of it with Bruce shouting with all his might, demanding, "I wanna know! Well, I wanna know!" Over and over, pounding it in, as if by the act of singing this song and *getting it right* he could revive all the lost hopes and wasted lives.

They played the whole show that way, pounding through remarkable versions of "Prove It All Night," "Darkness on the Edge of Town," "Trapped," "Badlands," "This Land Is Your Land," and "Hungry Heart." This was the band that played every note, every night, as if it counted. Still, it must have been news even to them that they could play a whole set at such a peak. Given an occasion, even something so slight as a birthday, Bruce always rose to the moment. Given lives at stake, he could take those lines from "The Promised Land"—"Take a knife and rip this pain from my heart"—and make them bleed.

When they came out for the first encore, he spoke again through the music of another. The song was the Byrds' "Ballad of Easy Rider," another song written for a contradictory purpose but adopted by vets who had no songs of their own. Roger McGuinn and Bob Dylan's plain lyrics said next to nothing, but the song told everything there was to know.

What was amazing was the gentleness with which Bruce sang. After four hours of frenzy and fifteen years of madness, it came down to this almost still moment in which the wound began to heal through nothing more and nothing less than the beauty of the music. Five years later, talking with Muller about old times, Springsteen explained that he had always wanted his music "to be useful," to help people who needed it. "When I did that benefit for you guys was the first time I got to do that," he said. If there's an explanation of why the night rose so high, maybe that's it. Bruce Springsteen wasn't doing the Vietnam veterans a favor; they were working *together*. And so when he sang those lines from "Easy Rider"—"Well, all he wanted was to be free/And in the end, that's how it turned out to be"—he was saying something for himself as well as for them.

It would still be years before Vietnam veterans began to get the respect they deserved, and when they did, it was often for all the wrong reasons: as an attempt to deny that the war had been lost for good reason, as a set-up for the nation to wage similar battles once again. But in the music made that night, you could hear a different process beginning—the wounds starting to heal. So believe Bobby Muller when he says, "Without Bruce Springsteen, there would be no Vietnam veterans movement."

Bruce also turned a corner that night. Not so much because he'd come out and made a political statement, or even because he'd spoken his mind so clearly about a complex issue and been understood. It was because he'd made his dream tangible.

"I know this is idealistic," he once said, "but part of the idea our band had from the beginning was that you did not have to lose your connection to the people you write for. I don't believe that fame or success means that you lose that connection, and I don't believe that makin' more money means you lose it. Because that's not where the essence of what you are lies. That's not what separates people. What separates people are things that are in their heart. So I just can never surrender to that idea. Because I know that before I started playing, I was alone. And one of the reasons I picked up the guitar was that I wanted to be part of something. And I practiced and I studied and I worked real hard to do that, and I ain't about to give it up now."

More than that, maintaining his connections was a form of self-protection. "One of the things that was always on my mind to do was to maintain connections with the people I'd grown up with, and the sense of the community where I came from," Bruce remarked a couple of years later. "That's why I stayed in New Jersey. The danger of fame is in *forgetting*, or being distracted. You see it happen to so many people . . . The type of fame that Elvis had, and that I think Michael Jackson has, the pressure of it, and the isolation that it seems to require, has gotta be really painful. I wasn't gonna let that happen to me. I wasn't gonna get to a place where I said, 'I can't go in here. I can't go to this bar. I can't go outside.' " The only sure way—the only way at all—to keep things in perspective was to keep a visceral connection with everyone else.

Yet Bruce faced an even more difficult obstacle to keeping life "normal": his wealth. "Most rich men will tell you that money don't mean a thing," he said. "But that's not true. It's freedom. But you also got to keep that up-from-under-thing that rock and roll has always been about. That's the constant vigilance . . .

When Steve and I were young, we said we wanted to be as big as the Rolling Stones, that we'd have all the girls we wanted, fancy clothes. That's all we wanted. Well, when you get there, sometimes the pants don't fit. Or maybe we've grown up too much to enjoy it or want it."

It was this resistance to decadence that earned Springsteen the respect of even doubters like critic Carson. "The limitation of rock-as-rebellion, and even of rock-as-fun, was that both equated rebellion and fun with youth, or at least youthfulness," wrote Carson. "But to Springsteen, with his belief in rock-as-*life*—not to mention a capacity for one-plus-one thinking—a far from negligible asset—it seemed purely natural and obvious that if people grew up, rock should encompass that, too. And once he saw that, he had to open himself up to lives where rock might tell the tale but couldn't provide the salvation."

Springsteen had begun to imagine such lives in the songs of *Darkness* and *The River*. "I wanted to make the characters grow up," he said. "You got to. Everybody has to." There is no more concrete refutation of the premise of bohemianism. But to Bruce, no theoretical question was involved; for better or worse, he lacked much interest in that kind of abstraction. After *Born to Run*, he remembered, "I said, 'Well, how old am I? I'm this old, so I wanna address that in some fashion—address it as it is in some fashion,' and I didn't see that that was done a whole lot."

It didn't occur to him to ask why—or at least, asking why and getting back answers like Carson's didn't deter him. "To me it seemed like, hey, it's just life, you know. It's nothin' but life. Let's get it in there."

His involvement with VVA was a significant extension of the same idea. By striking the first public blow for a group of Americans robbed of their health, their identity, their right to stand free, Bruce had done more than live up to his own ideals. He had begun to live them out. So when the tour finally ended three weeks later in Cincinnati's hockey rink, it was the most joyous conclusion anyone could have wished to see, a funny extravaganza.

But the tour didn't really finish until dawn the next day. Bruce kept the entire touring party and a couple of dozen visitors up all night, drinking and dancing to Dave Clark Five hits. In the end, he laid 'em all to waste and retired, having boogied two consecutive crowds straight into the ground. He made his plane back to Newark the next morning with a smile on his face. After it landed, he had time on his hands for the first time in three years.

5 ON FIRE

M idway through the show now, and Bruce stands soaked in sweat. He wears nothing more than t-shirt, jeans, and boots. All are sopping. From the floor, he looks so wet you want to check for rain.

Out in the seats, a night breeze fades the day's heat. Onstage, hot white spots and barely cooler red, blue, and yellow gels lock the band in an inferno. But even the musicians escape for a moment or two between songs or during the solo numbers. Not Bruce. He does his three-hour show without ever leaving that spotlight glow—and pays the price.

Heading into some slow numbers, the fatigue—not just tonight's, but the accumulated weariness of nineteen months of campaigning—begins to tell. Bruce stumps to the microphone, his right leg dragging a little from his old motorcycle wound, and you can see him catch his breath, reach out to adjust the pace, gather his thoughts. He's visibly incorporating that weariness into his demeanor, making it part of the show, as if to say, "Okay, that was the *tough* part. Everybody's a little winded now."

Bruce dedicates his song to Little Steven "and my band, because—" Cheers stop him before he can continue. He laughs right along, the show out of his hands for a second. "We're gonna get kinda sentimental tonight, now—it's the last night." Then regaining command: "There's no way I can ever measure what their friendship has meant to me over the years. So here's to my band . . . and here's to friendship." Gently, carefully, he sings "No Surrender," his song about what it meant to be a desolate kid in the Sixties and join a band—teaming up not just with fellow musicians, but entering into the kind of community from which he'd always feared himself excluded.

Sung with no accompaniment save his own guitar and harmonica, the song's most outrageous pronouncements are presented as flat fact—"We learned more from a three-minute record than we ever learned in school"—and its boldest hopes glimmer brightly before beginning to fade toward today: "Out on the street tonight, the lights are growin' dim/The walls of my room are closin' in/But it's good to see your smilin' face and to hear your laughter again/Now we can sleep in the twilight, by the river bed/With a wide open country in our hearts and these romantic dreams in our head." On record, backed by the band at full throttle, these words have an edge of desperation; the song's a reluctant farewell. Sung without the rock backing, the lines are weary and lonesome; if anybody's sleeping under the stars, it's not because they're running away but because they've earned a rest.

Quietly, the band files back into position. Bruce turns alongside the mike in its stand and faces the crowd, still drenched, hair limp, his arms hung down from shoulders squared but sagging. Turns and looks at the crowd, piercing them with a gaze that would be fierce were it not simply pained. Behind him begins the music, a guitar strangling in its own electronic echoes, followed by synthesizer moans.

He picks up the microphone and speaks in a hush. "I remember growin' up, my folks always havin' to work so hard all the time. I remember my dad in the morning, goin' out in the back yard, under the hood of one of the old cars he bought, tryin' to get it started to go to work." He pauses, stares out, says nothing but looks as if he wonders how to get through. The music continues. "And my mom goin' down to the finance company, borrowin' money for Christmas, and gettin' it paid back in time to borrow money for Easter, gettin' it paid back in time to borrow money to get us clothes to go to school in."

He stops again and looks bleakly out into the crowd, as much as to say that probably no one believes him. After a moment, despairing of explanation, he continues anyway.

"When I was really young, I don't remember thinkin' about it much." A brief pause. A sigh. "But as I got a little older, I watched my father . . . how he would come home from work and just sit in the kitchen all night. Like there was somethin' dyin' inside of him, or like he'd never had a chance to live." He emphasizes this last word ever so slightly, in such a way that you can't tell whether he is puzzled or bitter or both. "Until I started to feel there was somethin' dyin' inside of me. And I'd lay up in bed at night and feel like, if somethin' didn't happen . . . I was just gonna . . ." He takes a breath, squeezes it out; his voice is beginning to crack. "That someday I'd just . . ." Breathing harder now as if struggling with some massive weight that continues to press him down, he pushes on: "I felt like I was just gonna . . . If somethin' didn't happen, I was just . . . I felt like I was just . . ." Now he pants, pushing out his breath, gasping, gulping, forcing the words. "Like I was just gonna . . . just gonna . . ."

One last push and the song is born from his breath, the guitar melting into melody, the synth figure losing its sinister cast and becoming a beckoning horn. Now only the words are nasty:

> At night, I wake up with the sheets soakin' wet
> And a freight train runnin' in the middle of my head

Toward the end, he abandons the lyric for a kind of mumbled prayer: "Won't you shut out the lights . . . Yeah, won't you shut out the lights now . . . Won't somebody shut out the lights . . . Someone shut out the lights now . . ." Then he simply walks away from the mike and leaves it to the band, ticking the song away, beat by beat, like a transfusion.

6 MIDNIGHT SPECIAL

I never knew anybody who was unhappy with their job and was happy with their life. It's your sense of purpose. Now, some people can find it elsewhere. Some people can work a job and find it some place else . . . But I don't know if that's lasting. But people do, they find ways.

Or else. . . ?

[Long pause] Or else they join the Ku Klux Klan or something. That's where it can take you, you know. It can take you a lot of strange places.

—from an interview, 1980

Only a few days after the tour ended, Clarence Clemons flew to Maui to be married. Bruce flew out a little later; he'd be the best man. Many of the other band and crew members also attended. Conspicuously absent was Steve Van Zandt, already back in the recording studio, preparing a second album for Gary "U.S." Bonds and quietly working on a project of his own.

Clarence's decision to remarry was a shock. He was married and the father of two when he joined the E Street Band in 1971, employed as a youth counselor and playing sax only on weekends. Bruce and the band members were making fifty bucks a week—when times were good. Amidst the scuffling, Clarence's marriage soon disintegrated, and for ten years Clemons was the epitome of the party-hearty rock musician. ("I'd just lie back and watch the house jump up and down the block," he later said of those days.)

But in Stockholm during the European tour, Clarence again met Christina Sandgren, a Swede ten years his junior whom he'd first encountered while in Stockholm in 1975. Clarence and Christina (called Tina) hadn't seen one another in the intervening eight years. During that time only one brief letter had passed between them. Yet Clemons later said that he had returned to Stockholm determined to find her, and while in Sweden he asked her to marry him. She immediately came to the States and traveled with Clarence through the summer tour of America. Their wedding was held in Hawaii partly because Clarence had been there previously and loved it and also because the Big Man's brother was a minister in the islands.

"You got to be ready to want to do it," said Clarence of his reasons for changing his attitude. "I think that those eight years that we didn't see each other were perfect. She lived her life, I lived mine. We needed this time to grow up. I hadn't grown up at the time of my first marriage. People have to experience life before they do something. You'll always wonder what's out there if you don't." Clarence was not inexperienced.

In 1984, during the midwinter break in the *Born in the U.S.A.* tour, Tina Clemons gave birth to a boy, Christopher Nicholas. Since their marriage, Clarence had spent his non-E Street Band time operating and folding his Red Bank nightclub, Big Man's West (a Big Man's East had been half-jokingly planned for Stockholm; the Red Bank version lasted until early 1983); forming a band, the Red Bank Rockers, with boyhood friend J. T. Bowen as the outstanding lead vocalist; making two albums, the first an excellent retro-soul package featuring Bowen, which flopped commercially, the second a pop-oriented set containing the hit single "A Friend of Mine," a duet with Jackson Browne; and being converted to the teachings of guru Sri Chinmoy, through whom he met Narada Michael Walden, who produced his second album and used him as saxophonist on Aretha Franklin's comeback hit "Freeway of Love."

Shortly after the wedding, Bruce flew back to New Jersey. He didn't "go home," because he didn't really have a home to go to. Although now a multimillionaire, he didn't own a house. Well, he'd purchased a place in Los Angeles, but that was easy. He still lacked a home at home, though. The lease had run out on the farmhouse on Telegraph Avenue in Holmdel—just behind the Garden State Arts Center, "the opera out on the turnpike" of "Jungleland"—where he'd lived while working on *Darkness* and *The River*. Since then Bruce had bounced around quite a bit whenever he wasn't holed up in a Manhattan or Hollywood studio or out on the road.

This lack of a house wasn't entirely a matter of being unable to find a suitable place. It was just about a point of principle. "I always want to have a feeling of leanness, of not dragging too much stuff around," Bruce told his friend British journalist Michael Watts in 1981. "I guess that's one of the reasons why I've avoided buying a house—things just clutter up your life."

That attitude hadn't altered over the years. "I throw out almost everything I ever own," he'd told *Melody Maker*'s Ray Coleman during his first visit to England. "I don't believe in collecting anything. The less you have to lose, the better you are, because the more chances you'll take. The more you've got, the worse off you get." And Bruce's philosophy applied to a lot more than houses. When his friend George Theiss, the lead vocalist of their first band, the Castiles, got married in 1969, Bruce told him flat out, "Man, you'll never make it now."

It was an icy comment, but in those days Bruce could be equally cold about himself. "You know, you have to be self-contained," he proclaimed in the mid-Seventies. "That way you don't get pushed around. It depends on what you need. I eat loneliness, man. I feed off it. I live on a lotta different levels, y'know, because I've learned to cope with people, which is—be cool all the time . . . I can roll with the punches. It's a way of getting along."

That idea helped make Bruce self-sufficient in his twenties. But he was entering his thirties now, and some of his dogmatism seemed dubious, even to himself. Unlike Clarence, his shyness of marriage applied exclusively to himself. But there were still blocks and barricades about the possibility of domesticity in his life, and he'd put them there himself.

The contrast with the ideals of his concerts and songs was unmissable. Even Bruce knew that. "All my houses seem to have been way stations," he said many months later. "Which is funny, because the things that I admire and the things that mean a lot to me all have to do with roots and home, and myself, personally, I'm the opposite. I'm very rootless in that sense. I never attach myself to any place that I am.

"I always felt most at home when I was like in the car or on the road, which is, I guess, why I always wrote about it. I was very distant from my family for quite a while in my early twenties. Not with any animosity; I just had to feel loose. Independence always meant a lot to me. I had to feel I could go anywhere, anytime, in order to get my particular job done. And that's basically the way I've always lived.

"I think when I was young I did it intentionally, because I knew I only had sixty dollars that month, and I had to live on sixty dollars, and I couldn't get married or I couldn't get involved at the time. And then it just became my way of life."

The professional requirement to travel was also a convenient excuse, one for which Bruce had developed the perfect rationale—big-hearted, idealistic, functional, and abstractly accurate: "Part of the idea of rock and roll is to go on the road. There's a very different feeling that happens when you get out there in the Midwest, really out there where there's nothing for miles and miles around. The thing we got the most from was touring, getting people to come out, to leave their houses and come down to the show.

"Unless you can win an audience, you're in for a tough time. That's the most challenging thing, to play the kind of music you want to play, do the kind of shows you want to do and win an audience—win people who will listen to you, win people's ears— all kinds of people and all sorts of people. And then to sustain that relationship by being responsible about it. That's the most important thing."

But whatever the justification, Bruce was coming off the road, where he'd been happily surrounded by band, crew, and crowds for over a year, and returning to a house he'd rarely slept in. It was a nice place overlooking a reservoir in Colt's Neck, the heart of Monmouth County's horse country. But it wasn't a home.

Mythologically, home was Asbury Park, over on the shore, a beat-up beach town with mystique, where Bruce had made his bones as a bar-band rocker and where he'd found almost all of his bandmates. In truth, home was Freehold, fifteen miles inland, a pre-Revolutionary War tank town of 10,000 souls divided— black from white, rich from poor—by railroad tracks. The town of Freehold is in turn surrounded by Freehold Township, which has a wealthier landscape of large suburban homes and horse and truck farms. Freehold is the kind of place where the inferiority complex is built in, rubbed in the face of residents every time they hit Route 33 and head on past the city limits. It has none of Asbury Park's faded charm.

"It's just a small town—it's just a small, narrow-minded town," Bruce remembers. "No different than probably any other provincial town. It was just the kind of area where it was real conservative. There was a time in the late Sixties when I couldn't walk down the streets, you know, 'cause of the way you looked. It was very stagnating, there were some factories and some farms and stuff that, if you didn't go to college, you ended up in. There really wasn't that much, you know; there wasn't that much."

Bruce grew up in a working-class neighborhood of Freehold, where families who'd been in Jersey for generations lived alongside transplanted Southerners and recently arrived blacks, all working at the A and M Karagheushian rug mill, a Nestle's chocolate plant, a 3M factory, or various smaller factories and businesses. All were located within a mile or so of the Springsteens' various homes, not far from the center of town. When the *Asbury Park Evening Press* for Saturday, September 24, 1949, wrote, "Mr. and Mrs. Douglas Springstein [sic], 87 Randolph Street, Freehold, are parents of a boy born yesterday at Monmouth Memorial hospital," any local would have known by the address that they lived in a working-class neighborhood of neatly kept but poorly appointed houses. In fact, the house had been in the family of Bruce's paternal grandmother for a couple of generations, and Doug and Adele Springsteen were living there in part to take care of his parents.

When Bruce was six years old, the younger Springsteens moved nearby to Institute Street, where they lived in a two-bedroom cold water duplex. Later, when Doug's parents again needed to live with them, they moved to a house on South Street where Bruce spent his high school years.

In the 1950s and 1960s, when Bruce Springsteen was growing up, working men and women in industrial towns all across North America took for granted the ability to purchase a second car—perhaps a boat, or even a second home—to make enough between wages and overtime to set up some kind of side business (and to work in conditions that left them in some kind of shape for leisure or personal investment). Workers came to welcome short, seasonal layoffs or brief strikes as opportunities. Wages rose; hours shrank. For almost twenty years, even with periodic "adjustments" for recession, American industry provided a majority of workers a standard of living beyond anything previously known.

As long as it's recited in extremely precise terms, this conventional picture of U.S. life in those decades is accurate. But prosperity didn't reach everyone. Few black and Latin workers found things so fat. And even among white workers, there were those who slipped through the boomtime cracks and never found work steady or life satisfying.

Doug and Adele Springsteen both worked, Adele in the same job as a legal secretary throughout Bruce's childhood, Doug at a variety of jobs: taxi driver, rug mill worker, bus driver, guard at the county jail. But they were supporting not only themselves, Bruce, his younger sister, Virginia, and later, when Bruce was in junior high, his sister Pam, but also Doug's parents. The Springsteen kids always had the necessities, but there was little room for luxury, especially since Doug's work was often unsteady.

The key to the family's stability was Adele. "My mother is the great energy—she's the energy of the show," Bruce said. "The consistency, the steadiness, day after day—that's her. And the refusal to be disheartened, even though she was really up against it a lot of the time.

"My mother lived with an immense amount of stress and pressure all her life and she was a person of immense control. It was she who created the sense of stability in the family, so that we never felt threatened through all the hard times." Onstage, Bruce has often told stories of his conflicts with his father, but it was his mother's love of radio music, especially Elvis Presley's, that shaped the joyous side of his sound.

To describe Springsteen's childhood as ordinary, which in the case of male adolescents usually means feeling like a misfit, misses the mark. Compared to most people in America (especially those who grow up to report and interpret events), Bruce's early life was abject but, equally importantly, eccentric: "The loner thing started from the very beginning," he said. "My father's entire family were outsiders." His grandfather, the radio man, restored second-hand appliances and sold them to the laborers in the work camps outside of town. Bruce's night-owl hours began before he started school, and he was imbued by his grandparents with an extreme sense of independence. "They didn't give a damn what anybody thought," he said. On the other hand, he was imbued with a sense of hard work by his parents, especially Adele, who was working a steady job and also having to maintain a household for six people.

Make no mistake, Doug and Adele Springsteen didn't miss out on the luxuries of postwar America because they were lazy. They missed out because there was only a limited amount of room in that abundant society. Bruce, whose public recollections of his childhood have sometimes been bitter, also knew the other side: the frustrating battle just to make little things work. "My father worked a lot of jobs that take everything from you and give you barely nothing back," he said in 1980. "Some people get a chance to change the world, and other people, they get the chance to make sure the world don't fall apart." That was even more the case with Adele Springsteen, whom Bruce describes as "real smart, real strong, real creative—what I am doing today is directly connected to my mother." So Bruce was taught the inadequacy of the best intentions from the very beginning.

It was only at the beginning of the Eighties—just a few months before Doug's stroke—that Bruce was able to begin sorting out bad from good in his upbringing and to laugh about it some. Before *The River,* his stories of adolescence had been all hurt and anger. He couldn't really explain the change, except to say, "I sort of have a perspective on those times, right now, maybe more than I did then." He didn't seem to understand why he felt so obsessed by his past, why he kept mulling over old times, why so many of his onstage raps began "When I was growin' up . . ."

He'd turned thirty but he was no nostalgist. America was entering a political and economic phase in which a lot more lives were being wasted as the Springteens' had been and a lot more intelligent, talented kids like Bruce were being manhandled by a system completely insensitive to their needs. The real horror, as Bruce later realized, was that the lives didn't die, even though expectations might strangle. "My father sat there every night for, I guess, about eighteen years, and I never once asked him what he was thinking about, what was on his mind. I always felt he was cutting me short, and I guess in a lot of ways I was cutting him short. 'Cause I thought he didn't dream no more, and I was real wrong about that."

He dreamed better lives for his kids, for one thing. One way or another Doug and Adele found the money to send their kids to the nearby parochial school, St. Rose of Lima. Unfortunately, it was an extravagance neither Bruce nor the nuns appreciated, and one that turned grade school into a battleground of further humiliations. And not only because of the nuns. "I was a big daydreamer when I was in grammar school. Kids used to tease me, call me dreamer. It's something that got worse as I got older, I think—until I realized that I felt like I was dying, for some reason, and I really didn't know why." In ninth grade Bruce transferred to the public Freehold Regional High School.

Bruce didn't fit in there either. "I didn't even make it to class clown," he claimed. "I had nowhere near that amount of notoriety." Nevertheless, in the end he had to skip his own graduation, according to Robert Hilburn, because "one of the school's teachers thought Springsteen's long hair was disrespectful, so she appealed to his classmates. If they let him go through the graduation lines with hair that long, she said, they would be telling the whole community that a high school degree wasn't worth respect. No one came to Bruce's aid."

Bruce's teenage social problems are rather difficult to understand at this distance. In a sense, it was all mystifying even to him. "I was the kind of kid that never got into trouble, but trouble would gravitate around me—not even serious stuff, ridiculous kinds of things. I didn't have anything to hold on to, or any connections whatsoever—I was just reeling through space and bouncing off the walls and bouncing off people." He was drug-free and neither boisterous nor troublesome. True, his hair fell frizzily past his shoulders, and in those days that could be enough for ostracism—by adults. Maybe the trouble was just that he didn't make—or even know how to make—any special effort to socialize and that the students at Freehold Regional were just like kids everywhere else: brutal conformists whose instincts were to stamp out whatever failed to fit in. Bruce later dropped out of Ocean County Community College (which, like all such two-year institutions, had a high school atmosphere), but only after his fellow students petitioned for his dismissal on grounds of unacceptable weirdness.

One result was that Bruce remained in some ways innocent of his own times. Explaining the complete lack of appeal drugs had for him, Bruce said, "When I was at that age when it was popular, I wasn't really in a social scene a whole lot. I was practicing in my room with my guitar. So I didn't have the type of pressure that kids might have today. Plus, I was very concerned with being in control at the time."

He found more than solace in his solitude; he found advantage. As he said in 1978, "It was like I didn't exist. It was the wall, then me. But I was working on the inside all the time. A lot of rock and roll people went through this solitary existence. If you're gonna be good at something, you've gotta be alone a lot to practice. There has to be a certain involuntariness to it. Like my youngest sister, she could play if she wanted to. But she's too pretty. She's popular, you know what I mean? She ain't gonna sit in the house in her room no eight hours a day and play the piano. No way."

The few friends he made were among fellow rock and roll musicians who hung out at a late night teen club called the Upstage, in Asbury Park. The kids Bruce met there had to reckon with him because he was the best musician they'd ever seen, a great guitarist who could figure out how to play the latest licks in an instant. Musically, he was, of all things, a *leader*—though, of course, the rock and roll he perfected was as socially disreputable as he was. In the loving liner notes he wrote for Southside Johnny's first album, *I Don't Want to Go Home*, Bruce speaks of the Upstage as his greatest teenage refuge: ". . . you could work it so you'd never have to go home, 'cause by the time you got out of there it was dawn and you could just flop on the beach all day, or you could run home before it got too light, nail the blankets over the windows of your room, and just sleep straight through till the night."

To top his misery off, he was receiving an education guaranteed to murder any desire to learn. Bruce was a poor student—he got Bs and Cs when things were going well, but could do worse—and the school gave him no incentive to do better. Like a lot of kids back then, he probably finished high school at least partly because it kept him out of the Army. Years later, when he wrote in "No Surrender," "We learned more from a three-minute record than we ever learned in school," the line was publicly chastised by voices as various as Elvis Costello and John Fogerty. "It must have been a pretty good record," remarked a rock critic. Anyone who attended a working-class high school knew the punchline: ". . . or a pretty bad school."

Bruce's own perspective is less jaundiced. He focused, as he preferred to do with most things, on the positive side of the question. "There's a lot of people who just fall through the bottom of the educational system. Not because they're stupid but because people don't know how to reach them, number one, and number two, the kids themselves don't know how to open up their own consciousness. Which is what rock and roll did for me. It was like it just opened up my consciousness. It gave me a much wider sense of awareness."

This sense of rock and roll as revelation is an important part of what set Springsteen apart from the beginning of his career. Even as late as 1984 he told *People*'s Chet Flippo, "I know that rock and roll changed my life. It was something for me to hold onto. I had nothing. Before then the whole thing was a washout for me. It really gave me a sense of myself, and it allowed me to become useful, which I think most people want to be."

To Bruce, the music was an answer to anonymity, not only in his own life but potentially in everyone's. "I never look out at my crowd and see a bunch of faces. It's never happened. Any night I've ever been onstage, I see people—individual people in individual seats out there. That's why, before the show, we go out and we check the sound in every section of the room. Because there's some guy sittin' back here, and he's got a girl with him, and, you know, it's like this is their seat. And what you hope for is that the same thing goes the other way—that when they look up at you, they don't just see some person with a guitar." Always, he has delivered his music and his ideas with the sense that there could be someone just like himself out there, lacking only one small inspiration to begin the process of self-transformation. Always, he has played with the sense that he needs them at least as much.

Many other arts could have reached Bruce, but it makes a big difference that the one that did was rock and roll. First of all, rock was *there*—in the air, on the radio, in the car—available, inescapable, everywhere one went. Then, too, rock spoke in ways with which Bruce was familiar: In those late Fifties, early Sixties Top Forty hits, you could hear not only the voices of teenagers but the accents of the blacks and white Southerners who had migrated to places like Freehold. So it could have been any other art, but it isn't surprising that rock and roll is what it was. Nowhere else in the arts and media (much less the educational system) did such people speak—much less talk on their own terms. That's one reason Bruce latched onto American singers like Gary Bonds and the Ronettes at least as enthusiastically as the English rock bands on which his kind of rock band music is more often modeled. And it was partly by using American girl group and soul models that he set his own style apart. There was vision in all of the rock and roll of his youth; he related more closely than most to that which derived from lives close to home.

Rock and roll has so often been described as a music of youthful rebellion that it's easy to miss a contradictory fact: namely, that for many of its greatest practitioners—think only of Elvis Presley or any black man or woman who's ever stepped to the mike—it was a way of finding a place to stand in the everyday world. In the spring of 1986, Bruce put it more bluntly: "I started playing music because I wanted to *fit in*." The fact that white rock was taken over by bohemians in the mid-to-late Sixties couldn't change the fact that for many working-class kids it remained a vehicle to forms of success, and possibly even respectability, they otherwise could only dream about. One reason Bruce found

being the best rock musician in his area so fulfilling was that
when others had to come to him to learn things, he could keep up
his loner's facade but still have some sense of connection—a
setup a live audience only intensified. On his own, everything
told him he was nothing and nobody; in these situations, he was
somebody.

Finally, there was what rock and roll did not ask him to do. It
didn't require any betrayal of his working-class roots or even of
that environment's deep-seated anti-intellectualism, which in-
fected Bruce as much as the next kid. Playing music was a *job*.
You sweated while you did it; it was (or at least, Bruce made it)
an extremely physical form of labor. He could avoid the fact that
the foundation of all the stress and strain was—maybe before
anything else—his songwriting and his conceptualizing of the
show, which are sweatless and extremely mental forms of work.

Most of the time, playing rock and roll didn't pay very well,
which meant that the most extreme contradiction of all—the
contradiction of the working man grown wealthy—could be safely
ducked for a very long time, although after the multi-platinum
sales of *The River* and the highly profitable tour, that was no
longer true. But that didn't mean Bruce was ready to reckon with
such consequences. That was another thing not owning a home
was all about.

Bruce's fear of becoming just another rich guy only led back
to the most deeply seated contradiction of all. As hard as he'd
worked to become a rock star, he mistrusted his own fame and
fortune as badly as he wanted them. "During the lawsuit [with
Appel], I understood that it's the music that keeps me alive. That
and my relationship with my friends, and my attachment to the
people and the places I've known. That's my lifeblood. And to
give that up for, like, the TV, the cars, the houses—that's not the
American dream. Those are the booby prizes. And if you fall for
them—if, when you achieve them, you believe that this is the end
in and of itself—then you've been suckered in. Because those are
the consolation prizes, if you're not careful, for selling yourself
out or lettin' the best of yourself slip away. So you gotta be
vigilant. You gotta carry the idea you began with further. And you
gotta hope that you're headed for higher ground."

On the other hand, Bruce was not prepared to follow the

punks in abandoning attempts to relate and communicate. That was not what the guy who wanted to become one of the guys did. "I always felt that *Born to Run* was my birthday album. All of a sudden, *bang!* Something happened, something crystallized, and you don't even know what. And now what are you gonna do? That's the big question. You have an audience; you have a relationship with that audience; it's just as real as any relationship you have with your friends."

If there was nothing wrong with harboring a lust for recognition, there was nothing irrational about being afraid of what fame could do. After all, every role model anyone could point out had too quickly washed up on the shores of indulgence and confusion. In the end, the one thing Bruce Springsteen was most determined to do was avoid ending up like his inspiration. "I think about Elvis a lot and what happened to him. The demands that this profession make on you are unreasonable. It's very strange to go out and have people look at you like you're Santa Claus or the Easter Bunny.

"It's a confusing experience for them, too. Who are they meeting? They're not quite sure. If you don't respond exactly as they imagined or something, which you're not gonna . . . it can be a strange experience. If you expect it to be a reasonable thing, it can drive you crazy. The answer is trying to stay healthy— mentally, physically, spiritually—all under a lot of pressure."

In the autumn of 1981, thrust once more into isolation, it seemed that it was time to stand back and confront many things. It was time to write some songs and figure out a way to make a record of them.

■

You know the old saying: Trust the art, not the artist. I think that's true. I think somebody can do real good work and be a fool in a variety of ways. I think my music is probably better than I am. I mean, like, your music is your ideals a lot of times, and you don't live up to those ideals all the time. You try, but you fall short and you disappoint yourself.

For Bruce Springsteen, record-making is a way to illuminate the dark corners of highly personal issues and situations. He does this in a highly metaphorical way that emphasizes the universality of such problems, but the records are inextricably connected to the things he has felt and experienced and is trying to figure out. As producer Chuck Plotkin said, "With Bruce, the album actually is about something. It may not be about something that you can reduce to some paragraph of exposition, but it's about something."

For Plotkin that was the central advantage of working with Bruce. "There was nothing too serious or too strange or too remote or too apparently disconnected from record-making that couldn't be talked about with a sense of its relevance to the record-making process. The records were *about something*, and anything that you knew about anything relevant was fodder for the record-making mill with Bruce. Something that happened on the street on the way to the studio that sensitized you to some issue that you felt deeply about and that was related to some thing that one of the songs was dealing with. Nothing was irrelevant."

On the other hand, all this information was digested and distilled into songs that were utterly personal. This was true even though Springsteen could be the most derivative of rock artists (and rock is an enormously derivative medium). His songs bristle with quotations and allusions, musical and lyrical.

Bruce's first two albums spoke in such a clash and babble of metaphor that it was easy to miss the true topics of their songs, not to mention their revealing aspects. Beginning with *Born to Run*, however, Springsteen made a leap. By his own account, *Born to Run* "really dealt with faith and a searching for answers. . . . I laid out a set of values. A set of ideas . . . intangibles like faith and hope, belief in friendship and in a better way." That was his story, he later said. So it ended triumphantly—*he* had pulled out of his "town full of losers" and won.

But Bruce added a note of warning. "You don't really know what those values are worth until you test them," he said.

It's tempting to conclude that this test began with the lawsuit between Springsteen and former manager Mike Appel, that the stresses it applied caused Bruce to question the emotional *laissez faire* articulated in *Born to Run*. In fact, Bruce said, the summer of the lawsuit was one of the best of his life. "I had a truck and a motorcycle; I was living out there in the farmhouse; we had a pond and a pool. Every once in a while, I'd have to go up to the city and talk with the lawyers, but that wasn't so bad—it was just a different thing to do, you know." The legal complications—Appel, as well as obtaining an injunction forbidding Bruce to record, had the CBS royalties for Bruce's first million-selling album tied up—kept money tight, but being broke was nothing new.

For Bruce, the test took the shape of an internal struggle. "I guess in a funny way I began to do that test after *Born to Run* and through *Nebraska*. Those records were kind of my reaction, not necessarily to my success, but to what I was singing and writing about and what I was feeling—what I felt the role of the musician should be, what an artist should be. The one thing I did feel after *Born to Run* was a real sense of responsibility to what I was singing and to the audience. I didn't have an audience before that, not much of one. I was concerned with living up to that responsibility.

"So I just dove into it. I decided to look around. I decided to move into the darkness and look around and write about what I knew and what I saw and what I was feeling. I was trying to find something to hold onto that doesn't disappear out from under you."

Maybe Bruce believed he was just poking at the tattered edges of other lives, but he was really toying with more explosive forces. Each of his albums asked more probing questions, not only about the state of America but about the meaning of life. Whether he knew it or not, he was trying to rationally resolve questions that don't have rational answers. When anyone does that, one consequence can be that what you've taken for common sense stops shaping the world into a believable picture.

"Stolen Car" and "Wreck on the Highway," two of the key songs on the second disc of *The River*, seem central to this probing process, because they represent a break in mood from Springsteen's earlier work. Previously Bruce was as unfailingly optimistic in his songs as he was in his everyday interpretations of events. Not only was he the sort of person who could see opportunity in a lawsuit that prevented him from recording and hampered his touring for more than a year, he was the sort of artist who could describe life's most brutal moments of defeat and frustration—as he did over and over on *Darkness on the Edge of Town* and *The River*—and still find a way to turn those songs into affirmations. "What happens to most people is when their first dreams get killed off nothing ever takes its place," he said. "The important thing is to keep holding out for possibilities, even if no one ever really makes it."

The protagonists of "Stolen Car" and "Wreck on the Highway" are past the point of holding out. It's not just that their stories are so grim, though they are that: In "Stolen Car" the singer's loneliness has driven him to compulsive car theft (a kind of joyless-riding), while the protagonist of "Wreck" is kept awake at night by the memory of finding a hit-and-run victim on a rainy, lonesome highway. What really makes these songs spooky, though, is their haunted music. "Wreck" aspires to country (it's modeled after Roy Acuff's song of the same name, though without recourse to Jesus or Mothers Against Drunk Driving moralism), but it never makes it. Its very cadences reject the sentimentality a country song could never abandon. In "Stolen Car" Bruce sings against piano, synthesizer, a few muted voices—all of it ectoplasmic, except the drums, which thump like tympani or a shattered heartbeat. When Bruce sings, "I ride by night and I travel in fear/That in this darkness I will disappear," there is nothing left for the music to do but fade away, which it does without a nuance of reluctance. There is nothing more here—just a waste of life and a man brave or stupid enough to watch it trickle away.

Those stories are true to life, and yet not much else in rock and roll (let alone the rest of popular culture) was willing to face up to them. Bruce said he heard such tales sometimes in the music of punk groups, particularly the Clash, but in general, as he noted in the midst of the *River* tour, "there wasn't too much stuff in America happening. It just seemed to me that's the story. But there was a crucial level of things missing, and it is today still. Maybe it's just me getting older and seeing things more as they are."

It was more than that. The artistic success of *The River* as a whole lay largely in Springsteen's finally achieving some kind of balance between songs and topics he considered trivial and those obviously heavier. Songs like "Cadillac Ranch" and "Ramrod" made dinosaurs dance, and more portentous songs like "Point Blank" were offset by escapades like "I'm a Rocker." Springsteen was finally letting some of the songs he'd suppressed see the light of day, relinquishing a smidgen of control in order to build a broader and thus truer picture of the world he wanted his records to represent.

"When I did *The River,* I tried to accept the fact that the world is a paradox, and that's the way it is. And the only thing you can do with a paradox is live with it. On the album, I just said, 'I don't understand all these things. I don't see where all these things fit. I don't see how all these things can work together,' " he said when the eighteen-month agony of assembling it was finished. "It was because I was always focusing in on some small thing; when I stepped back, they made a sense of their own. It was just a situation of living with all those contradictions. And that's what happens. There's never any resolution. You have moments of clarity, things become clear to you that you didn't understand before. But there's never any making ends meet or finding any kind of longstanding peace of mind."

When Bruce began writing songs for his next album, just after he returned from Hawaii, these were the things he felt compelled to explore, the mysteries he wanted his music to help him reconcile. Already, during the later part of the tour, he'd written one new tune, "Mansion on the Hill," which had some of the dreamlike quality of "Stolen Car" but was written much more concretely. This was what Bruce was shooting for in his new lyrics. After seeing Huston's *Wise Blood,* he'd begun reading Flannery O'Connor's stories, and he was especially impressed by their minute precision, the way O'Connor could enliven a character by sketching in just a few details. And the way she used those details to create a world of claustrophobic lower class Catholic guilt must have seemed especially familiar to the reprobate of St. Rose of Lima.

Bruce also saw (on television) Terence Malick's 1974 film *Badlands,* a barely fictionalized account of the 1958 spree during which Charles Starkweather and Caril Fugate killed ten people in eight days across the barren landscape stretching from Lincoln,

Nebraska, to eastern Wyoming. The movie led him to Ninette Beaver's book, *Caril*, the definitive Starkweather account. Impressed, Bruce called Beaver, now a fifty-year-old assignment editor at KMTV in Omaha.

"Honest to God, I know I should know who you are, but I'm just drawing a blank," Beaver remembered saying after Bruce's song "Nebraska" came out and she knew. They talked for a half-hour about Starkweather (executed in 1959) and Fugate (who served eighteen years in prison and was paroled in 1976). Playing Lincoln in 1984, Bruce dedicated the song to Beaver, who attended as his guest.

Punk bands and their New Wave successors had been writing songs about characters like Starkweather for years. The obvious examples are the Adverts' "Gary Gilmore's Eyes," about the Utah prisoner who demanded a public execution, and the Boomtown Rats' "I Don't Like Mondays," about a California teenager who shot up her high school's faculty and some of her classmates, then offered that line as her explanation. In a way, though, "Nebraska" was closer to the Sex Pistols' "Holiday in the Sun":

> I don't want a holiday in the sun
> I wanna go to the new Belsen
> I wanna see some history . . .

Even if Bruce had regularly trafficked in shock and outrage, "Nebraska" wouldn't quite have fit the stereotype. His song spoke in a horrifyingly blank first person voice, and it went on to meet questions head-on that the others merely skirted or tackled at an angle. Bruce's Starkweather recites the facts of what he has done without much emotion; he's more excited by the memory of first seeing his girlfriend and by the anticipation of his own execution, which he greets as a chance to realize some wishes, including the hope that Fugate will find herself "sittin' right there on my lap."

But in the final verse, the song shifts gears. Starkweather speaks of the greatest consequences of all, with no more sorrow than a man remembering a pet lost in childhood:

> They declared me unfit to live, said into that great void my
> soul'd be hurled

They wanted to know why I did what I did
Well, sir, I guess there's just a meanness in this world

Charlie Starkweather never said or thought any such thing. He was all but illiterate, and he killed as he did in part because he was superstitious as only a half-wit can be. Starkweather certainly never harbored hope of any judgment anywhere so neutral or mystical as the "great void." Nor was he that matter-of-fact about the murders. He claimed that he killed in self-defense, and he made sure he dragged his girlfriend down with him. Starkweather, said one of the psychiatrists who testified at his trial, "tends to perceive things in a somewhat distorted way. He will pick out things which are not important because of his particular way of looking at things. The act of killing meant to him no more than stepping on a bug." Starkweather later told another psychiatrist that he wished he had a bomb so he could kill the first shrink.

That isn't the man who sings that last verse, and Bruce had done enough research to know it. The man who'd weighed those final lines and found they fit was Bruce Springsteen. It was as if Bruce had recast himself mentally, portraying what could have happened if he had not imagined his way out of the dead ends of Freehold, what the consequences would have been of hearing only static on his late-night radio. In 1975 critic Greil Marcus suggested that the source of "Born to Run" was the old juvenile delinquent tattoo "Born to Lose." "Nebraska" brought to life that tattoo and all it implied, and the person who had to live with its excruciatingly specific detail was the songwriter himself.

Bruce wrote a whole series of such songs: "Atlantic City," "Reason to Believe," "Johnny 99," "Highway Patrolman," "State Trooper," "Open All Night" were all songs of complete despair. All of them imagined the worst things happening, often to characters very like the most lovingly familiar people in his earlier songs. The guy begging the state cops not to bust him on the Jersey Turnpike could have been the lonesome joyrider from "Stolen Car," the man roaring to meet his baby in the middle of the night on the same highway was "Ramrod" revisited, the loser daring the big score in "Atlantic City" was a near relation to the one in "Meeting Across the River," the brothers in "Highway Patrolman" were a doomed version of the dragstrip partners in "Racing in the Street." What the new folks all had in common was being locked into situations in which there was no hope, no moment of relief or respite, from which there was no escape. There was nothing good in their lives and whatever had once been good had rotted.

Bruce wasn't sure exactly where the songs came from. "I wrote 'em real fast. Two months, the whole record, and for me that's real quick. I just sat at my desk, and it was something that was really fascinating for me. It was one of those times when you're not really thinking about it. You're working on it, but you're doing something that you didn't think you would be doing."

But certainly, rapidity and lack of self-consciousness weren't the major mysteries about these songs. They represented a rupture with Bruce's previous perspective. "It just seemed to be a mood that I was in at the time," he told interviewers in 1984. "I was living in a house on this reservoir, and I didn't go out much, and for some reason I just started to write. I wrote 'Nebraska,' all those songs, in a couple of months. I was interested in writing kind of *smaller* than I had been, writing with just detail."

He acknowledged that he was "going through some things" at the time, but declined to discuss them other than to say, "It was just kinda growin' up, growin' into the particular shoes I was wearing."

In fact, what was troubling Bruce personally was not far removed from what he'd already conceived as the central problem *The River* had tried to tackle: "People want to be part of a group yet they also want to disassociate themselves. People go through those conflicts every day in little ways: Do you wanna go to the movies tonight with your friends, or stay home? I wanted to get part of that on the record—the need for community, which is what 'Out in the Street' is about. Songs like 'The Ties That Bind' and 'Two Hearts' deal with that, too. But there's also the other side, the need to be alone."

Bruce was beginning to feel the downside of his loner's life— his need to be alone was becoming something tougher, more pernicious: loneliness. He later compared his emotions to the scene in *The Grapes of Wrath* in which an Okie farmer who tries to hold off eviction with a shotgun, only to be told that the men he wants to shoot are faceless, hidden away in boardrooms hundreds of miles away. "I felt the same way he did: Where do I point the gun?" Bruce said. "In the Seventies and Eighties, especially compared to the Sixties, it became awfully hard to identify an enemy." Right now, though, Springsteen was fighting the enemy within.

There was more to it than that, though. Bruce was also responding to many things that were happening in America at this time. Maybe playing in Europe had helped him see the stark contrast between the land of his ideals and what the country had become. This was a response to the Age of Reagan, but it wasn't only Reaganomics to which he was responding. It was something more basic.

"In America there's a promise that gets made, and over there it gets called the American Dream, which is just the right to be able to live your life with some decency and dignity," he'd told the crowd that final night in Stockholm. "But over there, and a lot of places in the world now, that dream is only true for a very, very few people. It seems if you weren't born in the right place or if you didn't come from the right town, or if you believed in something that was different from the next person, y'know. . . .

"Right now in the States, there's a lot of hard times, and when that happens there's always a resurgence of groups like the Ku Klux Klan and the National Socialists, and it seems like hard times turn people against each other, people that have common interests, people that don't understand that the enemy is not the guy down the street who looks different than you. But it's hard in the States, because the enemy is something that when you're brought up as a kid you're taught to respect. And it's something that you can't see; it's something that works on you and eats its way inside every day of your life and twists the good things that you have in you into nothing." And he sang "This Land Is Your Land," which he called "a song about living free, about the land that you live in, that should belong to each and every one of you, and that you have a right and a promise to life, to fulfill yourself inside."

In the songs of *Nebraska*, Bruce found himself exploring what happened to those basic values in such a society, looking for hard answers and recoiling from what he learned. "I think you can get to a point where nihilism, if that's the right word, is overwhelming, and the basic laws that society has set up—either religious or social laws—become meaningless," Bruce said of his fascination with Starkweather. "Things just get really dark. You lose those constraints, and then anything goes. The forces that set in motion, I don't know exactly what they'd be—I think, just a lot of frustration, lack of findin' somethin' that you can hold onto, lack of contact with *people*, you know? That's one of the most dangerous things, I think—isolation. *Nebraska* was about that American isolation: what happens to people when they're alienated from their friends and their community and their government and their job. Because those are the things that keep you sane, that give meaning to life in some fashion. And if they slip away, and you start to exist in some void where the basic constraints of society are a joke, then life becomes kind of a joke. And anything can happen."

It would be misguided to suggest that Bruce understood all this in late 1981 (the quote is from 1984), and it would be even more misleading to suggest that the songs of *Nebraska* were primarily a political response. Undoubtedly, what Bruce was doing, as he wrote and then taped, was responding to the changing context of his own life. In 1982 it meant something very different to be a loner in America—it meant facing up to a society in which the isolation was built in, perhaps even promulgated. As he later put it, "In a way, I felt like the album had the tone of what it felt like when I was a kid, growin' up. At the same time, it felt like the tone of what the country felt like to me at that moment. That was kinda the heart that I was drawing from." The two factors are inextricable.

And though Bruce has described himself as "a thinkin' fool," a person who analyzes almost everything, his concept of where such ideas came from was probably no more concrete than the songs that expressed them. It may even have seemed that his loneliness would end as soon as he got into the studio with his bandmates and other collaborators. His response to the mysteries of this music was to throw himself deeper into his work. By

Christmastime of 1981 Bruce had completed writing a cycle of songs that he felt would form the body of his next record, and he set to work getting them in shape for the studio.

One of the things that concerned Bruce was the length of time it took to make his records. *Born to Run* had been a year-long struggle; even subtracting time off for the lawsuit, *Darkness on the Edge of Town* had taken about fifteen months; *The River* had been more like two years. The first Springsteen album came out in 1973; so did the second. The third arrived in 1975, followed by records in 1978 and 1980. Even though Bruce claimed that he was reconciled to these intervals, he hoped to move faster now.

"I told Mike [Batlan], the guy that does my guitars, 'Mike, go get a tape player so I can record these songs.' I figured what takes me so long in the studio is not having the songs written. So I said, I'm gonna write 'em and I'm gonna tape 'em. If I can make them sound good with just me, then I know they'll be fine. Then I can play 'em with the band. 'Cause if you rehearse with the band, the band can trick you. The band can play so good you think you've got something going. Then you go in and record it, and you realize the band's playing really good, but there's no song there. So I'd record for a month, get a couple of things, go home, write some more, record for another month—it wasn't very efficient.

"So this time, I got a little Teac four-track cassette machine, and I said, 'I'm gonna record these songs, and if they sound good with just me doin' 'em, then I'll teach 'em to the band.' I could sing and play the guitar, and then I had two tracks to do somethin' else, like overdub a guitar or add a harmony. It was just gonna be a demo. Then I had an old beat-up Echoplex that I mixed through, and that was it. It was real old, which is why the sound was kinda deep.

"And so, that was the idea. I got this little cassette recorder, plugged it in, turned it on, and the first song I did was 'Nebraska.' I just kinda sat there; you can hear the chair creaking on 'Highway Patrolman' in particular. I recorded them in a couple of days. Some songs I only did once, like 'Highway Patrolman.' The other songs I did maybe two times, three times at the most.

"I put the tape in my pocket, carried it around a couple of

weeks, 'cause I was gonna teach the songs to the band. After a couple of days, I looked at the thing and said, 'Uh-oh, I'd better stop carrying this around like this. Can somebody make a copy of this?' "

Bruce made the tape on January 3, 1982, and mixed it over the next few days. First to hear it was Jon Landau. "He came up to the office one day—he'd let me know he was gonna have something—and he gave me a notebook and a cassette," Landau remembers. "And it was all the *Nebraska* songs, except for 'My Father's House.' And the tape had many other *Nebraska*-style songs, performed in the *Nebraska* style. There were versions of 'Downbound Train,' 'Born in the U.S.A.,' and, I think, 'Working on the Highway.' But basically it was the *Nebraska* album and other *Nebraska*-style songs. That's what he presented to me at that time, with this notebook, saying, in effect, 'Here it is; here's where I'm going with the next album.' "

Landau was tremendously moved by the tape, finding both songs and performances "surprising and very beautiful." However, he was somewhat taken aback at the dark tenor of so much of the material. "On *The River* tour Bruce was able to enjoy what he'd accomplished, more than at any other time I'd known him— to enjoy, for example, opening the Meadowlands. And in a funny way, these songs were so dark that it concerned me on a friendship level."

A few days later Landau drove down to New Jersey to confer with Bruce about the songs and how to prepare to record them. He already had some specific ideas.

Landau had been involved with the folk music revival in Boston, his hometown, and, as he put it, "I had some fairly developed ideas, when you get into that folk music area—not that I would strictly speaking call *Nebraska* folk music, but let's call it a folk-related style—about when the application of things like drums and a full rhythm section and so forth is suitable: When is it likely to sort of desensitize the material as opposed to when is it likely to add something? And I was somewhat skeptical right from the beginning that some of this material was gonna function better with a full rhythm type thing. The immediate thing that came to mind, going on the assumption—as we were—that most of this stuff was gonna take the . . . well, gee, the band is gonna have to play very differently than they've ever played before for this to work."

Landau felt that certain songs could easily be given arrangements that would enhance them; he suggests that "Nebraska" itself could have worked with the kind of somber arrangement used on James Taylor's "Fire and Rain": string bass, piano, brushed drums. But he also understood that the way the material was voiced and sung on the tape, which was clearly a substantial part of its power, argued against a full rock group.

"On the tape that became the album, Bruce basically sings unusually softly. As soon as you're talking about having drums, you're talking about having to sing out—not necessarily singing loud or harshly, but you must sing with a certain amount of force. If there's no drums, it's easier to sing in a purely conversational fashion. And when you hear the *Nebraska* songs done even with a modest arrangement, in the show and on the live album, Bruce has to push harder. It's just a natural thing to do. But on *Nebraska*, he's almost singing to himself."

But even with that in mind, it was still terribly unclear how the majority of the songs would function as Bruce Springsteen music. Landau certainly didn't have any idea yet how to make the music add up as an album. But then, he probably didn't expect to. Even if Bruce felt that cutting demos would expedite the recording process, Jon had been through three previous albums with him and wasn't expecting a rapid resolution of anything.

Landau and Springsteen spent some time talking about arrangement ideas, which songs seemed most likely to work out, which were probably not destined for the record—like any demo, this one had its false starts and dead spots.

"I remember one thing we talked about," Landau said. "This *Nebraska* version of 'Born in the U.S.A.' seemed to stand out as the one song that just didn't seem to be working in this context. And in fact, to me, when you heard just the acoustic guitar version, it didn't even seem like a particularly good song. It was a real odd thing, and it was not like anything else on the *Nebraska* album. And it was not like any other thing I've ever heard from Bruce—it sounded alien. It just didn't sound like it fit. I knew it was a great idea for a song and there were great things about it, but basically we had so many other good things goin' on the *Nebraska* tape that the song disappeared from consideration fairly quickly."

In the *Nebraska* demo version, "Born in the U.S.A." (the title inspired by an unproduced filmscript by Paul Schrader and by Ron Kovic's *Born on the Fourth of July*) was much faster than it finally turned out to be, and it had a different melody, although the lyrics were the same. Speeded up and played on an acoustic guitar, it was just a protest song, and that was the opposite of what Bruce wanted or needed.

There was no immediate progress toward making a record out of the demo in the first few months of 1982, anyway, because Bruce got caught up in recording the second Gary Bonds album, *On the Line*. Bruce wrote seven out of the record's eleven tracks, notably "Rendezvous," a perennial near-hit that had been kicking around since before *Darkness;* "Angelyne," a reprise of the "Jolie Blon" theme; "Out of Work," a mock-topical single; and a scathing soul ballad, "Club Soul City," which Bonds sang as a duet with fellow soul veteran Chuck Jackson. Bruce played a greater role than he had on *Dedication,* and his presence added a much darker cast to the music.

When it came time to mix the album, neither Bruce nor Steve Van Zandt could get a proper handle on it. So they called Chuck Plotkin in Los Angeles. Plotkin had served as mixer of Bruce's last two albums, and he was slated to be part of the next album's production team as well. Plotkin had some time on his hands, and he agreed to take on mixing the Bonds album.

Meantime, Van Zandt was nearing completion of his solo project. The idea for a Miami Steve solo album had been brewing for years. Steve was a talented songwriter in his own right; he could sing and he'd functioned as producer and even manager of Southside Johnny and the Asbury Jukes. When Gary Gersh, who was in charge of the Bonds albums at EMI-America Records, indicated the label would be interested in a Van Zandt solo effort, Steve was intrigued and, as soon as the 1981 tour ended, began to pursue that possibility.

Steve was Bruce's oldest friend, but he was every bit as brash as his buddy was cautious. Burning up with the idea of an album of his own, he set to work on it without waiting for a contract to be signed, which meant without a company to foot the bills for studio time. In the meantime, Steve decided he didn't want to embark on a solo career under the name Miami Steve, which is how he was known to E Street Band fans. To him that smacked too much of piggybacking on the Springsteen reputation. So he became Little Steven.

Then he decided that he ought to have a full-time band, replete with horn section. (Among Steve's salient virtues was an ability to organize proper Stax-style horn charts.) That meant a big band, and *that* meant heavy expenses; it also meant that the group would have to go out and work if Steve wanted to hold it together. Steve found some excellent players, centered around himself and the Miami Horns—an ad hoc aggregation he'd put together for Bruce to use on the occasions when Springsteen wanted to add horns to his show—plus Dino Danelli, the rhythm sparkplug of the Young Rascals, on drums. The group was filled out by a cast of talented unknowns, including bassist Jean Beauvoir, who later went on to a solo career of his own.

Steve finished the tapes for his album around the same time as the Bonds record. But he had even more trouble mixing them. He, too, called Chuck Plotkin, and Chuck agreed to take a crack at them. Steve sent out some material and Plotkin came up with ideas that resolved some of the mixing difficulties. They agreed to do more when Steve reached L.A.

Meantime, a friend of Landau's, record executive David Geffen, asked if Bruce would be interested in writing a song for Donna Summer, who had just been signed to Geffen's label. Summer was recording her first album with producer Quincy Jones, who was hot off making Michael Jackson's *Off the Wall*. There was even some talk of Bruce and Donna performing a duet. It was an intriguing idea: the King of Rock and Roll recording with the Queen of Disco. Bruce wasn't entirely certain how he wanted to proceed, but he did write a song. While in the studio with Bonds, he gathered the E Street Band for a demo session.

When Jon Landau heard the result, a song called "Cover Me," combining Springsteen's rock combustion with a sledgehammer version of the typical Summer dance beat, he smelled a hit. Bruce had played a tremendous guitar solo, and though the band had hurried through the song (this was just a demo, a guide for somebody else), the track was a keeper. "You aren't giving this one away," he told Bruce. Bruce didn't think much of the song, but he took Landau's idea seriously enough to write another number around a similar idea. "Protection" was sent to Summer and Jones, and while the idea for a vocal duet was discarded, it was arranged that Bruce would play guitar on the track while he was in Hollywood. (The Summer record didn't come to much, although Bruce played another hot solo, and he and Jones struck up a friendly acquaintance. Jones called Bruce "one of the nicest people I have ever worked with. He had an open mind. No preconceived notions. The man has more musical knowledge than a lot of people think and has a deep sense of commitment to music. You could feel his spirit in the sessions. He did every take like it was the last show at Madison Square Garden. He really gave it up. Instead of fading the song, he gave every song an in-concert ending. Fantastic.")

So in February, Steve and Bruce flew to California to work with Plotkin for a few weeks. Bruce's album project stayed on the back burner until late April.

■

Back in New Jersey that spring, Bruce slated band rehearsals to prepare for recording. In late April Chuck Plotkin flew in from Los Angeles, where he'd finally finished his other assignments.

"This was the first album that I came out to work on from the beginning," Plotkin said. "I lived in Los Angeles at the time, and I wasn't generally available to work in New York." He'd begun his association with Landau when Jon was producing Jackson Browne's *The Pretender* for Asylum Records, where Plotkin was then head of A&R. When *Darkness* was entering the mixing phase, Plotkin was spending considerable time in New York making a Harry Chapin record, *Living Room Suite*. Jon had then suggested Chuck to Bruce as somebody who could be of help mixing *Darkness*.

Plotkin never quite saw it that way. "I wasn't really a mixer, and I always felt somewhat miscast as a mixer. My background had been record production; I didn't even mix my own albums. *Darkness on the Edge of Town* was the first album I ever mixed, because they needed a mixer. It's just that what was left to be done when I joined them on *Darkness on the Edge of Town* was to mix the record."

Within the tight-knit world of the Springsteen camp, especially in the first months after Bruce's liberation from Mike Appel, the introduction of any new face was a major and potentially traumatic event, to be approached with great caution. What must have recommended Plotkin to Landau for this task was Chuck's ferocious attention to detail and his interest in the process of record-making itself. For Bruce, part of the task of making records—especially around the time of *Darkness*—was learning the process, getting an education.

"Essentially when you work with Bruce, that's basically what you do: You're available to communicate with him on various different levels about whatever it is that's going on," Plotkin said. "I think Jon perceived that, given the way Bruce worked, hiring some fancy mixer to come in and mix the record was not really what they needed. They needed to have somebody who was essentially sympathetic to the artist's role in even something like mixing—and someone who understood that, among other things, the process, for Bruce, was learning about how all this stuff worked. I mean Bruce, as accomplished an artist as he was even at that time, had only made four records."

In the process of mixing *Darkness* and then *The River*, which took six months and involved some re-recording and restructuring of songs, Bruce and Plotkin found a friendship that their work only deepened. "Both of us seemed to both be able to and interested in staying in the saddle until the thing was right," Plotkin said. "Neither one of us was afraid to work and neither one of us was the least bit disinterested in the subtle refinement of all kinds of details. I mean, after twelve hours we were both still there working and not becoming disinterested in the things we were learning about a particular piece of music while we were putting the mix together."

In some ways, Plotkin's background was even more different

from Bruce's than Landau's. He'd lived in California all his life, he'd attended prep schools, he was married and the father of a then three-year-old son. Gray-haired and gravel-voiced, Chuck provided a sharp contrast with Bruce, who seemed in some ways younger in the early Eighties than he had been five years before. Plotkin had worked for a record company, and he'd made a couple dozen records, working almost always with new artists; he was a part of the record industry in a way that Springsteen and Landau were not. What he shared with them, in addition to a cutting sense of humor and a trencherman's appetite, was a ferocious commitment to the idea that what they were doing was not merely entertainment and an equally strong resolve to get the details right.

"Bruce was the first artist I had ever met or worked with who took this art form as seriously as I did," said Plotkin. "I've thought to myself many times that if I hadn't met Bruce when I did, I might very well have stopped making records at some point soon after that. The guy was able to bite off some amazingly thick, complex things and work at them in this medium. It just revitalized my sense of what could be done with popular music and encouraged me to believe that there was at least somebody out there working with whom I could actually bring everything that I knew about everything into the process of making records.

"It's like for years I remember having said to various different people—about theater, about motion pictures, about records— people who talked about, 'Well, you've got to be entertaining.' Well, what entertains me is a beautiful, deep, rich, difficult exposition in some form or another of some deep and important human question or human experience. The other stuff just doesn't hold my attention. And it didn't hold his, either."

However, the Springsteen production team was crowded and it was unlikely that there would be any dropouts. *The River* was credited to Springsteen, Landau, and Van Zandt—that is, the artist and his two best friends. Plotkin was recognized as mixer, together with engineer Toby Scott, even though that wasn't a fully accurate description of his contribution. But credit wasn't really the issue.

"At the end of *The River*, when Jon and Bruce were taking off,

e Aurora is rising behind him.

The wildest things they'd ever seen

(JIM MARCHESE)

At a soundcheck in Europe, 1981. A nightly ritual that emphasized commitment to quality, from the top down.

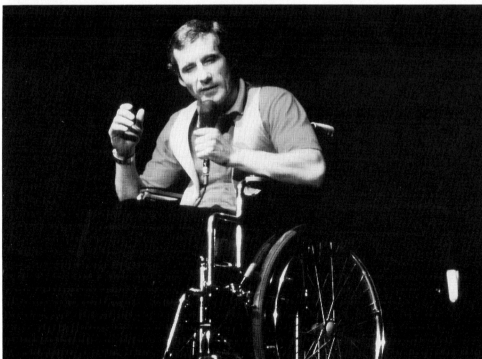

Bobby Muller of the Vietnam Veterans of America introduces Bruce at the Los Angeles Sports Arena benefit, 1981: "When you remember the divisions within our own generation about the war, it's a little bit ironic that it ultimately turns out to be the very symbol of our generation—rock and roll—that brings us together."

n the backstreets of Amsterdam, 1981

The Fender Esquire becomes Excalibur.

From left: Clarence Clemons, Danny Federici, Steve Van Zandt, Garry Tallent, Max Weinberg, Roy Bittan

From left: Clarence, Max, Bruce, Garry, Patti Scialfa, Roy, Danny

With Billy Joel and Cyndi Lauper during a break at the U.S.A. for Africa session

With Arthur Baker at the Sun City session

During the filming of the "Dancing in the Dark" video

standing around thinking about it during the filming of the "Glory Days" video

In Tokyo's Ginza district, 1985   (NEAL PREST●

Racing through the aisles, Kyoto   (NEAL PREST●

Boarding the train to Kyoto. Later, these fans crowded against Bruce's car while it stood on the platform, cameras flashing. Springsteen shot his own photos back through the windows.

(NEAL PRESTO

I said, 'Hey look, you guys, next time I'd like to show up for appetizers and the main course as well'—just because there were certain things we were dealing with in the mixing that if I'd been there from step one, the presumption was that we might avoid some of the technical problems. And also just . . . you know, being involved from early on and helping to conceptualize the piece and set a kind of sound picture for it. As much for the pleasure of the experience as anything else—just being able to be involved from the beginning."

The *Nebraska* sessions promised to be different. In late January 1982 Plotkin was called and asked to come to New York in May to begin working on the new album. He was a welcome addition for several reasons: First, given that the essence of producing a Springsteen record is "staying in the saddle," he'd proven that he was as well or better suited to it as either Landau, with his management duties, or Van Zandt, whose idea of production was to keep things swift and simple in the first place and, anyway, who was increasingly wrapped up in his own solo career.

Meantime, however, Plotkin's preproduction time was not spent preparing but in working on the Bonds and Little Steven mixes and helping Steve through the last stages of his contract negotiations at Los Angeles-based EMI. "All of the time between that initial call and the beginning of Bruce's record was just eaten up with a vengeance—and I mean a *vengeance,*" Plotkin ruefully remembered. "There were two records to finish, and I had meetings with the lawyers and then picking singles for the Bonds record and mastering. I was just exhausted. And I realized I had to get out of L.A. and go back and literally sleep for four days."

He checked into the Molly Pitcher Inn in Red Bank, in order to be near the rehearsals. Exhausted, he slept for three days. Refreshed, he began listening to a cassette copy of Bruce's original demo tape. "I got ahold of these tapes and I was transfixed. They were Bruce's original home mixes of the demos; he'd do three or four different mixes of a thing, and they were all on the cassette. The first thing I heard was four renditions in a row of the song 'Nebraska.' "

Like Landau, Plotkin was taken aback by the emotional

atmosphere of the songs. "It was frontier material for all of us—it was on the front edge of what Bruce had been doing for the six months before we started. And he had fetched something that was at the time mysterious to him. I think in some way it remained mysterious for a long period of time," Plotkin said. "It came from a place that was so deep inside himself and had been so unexplored prior to the exploration that flowered into those songs that he really just didn't know where it came from. The sound of his voice—he found a new voice!"

It was true. What was startling about the demo cassette was not just the unrelenting bleakness of the songs themselves. It was also the performances. Bruce had been signed to Columbia Records by John Hammond (discoverer of Aretha Franklin, Billie Holiday, Count Basie, Benny Goodman and, most relevant, Bob Dylan) at the height of the singer-songwriter era; and Hammond heard him as a solo artist. But aside from a few gigs around that time, Bruce had never been a "folk" singer. His background was entirely in rock and roll and rhythm and blues: band music. Bruce insisted on making his first album with what became the E Street Band and never looked back.

But around the time of *The River* and all through the tour that followed, Bruce had listened to music he'd never heard before: Jimmie Rodgers, Hank Williams, Woody Guthrie, the obscure singers on the Folkways *American Folk Music Anthology*, stuff he dug up for himself and on tapes given to him by friends. As a result, the *Nebraska* demos had the quality of stillness associated with the great Library of Congress folk recordings of the 1930s and 1940s, by performers artfully described by critic Paul Nelson as "traditional (and nonprofessional) singers and musicians you've probably never heard of: poor folks, mostly from the rural South, just sitting at home in front of that inexpensive tape or disc machine and telling their stories, sometimes artfully and sometimes artlessly, undoubtedly amazed that anyone from the urban world would place any value on what they were saying or how they were saying it . . . You did the song once, the way you'd been doing it your whole life, and that was it. That was it, all right: the song, your whole life, and every so often, a considerable piece of Americana. Like an aural FSA photo."

The *Nebraska* demos turned the idea of urban folk music on its head. Rather than appropriating the folk songs themselves, Springsteen worked with his own characteristic melodic ideas and lyrics that were utterly contemporary. The touches that felt like folk music came from the doing: the guitar trills that rang like mandolins, the strange diction of lyrics in which the listener was so often addressed as "sir," the blank directness of that intimate singing voice, which sounded more relaxed and easy—if not confident—than any rock and roll vocals Bruce had ever sung.

Everyone heard the new material as a departure. Steve Van Zandt remembered Bruce giving him the tape and saying, "I don't know what this is. It's just what's on my mind. I did this in the house. Whaddaya think?" What Van Zandt thought—everyone recalls his reaction—was, "I love this. This is an album."

As Steve points out, "There was no basis for anyone to think about it that way. [But] it was a special moment. An artist could never get closer to his audience than this. Not because it was done with an acoustic guitar, but because he was literally singing for himself. It's like the most direct, personal, accomplished artistic statement that you can make." And like Landau and Plotkin, Steve had his doubts about how much the demo tape could be improved. But he knew they were going to try. "At that point, I felt, we were just going in, it would probably be another year before something came out—realistically, at least that long. Looking at the pattern of recording, you could safely say two or even three."

Initially, it didn't seem that way, not because Bruce's demos had accelerated the process but because the band was so hot. The rehearsals ended almost as swiftly as they began. "We became aware after the second day of rehearsals that we were gonna start squeezing some of the vitality out of this stuff if we continued this process, and there was no reason to do it," said Plotkin. "The first time something came out great in a rehearsal, which was either the first afternoon or early the second afternoon, we all went, 'We should have had the tape running. This is crazy. Let's not waste ourselves here.' "

So the sessions moved to the Power Station recording studio

on New York City's West Side. Bruce's ways in the studio are peculiar, an uneasy amalgam of what's instinctive and the height of calculation. A session might be devoted to a number from the demo tape but there was an equal chance that it would be given over to something that Bruce showed up with that night. Or songs could simply pop up as Bruce stood in the studio fiddling with guitar, piano, or microphone. Such a song might disappear after the first take, or it might be worked on intensely for several days, after which it might become lost in a black hole or even resurface many months later. A song might be *finished* after the first take, and that was increasingly the case.

For all these reasons, Toby Scott kept a two-track tape machine running at all times, and when the action heated up even slightly, the twenty-four-track master tape began to roll.

This practice paid off one May night during a dinner break. Whenever Bruce had a few extra minutes during such quiet times he'd often stand at his vocal mike, leafing through the pages of the spiral-bound notebook containing his lyrics. On this particular evening, he started a somber riff and then stopped just as Roy Bittan and Max Weinberg came back into the studio. "Let's do something with this right now!" Landau said excitedly from the control room. Max and Roy quickly fit themselves into the song, which they had never heard before, and several takes were cut on the spot, without any bass or the rest of the band. The result was "I'm on Fire."

Bruce could come up with such material almost effortlessly, it seemed, and by now the band was able to keep up in the same spirit. Every song they cut showed it. Max Weinberg, in particular, had spent months practicing drum rudiments, regaining a sense of nuanced time that tended to get buried in the excited rush of stage shows but was crucial to record-making. Bruce was belatedly becoming interested in synthesizers; Roy Bittan, by several miles the most technically accomplished player in the band (Landau said he remembers Roy making two mistakes in ten years of recording), was already proficient with them. "I'm on Fire" is a good example of the highly atmospheric use Bittan made of the new machines. Garry Tallent's bass-playing had begun to come into its own on *The River*, and it stayed at a very high level. With the addition of Bruce's guitar, this four-piece ensemble was the core of the new music they were making. Steve, Danny, and Clarence added their distinctive touches as coloration, but it was the basic four-piece rock band set-up of guitar, bass, drums, and keyboards that drove the sound.

Even as Bruce was reaching for a greater sense of detail in his lyrics, the band's arrangements were taking on a similar cast. His earlier wall-of-sound approach, in which all parts coalesced into one gigantic Spectorian noise, was replaced by one in which every sound stood out sharply and the whole built from the integrity of these parts.

Be that as it may, the fact was that the material on Bruce's demo cassette wasn't going anywhere. For two weeks, they slugged it out with the same tunes. "I remember the main one we kept whackin' away at was 'Atlantic City,' which was a song that sounded like it was gonna really lend itself to the band," said Landau. "That was one song that seemed like it wasn't gonna be any problem. And *that* was goin' nowhere. No way was it as good as what he had goin' on that demo tape. Then we tried 'Nebraska' for a while, and Bruce had a whole little arrangement for it that had been rehearsed." Again, no success.

They tried other songs, notably "Mansion on the Hill," with an equal lack of results. "The stuff on the demo tape was astounding. It was an incredibly evocative piece of work. And we were losing more than we were picking up," said Plotkin. "I wouldn't even say that the stuff didn't come out beautifully. But the big thing was gone. The stillness was gone, the intimacy was gone. It was being scaled incorrectly."

After two weeks of frustration, Bruce agreed to put aside the material on the demo cassette and work on the songs he'd written since then. The earlier material wasn't being abandoned, however. As far as Bruce was concerned, it was still what his next record was about. It was just being put aside for a time, while other strategies for arranging and recording it were devised. It was senseless to waste studio time getting nowhere, and since the studio time was already booked, it was time to try some different material. (Unlike most other performers, Bruce never suffered any shortage of songs—it's hard to think of a more prolific writer.)

So they went back in the next Monday evening to try to salvage something from the remaining sessions.

The first thing Bruce called for was "Born in the U.S.A.," which shocked everyone. Landau had forgotten about the song, it had been cut from consideration so long before. Plotkin hadn't paid it any special mind on the demo; Steve didn't even remember it being on his cassette. The band hadn't rehearsed.

"To me, it was a dead song. It was one of the lesser songs on the *Nebraska* tape. Clearly the words and the music didn't go together," said Landau.

"What turned out to be the case was that Bruce, who had not forgotten about it, had discovered the key, which is that the words were right but they had to be in the right setting. It needed that turbulence and that scale—*there's* the song! He needed music that could evoke the emotional center of the character; he needed evocative music. In other words, an acoustic guitar wasn't gonna get you there on this song. He needed a band that could feel the way this song was supposed to feel.

"Well, we go through this thing, it was just a quick run-through. And even that is just basically 'Get your parts,' so you're not really getting a feeling for the thing. They started to play this thing and for everybody there, I know to this day, it was the most exciting thing that ever happened in a recording studio."

"We just kinda did it off the cuff," Bruce remembered. "I went in and said, 'Roy, get this riff.' And he just pulled out that sound, played the riff on the synthesizer. We played it two times and our second take is the record. That's why the guys are really on the edge. You can hear Max—to me, he was right up there with the best of them on that song. There was no arrangement. I said, 'When I stop, keep the drums going.' That thing in the end with all the drums, that just kinda happened."

"We did about five takes of it," recalled Landau. "I think the take that we used was actually the second complete take. The first take could have been used—I mean, they were all incredible. It was just one of those things where it happened real fast, and it was one of those deals where nobody had anything to say. I mean, it was like your producers and engineer just sitting there and it's unfolding . . . I was in complete shock.

"To me it was one of the most ultimate things of Bruce's gift, the way he had not let go of this song—he had so fully seen its potential and he had just somewhere on his own, instinctively, found his way to the solution. Because it was the same words, the music was different."

Different, certainly, from anything Bruce had ever done before. In some strange way, the song echoed the Rolling Stones' "Jumpin' Jack Flash" and "Street Fighting Man," but then again, Bittan's hastily conceived synthesizer part evoked a martial fife and drum right out of a corny Revolutionary War engraving, played at intervals that suggested Asian music. And in another way, the song just took in everything spread out between those landmarks and slammed it home into something new, something different, with all the high-impact force of Max Weinberg's drums. The song began with a resonant bass chord, which thrummed through the bottom of the first verse as the snare drum beat mercilessly against that fifelike synthesizer figure and Bruce chanted out the words at the top of his lungs.

At the top of the second verse, the rest of the band thundered into life and the turbulent story that the lyrics told—a kid who gets into trouble is sent to the Army and then to Vietnam, where he survives to return home and face facts—is matched by the metallic clash of drum against synthesizer. All through the middle of the song, this struggle for control continues and no one's winning the battle. The words are brittle images torn from the pages of a life gone to seed, and they tell the truth that America was still afraid to admit about the war, the truth that's just about all this vet has left to his name:

> Had a brother at Khe Sanh, fightin' off the Viet Cong
> They're still there; he's all gone . . .

The music rises to a flourish; the singer just stops—there is no finish to this thought. The next image follows immediately:

> He had a woman he loved in Saigon
> I got a picture of him in her arms now

Then the music breaks down again—just that drumbeat and the synthesizer like a call to arms and the voice bawling out its hopes

and fears, shattering against its own best intentions: "Bawwwwn
inna Yewww Esss Ayyy/Bawwwwn inna Yewww Esss Ayyy/
Bawwwwn inna Yewww Esss Ayyy," until the singer makes his
final, impenetrable declaration, biting down hard on each word:

> I'm a cool rockin' daddy in the U.S.A. now.

Who knows what this means? And yet, it seems the truest
residue not only of this war but of many, including the war
between Bruce Springsteen, Rock and Roll Natural, and Bruce
Springsteen, Thinkin' Fool. The music slashes and burns on for
another ninety seconds of rock and roll pyrotechnics—guitar
feedback, drum breakdowns, bass swoops, whooping vocaliza-
tions and imprecations—but it is never resolved, it just fades
away as old, discarded soldiers do.

That night they knew they'd really begun making an album.
And over the next three weeks, one song after another fell into
place, usually in just a few takes: "Glory Days," "Downbound
Train," "Darlington County" (a song they'd originally done during
the *Darkness on the Edge of Town* sessions in 1978!), "Working
on the Highway" (recast from its *Nebraska* arrangement), "I'm on
Fire," "I'm Goin' Down." A little more than half of what became
the *Born in the U.S.A.* album, released in 1984, was recorded in
those few nights in May 1982. All cut live, in the studio, and
eventually released with few, if any, overdubs. Plus a hilarious
"Working on the Highway" companion piece; the brutal "Murder,
Inc"; "Frankie," another *Darkness* leftover; and several others
that were of release quality but never got out.

Things were going great, everyone was ecstatic—except
Bruce. He was still fixing his attention on the first batch of songs,
the material from the demo cassette. Landau remembered thinking, "He's sending me a signal saying, 'Hey, I know everybody's
excited about how great this rock and roll stuff is, but this stuff
over here is what's really important to me right now. And I'm not
dealin' with this stuff until I figure out what I'm doin' with that
stuff.' "

The initial, obvious idea was to mix the two batches of
material together, which wouldn't be easy, since some of the

moods contrasted so sharply. But even that prospect was stymied by the incontrovertible fact that the band versions of the *Nebraska* material lacked the intrinsic atmosphere that made the demos great.

If it had been up to anyone else, they could have progressed with the material that had burbled up during the second set of sessions and made the rock and roll record everyone had shown up to record. "If at the end of the evening, your night's work is you cut 'Born in the U.S.A.' or 'Glory Days,' you feel pretty good. We knew what we had at the time. You go in and you spend six hours cutting 'Atlantic City' and at the end of the night you play the demo against what you did for the last six hours and you're nowhere, you feel pretty bad," said Landau. But Bruce remained adamant about wanting to make the core of his next album from the demo material.

No one had much idea what to do. So the era of uneasy feelings went on. "I was troubled by what was happening," said Plotkin. "The problem was that the demo tape was great and our treatments of the *Nebraska* stuff in the studio were adequate and they were less meaningful. They were less emotionally compelling, they were less honest; we were reducing the stuff, we were making less of it. We ran into a brick wall. Two-thirds of the stuff isn't working. We're screwing it up. What do we do here?

"There was a meeting one night that I remember, in the studio. And I think Jon had pretty much made up his mind—Jon had pretty much decided himself or thought his way through the issues and had pretty much decided himself that he thought we could and ought to treat this thing as an album."

Not exactly. In fact, Landau was thinking out loud, responding, he later recalled, to what he felt *Bruce* had already concluded. He and Bruce started talking in the empty studio at the end of the night's work. As they talked, Chuck and Steve wandered into the room. They all sat around a table while Bruce, ordinarily the quietest of them, expressed his frustration and a desire to finally nail the *Nebraska* songs down.

Landau had been mulling the problem over himself. He had come to no conclusions, but suddenly he found himself blurting out an idea he'd never intended to articulate. "Well . . ." he said.

"We can just put the demo out the way it is." Bruce shot Landau a look, a mixture of uneasiness and relief. He'd already had similar thoughts himself but had been unsure how to go about saying so, especially since Jon seemed "a little bit resistant." Was Landau serious?

"I wasn't serious and I wasn't not serious," he said later. "I was thinking out loud, and basically I'm in a position of figuring out, Hey, we have this stuff. I know it's great, Bruce knows it's great, Chuck knows it's great, Steve knows it's great, and it needs to come out. We tried very hard with the band, who have always been able to successfully render anything that we wanted to get onto a record, and we haven't been missing by a little. If we were missing by a little, we could figure that out. But we're not in the ballpark. We're not even close."

Landau's folk background again came into play. "I had a lot of familiarity with music that doesn't have drums. Voice and guitar can be a completely satisfying record to me. I have many many such records, and everybody knows a few—everybody's heard some Robert Johnson, and that's all that is. Not to make any extreme comparisons, but to me it's an utterly tenable idea that you can put a record out that's essentially voice and guitar."

They talked for a long while. All of the obvious questions came up. Musically, such material might be satisfying. But was it possible to release such music in the Eighties, at a time when the entire trend in pop was toward high-tech electronics—synthesizers, computer technology, video? People were writing articles wondering if the *guitar* was outmoded, and Bruce Springsteen was going to release an album of acoustic guitar and vocals recorded in a creaking chair in his bedroom on a portable tape deck?

Well, yeah, as a matter of fact he was. Columbia Records might not be pleased—although Landau maintained that they would readily release this album—and radio might have a hard time finding tracks to play. But as the conversation moved along, Landau became more and more convincing in his arguments. In the end, Steve Van Zandt's perception of the possibility of an album in the demo tapes became an unorthodox decision, put forward by the member of Bruce's production team—his manager—who was supposedly most concerned with Bruce's art as a commercial transaction. It was a perfect illustration of what made the relationship between Springsteen and all his collaborators, but especially Landau, so different from run-of-the-mill show business.

Anyway, the decision was really only succumbing to what was obvious. "I think it had become clear to everybody that this stuff was not going to be bettered," said Plotkin.

"One of the great things about the process the different groups of us working on Bruce's stuff have managed to evolve is just: You listen to the music. The music speaks to you. If you listen to it, it speaks to you. Whatever you think you're doing doesn't make any difference. It's what you are *in fact* doing. And if you listen hard enough, you can *hear* what you're doing; you can *hear* what you've done, which tells you what to include and what not to include—which take of a thing to use, which songs, which renditions. That's the whole thing. That's what you do: You put some music down and you listen to it.

"I think that it's one of the things that distinguishes Bruce from a lot of other artists. He, in fact, listens to his own stuff. He actually listens—in a way that's rather special, I think, for people who also write and play and sing. There is the feeling and ideas that go into creating the music, and then there is the process of stepping back and actually being able to hear what you've done as if you haven't just done it. Sort of separate yourself from the emotional rough and tumble of the creative process and listen. Listen hard.

"There's a fair amount of analysis that goes into it, but it's a very emotional process. There's a lot of flat notes on a lot of the records; there are things where the tempo isn't real solid. It's just, 'Does this thing make me feel my life in some deeper way that I otherwise would, in some new way than I otherwise have before?' And if it does, that's its job."

Bruce Springsteen is a cautious, conservative man, but he does not hedge his bets. Once the decision that the demo tape should become his next album was made, he held to it all the way. Someone proposed putting out the two sets of music together, as a double album. "Gee," Bruce said, "then most people would probably just listen to the other record. These songs will never get a fair hearing if we put them with the band stuff. This isn't the normal thing; it'll take more time. That's okay."

But, ran the argument, packaged together, more people would hear the *Nebraska* material.

Bruce was bemused. "I'm not worried about how many people get the record in their hands—I'm concerned with how many people *get it*. At least this way, I know if they're buying this album, they're buying it to get this album, not to get some other album."

So Bruce and Chuck Plotkin went to work turning the demo cassette into his next album.

Ordinarily, the hard part of finishing an album is mixing, placing the sounds so that they're heard in the proper proportions and perspective. Mastering, the final step, ordinarily is straightforward. Cutting a master disc from whose grooves LPs can be created is complicated and vital to the quality of the end product, but provided you're working with skilled technicians, the issues are mainly mechanical.

In the case of the tape that became *Nebraska*, nothing was nearly so simple. The tape deck on which Bruce had made his demo was a Tascam "home studio" that recorded at three and three-quarters inches per second (i.p.s. in studio parlance), double the speed of a nonprofessional machine. But in a recording studio, there are no such tape decks—the forty-eight-track master tapes there are two-inch reel-to-reel monsters rolling at thirty i.p.s., which are then mixed down to quarter-inch reel-to-reel "two-tracks" moving at the same speed. So the first job was to haul Bruce's Tascam deck into the studio and wire it up to the control board so its four tracks could be transferred to four tracks of a high quality studio tape rolling at thirty i.p.s. The idea was to mix the material from these tapes, using standard high tech studio equipment, echo, equalization, and other processes.

But they quickly discovered that these "pro" mixes were, as Plotkin puts it, "also disruptive to the sensibility of the thing." What they were trying to do was not just reproduce the music accurately but retain its atmosphere, an intangible they couldn't even describe to each other very well, much less to anyone who hadn't experienced the failed sessions with the band.

At one point they even tried sending Bruce into the studio on his own with an acoustic guitar to re-record the songs, but even then the songs didn't come out the same. Surrounded by the bright lights and huge machines controlled by studio professionals, they lost their feeling of isolation and became just stark and moody pieces, without the hair-raising quality of the originals. As Plotkin put it, "The better it sounded, the worse it sounded."

But that wasn't the worst of it. In order to play the three and three-quarters i.p.s. tape back on a conventional cassette player, Bruce had mixed it down by plugging his own conventional cassette machine into the back of the Tascam. Furthermore, it didn't have any alignment mechanism (by which the heads of one machine are matched up electronically to an industry standard), not that Bruce would necessarily have thought to align the heads if the facilities had been available. But then, that hadn't mattered, when all he was making was a demo. On Steve's machine, or Roy's or Clarence's, the stuff would sound good enough. It was only when you wanted to make several hundred thousand copies of those signals that you ran into trouble.

In January it didn't make any difference whatsoever that Bruce had mixed onto what Plotkin called "this completely screwed up, old battered blaster." But it mattered in late May, and sometime in the interim that machine died. "We never discovered the secrets of that machine," Plotkin sighed. They did know that it ran a little fast; they could tell because when they played the original Tascam master back through the studio board, the pitch was slightly elevated from the mixdown version, and that pitch shift could only have come from the machine that Bruce mixed with. So they were stuck.

"Once we discovered that these wonderful mixes that we were doing in the studio, where we brought in and remixed the stuff, were also depriving the stuff of some important element of its particularness, then we had no choice left but to take his original cassette mixes and try to master them," Plotkin explained. "So we got stuck with a very complicated set of technical problems."

Well, now at least they knew what they were going to try to master. So they took a thirty i.p.s. dub of the cassette to Sterling Sound and Bob Ludwig, the most experienced mastering engineer on the East Coast. And struck out.

"The cassette itself sounded fine," said Plotkin. "The problem is, cassette tape running across a head is one way of having the music transferred into a box that will give a signal and send it to a speaker. Another way is having a needle track a groove. A tape is soft; a needle's hard, vinyl's hard. And the mechanics of the contact between a needle and a groove are different than the mechanics of the contact of a smooth piece of tape passing over a smooth head.

"There was a kind of slap effect that Bruce got out of a little box—an Echoplex, the kind of little box that a guitar player ten years ago would have plugged his guitar into in order to get some slap on his guitar . . . When you take a noise like the beginning of 'oh' or 'uh,' and run it through a slap so it repeats . . . The needle would not reproduce that so that it sounded musical. It sounded like electronic distortion. It didn't sound like a throat. It was breaking up. It sounded like a piece of electronic gear crapping out."

They decided to try it in Los Angeles, so Bruce and Chuck flew to California and worked for a few days with Stephen Marcussen at Precision Lacquer. They learned a few things early on, and after several more days, they felt that they had it licked. They cut a reference disc. They played it all the way through, and the needle tracked and the voice didn't break up. They flew back to New York and played the disc for Landau. The problems returned. Bruce was reduced to the verge of tears; Landau and Plotkin weren't far behind him.

"Oh, it was just the most depressing thing," said Plotkin. "Here Bruce Springsteen, who takes years making records, has finally made an album in three days. And five weeks into the mastering process we haven't figured out how to get it on a disc. It was like God was looking down: 'Bruce, you cannot have anything fast. You have not suffered enough. You have not worked enough on this. *You* can't make a record in three days.'

"So we figured we just had to try something else." For a

while, they discussed releasing the album only as a cassette. Cassettes were becoming the dominant musical medium anyway, outstripping sales of LPs by ever-lengthening margins. But putting the album out that way would make it look even more like an oddity, and Bruce wanted the music to be heard as open-mindedly as possible. And anyway, despite everything else, Plotkin knew they were getting closer. He wanted to try working more or less on his own at a less specialized mastering facility.

Plotkin called Atlantic Records studios, and engineer Jimmy Douglas agreed to work with him in their mastering room. Atlantic's mastering room was primarily a convenience for its patrons, and together with Douglas and Dennis King, Plotkin could pretty much do as he pleased there. He used what he had learned about how radically the record's peak sounds had to be limited, but he also took even more unorthodox steps. "And," he said, "I wanted to do it someplace where my high tech mastering cronies were not gonna think I was outta my mind. I wanted to experiment someplace."

Plotkin was no more an expert at mastering than he was at mixing. What he did know was that the normal standard level for cutting a master was zero—that is, a record's grooves were cut so that on the peaks, the v.u. meter on a tape machine would kick right to the edge of the red. It was even considered desirable to cut things a little "hotter" than that, to push the peaks up to $+1$ or $+2$. Records cut with a higher relative volume sound louder and more alive at the same playing level, and hotter sounds disguise a multitude of sins, burying hiss and other noise.

The tape that they were mastering from was two generations down from a cassette master, and cassettes are inherently much noisier than reel-to-reel tapes. The way Bruce had recorded was, compared to recording in a professional studio, also fairly noisy. No mastering engineer in his right mind would consider trying to cut a super-low-level master from such material, for fear that the pops, clicks, and hisses would make him a laughingstock. A completely reasonable attitude, but that's where Plotkin had an advantage—he was not a mastering engineer. For him, the only significant issue was to get a master that would track without the sounds cracking up. And so he pushed the level farther and farther down—they'd already tried cutting a -2 and a -3 disc at Precision—until finally he got something that worked. The peaks were only pushing the needle up to -7 (take a look at the meter on any tape deck), meaning that most of the music was recorded even more softly than that, but he had a master.

They played it a few times to be sure, and then they played it for CBS Records President Walter Yetnikoff, who was very moved by its personal quality and wound up telling them tales of his own childhood. Then they went out to Bruce's favorite New York steak house and celebrated.

7 REASON TO BELIEVE

Take a good look at my face
You'll see my smile looks out of place
—SMOKEY ROBINSON

Nebraska became an album for the best reason: When he'd switched on that Tascam tape deck in his bedroom, Bruce Springsteen had plugged into far more than he'd intended. As Quincy Jones noticed, every time Bruce played, he went as far as ability, instinct, and judgment could take him. At best, that meant discovering new territory every chance he got.

That doesn't mean *Nebraska* didn't rework a lot of familiar territory: The cars and highways, the guilt and quest for redemption—all the things that naysayers claimed were excessive in his writing—were abundantly present. In some respects, even the characters were extensions of those on the cycle of albums from *Born to Run* through *The River*. Joe Roberts and his brother, Franky, are adult relatives of the men in "Racing in the Street," "The River," and "Born to Run"; the narrator of "Atlantic City" relives a version of "Meeting Across the River"; the haunted wild men of "State Trooper" and "Open All Night" are virtually indistinguishable from the outmoded cruisers of "Ramrod" and "Stolen Car." You could even say that the dreamer of "My Father's House" is the same man whose nightmares are recounted in "Darkness on the Edge of Town" and "Wreck on the Highway."

All these links and many more are firmly, even obviously, established. But even though they're connected, *Nebraska* didn't go where *The River* most logically would have flowed.

Nebraska gave Springsteen a new voice and his music a different feel; it also changed the population of his landscapes. Missing from the cast was the central character recognizable in "Badlands," "The Promised Land," "Hungry Heart," and "Thunder Road." Or maybe he wasn't missing—perhaps he'd just been warped beyond recognition. Springsteen and his characters had been rock and roll fundamentalists. Both *Born to Run* and *Darkness on the Edge of Town* opened with proclamations of faith and vitality: "This is a town full of losers, I'm pullin' outta here to win" ("Thunder Road") and "It ain't no sin to be glad you're alive" ("Badlands"). Now Springsteen stood those statements on their heads. In two of *Nebraska*'s first four songs, men virtually beg to be executed, and in the album's most heartbreaking moment, the protagonist of "Used Cars," a bright kid embittered by the humiliations of poverty, sings of a town full of losers from which he has no hope of pulling out: "My dad sweats the same job from mornin' to morn / Me, I walk home on the same dirty streets where I was born." This wasn't Bruce Springsteen's story; it wasn't the story of those whom he'd written about previously. It sounded different because, despite all the reference points, it was something new.

In part, the new album found its voice in the American folk and country music to which Bruce had listened so intently, especially Delta blues singers like Robert Johnson (whom Bruce first heard around this time) and bluegrass groups like the Stanley Brothers.

Folk music is palpably present in *Nebraska* as a wellspring of its energy and its stillness. Even "Open All Night," the closest thing to an all-out rocker on the disc, harks back to proto-rockabillies like Harmonica Frank Floyd and Hank Mizell rather than Chuck Berry and the R&B singers who inspired Bruce's usual songs. *Nebraska* is a species of folk music, but not since the first three Bob Dylan albums had any performer extended the folk tradition so effectively. Like Dylan, Bruce accomplished the feat by bursting through every rule and boundary folk cultists had established. But where Dylan was the product of a self-conscious community of urban folk singers, Springsteen was still not the folk-based singer/songwriter that John Hammond and Mike Appel thought they'd found in 1972. On *Nebraska* Bruce was responding to a more basic fact. He'd stripped his music until he laid bare the folk roots of rock and roll itself.

If folk tradition was the most significant musical influence on the *Nebraska* performances, it was hardly the most important force in shaping the album. Far more crucial was Bruce's recent personal experience. With *The River*, "Hungry Heart," and the ensuing tour—his graduation from a rapt cult to a truly mass audience—Bruce confronted the greatest challenge rock stardom presented. While out there working, he'd made the transition without dissolving or diluting the rapport between himself and his fans. Now he faced the moment of greatest dread.

Track the trajectory of all the rock and roll heroes who ever scaled the heights of fame Bruce now occupied and there comes a point, in every story from Presley's to Jagger's, where the line drops off the map. This moment arrives when the star's career is at a peak of commercial acceptance, acclaim, and often of artistry. It's as if each star looked his audience in the eye . . . and fled. For Elvis the moment came, perhaps, when he was seduced by Colonel Parker and Hollywood, or maybe when he returned from the Army—or for that matter, it might have been the day he quit his job at Crown Electric. With the Stones, you could locate it exactly—that grisly instant at Altamont when Mick Jagger emerged from his dressing room and found himself not revered but punched hard in the mouth.

In dozens of bad rock novels, the denouement is a Corn King ritual in which the audience slays the performer, usually because he has overexcited them erotically. It's interesting that this archetype has persevered through all the changes in popular culture since the 1950s (when the first such novels were written). After all, the fact is that every dead rock star but Lennon died a lonely, isolated death from drink, drugs, or a plane crash. But the facts have nothing to do with the legend. The myth finds its power in the basic relationship between the individual star and a truly massive audience. For all its thrilling potency, direct contact with such a crowd is also frightening, threatening every individual in its path with psychic, if not physical, extinction. For the performer who's the focus of all that attention, the threat is palpable—retreat from the spotlight glare and you're anonymous again, but holding your ground means risking being overrun by the crowd and its demands. Whatever would *really* happen, what feels most likely is death by catastrophe, and it feels that way not only to inept novelists but to dozens of rock stars swaddled in bodyguard "security."

In the face of this puzzle (which has faced all artist-celebrities since Picasso), retreat is the only available tactic. *Nebraska* was an accidental album, but it was an accident waiting to happen. Bruce needed to draw back and reassess what he'd been doing and how the world had responded. *Nebraska* was a reflection of that need, giving him space in which to relocate his public identity in a way that another rock and roll album, no matter how finely crafted, wouldn't have done.

Nebraska was at most a sideways step in the pattern of Bruce's work and career, since its very nature ensured a limited audience, while the essence of what he'd done until then had been the broadest possible outreach. Yet to proceed on that line at that moment would have threatened to reduce Springsteen's rock and roll idealism to the status of careerist opportunism, giving the people what they wanted for all the wrong reasons.

The enormous power of the mass audience can quickly become dictatorial, restricting performances to rote repetitions of outgrown rituals. Mass audiences are less rapt, not so universally willing to put up with the more reflective aspects of the show, and they invariably pull the performance in the direction of the known. When it comes to sheer rocking out, a mass crowd is unmatchable, but simply meeting its demands is a trap. In the same way that not outgrowing cult status means withering and dying, giving in to the collective will of the mass audience— letting the crowd, in effect, determine creative decisions—can be devastating. Retreat in order to regroup is the only way for the artist to reassert control.

Once in retreat, most stars never make it back. Even if they stay famous and make hit records, the tendency is to avoid a repetition of the situation that caused them to retreat in the first place. The essential spirit of interaction with the audience disappears. Artists as influential and fascinating as Pete Townshend and Neil Young became lost in a maze of their own suspicion and dread. The Stones grew cynical, Lennon and McCartney just dropped out: one from playing music, one from trying very hard. Elvis mingled confusion, resentment, and terror of his own condition. Dylan blundered from pillar to post. By the early Eighties, the pattern seemed so irrevocably fixed that the new generation of rock stars became obsessed with keeping their careers within bounds so as to avoid any such moment of confrontation, willing to make music that promised nothing just so that the debt would never be called in. It was the heyday of the "semipopular."

On tour Bruce had been able to ignore or at least overwhelm these facts through an act of faith. He really did believe, to use Greil Marcus's words, "that rock and roll . . . has a coherent tradition which, when performed, will reveal possibilities of rock and roll the tradition did not previously contain." And he honestly felt that the source of all his fame and wealth was his talent for delving into just such questions while inviting damn near anybody who asked along for the trip. Yet, whether he was conscious of it or not, the crowds on the final leg of the American tour sent a message that disrupted this faith. They wanted to rock; they weren't especially interested in sitting through the somber songs that set up the explosive rock numbers, and they didn't try to hide their impatience. Springsteen was sufficiently willful to do what he needed to do anyway, and his moodier pieces were compelling enough to keep an unexpectedly high proportion of the audience involved. But audience rapport was an important part of the show, and although that never disintegrated, it was noticeably diminished. *Nebraska* didn't drive the mass audience away, but it certainly taxed its attention, and it served notice—to Bruce himself if no one else—that the dictates that ruled his life and music were still his own. This didn't solve the problem of how to regain contact with the mass audience, but it at least bought Bruce some space and time in which to figure out his next moves.

But even though *Nebraska* remains a rearguard action, it would be a mistake to dismiss the growth it exhibited, particularly in Springsteen's writing and singing. In their details and especially in their characterizations, songs such as "Used Cars" and "Highway Patrolman" are the most lifelike songs Bruce has ever written. Comparisons are difficult because the styles are so different, but on a purely lyrical level, for instance, these songs are more intriguing in their intricacy than those on *Born in the U.S.A.*

Nebraska's songs are about the utter inability to communicate and the isolation that results. In that sense, it's a pure product of Bruce Springsteen's critical condition as a pop star. But it is also about family betrayals and failures, dreams that are wasted, hopes that are blasted, a longing for death as a release from the pitiful consequences of this life. The best of its songs—"Nebraska," "Highway Patrolman," "Used Cars," "Mansion on the Hill," "Reason to Believe"—are as horrifying as they are beautiful, not just because so many people die but because those deaths are so welcome to the singer, such a confirmation of his own despair. But the singer obviously didn't feel that disarrangement of all order simply because fans clapped and stomped through "Independence Day." Other, greater estrangements were at work.

■

Anybody who traveled America in 1980 and 1981 would have been thrown out of kilter. Double digit unemployment was only the most accessible measurement of the greatest economic disaster since the Great Depression. The United States was no longer the land of plenty, it was a land of limits; it was no longer the home of a dream of equality but of a nightmare of inequity. If Americans expected nothing else, they expected a surfeit of personal possessions. Now hundreds of thousands had lost their homes, their jobs, and in the ensuing confusion and disruption, much of what they had thought was eternal. Families fractured, communities crumbled, tempers once sweet turned sour. An ugly spirit ascended, the most perverse rendering of "every man for himself." The greed behind it all wasn't anything new—in part, it was as old as the earliest European settlement on the continent—

but it had rarely stood so naked and unapologetic. In this world, all men saw each other not as brothers but as incomprehensible, threatening aliens.

In Europe, also in the throes of a new Depression, Bruce and the band experienced another kind of disparity, because the tremendous respect and devotion audiences there paid them wasn't based only in Bruce Springsteen's personality but also in his stature as a representative and disseminator of a shared version of the American dream, or at least a shared dream that was associated with America. The depth of their listening, which accepted all Bruce had to say and urged him on, said so decisively.

It's not entirely clear when Bruce Springsteen realized that he was writing about America, although since he was both ambitious and a native of the first country that was an idea before it was a nation, the topic was inevitable. Certainly, that must have been part of what drew him to John Ford, the greatest poet of the American cinema. But long before that, you could hear Bruce struggling to express something about it. When his storied Jersey Shore band, Steel Mill, played the Matrix in San Francisco in 1969, *San Francisco Examiner* reviewer Phil Elwood was struck by a tune called "American Song," composed of "political-military observations, ranging from Concord Bridge to the present." A similar number was prepared for Bruce's first Columbia album but dropped. Beginning with *Born to Run*, however, the idea of a specifically American dream began to loom larger and larger in Bruce's work. And beginning with *Darkness on the Edge of Town*, the frustrations of trying to realize that dream became Bruce's central subject.

That doesn't necessarily mean that Springsteen had grown especially political. In November 1976, playing a series of New York shows during the lawsuit period, Bruce treated the forthcoming presidential election as an occasion for jokes; his attitude seemed to be that politics was just something that could get in the way if you let it. But in November 1980 he took the stage at Arizona State University in Tempe on the night after the right-wing landslide and opened the show by commenting, "I don't know what you thought about what happened last night, but I thought it was terrifying." And by that time, he had released *Darkness on the Edge of Town*, an album suffused with class consciousness.

Even at that point, though, what made Springsteen so specifically American was less what he said than how he went about his business. On the surface he was almost childishly guileless, and the virtues of his show resided in straight-from-the-shoulder plainspokenness, the restriction (which sometimes amounted to abolition) of irony, and the creation of drama without extravagant theatrical mechanisms. (Theatrical devices of a less tangible sort were everywhere, of course.) Furthermore, Springsteen developed a songwriting style that spoke in an unmistakably American fashion. The language of even his most arch and artful songs—"The River" is the best example—is completely vernacular. And of course, his singing voice, with that odd combination of soul hoarseness, rockabilly twang, and Jersey nasality, was as unmistakably American as David Bowie's was British, and in the early Eighties that was uncommon in white rock.

But if America is a presence in Springsteen's songs before *Nebraska*, it's mostly through his remarkably specific sense of place. Looking back, it makes sense that he called his first album *Greetings from Asbury Park, New Jersey*. From the start, Springsteen's songs have been peppered with unforgettable places, although most are fictitious: Greasy Lake, Jungleland, "a rattlesnake speedway in the Utah desert," Stockton's Wing, the Trestles, Thunder Road, Bluebird Street, "that dusty road from Monroe to Angeline," "the fields out behind the dynamo." Often evoked just in the way Bruce sings their names, these places are vivid out of all proportion, compellingly rendered in the inflections of Springsteen's singing and recognizable archetypes for every American and everyone familiar with the landscape of American pop fiction, movies, and music. And because these songs are unified by their emotional portraits, even "Badlands" and "The Promised Land" are genuinely international beyond the bounds of their all-American titles.

Nebraska is different in many respects. Even its most specifically sited songs are primarily character studies. Several are directly grounded in the new depression of the early Eighties. In both "Johnny 99" and "Atlantic City" the protagonist complains of "debts no honest man could pay" and resorts to acts of desperate futility. Poverty is ever-present, and it's not the romantically bohemian poverty of the rock and roll singer in "Rosalita," soon to be dispelled by a grant from a large corporation, but poverty so crushing in its permanence that it saps all strength from the soul. There's not just a scarcity of jobs, as in "The River"; in "Johnny 99," when "they closed down the plant in Mahwah," it stayed shut. Bosses run wild over workers, and while one class hides behind "gates of hardened steel," the other works the night shift for penance and punishment.

In even the most glum of Springsteen's previous songs, people survive because they have roots, often connected to a love affair but always related to a dream. *Dream* was one of the biggest words in Springsteen's onstage vocabulary, and it was always linked with the redemptive power of rock and roll music and, through that music, to the entire purpose of playing and gathering. You could say that *Nebraska*'s story begins with "The River," when Springsteen finally imagines a character asking, "Is a dream a lie if it don't come true/Or is it something worse?" In Springsteen's universe, that is a very dangerous question because it dredges up an irreconcilable contradiction. And *Nebraska*'s characters have found the answer; it's about the only question to which they could respond in the affirmative. For these lost souls it's all over but the shrouding. In a vicious climate men go mad, turn viciously crazy, and nothing is left to check their casual cruelty. Faith, hope, the possibility of redemption—all the concepts lurking behind Bruce's "dream"—are nothing less than absurd. In "Atlantic City," the singer toys with the idea of reincarnation as a signal that he's ready to test its truth. In "Reason to Believe" the idea of a life after death is seen as no more ridiculous than the idea that people will behave decently in this one.

It's not just that some of the characters are afflicted this way. They all are, even a stolid center of gravity like Joe Roberts, the highway patrolman. "Highway Patrolman" is *Nebraska*'s finest story; Roberts is Springsteen's most fully and lovingly drawn character and the performance is as beautiful as it is exhausted. Caught between family and responsibility, duty and love, Roberts obeys his most decent instincts and finds his life ruined by impossible choices. As he allows his brother's car to escape, he also watches himself cross the border into the forbidden. Springsteen's voice quakes as he sings the final verse, and when Joe finally watches his brother's "tail lights disappear," the voice breaks and Bruce fumbles the guitar pick, which he has otherwise strummed steadily throughout the song. In the universe of Springsteen songs, making the right choice is always of the essence, but now he's telling a story in which right is not an available option and it feels absolutely shocking.

Nebraska's other great character sketch is "Used Cars," told in a child's voice (a voice not far from those O'Connor stories). It's a bitter tale, clearly drawn from life in a way that "Highway Patrolman" could not have been. "Highway Patrolman" has the atmosphere of a movie; "Used Cars" stinks of everyday reality and it's just as brutal in depicting lives so impoverished they feel counterfeit. Everybody is faking it, even the kid who makes another of Springsteen's breakout vows: "Now mister the day my number comes in/I ain't ever gonna ride in no used car again."

Springsteen spoke so often in his shows about his family's run of junkers that the personal context of "Used Cars" is unmistakable. It's as if, having imagined his way out of the trap, he now returns to his despised neighborhood and "walks home on the same dirty streets where I was born," trying on the shoes of those who didn't escape . . . or, maybe, wondering how much of himself made the break.

"Used Cars" isn't the only bit of elemental autobiography on *Nebraska*. "Mansion on the Hill" refers to an actual place Doug Springsteen and his son used to visit near Freehold, while "My Father's House," in which father and son achieve reconciliation in sleep that they cannot reach awake, is archetypal as only real dreams are.

And that's the final context in which *Nebraska* must be understood: as a deeply personal exploration of the private demons tormenting Bruce Springsteen. *Nebraska* is a study in crisis, and while a portion of that crisis was professional and a portion was political, another part was personal.

Born to Run proved that rock and roll dreams could come true. The albums that followed grappled with what happened when dreams were fouled. But all those records were predicated on the premise that the world is basically a decent place. *Nebraska* is not only bold enough to admit that it isn't, but that, in fact, living in it is an act of folly.

This might have been easy to ignore; it wasn't Bruce Springsteen's problem. But looking back over his life, he saw how thin the margin truly is. That is what accounts for the complete lack of distance with which he speaks through Charles Starkweather in "Nebraska," and for his almost eager acknowledgment of the other disasters and tragedies in these songs. When his career began, Bruce conceived himself as an explorer, and his searches had taken him not only all over the world but deeper into his own psyche than it was perhaps prudent to venture. Bruce describes himself as a basically psychological person, by which he means introspective and analytical. Since he always thought big, he found himself asking gigantic questions on that score, too. But when you get down to asking about life's meaning, you encounter questions that will not surrender to rational analysis. Now, pondering how it was that others got through life without his basic faith, the answer that came screaming back was *maybe he shouldn't be quite so sure*.

"Reason to Believe" stares down all of Bruce's rock and roll idealism and mocks its certainty. This happens in the specifics of the song, not on its surface, for this excavation of the potential purposelessness of existence is ironically one of *Nebraska*'s jauntier numbers. The irony is that the title phrase could serve as an epitaph of his career. Its images are as bizarre as anything in *Wise Blood*: A man stands by the side of a highway, poking a dead dog as if he hopes to revive it. A woman stands at the end of her driveway every night, waiting for the return of a man who didn't care for her much when he was around, then left without notice. A child is baptized in the same instant that an old man is buried.

A groom is left waiting at the altar and long after everyone else
has gone, still stands there refusing to face the fact. And after
each of these verses, Bruce puts the knife in:

> Struck me kinda funny, seem kinda funny sir to me
> Still at the end of every hard-earned day people
> find some reason to believe

As on so many of the songs here, the phrasing is flat not
because the singer doesn't care but because his reserves are
exhausted. But this time there's nothing ambiguous about the
comments. If this stuff really strikes him funny, it's a cheerless
joke. "Oh Lord won't you tell us, tell us what does it mean," he
inquires after the baptism and funeral, but this time Bruce
Springsteen, who has provided answers to such questions with
every note of his best music, doesn't even pause long enough for
God to get a word in. He just strums harder and keeps on singing.
The stories and images rush out so fast that it's hard to take them
all in. It takes a while for that verse to sink in, for example, to see
that what passes in the instant between its second line and its
third—between birth and death—is an entire lifetime, that the
baby dunked in water and the old man flung back into the earth
are the same person.

What Springsteen was saying contradicted almost everything
implied in his other records, and it's impossible that he didn't
know it. Maybe he could still stomp and shout, "It ain't no sin to
be glad you're alive," each night during "Badlands," but he now
also found himself able to see justice on the other side of the
story.

Because in earlier songs Springsteen often found reason for
optimism in the most terrible circumstances, many listeners
(particularly reviewers) took the chorus of "Reason to Believe" to
be an affirmation. But "Reason to Believe" said yes to nothing. It
stared straight into the void about which Springsteen-as-
Starkweather spoke and found there exactly what was expected:
nothing at all.

If there's another song much like this in American music, it
must be the Stanley Brothers' haunting bluegrass hymn "Rank

Strangers," in which the singer returns after a long absence to his boyhood home in the Blue Ridge and finds there not one familiar soul:

> Everybody I met seemed to be a rank stranger
> No mother or dad, not a friend could I see
> They knew not my name and I knew not their faces
> I found they were all rank strangers to me

It's a song suffused with mysticism and terror, but in the end the singer is reassured by "the voice of a stranger" who assures him that he will rejoin his loved ones in heaven, "where no one will be a stranger to me." In Bruce's song, such hope of reconciliation was beyond consideration. His thoughts had now taken him closer to the Old Testament than the New, to the voice of that cranky old preacher Ecclesiastes, who despises life and all its activities and concludes, "Vanity of vanities . . . all is vanity."

If you were willing to admit what it was saying, it was frightening to listen to "Reason to Believe." But if it was scary to hear, it's hard to imagine what it must have been like to have to live it every day. And it would be a while before these badlands started treating their creator good.

8 BADLANDS

You broke my heart 'cause I couldn't dance
You didn't even want me around
And now I'm back to let you know
I can really shake 'em down
                    —THE CONTOURS

Finally having a master didn't mean that *Nebraska* was ready for release. Springsteen and art director Andrea Klein spent the better part of the summer working up an album cover. Bruce wanted something more evocative than a portrait of himself, something closer to the pictures he'd found in a rare copy of Robert Frank's 1958 photo essay, *The Americans*. Frank was known to rock and roll fans as the creator of the *Exile on Main Street* album cover. His long out-of-print book explored, in the words of Jack Kerouac's introduction, "that crazy feeling in America when the sun is hot on the streets and music comes out of the jukebox or from a nearby funeral." Its portrayals were in a style of photography that directly connected to the *Nebraska* songs—staring without flinching at painfully mundane scenes and stirring the swarming life beneath.

Klein introduced Springsteen to the still-life and portrait photos of David Kennedy, and they arranged a marathon photo session at Kennedy's house in Brewster, New York. Three pictures emerged. Two are of Bruce. In one he's caught gazing apprehensively through a doorway; in the other he sits quietly at Kennedy's kitchen table. But the photograph that wound up on the cover was one that Kennedy had taken some time before, a shot of two-lane blacktop in the Midwestern flatlands that he'd grabbed through a windshield. Although the perspective is different, Kennedy's picture bears a startling resemblance to Frank's "U.S. 285, New Mexico," from *The Americans*. It also resembles pictures that Springsteen and photographer Eric Meola took in the Western desert in 1978. Its bleak tone succinctly sums up *Nebraska*'s mood.

Even with a cover, the album lacked a title. The record was slated to be released in early October, but Bruce debated about what to call it until nearly Labor Day. About half the song titles were considered; *State Trooper, Used Cars,* and *Reason to Believe* were among the finalists. But in the end, it was the first song, which was also the first one that Bruce had recorded, that set the mood and told the story. So the album became *Nebraska*. Columbia announced its release to a puzzled record world.

Nebraska wasn't a gimmick. Bruce didn't have a commercial need to get a record out. His core audience wouldn't drift away if it took him a long time to make his next album; most fans probably expected him to take two or three years in the studio. Even so, the new album had to be presented properly to whatever audience it could find. Oddment *Nebraska* might have been, but it still had to be marketed.

That wouldn't have been easy in any circumstances, and it was harder than ever in late 1982. The record business was in its greatest slump since before the advent of the Beatles; the mega-platinum boom years had been waning since 1979, and they'd ended with a thud in 1981. Even superstar sales expectations were typically cut in half. Increasingly, album-oriented radio (AOR) stations were crowded out by singles-based competitors who simply moved Top Forty to the FM side of the dial, and the AOR stations that survived lasted by being programmed ever more rigidly. Because broadcasting dictated what music sold, records became equally conservative, and the result was a quagmire of stagnation: boring radio, boring music. Bored fans found other ways to spend their dough. In this climate, to release an album like *Nebraska*—an album without singles or prefabricated thrills—seemed next to suicidal. Experienced record businessmen guessed it would sell only 200,000 or 300,000 copies, less than a quarter of *The River*.

Yet Jon Landau, who as manager was responsible for such facets of Springsteen's career, was remarkably confident. "What I thought and knew was that we could put this tape out and it would be a sensational record." he said. "That's what I knew. I didn't know what would happen to it—how many people would hear it, what room there was for it on radio. All those things obviously required thought, but that wasn't the key decision. After all, even if we had gotten the band on all the *Nebraska* material, nobody thought that this was the most commercial stuff Bruce had ever written. That was not one of the reactions anybody ever had."

Springsteen and Landau adopted the attitude that the album would get enough airplay for people to know it existed and that it would sell enough to justify releasing it. "Clearly, it's something different; clearly it's not for everybody," Landau remembers thinking. "We're not going to try and pretend that this is the follow-up to *The River* in the normal sense. At the same time we're not gonna promote it in a fashion that makes it seem we're apologizing." So when someone proposed that the record be released in Columbia's budget-line series for a reduced price, Bruce simply laughed and asked whether it was now the policy to price albums based on how many musicians played on them. On the other hand, this was the sixth album he'd released but the first for which he did not plan an immediate concert tour; he also decided to shun the typical postrelease series of press and radio interviews. This time out, the music really would have to speak for itself.

Then again, if *Nebraska* was to find any audience at all, CBS needed some promotional tools. Dark as days were in the record business, there was a prosperous new phenomenon: MTV, the twenty-four-hour cable television channel broadcasting "music videos," short film clips designed to promote singles. Such clips had been a highly effective sales device in Europe for years. At a time when other forms of broadcast exposure for music were smothering innovation, MTV opened its programming to much that was new—it had to, because not that many videos existed. As a result, it had begun to capture a larger audience that bought impressive quantities of records. Record labels were eager to take advantage of its potential, although albums like *Nebraska* weren't what they—or MTV—had in mind.

That autumn Landau was visited by Arnold Levine, who headed up the in-house video department at CBS in the Seventies. Levine had filmed parts of a Springsteen concert in Tempe, Arizona, in August 1978, and the clip he made of "Rosalita" had been used in England and Europe, where it was an important factor in creating anticipation for the tour. (Although a snippet appeared in Malcolm Leo and Andrew Solt's 1981 ABC television special "Heroes of Rock and Roll," the full "Rosalita" video didn't air in the States until 1984.)

Levine, now a freelance video director, approached Landau to inquire about making a clip of "Atlantic City." He had been told that getting Springsteen to appear in the video was probably out of the question. But that was the case not because Bruce was hostile to the concept of video clips (in fact, he was intrigued, although plenty wary of the medium's ability to flatten imaginative content) so much as because he was heading for California to mix his rock and roll material. What Levine proposed was shooting street scenes in Atlantic City and putting together a video that would contrast the wealth of the casino strip along the boardwalk with the destitution of the rest of the town.

Springsteen agreed to let Levine try the idea, but everyone was extremely skeptical about winning Bruce's approval for something in which he'd have so little involvement. ("The only direction I gave was to say that it should be kind of gritty-looking, and it should have no images that matched up to the images in the songs.") In general, the watchword of the entire Springsteen camp was *control*, and letting Levine work on his own was, for them, a step as unusual and almost as daring as *Nebraska* itself. But what Levine created was simple, tasteful, and evocative, making its point without bludgeoning the viewer and working at an angle that didn't detract from the lyric narrative. Shot in black and white, it was one of the most impressive music videos anyone had come up with and, after Bruce gave his okay, universally well received. MTV played "Atlantic City" frequently, and the song's exposure there undoubtedly won the album many listeners it otherwise wouldn't have had.

The response to *Nebraska* was surprisingly intense. Before release, doubts ran rampant. When producer Jimmy Iovine, who had engineered *Born to Run* and *Darkness* and remained a close friend, heard the tape Landau sent him, he turned to Bob Seger, with whom he was working, and insisted, "This can't be it. It must be the roughs." Commented Bill Hard, editor of *The Friday Morning Quarterback Album Report*, an influential AOR tipsheet, "I think it's gonna do one of two things. Either it's gonna continue a trend toward softer, more personal music being accepted by radio, or it's gonna be a complete bomb."

In fact, neither happened. *Nebraska* was part of no trend—it flew in the face of the most important trend of 1982, which was synthesizer-oriented British pop. But as AOR radio programmer Lee Abrams, an extremely conservative practitioner, remarked, "With an artist of Springsteen's prominence, you owe it to the audience to expose it and let them make up their minds. I can't imagine a station's not playing it. You've gotta give it a shot." Most AOR stations did play it a bit, at least in the first couple of weeks after release. Audience reaction was divided—WMMS in Cleveland, a long-time bastion of Springsteen mania, reported that its call-in comments were split evenly between those who loved the album and those who hated it—but the response was there. And when *Nebraska* was played, it sold remarkably well for such a commercially off-the-wall venture, reaching Number Four on the *Billboard* album chart and selling about 800,000 copies in the United States alone.

Critical opinion was overwhelmingly in *Nebraska*'s favor. Even such long-time Springsteen naysayers as Robert Palmer of the *New York Times* had kind words for it. In the annual *Village Voice* critics poll, the album placed third (behind Elvis Costello's *Imperial Bedroom* and *Shoot Out the Lights* by Richard and Linda Thompson). *Rolling Stone* named *Nebraska* among its albums of the year and termed Springsteen artist of the year, top male vocalist, and best songwriter.

Reviews were exceptionally important to Springsteen. He was aware of the role critics had played in his early career, and he'd come to know several writers around the country and to count on their comments to help translate the more serious side of his work. If he was truly concerned not with how many people got the album but with how many *got* it, he must have felt as if he'd cashed the bet when he read the reviews.

Paul Nelson, who reviewed the album for *Musician,* was a folk music expert (he'd edited *Little Sandy Review* in the early Sixties and had the distinction of being one of the first people to play Woody Guthrie records for Bob Dylan). Nelson had known Springsteen since before the release of Bruce's first album. His review opened with an acknowledgment of how difficult the album could be to hear, because it "sounded so demoralized and demoralizing, so murderously monotonous, so deprived of spark and hope. . . . Springsteen had the courage of his convictions, I decided, and had made an album as bleak and unyielding as next month's rent. Only one problem: I didn't want to hear it. So day after day, I circled *Nebraska,* attempting to listen, trying to escape."

Unlike most others who were initially so put off, Nelson finally found a way to get to the guts of it, tracing the record's roots to recent work by Neil Young and Bob Dylan, to Guthrie, and to those Library of Congress field recordings. Of course, few others had the background to place the album in such a broadly historical context.

But some critics found the record more accessible—after all, it did tap a mood astir in the nation. "A dark-toned, brooding and unsparing record, *Nebraska* is also the most successful attempt at making a sizable statement about American life that popular music has yet produced," wrote Mikal Gilmore of the *Los Angeles Herald Examiner*. Gilmore praised Springsteen's growth as a writer, particularly his use of vernacular language and the record's "submergence in point-of-view. . . . When Springsteen tells Charles Starkweather and Johnny 99's tales, he neither seeks their redemption nor asks for our judgment. He tells the stories about as simply and as well as they deserve to be told—or about as unsparingly as we deserve to hear them—and he lets us feel for them what we can, or find in them what we can of ourselves."

Others homed in on the album's politics. In a review presciently titled "Born in the U.S.A.," Greil Marcus wrote: "*Nebraska* . . . is the most complete and probably the most convincing statement of resistance and refusal that Ronald Reagan's U.S.A. has yet elicited from any artist or any politician.

Because Springsteen is an artist and not a politician, his resistance is couched in terms of the bleakest acceptance, his refusal presented as a refusal that does not know itself. There isn't a trace of rhetoric, not a moment of polemic; politics are buried deep in stories of individuals who make up a nation only when their stories are heard together. But if we can hear their stories as a single, whole story, they cannot. The people we meet on *Nebraska* . . . cannot give their lives a public dimension, because they are alone; because in a world in which men and women are mere social and economic functions, every man and woman is separated from every other."

To Marcus this was a definition of what had taken place as a reactionary regime unraveled the accoutrements of liberal tradition, and the consequences were unmistakably totalitarian. "The only acts of rebellion presented on *Nebraska* have to do with murder," he concluded. "They are nihilistic acts committed by men in a world in which social and economic functions have become the measure of all things and have dissolved all other values. In that context, these acts make sense. And that is the burden of *Nebraska*."

Others, however, discerned that Bruce might be carrying extra weight. "Any artist who confronts the world around him in an attempt to define a set of values and a reason for living is running a risk," Robert Palmer concluded. "What if the world simply doesn't make sense? What if there is no reason for living? Several of the songs on *Nebraska* circle around these disquieting possibilities, and its final song, 'Reason to Believe,' attempts to come to terms with them. 'At the end of every hard-earned day,' it concludes, 'people find some reason to believe.'

"But 'people' and Bruce Springsteen are not necessarily the same thing, and the song fails to dispel the mood of profound unease engendered by the rest of the record. It's been a long time since a mainstream rock star made an album that asks such tough questions and refuses to settle for easy answers—let alone an album suggesting that perhaps there *are* no answers. Facing that possibility has driven more than one sensitive soul right up to the edge of the abyss, and over it. One can only hope that Mr.

Springsteen will either find 'some reason to believe' or learn to live without one."

■

The plan was for Bruce to come to California and spend several weeks mixing the rock and roll material with Plotkin. At the same time, Bruce arranged for Toby Scott to install a more elaborate twenty-four-track home studio in an outbuilding at his Los Angeles house. But it wasn't quite that easy to change gears from the gloomy and insulated world of *Nebraska* to the more open and friendly space of *Born in the U.S.A.*

For one thing, Springsteen's tightly managed world was in turmoil. Bruce was able to retain such complete command of his work in part because the community within which he made music had for years been stable and protective. There had not been a major change in the band or management since the lawsuit, five years before. Now Steve was off working on his solo project, preparing to tour and planning his wedding for New Year's Eve, in the process completely absenting himself from the planned mixing sessions. Over Labor Day weekend, Landau was married to former *Rolling Stone* editor Barbara Downey, and he, too, stayed behind in New York. Plotkin had been separated from his wife and son in Los Angeles for months; he had some serious catching up to do. Bruce had broken up with Joyce Hyser, his girlfriend since 1978, soon after the tour ended, and he'd been mostly on his own since then. Aside from Steve, he socialized with the band infrequently, and he didn't have the circle of musician cronies common to most other rock stars. He was back to being a full-time loner.

Single-mindedness had made Bruce Springsteen rich and famous, an idol to millions, virtually King of Rock and Roll. But just as his music had matured, so had he, and now the loner was beginning to experience his condition in a different way—as nothing more than loneliness.

"That whole *Nebraska* album was just that isolation thing and what it does to you," Bruce said many months after the ordeal was over. "The record was basically about people being isolated from their jobs, from their friends, from their families, their fathers, their mothers—just not feeling connected to anything that's going on—your government. And when that happens, there's just a whole breakdown. When you lose that sense of community, there's some spiritual breakdown that occurs. And when that occurs, you just get shot off somewhere where nothing seems to matter."

It would have been difficult to deny that there was a more intimate connection. Bruce didn't even try, although he was never very forthcoming about how deep and immediate his own sense of emptiness ran and how difficult it proved to dispel. "The *Nebraska* record sounds a lot like me, in the sense of the feeling," he said. "I don't mean in the particular details of the stories, but the emotional feeling feels a lot like my childhood felt to me, a lot of the people I grew up with, the tone. . . . The whole thing is, when you tell a story, a story is only good if it's your story in some fashion. Even *Nebraska*, which is extreme emotionally, the thing that makes it real is knowing what that feels like. In a funny way, I feel it's my most personal album."

Wrapped up in his own thoughts, Springsteen thought to clear his head by doing what he always did: Get out and drive. Rather than flying to Los Angeles, he traveled by car, accompanied by his friend Matty DiLea, proprietor of a North Jersey motorcycle shop. They took their time with the trip, lingering in the vast empty American landscape Bruce loved. "And when we got to my house in Los Angeles," Bruce remembered, "I wanted to get right back in the car and keep on going. I couldn't even sit down."

It seemed imperative to keep moving, to try to outrace whatever demons *Nebraska* had dredged up. But as Bruce traveled through the middle American badlands, he felt cut off from real life, so lonesome he could cry.

Springsteen was certainly a person of black moods, but he had never encountered a cloud that rocking out couldn't disperse. Now he'd run into a darkness that floated in off the music itself. A complicated network of forces were at work—his own loner's life-style in conjunction with his remarkable antennae for touching the mood of his generation, coupled with the wrenching emotions of making the transition between *Nebraska*'s sombre music and the ecstatic rock and roll represented by "Born in the U.S.A." "I thought, 'This can't be happening to me. *I'm the guy with the guitar,*' " Bruce recalled, as if that should have rendered him immune to the consequences of dwelling upon cosmic questions.

As far as he could tell, music had always given him a kind of immunity from despair. The guitar had been an effective weapon in forging a better world for Springsteen, and he continually celebrated this. It was hard for him to imagine that it had also served as a protective shield. In truth, Bruce exercised such remarkable control over his work environment not only to enhance the quality of the music he created but also because he wasn't especially eager to be reminded of how many aspects of life—especially home and family, themes central to his work—he had closed off. As long as Bruce believed that he'd found a meaningful pattern to his existence, the trade-off was workable and beneficial. But the moment doubt crept in, the edifice crumbled and, with it, his remarkable assurance about how the world worked.

As a kid, he'd been smart enough to see that the order life had was generally imposed on it, and he'd been strong enough as an adult to work through his vision. But at the bottom of the questions he was asking—about what people believed and why and what happened to those who didn't believe at all—was a sense of the underlying fraud of all order, the undeniable fact that the universe contained as much randomness as structure.

The central tenet of everything Springsteen had ever done was hope. Bruce had always had his doubts that what worked for him would work for everyone else—he knew how extraordinary his own story was. But he believed in the validity of effort. Now, though, the rituals that made sense of his life had stopped working even for him. Things were spinning out of control.

"I guess for the *Born to Run* record I kind of established a certain type of optimism. After that I felt I had to test those things to see what they were worth. I guess in a funny way I began to do that test after *Born to Run* and through *Nebraska*. Those records were kind of my reaction, not necessarily to my success, but to what I was singing and writing about and what I was feeling— what I felt the role of the musician should be, what an artist should be. The one thing I did feel after *Born to Run* was a real sense of responsibility to what I was singing and to the audience. I didn't have an audience before that, not much of one. I was concerned with living up to that responsibility. So I just dove into it. I decided to look around. I decided to move into the darkness and look around and write about what I knew and what I saw and what I was feeling. I was trying to find something to hold onto that doesn't disappear out from under you. Eventually it led up to *Nebraska*, which was a record about the basic things that keep people functioning in society, in a community, or in their families or in their jobs. The idea is that they all break down. They fail. The record was a spiritual crisis—families fail, your job fails, and then you're gone, you're lost, you don't have any connection to anything. Everything just goes out the window.

"I was interested in finding out what happens then—what do my characters do, what do I do?" In the opening months of 1983, the question was not altogether rhetorical.

In a way, the problem wasn't even that grandiose. Maybe it was just the natural response of a guy in his thirties watching all his friends settle down into domestic routines and feeling himself odd man out. At some point, after all, life as a loner mutates into a life that's just lonely. At thirty-two, Bruce Springsteen seemed to have reached that point. He felt more than ever connected to the image of John Wayne at the end of *The Searchers,* turning away from the site of domesticity and returning to the bitter wilderness.

What he didn't do about it was follow his impulse to jump in the car and drive back East as soon as he'd hit L.A. Instead, he thought for hours about what had happened and began an even more basic questioning of his beliefs and motivations.

"It was very strange, because I felt that I'd done some of my best writing, and creatively I felt real vital. But maybe the thing that I was looking for from music, rock and roll . . . in some fashion it was either letting me down or it wasn't there, or I was demanding too much or . . . or . . . Something was wrong; something was dramatically wrong," he said a couple of years later.

"I think in the end, it was a real liberating experience. 'Cause

I said, Whoa, I've made a big mistake here. I always had the idea that rock and roll will *save* you. It will do this, it will do that. Well, it won't. Not in and of itself it won't. It's not gonna. It's not gonna. That's all there is to it. It can't do it for me.

"It doesn't make anything less of it. It's just reality. I had a new sense of realness. And for the first time, I had maybe a sense of limitation, and it was a healthy sense of limitation. I know I walked on with a lot of different expectations after that moment. It did not in any way affect my devotion to my job or my work or what I wanted to do with it. But it may have been something that was as simple as, Gee, there's more to life than this. It's just cliché, but that, in a funny sort of way, is it. Knowing that there are things I need that can only be provided by people. By contact. By . . . women. By . . . friends. You can't be the guy just blowin' the horn on the mountain."

But before Springsteen reached that realization, he needed more time alone, time in which he threw himself back in his work. But not the work of completing the rock and roll album that "Born in the U.S.A." had begun. He worked by himself in his Los Angeles home studio, creating a series of songs descended from *Nebraska*.

It wasn't that he necessarily wanted to linger in that gloomy world. It was more that he couldn't escape it until it was through with him. Meantime, the joy of rock and roll belonged to a separate universe, one in which Bruce Springsteen had temporarily lost interest.

"Whenever you start another record, you start from the point you stopped at," he said. "And when I stopped the *Nebraska* record, I just continued in my garage, in Los Angeles. I improved the recording facilities somewhat; I got an eight-track board. I drove across the country and I got to Los Angeles and I just set up shop in my garage and I just kept goin', you know. That's when I did 'Shut Out the Lights' and 'Bye Bye Johnny,' and I did a version of 'Follow That Dream' and I did a whole bunch of other things. So I just continued because I was excited about the fact that I felt the *Nebraska* stuff was my most personal stuff."

For Bruce, *Nebraska* delivered the goods. "I enjoyed the record a lot, it was easy to make, for the most part; it was a real private kinda record, it was my most personal record, I didn't have to go to the studio to do it. I felt that the distance between me and the audience had been stripped, basically, to its minimum. That the distance between the actual creation of the music and the audience had been stripped down about as close as you could conceivably get it. There was no production values in the way; there was no band; all of these things became non-issues."

But of course, if the gulf you're trying to cross isn't just artistic but also personal—and in a broader way, social—things don't work out so neatly. "The other side of the coin was that the record seems accessible to me but it obviously wasn't as accessible as *Born in the U.S.A.* or *The River,* for that matter," said Springsteen, looking back. "Maybe just because of its subject matter, that alone. Or maybe it came out at a time when you didn't hear a lot of anything like that on the radio.

"I had a kid come up to me after the record came out and tell me it was too mellow. It was a young girl and I understood what she was saying; what she meant was that it didn't have a lotta loud noises on it. You know, it didn't have drums and all that thing, and hey, she was sayin', that's what she likes, you know?" He laughed.

"I'm always somebody who has a lot of ambiguous feelings about, not necessarily what I want to do but the style that I want to do it in. And the *Nebraska* album offered me a lot of privacy. I made the record, it came out, I got in the car, I drove across the country, I might have been recognized once someplace or somethin'. And I was really happy with the record, I really felt that it was my best record to that date as far as an entire album goes. I felt that it was my best writing, I felt that I was getting better as a writer. I was learning things. I was certainly taking a hard look at everything around me."

So he stayed awhile on his mountain, blowing his horn, making soft noises.

■

Bruce briefly worked with Chuck Plotkin on rock and roll mixes, but his heart was elsewhere. The material everyone already thought of as the *Born in the U.S.A.* album just didn't

seem urgent anymore. What held Bruce's attention was the new
material he was writing, which sounded like a cross between
Nebraska, sketchy rockabilly, and some of Neil Young's more
melodic late-Seventies songs. As on *Nebraska*, Bruce built the
songs around guitar and voice, but he fleshed them out with a
Linn drum machine and comparatively extensive guitar and voice
overdubbing. The result was sketchy and moody. The songs
included "Shut Out the Light"; "Sugarland," a song about disenfranchised farmers (with very different music from the stage
rendition); and Bruce's rewritten version of Elvis Presley's "Follow That Dream."

As everyone soon realized, it was asking too much for Bruce
to psychologically roll from one record right into another. As Jon
Landau puts it, "Most artists who take their work very, very
seriously are saying something to themselves, and they need to
have time to just digest the experience. Having produced this
record, whether it took two minutes or two years, Bruce basically
seemed to be quite distracted right away. He was interested in
working but not in any heavy goal-oriented fashion." Wisely,
Landau and Plotkin pretty much left him alone.

After the holidays, Bruce called Landau and asked him to
come and listen to what he'd been up to. In early January,
Landau flew to California, listened, liked a lot of what he heard,
and realized they were back to square one: Bruce had composed
another group of songs that didn't blend naturally with the *Born
in the U.S.A.* rockers. Once again, he'd come up with material
that was for the most part ill-suited to the E Street Band.
Together, they sat down to assess the situation.

Landau and Springsteen's relationship has little in common
with such storied pairings as Brian Epstein and the Beatles or
Tom Parker and Elvis Presley. As Bruce puts it, "There's
basically nothing ordinary about our relationship. I don't know of
any other situation even remotely like it."

Jon Landau has never been a typical manager—or even
record producer—any more than Bruce has been a typical rock
star. In the beginning, Landau wasn't especially interested in a
career as a manager. Even after he proved successful in the job,
and other artists frequently came to him, Bruce remained his

only client. As Bruce said, "The whole thing really evolved out of a unique type of friendship. Jon just happens to be my manager because nobody was my manager and I need a manager; there was nobody better for the job than him, but our relationship is not based around him being my manager. It's just one of the things that he does for me, and he does it real well. Before he met me, he had never managed anybody but it kinda grew out of the need of that situation."

Jon Landau is Springsteen's manager, then, because he is the person best able to communicate with Bruce and because he can handle the even more difficult and important task of effectively communicating Bruce's ideas to others. Those are considerable qualifications, but there's an even more important one. Landau also has a gift for helping Bruce understand many of his own ideas.

Landau grew up in Brooklyn and the Boston suburbs. After attending Brandeis University, he played guitar and banjo in rock and bluegrass bands and worked in a Harvard Square record store, where he met Paul Williams, editor of *Crawdaddy!*, the first rock magazine, which his reviews of rock and soul albums immediately improved. In addition to attending shows and concerts everywhere from the folkies' Club 47 to the hippies' Boston Tea Party, Landau befriended many musicians, particularly such Boston stalwarts as Peter Wolf and Barry Tashian. In his early writing, however, he emphasized rhythm and blues taste above everything else, dwelling especially on the virtues of the records made by Stax/Volt in Memphis and by Motown. At a time when no other major critic paid anything close to sufficient attention to black rock, this made him stand out, particularly since his reviews were more likely to dwell on specifically musical—as opposed to social or lyrical—questions. Later, as editor of all *Rolling Stone* record reviews, a position of great authority in the pop world, Landau was also an early champion of the singer-songwriter movement. The catholicity of his taste was indicated by the first artists he produced. There was an unreleased session with Wolf's blues-based J. Geils Band, the proto-punk of the MC5, and the laid-back singer-songwriter stylizations of Livingston Taylor. Landau also served as *Rolling Stone*'s film critic for a time.

Landau was much more sympathetic than his critical peers about popular music as a business proposition. Coupled with his *Rolling Stone* tenure and his production experience, this gave him considerable clout within the rock industry. His friendship gave Springsteen's career its biggest boost since Bruce's discovery by John Hammond.

The intensity of their friendship stemmed from the very first time Landau saw Springsteen perform, in April 1974 in a tiny bar in Cambridge, Massachusetts. (Another show, about a month later, inspired the famous "rock and roll future" column.) Their friendship rapidly blossomed through a series of hours-long phone calls between Boston and New Jersey, in which Jon and Bruce talked about everything from the nature of the art to the details of record production to the mysteries of Gene Pitney's hit singles. Its first fruit was the production of *Born to Run*.

But all of that is only the relatively public aspect of their story. In the end, there were deeper and less tangible bonds. When he met Bruce Springsteen, Landau was thinking about leaving *Rolling Stone* to become a full-time record producer. He certainly hadn't planned to limit his work to one artist; that was just how the situation developed. And he was willing to let it, because he had absolute faith in Bruce Springsteen's capacities, not just as a rock star but as an artist. Landau gradually became manager because there seemed no one else—certainly no established manager—who met all of Bruce's needs and desires, the greatest of which was to have someone he could trust and confide in, someone with whom he could play a role more vulnerable than the loner.

Even though Jon was ordinarily imperious, he was continually patient with Bruce. He offered his guidance without insisting on a result or even a direction, even if he'd already made up his mind about what he hoped would happen. "A lot of times he won't say anything," Bruce said. "He lets the thing raise itself, rather than letting his opinion or his taste or his own prejudices get in the way. And that creates a tremendous amount of trust in his opinion."

Landau was able to operate this way because he and Springsteen shared a taste for restraint, an aversion to making public relations gestures for their own sake and the desire to present

Springsteen's music with as much dignity as they felt the best rock and roll deserved. The same thing applied in private discussions. Consequently, when either was moved to make a stand about something, he spoke with cumulative force.

"The essential part of me and Jon's interaction is that either of us can argue intensely about this issue or that issue, but in the end the music does the talking," Bruce said. "And we argue until what's right reveals itself, whatever that may be and wherever it may come from. We don't argue until he wins or I win.

"We both have a dedication to the idea, and we're just a couple of guys trying to get to it. That's the essence of our process. I don't have a dedication to my viewpoint on any particular issue, and I don't believe that he does, even though he has his arguing position that he feels is right and I have my arguing position. And we'll go at it until what *is* right or what feels right reveals itself. And I don't know of any time that we haven't agreed on what that was. No one has ever said, 'Well, I think you're wrong, but okay.' That has never happened. It's always come to like, 'Well, all right. Yes,' or 'That seems like the right thing to do.' And I think that's because our dedication is to the idea.

"That's a real important thing about the way we work. And it keeps all the personal baloney that might normally come up in control. One of the things that keeps that under control is the trust we have in each other. From day one, when we first started to work together, I always felt Jon understood what I wanted to do and he was there to help me do that thing. It was as simple as that. He has always made me feel like he is there to help me do this thing that I wanted to do. He's just always made me feel like that. Consequently, when we get into various different arguments over this song or that song or even if we get frustrated with each other, eventually we work our way through to the answer. And I think that's a real different thing and a real important thing."

Imperious as he, too, may have been, when the chips were down, Springsteen had a musician's necessary knack for collaboration. (Songs may be composed in solitude, but they're played— and recorded—by groups.) He was able to grapple with and use the ideas of a diverse group of people, which is the only way he could ever have made coherent albums working with a trio of producers who had quite a bit less in common than Holland–Dozier–Holland.

A manager's job is to rationalize art, translating abstractions into marketplace terms. A producer's task is similar. Often as not, Springsteen and Landau worked together in just that perspective: artist and translator. But when it came to specific pieces of music, they again violated the cliché. Often it was Jon who worked on instinct, fighting against Bruce's innate conservatism and caution, willing to let a piece that just rocked stand on its own. Bruce tended to be wary of what came too naturally. Landau struck everyone who met him as an extraordinarily controlled and rational person, but he loved wild music, from "Tutti Frutti" to "Kick Out the Jams." It was this one streak of recklessness that often proved most useful in making records and furthering Springsteen's career.

While making *Born in the U.S.A.*, this conflict centered around one song, "Cover Me." Landau says he knew the song belonged in the next (rock) album the moment he heard what was supposed to be nothing more than a tossed-off demo. Bruce was indifferent to the track from the start, often outright hostile to it. It struck him as too light, too pop, too obvious. These were among its virtues, Landau insisted, and anyway, none of that belied the intensity with which Bruce whipped home the crucial line: "Wrap your arms around and cover me!" Although the song was closer to pop than rock—and in its rhythms closer to postdisco dance music than either—it had a stinging guitar solo. Landau loved its modern sheen; Bruce knew its value—he'd created it, after all—but he wasn't sure what it said about him. The more anachronistic shape of his soul and rockabilly-based tunes was secure and comforting. In all their discussions about the album, Landau kept dredging up "Cover Me" and Bruce kept kicking it back under the rug, radical manager against conservative artist.

When they got together in Los Angeles that January, Bruce wasn't really in a mood to take any decisive actions and Landau was shrewd and sensitive enough not to push too hard. "At the time I felt that maybe this [solo recording] is where the whole thing is going in some fashion," Bruce said. "Maybe the idea is gonna be to just keep the thing real stripped down right now, almost like a *John Wesley Harding* type of thing."

Bruce did have one song that he wanted to try cutting with the band, and in February he flew back to New York briefly and in a short session recorded "My Hometown" at the Hit Factory, the studio at which the rest of the album would be made. "My Hometown" had something in common with the squalid, somber worlds of the *Nebraska* characters, but it was almost quiescent in its portrait of an American worker who witnesses the flower and the rot of post–World War II prosperity. The man teaching the rituals of a dead-end town to his son in this song lacked the rage of Johnny 99, and while that gave him the strength to think about pushing on, it also created a feeling of acceptance akin to the world of "Mansion on the Hill," with its horror-show class rituals. Taken on its own, "My Hometown" is a highly ambiguous statement, fraught with fear and reconciliation and detailing defeat. But it isn't nearly as desperate as "Used Cars," its opposite number from *Nebraska*, even though the circumstances are more mean and frustrated. "Foreman says those jobs are goin', boys, and they ain't coming back/To your hometown" are lines that lurk and linger in the heartland of America in the Eighties.

Successful as that session was, Bruce still headed straight back to his Hollywood solitude, once more leaving manager, band, and producers up in the air about his plans.

"I was living in L.A. and Jon was living in New York and I'm not a big person on the telephone so our communication wasn't as steady as it might be during the course of making a record," Bruce remembered. "Really, at the time we weren't consciously making a record. The *Nebraska* record had just come out and we had the bunch of cuts from the studio *Nebraska* sessions. It was just sittin' there, waiting to be mixed, because nothing else ever really happened on it again. We did that in two weeks, the same two weeks we spent tryin' to record some new *Nebraska* stuff."

In retrospect, it seemed to everybody that the problem was isolation, lack of contact and interaction. Bruce put it down to "my new method, which was initially begun for purely economic purposes. What do I spend all the money in the studio on?

Writing the songs. I go in and record a hundred songs; some of 'em I finish, some of 'em I don't. It's a waste of time, it's a waste of everybody's time and money. Let's not do that anymore. I'll do that at the house.

"Now that I've begun to do that at the house, there's also something else happening. Nobody's seeing anybody else. The band's not seeing me, I'm not seeing the band, I'm not seeing Jon, Jon's not seeing the band or me. And it's been quite a while."

A few weeks after Landau went West, CBS Records president Walter Yetnikoff made a trip to Los Angeles and visited Bruce. Springsteen and the colorful record chief got along well and they met for dinner and had a great time. But Bruce didn't play anything for Yetnikoff, or even talk about his music.

When Yetnikoff returned to New York, he phoned Landau and expressed his concern. ("He never mentioned it to me," said Bruce, "but I do believe that he was concerned about me making another record in my garage or in my bedroom or wherever I was makin' it, you know.") Yetnikoff pointed out that although Springsteen was supposed to be working on his next album, that wasn't really possible, since his chief record producer and his band were a continent away.

Yetnikoff wasn't trying to pressure Springsteen, exactly. He didn't have much leverage, for one thing, since Bruce didn't need immediate transfusions of CBS cash. Anyway, it was inconceivable for him to make music under duress. What the record company president provided was an outside viewpoint that forced Landau and then Springsteen to face what was actually going on.

Jon phoned Bruce and they had a long talk about what they were trying to do. They agreed that the goal was still to make another album and that whatever else Bruce may have been accomplishing in California, that wasn't happening. "We realized that the studio is important because one of the things that happens is that everybody sees each other," Bruce said. "We get together and the band plays and sometimes we get something and sometimes we don't, but we do have a feeling that everybody's chipping in and working on a project. There's a little sense of something going on.

"So we had gotten into a very isolated fashion of working. Which can appeal to me because I can be a very isolated person. So we had a discussion on the phone, I think, and it wasn't just through my contact with Jon, it might have been through my contact with some of the other band members. Where I kinda sensed them feeling, 'Gee, what's going on?'

"In our conversation, I believe that Jon did bring up that Walter had said how are we making a record if we're not seeing each other. And that was a good point, because a lotta things that happen between me and Jon come in the course of just a day when nothing's happening. You talk about something and it'll just go in and sit there and then a few months later I'll recognize some aspect of it in something I've written, that this had something to do with our discussion.

"We talked about this; we decided, that's right. Summer was coming up, I'd been in California quite awhile. It seemed like it's time to get back, get in the studio, do it the old way. Get the band in, spend a little time in there. And that's what we did."

In early May, Bruce came home—by plane—and went back in the studio with the band.

■

Simply coming back home didn't end Bruce's turmoil. For one thing, his relationship with the band was still ambiguous. That was the chief reason Landau felt immediately making another *Nebraska*-style album could create serious problems. "To me, Bruce is the most unusual combination of talents that I know of, in terms of lyric-writing ability, music-writing ability, guitar-playing ability, arranging ability, band-leading ability, singing, everything," Landau said. "And when an artist has range, the most exciting thing is when you are doing all of the things that you know how to do, at the same time, at the peak of your ability. As I said to Bruce at the time, the problem with the *Nebraska* thing as a permanent approach or a main approach is that it is tremendous at what it is, but you have so many capabilities that are not utilized that it seems like it's less than you can be."

By making successive albums without the E Street Band, Bruce would seem to be signaling that he was no longer going to work with them. Furthermore, since he'd probably want to tour after the release of the next album, he would have the extremely difficult task of presenting twenty new songs into which the group didn't fit. Another round of enforced idleness might break up the group—players as skilled as Roy Bittan weren't going to sit on their hands forever. In any event, Bruce would be sending a very confusing signal to everyone concerned.

Landau wasn't absolutely opposed to making such changes, but he worried that Bruce hadn't thought everything through. "I just wanted to make sure that, if we were gonna go in this direction, all of these things were thought about. If Bruce had considered them all and said, 'Nope, this is really right; my thing with the band has changed; maybe I'm not gonna use them so much; maybe I'll do a tour without the band. . . . ' If he'd been prepared to make all those decisions, then fine. But I wanted to make sure that he understood that those were the decisions he was possibly making."

Bruce didn't want the group to break up, but he wasn't ready to get back into full-tilt rock and roll, either. As a method of music-making, *Nebraska* struck him right then as more than satisfactory. "There's nothing much more intimate than working with yourself," he said. "You're just working with your own thoughts and your own ideas. It is *not* something that you would want to do all the time, but at the time I wasn't exactly sure of that."

Bruce now needed to find music that reflected the ways in which he'd changed, and rock and roll still pulled him toward the same old mysteries, the same old ghosts. For the first time in his life, he felt wary of being in a band and rocking out.

"I think, and this goes to the general philosophy of the whole thing, the thing I liked about *Nebraska* was that it was kind of a private record. And in a way, I was able to maintain more privacy making that type of record. Basically, I'm a private person. So it appealed to me on a lot of different levels. And in a funny way, I'm somebody who has to be drawn out. That is one of the essential things Jon does for me, even in the face of my resistance.

"So I think that there was a point where I said, 'Gee, I could make a record like this, these types of records, and it's satisfying to me.' I was leading the type of life I was leading; it was totally suitable, it filled all my needs in a variety of different ways. I suppose I toyed with that idea because of the protection that it provides."

Furthermore, no matter what Bruce wanted, his relationship with the band *had* changed. The sessions called for in the spring and summer of 1983 were the first since 1975 without Steve Van Zandt on rhythm guitar. Even though Steve's presence was more often felt than heard, his catalytic personality had been an important component of Springsteen's relationship with the E Street Band, especially since Bruce often communicated with Steve even when he was basically noncommunicative towards everyone else. But that summer Steve was touring Europe in support of his first solo record and returning to New York to record his second album, *Voice of America,* in another part of the Hit Factory.

Steve Van Zandt had evolved his way in and out of Bruce's bands before, and this time he left without much discussion. "I felt that at that point I had something really significantly different to say," Van Zandt said. "Different enough that it would take full-time, it would take leaving. And also, I felt that I had contributed everything I could possibly contribute: We'd recorded live, with no overdubs whatsoever, which is something that I had always worked for right from the beginning. . . . It was just a matter of getting the craftsmanship to the point where you can do that.

"Bruce and I talked off and on during this period. And it was just a real obvious point where I was anxious to get on with this new thing, because it was new, you know. I'd dedicated seven years of my life to making that thing happen, and we had accomplished everything that I hoped we could accomplish. It had never occurred to me until then to leave." However, Steve didn't talk much with the rest of the band about his plans—"not until it was comfortable," which was after they'd already done a few weeks work without him. And in keeping with the Springsteen organization's penchant for secrecy, his decision wasn't communicated to the outside world until many months later, on the eve of the release of *Voice of America* and Bruce's own record.

One result was rumors that Springsteen and Van Zandt were having a feud. One story even claimed that Steve's tracks had been erased from Bruce's masters, something that was impossible, given the way the music had been recorded. As Van Zandt said, "I did the mandolin solo on 'Glory Days' into my vocal mike. How you gonna wipe *that?*"

Van Zandt interpreted the rumors as a sign of public confusion. "I guess people had a tough time figuring out how I could leave at that point, not knowing how I felt, not knowing my own potential. 'Why would he leave?' Of course, it's because I had something to say that no one specifically had ever said before, and how could they relate to that if they've never heard it."

But if people were confused, it was also because the split—however amicable—disrupted the mythology of the E Street Band. Steve Van Zandt wasn't only Bruce's oldest friend in real life; onstage the role he played was the Sidekick. In many of Bruce's yarns, rock and roll functioned on the buddy system, and through them he and Steve and Clarence had achieved a kind of group identity. In real life, of course, being the sidekick of the King of Rock and Roll might mean smothering your own talents or, at best, never getting a chance to discover what they were. As Chuck Plotkin put it in describing his own situation, "Anybody who works with Bruce can become overidentified with him. Your identity becomes subsumed in the identity of someone of Bruce's magnitude. It's difficult to get on with the next project, because the thing that people are interested in is how it was to work with Bruce."

Steve felt it necessary not just to leave Bruce's band and his production team but even to change his name from Miami Steve to Little Steven and eventually (with his second album) to abandon the soul music on which his earlier image was based. It was anything but the easy way out, but that was how he felt it had to be.

The absence of Steve Van Zandt didn't necessarily change Springsteen's rock and roll sound. The tracks without Steve's guitar include "No Surrender," "Bobby Jean," "My Hometown," and "Dancing in the Dark," which retain the same diversity of sound and feeling as the material Bruce recorded while Van

Zandt was in the group. But Steve's absence still added to Bruce's uncertainty, and having just had a successful experience cutting solo, he was still inclined to think in terms of recording without the band. As Plotkin said, "It looked for a long time like we could end up with *Nebraska II*."

With Bruce uncertain of his own direction, the music they made that summer lacked the confidence necessary for great rock and roll. They made some decent tracks in those long, hot weeks—"Stand on It" and a new version of "Pink Cadillac" (the one they ultimately released) among others—but nothing was up to the level of the material they'd recorded the previous May. Plotkin, the closest thing to a newcomer in the byzantine Springsteen recording process, felt almost estranged. He just couldn't hear the value in the songs they were cutting; he found them forced, the one thing good rock and roll can never be. Communication broke down.

Plotkin remembered the summer with a shudder. "Bruce would ask me what I thought about a guitar solo, and I'd say, 'I don't know. I don't know what the song's about. I don't know whether the guitar solo's the right guitar solo, because I'm not getting any hit off the song.' He'd say, 'Well, all right then, I'll just do this guitar solo.' After two or three of those responses, he just stopped asking me what I thought. I went through a period for about two months where we hardly talked. I was there every day and hardly ever expressed an opinion because he stopped asking me, and I didn't have any opinion about anything except the songs.

"It sounded like Bruce was trying to recover from *Nebraska*. He was trying to find some new footing, and he was writing stuff that was not really rocking, and it was clearly meant to rock. That was the main thing: He was ready to rock again; he wanted to and he knew that was what he was gonna have to do or he couldn't finish, and he made a valiant effort to get a series of things to rock that were written from a place inside of himself that was just not rocking."

Landau, who had gone through less drastic versions of the same process on three other albums, was more sanguine. "Chuck's job is such that he has always gotta be grappling with the music as it is right at the moment. That's the key to what he's doing," he said. "At those particular sessions, I was able to be less concerned about any particular song we were cutting (until we hit 'Bobby Jean') than I was about getting a process going, getting us back into an integrated working situation—the producers, the band, making this album together. In general, if I heard something that I didn't like or was not my favorite type of thing, I wasn't alarmed by it.

"Besides, the way we jump around is disorienting to anybody. Chuck was still getting used to songs that go into the black hole and you never hear from them again."

As the summer wound down, it became obvious that everyone needed a chance to get out and breathe, away from their nocturnal and pent-up studio existence. Bruce had spent the previous summer getting out almost every weekend to play with friends famous and obscure, joining bands like Beaver Brown and Cats at Jersey shore bars like the Stone Pony or sitting in with journeymen rockers like Nils Lofgren who were playing nearby clubs. He hardly took a day off all summer. Like everyone else, he'd clearly earned the chance to get some sun and to think about what they'd accomplished.

But workaholics don't make it so easy on themselves. As August approached, Springsteen proposed not that they needed a vacation but that they were finished with recording and ready to start final mixes. In retrospect, even Bruce doesn't quite understand his thinking. "When we started to mix the record, I don't really know what we thought we were doing. We must have thought we had an album."

The task of proving the point first fell to Chuck Plotkin, who began by asking Bruce to explain exactly which songs were on the record as he imagined it. "I said, 'Well, look, Bruce, you tell me what it is that we're gonna mix, what cards are on the table. I'll wade into the stuff and I'll take the best rough mixes that we have and let's string 'em together. I'd like to hear the record before we mix it.' " So Springsteen gave Plotkin a list of songs with a basic idea of their sequence.

Plotkin and Toby Scott went back into the Hit Factory by themselves and over five days assembled Bruce's version of the new album. What Plotkin heard confirmed his worst suspicions: They were a long way from finished. "And I was scared to death because our communication had just dwindled away to nothing," Plotkin recalled with a shudder. "That was one of the low points of my involvement with Bruce, because I was just scared to death. I was in a state. I strung the stuff together, and I said, 'I'm gonna master these rough mixes. Because I've got to figure out some way to get him to listen to this as if this is the record.'

"I'm talking to Jon every day about this. 'Jon, how can I tell him this?' 'You just have to tell him.' I said, 'My only hope is to get him to listen. I'm not gonna tell him anything. I'm gonna bring the disc down there, and I'm gonna say, "Bruce, look, let's just put this baby on and let's see how we're doin'." ' Real nice and easy. And hope that he can hear it. He'll see the disc—he's taken a week off, he'll know. 'Cause I just can't say what I have to say. I know he won't take it from me right now.' 'Well, just go down and do your best.'

"So we set up a meeting in New Jersey and I walked in with the reference discs. I said, 'Let's put this baby on and hear it.' Bruce said, 'What do you mean?' I said, 'Well, I've got this all put together here. Let's just listen to it. We don't need to talk about it.' He says, 'I don't want to listen to it.' He says, 'Charley, you just spent five nights all by yourself in the studio, listening to this stuff. Tell me where we stand.' And I wanna go, 'But Bruce, you haven't listened to a word I've said in the last eight weeks. We haven't talked. What difference does it make what I think?' I didn't say this, but that's what I was feeling. I said, 'Geez, I really think we oughta just listen to this stuff, you know. We'll just sit here together and we'll be able to hear what it is. You don't really want me to tell ya what I think.' He said, 'What the hell do ya think I hired ya for?'

"And I thought [*groaning*], 'He's not gonna listen to the thing. I'm gonna have to tell him.' So I said, 'Well, I can hear the album. I can hear the album we're making. This isn't it.' [*He laughs.*] Because I couldn't be negative. 'This isn't it but I can hear it; I know what this record is about. And I know what of what we have is working, and I know what isn't working and I know what's missing. And we're real close. I can make one great side out of your song list, but I can't make two great sides out of it. I can make a great opening side or a great closing side. But I have a feeling that what we have is sort of like marking posts.' I said, 'If you listen to "Born in the U.S.A." into "My Hometown," that's the whole thing. That's the record.'"

Against his better judgment, Plotkin had done exactly the right thing. It came back down to his vision of what it meant to produce a record with Springsteen. "It's simply caring enough about Bruce and his records to hang in until the record is right. That is, to hang in with him when his impulse is that it can be better and to force him to hang in with you when your impulse is that it can be better. It's the highest uncommon denominator. It's being able to hold your own in fairly strong company where the issue is, Is this thing as good as it needs to be yet? That's it. That's the job. Just somehow or another mustering the physical and emotional strength to stay at war until the thing is won. That's all. That's just . . . that's *it*."

"And he bought it—he bought the whole cloth."

What Plotkin was selling (with Landau's essential concurrence) was an alternative vision of where they were at. As the producers saw it, the problem with the album was twofold. In the first place, there weren't quite enough songs that fit together in order to make a great album. In the second, a great deal of the best material they'd recorded was *not* on these reference discs. Springsteen's interest in "Downbound Train" had recently revived; "My Hometown" was part of the story from the time it was recorded, and Bruce had always regarded "Born in the U.S.A." and "Glory Days" as the core of the rock and roll LP. But "Cover Me," "I'm on Fire," "Working on the Highway," "Pink Cadillac," "I'm Goin' Down," and "Darlington County," all of them recorded more than a year before, had been abandoned. Those songs were among the best Bruce had ever recorded because they felt almost effortless—not casual or throwaway but sung as if Bruce were for once performing without burdens. In the months since, Bruce had felt just the opposite, and the new songs, no matter how hard the rhythm section kicked, showed the strain. He needed some more songs and everyone simply had to wait until he'd written the right ones.

Bruce's response to their conversation, Plotkin recalled, was almost immediate. "Two nights later, we went into the studio and he said, 'I have a song I want to cut.' We cut 'Bobby Jean' and it was like the fever had broken."

The song was a breakthrough for Bruce in several ways. Its accents were more modern than his usual rockabilly and soul-fixated rhythms. Tallent's bass chopped against Weinberg's drums, while Bruce's rhythm guitar and Bittan's perfectly placed piano notes roiled up out of a virtual dance groove. The song surged but also almost floated. This simple, spacious music was the essence of rock and roll: effortless, joyous, deeply grieved. It was the sound they'd spent the summer searching for.

Bruce wrote the lyric as a letter to a departed friend, and he sang it with the same mixture of mourning, wistfulness, affection, and anger. His voice was open, "young," showing no strain even as it hit a couple of awkward lines (e.g., "talking about the pain that from the world we hid"). The song is a one-way dialogue and, obviously, many of the details must have come from the circumstances of Steve Van Zandt's departure: "You hung with me when all the others turned away, turned up their nose/We liked the same music, we liked the same bands, we liked the same clothes." But it was more than just Miami Steve that Springsteen's singing sent away with this odd combination of reluctance and eagerness. In the end, as he sings lines that mingle love, grief, and rancor, Bruce might be singing to the old self burned up in the crucible and aftermath of *Nebraska*:

> Maybe you'll be out there on that road somewhere, in some
> bus or train traveling along
> In some motel room there'll be a radio playing and you'll
> hear me sing this song
> Well, if you do, you'll know I'm thinking of you and all the
> miles in between and I'm just calling one more time
> Not to change your mind but just to say I miss you, baby,
> good luck, goodbye Bobby Jean

But just making "Bobby Jean" didn't settle the question. Shortly afterward, Jon Landau drove down to Bruce's house, and that night they did play the acetate of the prospective LP.

"It just wasn't a record; it just didn't sound like one," Bruce said. "I've got a whole bunch of strange little songs that really, they're interesting but they don't seem to be mixing. It wasn't that all the stuff wasn't good on it. We had 'Shut Out the Lights' on it and 'Follow That Dream.' Individually the things were good but they just didn't add up—it didn't sound right, it didn't come together. And the difference in sound quality from the garage thing to the studio stuff was too haphazard. It left you flat."

The process had again become mystified and confusing. As Bruce admitted, "Of course, that's the inevitable question: We have a lot of material, why don't we have a record? It's mysterious—like why? And you know time is beginning to tick on and we had seen this before and we didn't want the same type of situation that we had on *The River* and *Darkness*."

The problem was that Bruce had cast aside most of the best material, which remained the songs from the band sessions done during the *Nebraska* period. As he said, when they failed to get mixes of them in California, "then I really dumped on them."

"All the stuff that got thrown out is pretty good," Landau said.

"Aw, no, that's no good," said Springsteen.

"No, that's good stuff," said Landau and plunged a bit further: It had been thrown out while Bruce was in California; Jon hadn't really had a fair chance to work on it.

"Jon is good like this—he's patient, for one thing," Bruce said, laughing as he described it. "And he waits and he waits, and when he sees I'm down, then he makes his move. We reach a point of some confusion, then it's like, 'Hey, what about this stuff?'

"This was a central discussion that we got into one night. A lot of these songs had been thrown out without us really discussing the merits of them or whether they should be. And I had all my reasons why I didn't like it. I always have a million reasons. And they're arguable, you know; you can always make an argument.

"So that was when we sat down and we started discussing what type of record we were trying to make. The answer we came out with in the end was, we were making a rock and roll record. Before that we hadn't been trying to make exactly that particular type of record. A rock and roll band record. You know, with fast songs on it. Drums. Not too mellow. Something with loud noises on it.

"And this was a funny thing, because I had a lot of ambivalence about doing it. It's always a trade-off that you make. I guess part of it was I just wasn't sure that was where I wanted to go."

When it came to the actual composition of the *Born in the U.S.A.* album, Jon Landau had very specific ideas about where things ought to go. After their meeting in Rumson, Jon said, "I decided for myself that it was time to think about what my ideal album was, out of everything we'd so far recorded. It was something I'd never done before, but it seemed that it would be useful to have somebody's version of the record.

"So I made up a rough album sequence and sent it to Bruce with a letter, which was my own rave review of that sequence, giving all the ideas and arguments I could think of. In my own mind there was an element of provocation, because it was so unusual."

The letter ran five single-spaced pages of closely packed argument. Landau had arranged an eleven-song sequence. Side One consisted of "Born in the U.S.A.," "I'm Goin' Down," "Cover Me," "My Hometown," and "Bobby Jean." Flip it over and you got a still-unreleased ballad called "My Love," the revised "Follow That Dream," "Glory Days," Bruce's version of "Protection," the second song he'd written for Donna Summer, "Janey, Don't You Lose Heart," and "I'm on Fire." The idea, he wrote, was to make the album "a collage having to do with past, present, and future," with an eye toward expressing Bruce's current state of mind and opening doors for the future. "Born in the U.S.A.," Landau commented, "starts the album right in the middle—a man at the crossroads, by himself, disconnected from his past but not yet connected to any imaginable future beyond mere survival; a man at the beginning of a search."

Landau's letter also emphasized musical balance. He was encouraging Springsteen to step forward musically by using the dance rhythms and minor keys of "Protection" and "Cover Me." But most of all, he was concerned that the group of songs picked should reflect *adult* emotions.

Writing the letter was an eccentric approach to record production, but because Jon's positions were well-stated and cogent,
it helped break the bottleneck. "I think we all felt that we didn't
have anything to lose at that point," Landau said. "I think one of
the things that tape did was reintroduce the discussion of "I'm on
Fire," "I'm Goin' Down," and "Cover Me," songs in which Bruce
had seemed to lose interest."

Again, Landau had stepped in at a key moment to help
formulate a decision that felt like a step in the right direction. So
they went off on their break, scattering from California to the
Jersey shore, and returned refreshed for the next round in a battle
that still had a long way to go.

◼

"When we went back to work in September, there was a
looseness—there was an intensity but there was also a looseness," said Landau. "It opened up and everybody was shooting
their mouth off. Everybody, including Bruce, sensed, 'Hey, we
gotta figure a way to pull this all together and get it off our backs.'
And we gradually just sifted through the material in the fall.

"We started gravitating very clearly back to a lot of the earlier
stuff. Bruce was totally open-minded to it at this point: It's all on
the table, anything's possible now, let's work until we're done.
He took a lot of those songs and toyed with them and sort of
tweaked them and, I think, brought them more up to date with his
sensibility. He was more willing to look at some of that older
material and say, 'Gee, maybe it's not the song or the track;
maybe there's just something in the arrangement where if I can
move it from here to here, it's gonna sit a little more comfortably
for me.' And he wrote a couple of songs and he went and he did
those."

In November Bruce took the band into the studio without
Landau and Plotkin to record two songs, "No Surrender" and
"Brothers Under the Bridges." Both songs are basically "Bobby
Jean" turned inside out. Rather than dwelling on an old friendship at the moment of disintegration, Bruce's new songs surveyed
the entire relationship and the values that can grow out of intense
adolescent friendships and high school promises rashly made.

Both songs obviously reflect the departure of Steve Van Zandt from the E Street Band, but "No Surrender" is by far the more effective.

"No Surrender" recapitulates not only an adolescent friendship but a whole style of recording. Working as his own producer, Bruce came up with his first "wall of sound" arrangement since *Born to Run*. "No Surrender" emerges as (barely) updated Sixties trash rock, far from the crisp electronics of the other *Born in the U.S.A.* tracks: Thunderous drums and surging washes of guitar support a vocal chorus straight off a 1965 Searchers' album.

The song's declaration of faith in the transformational power of rock and roll struck some as naïve, which was fair enough. The song was written as a character study but was clearly an intimate portrait of Springsteen's own values (an idea reinforced by his repeated dedications of the song to the absent Van Zandt during the 1984–85 tour). It's really a last gasping breath of innocence from a rocker who has embraced adulthood. But juxtaposed with the newer sounds and curdled optimism of "Bobby Jean," Springsteen's other recent song, "No Surrender" became a restless farewell, mingling a sure knowledge of the inadequacy of idealism with a stubborn refusal to renege on ideals.

In that way the song resembles not "Bobby Jean" but "Born in the U.S.A." "Born in the U.S.A." is the anthem of a man who has surrendered to adulthood; "No Surrender" outlines the convictions that sustained him long enough to make that decision. Once that connection is made, it seems not only sensible but inevitable that these characters "learned more from a three-minute record than we ever learned in school." And it's the very vividness of his teenage recollection that makes Springsteen believable in the final verse, where he sums up his rock and roll dream:

> Now on the street tonight the light grows dim, the walls of
>   my room are closing in
> There's a war outside still raging
> You say it ain't ours anymore to win
> I want to sleep beneath peaceful skies in my lover's bed
> With a wide open country in my eyes and those romantic
>   dreams in my head

Brash as it is, "No Surrender" is perfectly confident as it lays out a purely "childish" set of values and acknowledges their continuing currency in adulthood. This is exactly the sensibility for which *Born to Run* was criticized, which means that "Bobby Jean" meets head-on the issues that had set Bruce to asking such hard questions of himself in the first place. Like the guy in "Born in the U.S.A.," he found himself running down the same road he'd always been on, albeit with a new look on his face.

Confident as he may have been, Springsteen was still unsure exactly which songs belonged on the record and what their sequence should be. The way that he makes records, those two steps—selection and sequencing—are the essence of the job. As Roy Bittan once said, "Bruce will throw a hit record off an album, as he did when we recorded 'Fire' and everybody agreed 'Fire' was one of the best songs he wrote for that album. But he would not put it on because it's not what he wanted to say with *Darkness*. Ninety-nine percent of the other artists in the business wouldn't *think* of doing something like that. But to Bruce, what he says is more important than the commercial benefits he could gain from the commercial material. That's the story. That's how he does it. And that's why his albums stand up so well. That's why ten years from now people will be able to play those albums and those albums will say something."

But Springsteen got away with such tactics only because his gifts were so broad. "The guy's a great writer, he's a great singer, he's a great player, he's got great arrangement ideas," said Plotkin. "It's not like producing somebody else's records, where all of those things occupy most of your time and energy and you just cut whatever damn songs the artist can come up with. Most people write eight or nine acceptable songs and that's your album. But with Bruce, there is *no song* that isn't dispensable, in and of itself. And what you're always looking for is, What are we up to with this? What is he saying? What's the guy on about this year? What connects these things?

"With 'Born in the U.S.A.,' the night he cut it, we knew we had just started the album. On *Born in the U.S.A.*, he actually found what he was going to be going on about before he even recognized it as such."

"When people wonder about what goes on when you make a record for two years, this is what goes on," said Landau. "In other words, the main thing that does *not* go on is taking one song and overdubbing on it for three months to get it. Earlier in Bruce's career, we sometimes did that. But the process now is the creation of this huge mass of material and then the incredible complexity involved in sifting through it and ordering it and finally creating an album. Because that is what we are doing—we are making an album.

"In other words, are there songs that are not on the album which if, compared in pure isolation—song X to song Y—might it be possible that song Y, which is not on the record, might be in some sense a better song than song X, which is on the record? Yes! But that is not the discussion. The discussion is what plays best as an album—where's the unity, where's the balance of forces? That song that's not on there might have been one ballad too many or it might have been one rock song too many. And if we had that instead of the song we might take it off for, it might have tipped the overall emotional weight of the side away from where we really want it to be."

So crucial was this process of selection and organization that even once recording was essentially completed there was a fair amount of disagreement about what the record consisted of. Landau and Plotkin both felt that the best possible album would build around the core material recorded in May 1982. Bruce hoped to use more of the 1983 stuff. The difference was extremely significant, not because it meant much commercially—as Jimmy Iovine once remarked to Landau, in order to sell all the album had to be was "Born in the U.S.A." and nine other songs—but because the material created with "Born in the U.S.A." had a cohesion of music and ideas that simply didn't exist among the songs from the other sessions. Certainly, nothing else fit so well with "Born in the U.S.A." and "Glory Days," which for Bruce were always the cornerstones.

Failing to persuade his coproducers, Bruce adopted an oblique stratagem. For the first time ever, he solicited a wide variety of opinions about song selection. The band was polled on its choices, which was the first time *that* had ever happened, but even more outlandish was Bruce's decision to solicit the opinions of assorted crew members and friends. Springsteen's penchant for secrecy made each of his projects something of a mystery even to insiders. Because some exciting songs didn't belong on any given album—though, as "Darlington County" proved, they might linger long enough to find their place—it was risky to have anyone hear them out of context. Now Bruce had not only decided to play about twenty assorted songs for people outside the production process, he was also inviting his friends to list their choices, in sequence if possible.

One by one, he brought folks to his little house on the Navesink River. Seating them at a small table with the notebook in which he kept his lyrics spread out before them, he'd plug them—and sometimes himself—into a Sony Walkman Professional and play selections from half a dozen cassettes containing rough mixes. Then he might leave them alone with the songs for a time while he ran errands or simply got out and ran his daily six miles. When Bruce returned, a short discussion ensued and then the moment of truth, listing the picks. Turning to the back of the notebook, he would inscribe each person's selections.

Bruce took the process very seriously, although exactly what he got out of it is anybody's guess. Maybe it was just another part of shedding his isolation. However intently he listened as each of his friends and associates told him what should be on the record, surely no one had the impression that he was going to put out what *they* wanted. On the other hand, it was his willingness to hear everyone out that was the point. As Chuck Plotkin said, "Just because you're bright and independent and self-possessed and self-contained and ambitious, that doesn't necessitate your locking everyone else out of your processes." That was something Bruce had always believed, but it was only now that he seemed open enough to really try to make it work. Though the final choices had to be his, he paid attention and that by itself was rare for any artist. And who knows, maybe the popularity of "Cover Me" in the listening sessions helped put it on the record, although it's more likely that sheer quality and everyone's months of plugging got it over.

"When we went back in the studio that fall, the process was

very focused," said Landau. "We put all this stuff on the table—a tremendous diversity of material—and we just kept playing all the different things, and over time there was a fairly natural consensus to go back [to the 1982 songs] because basically everybody involved came to feel it was the best stuff. It wasn't an ideological process at all. Hey, if there'd been more 'Bobby Jean's from that late group, that's what would be on the record."

But Landau also felt that the early material asserted itself because of an intrinsic superiority. "The beauty of the *Born in the U.S.A.* group was that it had internal balance. I mean, we start with 'Born in the U.S.A.'—this is so intense—and then 'Cover Me'—although it's pop on the one hand, it's in a minor key and it's very dark; the lyrics are very serious. You say, 'Well, we need some relief.' Well, you get 'Darlington County.' It's already there; a great deal of it's there."

By Christmas they were ready to start final mixes of the fourteen or fifteen songs still in contention. The process of final mixing is so delicate that outside ears are always called for. As a result, specialist mixing engineers had emerged within the major recording studios. However, because of his technical unorthodoxy and the availability of Chuck Plotkin, Springsteen had never worked with one. But Plotkin had been involved with the recording on this album from the beginning and was far too intimate with the music to provide the necessary perspective. So they worked with Bob Clearmountain, the best-known mixer in Manhattan.

Clearmountain was a perfect choice. A former bassist and mathematics whiz, he is among the most musical engineers in pop music history. Orginally based at the Power Station, which came to prominence in part because of his presence, Clearmountain earned his reputation working with Chic (Bernard Edwards and Nile Rodgers), who made some of the most high-tech recordings of the early Eighties, and with the Rolling Stones, who made some of the least polished. Clearmountain works fast but achieves remarkable results: extremely well-defined bass and electrifying drum sounds and vocals that are clearly intelligible and superbly integrated into the band sound. The latter was especially important in this instance because Bruce's records had often suffered from murky vocal mixes, not because Springsteen wasn't a good singer but because he was reluctant to fully expose his voice. Clearmountain knew just how to achieve the necessary balance between clarity and cover-up.

Yet as the mixing progressed, Landau remained uneasy. It struck him that even though they'd made an excellent record, it suffered from some of the same commercial flaws as Bruce's earlier albums. For instance, although there were plenty of hit possibilities, there was no sure-shot opening single. Equally important, the album lacked a clear picture of Bruce Springsteen at that moment. Clearly Bruce had undergone a great many transformative experiences since *The River*—or even *Nebraska*—but these weren't reflected in the songs they'd assembled for the new album. Even the newest material, "Bobby Jean" and "No Surrender," looked back rather than forward.

From the time they'd returned from the late summer break, Landau had adopted an unusually aggressive posture, something that only the manager/producer/best friend could do. "Part of Bruce's whole thing with Jon is that he has to bang into Jon," observes Plotkin. "Because Bruce is Jon's exclusive client, Jon really does get to take the position, 'Look, Jack, this is my career, too. I've spent the last three years of my life on this. Chuck made a Bette Midler record; everybody else has other things. But this is my record, too.' He gets to say things . . . He doesn't have to say, 'Bruce, you don't want to do this. You don't want to put out a record without an obvious opening single after all this time.' He just says, '*I* don't.' " It's not quite that easy, but the point is well taken nevertheless.

Landau confesses his own impatience. "I felt like, 'Let's get on with it now.' So I started to behave somewhat differently than I have in the past. At this point, we'd been working together for so long that I just felt I could say things in a real direct fashion. Bruce knows that I know that's he's always gonna make his own decisions; I'm gonna participate in them but he's gonna make them in the final analysis. And I'm gonna respect them, whatever they are."

In March, toward the end of the mixing sessions, Springsteen, Landau, and Plotkin spent a long Sunday reviewing everything they'd accomplished so far. It was an impressive body of work, and with the late substitution of "I'm Goin' Down" for "Pink Cadillac" (which was bumped to become the B side of the first single) they'd finally reached complete consensus on the song selection. Late in the afternoon, Plotkin left for the studio. Jon and Bruce would meet him there later that evening. Sitting with Bruce in Springsteen's room at the Lyden House, the East Fifty-third Street residential hotel where Bruce and Chuck had been periodically holed up since the previous summer, Landau blurted out what had been bothering him about the record.

Bruce recalled that Landau spoke "unusually forcefully," an understatement by Jon's own account. Landau wanted a first single, and by that he meant more than just a guaranteed hit. "When I used the word *single,* in my own mind I meant it in a much bigger sense. The type of single I was talking about was a single that would truly represent what was going on. And I was also searching for a way to express the idea that I wanted something that was more direct than any one thing that was on the record. As I said to Bruce, a song where a person who is a Bruce fan, who stayed with you on *Nebraska,* even if it was mysterious to him, a song where that guy's gonna say, 'Yeah, that's Bruce; that's what he's all about, right now, today.' "

"I don't have a song like that," Bruce said. Landau persisted, arguing his case strenuously and in great detail. "I don't know if I was doing it to be provocative or what. I was just doing it. I was saying things I hadn't planned to say," he remembered.

Springsteen balked, then exploded. "Look," he snarled, "I've written seventy songs. You want another one, *you* write it."

Landau took it on the chin but got in the final punch: The point wasn't just that he wanted such a song—although he frankly admitted that he wanted this as much as Bruce had wanted *Nebraska*—but that the album *needed* it, that it would be artistically incomplete until such a song existed.

By the time they left for the studio, Landau and Springsteen had calmed down, but both found the experience "weird," mostly because neither of them was given to such emotional roughhousing, at least not with each other. "It was a very explosive few moments, and it subsided very quickly and we went off and worked on the mix," said Jon. "It was as close as we get to almost the atmosphere of an argument, but it didn't hang in the air at all."

But later that night, alone in his hotel suite, Bruce found himself replaying the discussion. Sitting at the end of his bed in those hours before dawn that he still treasured most deeply, he picked up his acoustic guitar and began to strum a simple riff. He'd already thought up an opening line: "I get up in the morning," he sang and stopped. No, he thought, *I* don't wake up in the morning. What do *I* do? "I get up in the evening," he sang softly and thought, Well, how do I feel about that? ". . . and I ain't got nothin' to say / I come home in the morning, feeling the same way / Man, I ain't nothin' but tired, tired and bored with myself."

Telling the story even a couple of years later, Bruce still seemed a little bit in awe of what happened next. "It was just like my heart spoke straight through my mouth, without even having to pass through my brain," he said. "The chorus just poured out of me."

You can't start a fire, you can't start a fire without a spark
This gun's for hire, even if we're just dancin' in the dark

By sunup Landau had what he'd asked for: a song that summed up Bruce Springsteen's life in that moment. It was exactly what the album needed. But it was also far, far more—the most directly personal excavation Bruce had extracted from himself since "Born to Run," a song whose intimacies ran bitter and deep. Even the song's quotations from rock and roll classics were cuttingly ironic: Bruce Channel's mournful "Heeeey baby!" and Elvis's "Have a laugh on me / I can help" each mutated into a statement of frustration.

In a way, the song was about everything Bruce had withstood since *Nebraska*. Through it all, Bruce's songs remained stoically philosophical. In "Dancing in the Dark" he finally let his bottled-up confusion explode. Through its verses, "Dancing in the Dark" sounds not so much bitter or angry as just plain *irked,* ticked off at events.

When he recorded the song, Bruce snapped off every line as if it were so brittle it might well shatter, and as if he didn't give a damn. Lonesome as some of those lines were, they were aggressively sardonic, too. "I wanna change my clothes! my hair! my face!" he cries, bemoaning "livin' in a dump like this," attacking his own loathing and fear of aging and responsibility and competition and the unending tug of each of these things. "Dancing in the Dark" becomes a jeremiad, as well as a replay of his rancorous discussion with Landau, this time with Bruce playing both roles. Juxtaposed against "You can't start a fire without a spark" is the rejoinder: "You can't start a fire, worrying about your little world fallin' apart."

This is a protest song worth keeping—a marching song against boredom, a battle cry against loneliness, and an accounting of the price the loner pays. And on top of that, it's also the moan of an extremely physical person who can't wait to hit the road again: "There's somethin' happenin' somewhere/Baby, I just know there is," he sings, and again, "I'm dyin' for some action." He was well on his way to finding as much as he—or anyone—could handle.

■

Landau asked for a song about how Bruce was feeling. Bruce responded with a record that was about how he felt the second the song was proposed. In a way, "Dancing in the Dark" is about being caged in by one's own creation—its genesis is the desire to finish making *Born in the U.S.A.* Oddly, however, recording it proved difficult for Bruce. The session was one of the smoothest ever for the E Street Band—that day just Bittan, Weinberg, Tallent, and Springsteen, with Clemons's saxophone solo added later. But it came out as a record dominated by Roy Bittan's synthesizer and the supple drumming of Max Weinberg, while Bruce thought the song should be led by guitar. Over the next several days, he tried a variety of approaches to make it work that way. "In the end, it was just like any child," he said. "It was gonna be what it was gonna be, no matter what I wanted." Springsteen surrendered and the record was done.

The sequence quickly fell into place and changed little after mixing began. Side One included six songs, all recorded in 1982:

"Born in the U.S.A.," "Cover Me," "Darlington County," "Working on the Highway," "Downbound Train," and "I'm on Fire."

Side Two mingled material from 1982 with the work done in 1983 and 1984: "Bobby Jean," "I'm Goin' Down," "Glory Days," "Dancing in the Dark," and "My Hometown." Clearmountain finished mixing these songs in about three weeks, along with enough extras for several B sides, and they began preparing to master. And then Bruce began to reconsider. If he could just record another song or two, he suggested, the record would be much stronger.

Landau reacted vehemently. He pointed out that they'd already cut about seventy tracks, which was a ratio of about six to one. To get two more worth keeping—two better than the great-to-excellent material they already had—would likely require cutting about a dozen new songs. It was pointless to wait around to see if lightning would strike. *Born in the U.S.A.* spoke in the unified voice Bruce wanted for all his albums. It was time to let go of it.

The conversation ran deeper than that, though. In the course of it, Landau and Springsteen talked also about all the changes that had occurred since *Born to Run*. In a sense, the conversation was a way of reassuring each other about the new album's potential to create a massive, really disruptive success.

From the time they'd begun, Bruce had never been sure that he wanted to release such an album. "And then, of course, Jon tends to argue for the other idea, the louder noise. A lot of the things that I'm verbalizing now were implied at the time. And I'd bring up whatever—the ghost of '75—and say, 'Oh, that was a pain.' There were a lotta consequences that Jon was arguing for. And generally I guess I felt I'm the guy that has to face 'em," he said many months later. "And I was right." He laughed. "So on one hand, this always undercuts Jon's arguments in these areas, a little bit . . . but not that much," he added, sobering up again.

Bruce's arguing position was in favor of quiet, personal music—soft noises—that satisfied him and kept his profile low; it was all he needed to do. He stuck to it as he and Landau talked the matter through not one time or ten but over and over again for weeks. He simply wasn't sure that he wanted to be that big, that exposed.

"We had made a record that was pretty off center for me,

which I think is good. And I think those records should be made and I want to make other ones. But they're not the only records to make," Bruce said. "But that's where I was left—I was left out over there. And I spent a lotta time by myself, for a long time, where I did not have a lotta contact with everybody else. So I just kinda hung out there. That was part of the problem—it wasn't really that great a place to be left hung out at. But that's where it was and so then when we began to make a new album, the whole process was one of slowly kinda moving back, until bang! I locked in, I knew what we were gonna do, I knew what I really wanted to do. So Jon's place in this is he's just kinda there coachin' me. And we do this through arguing, and sometimes I just have to say a bunch of things and then once I say 'em, they're over. I'm arguing with myself is what I'm doin'.

"Part of myself is saying, 'Hey, don't do that, why do that? It's nice like this.' And then the other part of me is saying, 'Yeah, but if you could pull this off.' And then the other side: 'If you do that, you know, you're hangin' way out there and who needs it?' I'm sure it goes on inside of anybody who's a public figure and I suppose it goes on inside of everybody to one degree or another."

It went on with special relevance around the issue of what kind of record *Born in the U.S.A.* was going to be, however. The new trend in the record industry was for blockbuster albums keyed to a string of hit singles—Michael Jackson's *Thriller*, which produced seven Top Ten hits, is the archetype—resulting in mega-platinum sales: 5 to 15 million copies (*Thriller* sold 38 million). Coupled with the heightened visibility due to video exposure (in the wake of MTV, music video programs had proliferated from the networks to local cable channels), the result was the most intensely saturated sort of fame. Just the kind of thing that Bruce had been dodging since *Born to Run*.

As finally released, *Born in the U.S.A.* had numerous potential singles—seven of its songs became Top Ten hits and there were at least two others ("Bobby Jean" and "No Surrender") which would have had a good shot if they'd been issued on 45. Clearly, if Bruce allowed this music to reach the public, his public profile would soar, and that was something that always—and justifiably—made him skittish. One way of looking at the whole arduous process of constructing *Born in the U.S.A.* was that it was a way of avoiding the specter of such celebrity.

"But at the same time, the big question came up. I had worked hard to get through a certain door and I had an opportunity that I had created for myself." Consciously or unconsciously, Bruce's image of standing in a doorway, trying to decide whether to walk through, again threw him into the realm of John Ford's *The Searchers*.

In that film, John Wayne spends five years tracking his young niece, who has been kidnapped by Indian raiders who massacred the rest of her family. Wayne doesn't play an uncomplicated good guy; he is an unreconstructed Confederate soldier, there are indications that he may be a highwayman, he is a racist, and although he initially intends to rescue his niece, he decides to kill her when he finds that she's been taken as a wife by the Indian chief. But when he finally does catch up to her, after a long ride across the desert, he sweeps her up in his arms and brings her home.

In the film's final scene, all the other characters enter a house, but Wayne is left standing outside, framed in the doorway (scenes viewed through the dark side of such portals are the film's recurring motif). He adopts a noble posture, holding his left arm with his right, but the film ends with the door swinging shut on him, forever barring him from what's inside the house.

"The John Wayne character can't join the community, and that movie always moved me tremendously," Bruce said. But if the experiences *Nebraska* and its aftermath had dragged him through had any value, it was to reinforce his desire to belong to just such a community, to cut him loose from the illusion of the romantic loner, to make him understand that in real (not mythic) life, making your stand all by yourself is a miserable impossibility.

"In the end," Bruce said, "it was a variety of things that kinda threw the argument in one direction, but my feeling was that I'd created an opportunity for myself and why cross the desert and not climb the mountain?" So, at the last moment when he could have turned back from superstardom and its threatened betrayal of self, class, and quality, he pushed forward precisely because it seemed the only way to preserve those things he most cherished.

"This was '84 when this was happening and I started in '64, so that had been twenty years. And where I was at that moment was the result of thousands of small decisions that I'd made daily since I was fifteen. The decision to stay inside and play guitar, the decision to watch the band all night long instead of chasin' girls around the CYO or whatever. The decision to watch the guy's hands on the guitar. The decision to quit school, to take my chances. There were just hundreds, thousands of 'em, throughout my whole life. And we had 'Born in the U.S.A.'—we had that cut, and that was kinda sayin', 'All right, come on.'

"I knew that that particular song was just a song that comes along once in a while, even if you write good songs. It had some power to it that seemed to speak to something that was so essential, similar to the way that 'Born to Run' did. It's not that you have better songs or worse songs, but that's a particular type of song.

"And I wrote that song with an intent. I had an intent. And I put a rock and roll band together with an intent. And the intent . . . was a loud noise intent." He had been speaking soberly, but now he found himself cracking up at the very idea.

"I guess that I felt that the rock band is there for use by the public. It is a public service situation. And I felt that essentially when it came down to it, that was my idea from the very beginning, because that was where my roots came from. The people that I admired the most were people who did that or tried to do that or made that attempt. They did not back down. Or turn away. They took it as far as they could take it. For better or for worse."

Jon Landau was not insensitive to what an enormous decision he was prodding his best friend to make. On the other hand, he continued to push in that direction for a simple reason: "I believed with all my heart that Bruce could do this." As they tumbled around the issue, Jon reminded Bruce that they had created structures that could withstand everything a massive hit would bring, a protective community that would help deflect some of the superstardom mania and might absorb and productively channel the rest. It was a huge task and a bigger risk. The question was whether Bruce was ready to take it.

"Me and Jon sort of get into these types of arguments," Bruce said. "And what is happening at the moment is, the answer is already there. We're not figuring something out, really. I'm in the process of centering myself and Jon is assisting me in doing this.

"At different times in my life, because obviously you can't stay there all the time, I'll go off to this side or that side. And particularly when I'm out of contact with Jon for a long time. Basically I'm a guy [who has] extreme emotions and extreme feelings but I act right down the center, most of the time. My behavior and my actions tend to be very focused and very centered. They always have been. So I would say, Jon's daily job is essentially that he centers me. And if I get way out on one side, we may have a series of discussions and eventually I'll feel myself coming back to the middle. So at this period this is kind of what was happening.

"It gets me in contact with what my real feelings are, what I really want to do. So essentially, it came down to a pretty simple thing. In the end, as much as I hate to say it, but in the end, what we did, that was what I wanted to do. You know, even if I had very strong feelings in the other direction—and I did. And what I wanted to do was what I'd set out to do. And if I had the opportunity to do it, I really wasn't going to be able to do anything else."

In the end, then, Bruce Springsteen accepted the mass mania—and all its consequences, imagined and beyond belief— because he really did believe what his songs said, including the part that didn't just welcome everyone's participation but openly and actively solicited it. So he chose the Loud Noise, and *Born in the U.S.A.* was up and running.

■

Then Bruce played the assembled album for Steve Van Zandt, who was back in town from his European tour. Van Zandt loved what he heard. "Just that feeling of effortlessness, which is how you picture it when you first start playing—and you wonder why you can't do it. It's so frustrating. And there it was, man— the thing that you got into it for in the first place."

But Steve was also concerned. "I think he mentioned they were thinking about 'Dancing in the Dark' as the first single. And

I said, 'This is a big mistake,' " he recalled, shaking with laughter. "And he played me 'No Surrender' as a song that wasn't even on the album. I said, 'Wait a minute, you got these songs reversed. If you're gonna throw something out, throw that one out and 'No Surrender' should be the first single.' That's how much I know."

Steve felt that "No Surrender" was "the perfect way to introduce this new album—because it tied together the whole past. I mean, it had some of that *Born to Run* thing but a new message." And though he was clearly incorrect about the song's suitability as a first single—it would not have signaled a modernization of Bruce's music and ideas but instead would have heavily reinforced links to Bruce's past—he was absolutely correct that the song belonged. CBS already had the eleven-song sequence for the record, but it was quickly pulled back and remastered with "No Surrender" slotted in at the top of Side Two. "There was enough time for it on that second side," said Landau. "We just put it first; we didn't worry about 'Where does it fit?' It makes the whole side rock a little more."

Well, rocking a little more seemed to be the order of the day. In early April they turned the master over to CBS and circled three dates on the calendar: May 9, when "Dancing in the Dark" would be released; June 4, when *Born in the U.S.A.* would enter the stores; and June 29, when the tour would start in St. Paul, Minnesota.

9 STILL DANCING

The show's first set ends in a rush of light and energy, the chords of "Thunder Road" bursting open the somber mood established by the preceding songs and making a promise of better times to come. At the end, Bruce skids thirty feet on his knees to wrap himself in the arms of Clarence Clemons for a soul kiss.

Backstage during the intermission, several rock stars, a few TV celebrities, the odd movie mogul, but mostly just family and friends mill about in a tent with refreshments: a couple bottles of wine, some beer and soda, nuts and chips. The spread is limited in quality and quantity—one is invited to visit, not linger. Without a retinue of dope dealers, this backstage encourages less lurking about and less self-satisfied and attention-grabbing behavior than any other in rock. "Welcome to the Hardy Boys," someone remarked to *People*'s Chet Flippo near the start of the tour. But the atmosphere isn't squeaky clean; it's just business-like. And not wasteful. The food and drink runs out just about the time the second set is ready to start.

Those with more productive reasons to be here wait out the half hour break in the show's office, which is equipped with phones and computer terminals. Until tonight, this has been a

place of light banter and rare bursts of activity. With the tickets
sold out so soon after going on sale—a matter of minutes in most
places—and an experienced and sober crew, there simply hasn't
been much occasion for tension or dramatics. Good gossip has
been hard enough to manufacture.

Tonight, though, plans are afoot. Equipment has to be
shipped and warehoused; plane flights home have to be arranged
and next jobs located. And after eighteen months of intense
comradeship, there are farewells to be made. However, most of
the crew have worked together before and most will be together
again. For the past year and a half, these guys have done a
superbly smooth and efficient job pulling off the longest, highest-
grossing tour in rock and roll history without a single untoward
incident. Part of the triumph of *Born in the U.S.A.* is theirs, but
tonight they look back with ironic detachment. For the crew,
bread and butter is hooking up with the next tour as soon as this
one's over, and they'll move on with no regrets.

About ten o'clock, somebody goes to the Xerox machine and
runs off a few copies of a single sheet of paper before the show
shifts into gear again. It's a written set list, composed as a nightly
ritual by Bruce in his dressing room while cooling down after the
first half. The list is different every night; although there's a basic
structure to every show, only the opening and the closing are
fairly fixed.

In part, the intermission is there to give the band time to
replenish its energy. But it also gives Bruce (who is so supercharged by the show itself that he is virtually inexhaustible) the
time to calculate exactly how the rest of the night should run. The
second-half set list, scrawled in Bruce's looping schoolboy hand-
writing, puts what the night is about into focus for anyone who
reads it attentively. By choosing one song rather than another—
the fairy tale of "Growing Up" rather than the agony of "Backstreets," say—Springsteen expresses his sense of the occasion,
his reading of the crowd. Watching Bruce work, you can feel
these things, but what's amazing is that by half-time he's worked
out the gestalt of the evening well enough to write it down.

There's instinct involved, but equally there is intellect. It's
the blend that makes this the greatest show on earth. The set is

much more fixed than it once was, back in the club days, when Bruce was liable to call off just about any song he'd ever rehearsed and the only sure thing was "Rosalita" at the close. Now, when so much else is locked in, "Rosalita" is a variable element. Bruce is just as likely to end with something else, usually "Racing in the Street." In general Bruce has two shows— one for opening nights, which tends to concentrate on anthems, and one for the second night, which has a slightly larger proportion of oddities. (In cities where the band makes longer stands, all bets are off.) As it happens, a more predictable structure hasn't reduced the show's impact; the prominence of each night's variations is enhanced *because* the rest of the show is so tightly constructed.

Springsteen gives the set list to his major domo, Jim McDuffie, who sees that it's copied and passed around. The band studies it as hard as the *Daily Racing Form*, mostly to make sure they're prepared for any unusual songs. A number can drift into regular rotation and then suddenly be replaced by something the group hasn't done for months or even years, and when that happens it means quick changes in synthesizer presets and guitar tunings have to be made. The crew also gives the list a hard look, in order to know where to be at crucial moments. For McDuffie and a couple other crew members, there are cues to note: when to show up with the "Pink Cadillac" blackboard, when to don the bear costumes for "Growing Up."

Ready as they'll ever be, the band again sets out for the stage, Bruce's boots clicking on the concrete ever more decisively. Tonight the band seems caught between emotions. This is the end and yet it's a show they've done hundreds of times. They are friends destined for parting; they are also professionals. The show takes place in the intersection of those facts.

Strobe lights hit Bruce in a tableau of sweat, muscle, and guitar as Patti Scialfa creates an echoed obligato around the words *Cover me*. As her ghostly shrieks reverberate, the rhythm section kicks in and they're off and pounding again. The second set is designed to be light—"fun"; the first set is not. But "Cover Me" offers only a hint of this transition. The song has earned its place at the top of the last half of the night, it seems, because it suggests everything that has come before. It's a last bit of blues before diving into pure release. That release immediately presents itself through "Dancing in the Dark."

∎

A Springsteen concert is an event packed with rites, but as Bossmania developed in the wake of *Born in the U.S.A.*'s ten-times platinum success, Springsteen no longer dove into the crowds. He'd stopped doing it regularly even when he was still playing in arenas rather than stadiums, not out of fear, it would seem, but because there wasn't much mystery left to the act. Rather than serving as a way of personalizing the event, physical immersion in the audience had simply become another star turn. Yet Bruce still wanted something that physically symbolized his interaction with his listeners.

The replacement rite that evolved actually had its origins in the 1980 tour. When the band played "Sherry Darling," a frat-rock trifle from *The River*, Bruce would sweep into the front rows to pick out a girl and bring her onstage to dance with him through the final bars. It meant something quite different from Bruce leaping into the crowd. Rather than reinforcing Springsteen's stature as mythic Everyman, it suggested that stardom was as much a matter of position and good fortune as skill. But "Sherry Darling" wasn't always a regular part of the show, much less central to it.

It was music video that codified the dancer-from-the-audience as an important and inevitable part of the show. For his first 1984 video, Springsteen originally planned to collaborate with director Jeff Stein (who made the Who's *The Kids Are Alright* and worked with the Cars, among others). But after an abortive one-day shoot at Astoria Studios in Queens, New York, that project fell through. The concept simply wasn't working.

Stymied, Springsteen and Landau turned to their friend movie director Brian DePalma, whose films were mostly in the horror and thriller genres (*Carrie, Dressed to Kill, Scarface*). Although the stylistic disparity couldn't have been more complete—DePalma specialized in the overkill Springsteen disdained—it was outweighed by the virtues of working with a talented professional who could move quickly. "Dancing in the

Dark" was already out and streaking up the charts, the album was ready to come out, the tour was set to begin.

DePalma, who'd seen many Springsteen shows, got together with Landau and cooked up a story line. Three girls arrive late at Springsteen's St. Paul concert (the first of the tour), forgetting their tickets in the rush. They talk their way in, buy tour shirts from the merchandise tables in the hallway, and find themselves seated in the first row. Springsteen comes out to sing "Dancing in the Dark" and, as the song nears its conclusion, he points down at one of them, then sweeps her up to dance with him.

DePalma worked with Springsteen and the band during their final week of rehearsals at Clare Brothers Audio in Lititz, Pennsylvania. On June 28, the day before the first show, De-Palma worked with Springsteen, the band, a hundred extras picked off the Minneapolis/St. Paul streets, and his own crew, shooting close-ups and further rehearsing the interaction between Springsteen and actress Courtney Cox, who was playing the lucky concertgoer.

The next night, in the midst of his first show in almost three years, Springsteen opened the second set with "Dancing in the Dark," singing it with the house lights up full for the cameras, and when he was done announced to the crowd that they were making a "movie" and that he was going to do the song again. Since the single was Top Ten already, this was hardly an unpopular move, but it still struck an odd note. Never before had Bruce Springsteen allowed an outside agenda to interfere with the spirit of his shows. When Levine filmed "Rosalita" in Phoenix in 1978, his cameras were severely restricted in their movements, to prevent them coming between Springsteen and the audience. At the M.U.S.E. No Nukes shows, the film-makers were similarly constrained. Now Springsteen wasn't just giving the camera crew free rein, he was *lip-syncing*.

In the end, Bruce was dissatisfied. As he told English disc jockey Roger Scott, "Basically, the thing I didn't like about that [video] was it was lip-synced. Which is not what I want to do, because I think the best thing our band does is address the moment. And we go for authentic emotion and that gets all knocked out of whack when you're singing to something you recorded a long time ago. It was kind of an experiment."

In terms of rock iconography, the experiment was a failure. Although film critic J. Hoberman later praised DePalma's "sinister cool" and the video's "perversely radical realism" in presenting Springsteen as "a heroic model worker whose infinitely repeatable—and here artfully synthetic—rite climaxes with the dramatic selection of a partner out of the front row," from a rock and roll perspective that was just the problem. As Greil Marcus wrote, "On record, the song is about blind faith and struggle; here, as the comic Bob Goldthwaite put it, Springsteen looks like a member of Up with People. . . . Moving across the stage in seemingly choreographed, marks-on-the-board jerks, he grins like a supper club singer doing 'Gloomy Sunday' while communicating boundless love for the crowd. One is made to see a wide-eyed girl pressing against the stage; Springsteen takes her hand, lifts her up, and dances with her as the video fades out. From show to show, he really does this—but this girl is too cute, and the routine makes something that actually happens into something that could never happen. The next time you pay your money, enter a hall, and see Springsteen sing his songs, it will make you think the woman whose hand he takes is a plant."

DePalma took most of the heat for the video, but that wasn't fair. The fact that Courtney Cox was completely unconvincing may be pinned on DePalma, who cast her—as one Springsteen fan noted, there were plenty of attractive women in the house who would have been genuinely impressed by the opportunity, rather than expressing a distanced cool, as Cox chose to do. But what was really unsettling about the "Dancing in the Dark" video was Springsteen's interpretation of the song itself.

Springsteen's self-conscious dancing ("When he did that dance in high school, he used to call it the boogaloo," laughed Curt Fluhr, the bassist in Bruce's first band, the Castiles) and his enormous, brilliant grin (he'd had his teeth fixed between tours) simply didn't jibe with the anguish in the vocal. And that wasn't DePalma's fault. Because the track was lip-synced, what the listener heard was the dark urgency of the song. But when Bruce took the stage and sang about loneliness, the isolation the song portrayed disintegrated in the rush of the crowd's enthusiasm. He didn't feel miserable; he felt great. But pulling the song into the record's more "serious" mode might have resulted in a performance that was equally forced. The "Dancing in the Dark" video snagged on the most obvious pitfall of performance film, the discrepancy of effect among media—the simple fact that a song sung in the studio means something different than one sung under hot lights before a crowd. It wasn't just that Springsteen's lip-syncing wasn't convincing—it wasn't that bad—but the joyous look on his face denied the feeling in the studio version of the song.

However, the fact that the "Dancing in the Dark" clip was artistically unsatisfying (unless you were primarily a DePalma fan, in which case it *was* a good piece of work) didn't have anything to do with the way that most people experienced it. Video clips are advertisements, and what "Dancing in the Dark" was selling was a whole package: the song, the singer, the show. Picking a girl from the crowd and bringing her up to dance became a nightly drama in which the crowd took great delight, and not many thought that the dancers were "plants"—certainly not the women who paid ticket scalpers hundreds of dollars and jostled for space in those front rows, all for a chance to boogaloo with Bruce.

For them, at least, it seemed to be worth it, and looking on, it wasn't hard to figure out why. As the song ended, the stage went black and then the spotlights popped back on Bruce and the dancer, sometimes carried in his arms, sometimes swooning (one night in Tokyo, the girl fainted dead away), sometimes prancing too wildly to be held. Standing at the side of the stage one night at the Meadowlands arena you could read the lips of the teenage girl he'd dragged aboard, as she grabbed Bruce by the shoulders and pulled him close for a kiss. "I love you *so* much!" she gushed, then blushed and buried her face in her hands. But she'd only blurted out what all the others were feeling. Springsteen was supposed to sound downhearted in the face of *that*? Confronted with so much love, summoning just the memory of downhearted-ness was already an accomplishment.

■

Tonight, "Dancing in the Dark" rides in straight off "Cover Me," one riff picking up from the other, a smooth and abrupt transition from gloom to joy. Lately, Springsteen has been singing the song's blackest lines into the same echo used on "Cover Me." "You sit around gettin' older. . . . I wanna shake this world off my shoulders . . . there's a joke in here somewhere." Such morbid phrases rattle around the Coliseum for several seconds before the band kicks in, the echo drops out, and the real action starts. The song is now faster and looser than on record, Bruce hanging onto lines that he spat out in the studio. The song becomes undulating where the record is staccato, and the result is less a confession than the shadow of a memory.

At the end Bruce's voice is doubled by Nils Lofgren's wavering tenor. Then, just when the sax is supposed to kick in, Bruce picks up the mike again and declares, "Sometimes I feel . . . I get feelin' so downhearted . . . And I wanna reach out for some inspiration to somebody who . . . Heeeey, c'mon baby!"

But tonight, rather than reaching into the front rows, he turns to the wing stage right and pulls out Julianne Philips, his wife of six months. Swinging her around the stage as the Big Man resolves the song with his belated solo, Bruce looks as happy as a man can be. "Had to save the last dance for her!" he declares as Julie bustles back into the wings.

But that is hardly sufficient. Having had his personal fun, Springsteen gives the spotlight over to the whole crowd with "Hungry Heart." By now the crowd knows the ritual of singing the first verse without Bruce as well as the band does, but 80,000 voices in unison are startling and powerful even when you know what's coming. More than that, this crowd is burning with a sense of occasion.

The first set must have been just a warm-up for the audience. Although the response was strong by any standard, there's a frenzied edge now, like a football crowd invigorated throughout the game suddenly discovering new resources in its lungs during the waning moments of the fourth quarter. There are hundreds, maybe thousands out there who have been following this tour since the day it started, perusing accounts of it with the kind of attention ordinarily reserved for great sporting tournaments, and like those sports crowds, they rev themselves up and transmit their ecstasy to the players, whose exploits feed it back once more.

This crowd cheers Bruce Springsteen and the E Street Band, but in many ways it's equally celebrating its discovery of itself. As 80,000 throats grow hoarse, you can feel a great sense of satisfaction being released. However fragile and artificial it may be, right now this great spirit of community feels better than anything else in the world—especially in a world that spends so much time claiming that community is impossible to create. The rest of the show is turned over to celebrating the realization of the truth.

■

Whatever else it may be, *Born in the U.S.A.* is Bruce Springsteen's friendliest record, welcoming everybody along for the ride. Of course, a lot of the journey is through scary and depressing territory, where friends fall along the wayside and lovers time and again turn cold shoulders, but that doesn't destroy the sheer thrill of making the trip.

This isn't necessarily Springsteen's best album—a strong case can be made for the stylistic unity and raw emotions of *Darkness on the Edge of Town* or for the excitement and innocent exploits of *Born to Run*. *Born in the U.S.A.* is more diverse than unified, and alongside the two finest tracks Springsteen has ever created—"Born in the U.S.A." and "Dancing in the Dark"—is the weakest song he's released since the second album, the incredibly sloppy "Downbound Train." (The protagonist's three jobs in five verses are only symptomatic of its problems.) From peak to peak, however, this is the boldest music Springsteen's ever made. "Born in the U.S.A.," "Cover Me," "I'm on Fire," and almost the entire second side update his sound, working in synthesizers and more contemporary rhythms so subtly that the transition goes all but unnoticed until the unmistakably modern "Dancing in the Dark," the album's eleventh track, kicks in.

Partly, this is just the result of what Chuck Plotkin called "the craft issue." "Bruce is a better record maker now than he was ten years ago. It's as simple as that. Recorded music is an art form; he's working in a medium, and I think he's grown enormously as a record maker," the producer told *Billboard*. From the standpoint of performance and production, that's certainly true.

Roy Bittan's subtle use of synthesizers and his always magnificent piano playing, Max Weinberg's more fluid drumming, and Garry Tallent's supple bass work give these tracks a groove strong enough to match Springsteen's perpetual drive, and Clearmountain's mixes make what's going on brighter and more exciting. This lets Springsteen get away with even his slightest songs, far more than he'd been able to do on his previous three albums—compare "Darlington County" to "Cadillac Ranch," its sound-alike from *The River*. The result is an album that appealed to many who found his earlier, more elaborately anthemic records portentous. Springsteen had finally let loose his pop songs, and the explosion of hit singles and concurrent celebrity trappings were only to be expected.

Nevertheless, the subject matter of these songs is grim and unyielding. Although *Born in the U.S.A.*'s surface is hard rocking and joyous, the record begins and ends with songs about national tragedies, and in between there's not much solace. Muddled love affairs abound, from the bottled-up heat of "I'm on Fire," *The Postman Always Rings Twice* of rock and roll, to the frustrated horniness of "I'm Goin' Down." In both "Darlington County" and "Working on the Highway," everything seems swell until the very end, when the boom is decisively lowered. Despite its giddiness, "Glory Days" is as much about the fear of death as anything on *Nebraska*, while the rhythmic exuberance of "Dancing in the Dark" is just a frame for the depiction of an artist's nightmare. Throw in the shutdown friendships and closed-down dreams of "No Surrender" and "Bobby Jean," not to mention "My Hometown" and "Born in the U.S.A." itself, and you've got an album that's more painful than "fun." Those who heard only party songs and sentimental farewells were swimming in the ocean but ignoring the tides.

Then again, Springsteen's willingness to leave the story wide open signified how much he'd changed. And that's the real story of *Born in the U.S.A.* From *Born to Run* through *The River*, Springsteen's records spoke through a series of characters whose vulnerability was somehow exactly what made them indomitable. Those folks maintained their integrity *no matter what*. The alternative (glimpsed only rarely and in passing through such songs as "Racing in the Street" and "Jackson Cage") was a spiritual death no less immediate than a wreck on the highway.

On *Nebraska*, the everyday characters Springsteen had worked so hard to bring to life with dignity were dragged down and distorted by forces so far outside their control that vulnerability was an obscenely inadequate description of their condition. Joe Roberts, the highway patrolman, and that little kid in "Used Cars" aren't just subject to pain, they're animate wounds. Now, on *Born in the U.S.A.*, the characters partake of all this experience. Even the best of them can be vanquished and integrity is anything but an unquestionable attribute—after all, the guy in "Darlington County" rides right on by his buddy Wayne's arrest. But these characters aren't the bizarre manifestations of good and evil found in *Nebraska*. They're just folks again. Even though you could halfway imagine the guy in "Born in the U.S.A." as Frankie, the bad brother of "Highway Patrolman," nobody here starts that low in the pit, much less as far down as the guys in "Atlantic City" and "State Trooper." And that's exactly why, when these people get kicked around, they stay down for the count.

"Foreman says those jobs are goin', boys, and they ain't comin' back" and that's final. The thirty-five-year-old father who sings this central message in "My Hometown" talks of moving on, but he imagines no way out, for none exists. It's not like there's some town out there unaffected by all the things that have happened in his hometown. And unlike the gas-guzzling dinosaur of "Ramrod," he's mature enough to know it.

In the face of such circumstances, the defiant slogans of "Badlands" and "Thunder Road" would seem worse than false; shouting them now would have been a betrayal of everything that sticking to those slogans had taught Bruce Springsteen. It wasn't that statements like "It ain't no sin to be glad you're alive" were suddenly untrue, but that the inadequacy of such incantations by themselves was now exposed.

There is a progression of understanding embodied in "Born in the U.S.A.," particularly in those haunted final lines: "I'm ten years burning down the road/Nowhere to run, ain't got nowhere to go." The speaker is a Vietnam veteran but, given his Motown allusion and the highway imagery, he's also unmistakably Bruce Springsteen.

That progression—call it growing up—is also embedded in

the sequential structure of the album, which moves forward by oscillating between the desperate and the hysterical. "Cover Me" melts into "Darlington County," "No Surrender" becomes "Bobby Jean," "Glory Days" slides into "Dancing in the Dark," and that story erodes into "My Hometown," as if each speaker stopped the preceding one to say, "You think *you've* got problems."

It's tempting to see a basic contrast between the May 1982 material that comprises most of Side One and the later songs that make up the bulk of Side Two. But while there is a contrast, it goes back to the central 1982 songs, "Born in the U.S.A." and "Glory Days." At its heart, the difference is this: On Side One Springsteen sings through a variety of characters to whom he bears some relationship. On Side Two he most often sings as a version of himself. Side Two of *Born in the U.S.A.* is as personal as Springsteen's music has gotten. You can feel the transition edging in with "I'm on Fire," which closes Side One, and of course, Side Two opens with a restless farewell, "No Surrender," followed by a resigned one, "Bobby Jean."

The contrast is greater, though, the farther afield you gaze. Compare *Born in the U.S.A.* to earlier Bruce Springsteen albums, and you'll see as much difference as similarity. You can make a connection between the runaway kid on the bike in "Born to Run" and the middle-aged man in "My Hometown" or between the optimistic innocent of "Thunder Road" and the Vietnam veteran of "Born in the U.S.A.," but you can also see the discrepancy. Did the veterans of *Born to Run* fall so far? Did the expectations—much less the experiences—of the survivors of *Born in the U.S.A.* ever rise so high?

Move out a bit farther and try to fit these songs into the history of rock and roll. There is nothing about youth or juvenile experience in these songs. Almost every track on the album speaks of the experiences of young people but in the voice of someone much older and more experienced. The only teenage situation, in fact, is "I'm Going Down," and that song is written and sung with much more detachment and composure than any real teen could hope to bring to it.

The continuity lies elsewhere. *Born in the U.S.A.* is peppered with allusions to rock and roll history. Some of the links are obscure, as in the passing reference to Martha and the Vandellas' "Nowhere to Run" at the end of "Born in the U.S.A." and the pickup of a title from Chuck Berry's "Downbound Train," or the allusion to Bruce Channel's "Hey Baby," which provides the most grievous motif of "Dancing in the Dark." But others are unmistakable; the titles "Born to Run" and "Born in the U.S.A." are similar by design, just as they're purposely similar to other titles: Chuck Berry's "Back in the U.S.A.," any juvenile delinquent's tattooed "Born to lose." In a way, that's exactly what *Born in the U.S.A.* is about: people who have lived out every note of rock and roll, who have believed in its promises and threats and have tried to live them out, and what happens when they grow up. That isn't the only difference between the parent and soldier of this album and the reckless youth of its 1975 predecessor, but it's the most important difference.

And yet the best way to understand the development of the central theme of *Born in the U.S.A.* isn't to explode the record outward but to focus inward at just "Born in the U.S.A." and "My Hometown." Chuck Plotkin was right: The whole story *is* in those two songs. The former is melodramatic and distanced from anything Bruce Springsteen might ever have been (except in his worst nightmares). "My Hometown," just as much a fantasy of a life Springsteen never lived, is much more matter of fact, and despite its acceptance of a miserable reality, it's much more astute about the way things happen. In "My Hometown" broader, more material forces are at work, and even if the singer doesn't name them, he identifies them. Just as "Born in the U.S.A." contains the answer to the question implicit in "Reason to Believe" ("nowhere to run, nowhere to go," but you keep burnin' up the highway anyway), "My Hometown" extends "Born in the U.S.A.": When you take a good look around, you plant your feet—but that doesn't mean you can stop running.

This is a realm where the political and psychological come together in a grinding crunch. Too crazy to think straight, the poor fool in "Born in the U.S.A." finds himself dragged into a brutal and senseless war. Dwelling on what's been happening to his family and his town for generations, the discarded working-man of "My Hometown" feels every constant factor in his life wrenched apart. Both find themselves someplace they've never been before and without any choice but to accept it—for the time being. In the end, *Born in the U.S.A.* is about exactly the things that had plagued and preoccupied Bruce Springsteen for the past few years. If this isn't what made it popular, it's certainly what makes it fascinating.

■

More than most albums, what *Born in the U.S.A.* meant depended upon how it was heard. Because its themes would later be misappropriated by politicians and their stooges, it's easy to forget that the record had a separate life in the hands of rock fans, who struggled to make sense of what it had to say or found their senses swept away by the pounding beat. Some waved flags, some just danced past them, a few fought their way deeper.

What Springsteen's massive audience, old fans and new, thought, we can only guess. There were soon far too many of them to hazard a survey, and even when they came together for the concerts, there was no way of knowing if those sufficiently fortunate and well-heeled to get tickets were representative—or if so, of what. But if we can trust those who wrote about the record—at least those who wrote about it early, before it became the thing to do and general-interest windbags from Leon Weiseltier to Jack Newfield chimed in—then *Born in the U.S.A.* managed to dissolve some feelings of isolation, and in the heyday of the hegemonic semipopular (Ronald Reagan's "landslide" was achieved with the votes of less than a quarter of the eligible electorate), that was also a welcome relief.

No song could have been more wildly misread than "Born in the U.S.A." Jingoists took its superficial salute to patriotism as an assertion of dumbskull pride and latter-day revisionism; too many on the left, domestically and internationally, grasped at the same straw. Yet to anyone who listened attentively the story was clear. As critic Greil Marcus wrote, "The song is about the refusal of the country to treat Vietnam veterans as something more than nonunion workers in an enterprise conducted off the books. It is about the debt the country owes to those who suffered the violation of the principles on which the country was founded, and by which it has justified itself to the Vietnamese—or rather (because when he is on, Springsteen personalizes everything he touches), one veteran tries to make the link."

The key to "Born in the U.S.A." is its third verse—the incomplete, almost muttered verse in which the Viet Cong win the war: "They're still there, he's all gone." Springsteen isn't concerned that America lost; even Rambo knows that story. His concern is the lives that were lost and the facts that aren't being faced. It's hard to think of another postwar work of art in which the basic, irreducible fact of the war—that the Vietnamese won—is so plainly and forcefully stated.

In just the same way, after Ronald Reagan's attempt at expropriating Springsteen's image in a Hammonton, New Jersey, campaign speech, many leftists were confused about Bruce's nonconfrontational rejection of the President's kudos—he didn't make a speech, he just changed the way he expressed his ties to those the President despised. Yet at least one rock critic understood this perfectly. "I don't think the difference between the America of Ronald Reagan's landslide and the America of Laurie Anderson and Bruce Springsteen and Prince has anything to do with ideology or even values," wrote Steve Erickson in the *Village Voice*. "I think the difference is that Reagan's landslide was a colossal act of faith while these rock and roll records are, for the most part, acts of doubt—acts, I should say, of aggressive doubt. . . . Springsteen's record and tour find doubt and faith locked in protracted negotiations with no settlement in sight; the tour in particular seemed less a religious revival than a state of siege. Whether his fans get that same impression, I don't know. The media this year decided that Springsteen's importance as an American artist had to do with blue-collar economics; I think his importance has to do with the idea that doubt might be the antibody that saves a soul wracked by the toxics of blind faith."

This is true enough, as far as it goes, and prophetic, to boot, given what Springsteen had to say about "the toxics of blind faith" in the introduction to his 1986 hit single "War." But Steve Erickson and Greil Marcus are also a part of "the media," and they were far from alone. The great majority of press reviews of *Born in the U.S.A.* got most of the story right. You could almost draw a line between those who wrote about Bruce Springsteen because of his political agenda and those who wrote because they knew something about music. The music writers were the ones who got it right, and not because they ignored the politics. And this has nothing to do with whether they liked the record or not—aside from "Born in the U.S.A.," Marcus thought it "a piece of cheese." The best of what was written and discussed circled around the record itself and centered on what was happening in the environment in which *Born in the U.S.A.* existed, the environment that it helped create. This was true even of a review otherwise as single-mindedly zeroed in on musical artistry and songwriting craftsmanship as Stephen Holden's in the Sunday *New York Times*.

"If *Born in the U.S.A.* is an elegy to a vanishing breed of American, Bruce Springsteen represents a spirit that is also disappearing from our popular music," Holden wrote. "He is one of a very small number of rock performers who uses rock to express an ongoing epic vision of this country, individual social roots and the possibility of heroic self-creation. . . .

"Springsteen recognizes rock and roll as a product of the working class culture he writes about . . . [T]his hard Saturday night party music for the common people wasn't invented to help examine the hard realities of life but to find a release [from] those realities. But on *Born in the U.S.A.*, Springsteen uses the music to do both. He has transfused rock and roll and social realism into one another, and the compassion and the surging brawn of his music make his very despairing vision of American life into a kind of celebration."

A dozen critics picked up the pieces of this story, seeing in *Born in the U.S.A.* the culmination of the long yarn that began with *Born to Run*, finding threads of continuity amid the rubble of the lives the songs described. But most of all, the music critics got it right because they were rejoicing that there was, even in the heyday of the semipopular, a multi-platinum record that embodied more of rock and roll's virtues than its vices, a record whose mass appeal didn't cheapen either artistry or ideology. That is, critics were celebrating in Springsteen not their own good taste—many critics utterly uninterested in Springsteen or mainstream rock liked this album—but their audience's.

So more than anything, it was Springsteen's plain ability to communicate to a mass audience at all that people found inspiring. As Eric King put it in *Spin*, a magazine whose propensities unconsciously parodied the semipopular ethos, "If the '60s were supposed to be about the formation of a community that idealized rock music, Springsteen is the creator of a rock music that idealizes the idea of community."

When rock and roll criticism began—when people first began to admit, in public and in print, that they took this stuff seriously—one of its central precepts was that somehow the audience responded to the best stuff. But as time passed and some of what listeners sought out most avidly proved to be crap and some of what critics most favored was widely ignored, some critics came to revile the mass audience. But since, in the end, so much of rock's meaning derives from its use, that was a shaky position to occupy. In the end you were either a critic or fan of rock and roll, and to disdain the Loud Noise and its luxurious temptations meant surrendering the possibility that what you did would matter much.

Because almost everyone else had given up on getting through, it was impossible not to read enormous significance into Bruce Springsteen's proof that the ideal of balancing quality and success still held—if you were good enough to make it work and naïve enough to try. ("I was never much of a cynic, myself," Bruce said in one interview, almost apologetically.) People were invited to read as much into *Born in the U.S.A.* as they cared—or dared—*and so they did*. When that happened, they found out something about Bruce Springsteen and something about his audience. Those who most fully grappled with *Born in the U.S.A.* also found out something about themselves.

"I am a thirty-three-year-old man who has loved rock and pop music as foremost concerns for twenty years now, which is to say I have been fortunate to see great moments in American and English pop culture come, go, reignite and sometimes die off, in sad waste or injury," wrote Mikal Gilmore, who wrote a series of brilliant analyses of the record, the tour, and the Springsteen phenomenon for the *Los Angeles Herald Examiner*. "But when I see Bruce Springsteen reaching to his audience—to every corner of a large arena, to every mind in the hall—I find the kind of fulfillment and community that only the best friendships and kinships might bring one, which is to say, I see an oath of love and meaning played out with full heart."

In America, in those dark days of 1984 and 1985, when men had turned mean against one another and grubbing and greed were the order of the nation's business, such testimony was rare indeed. So Bruce Springsteen, who had himself walked cruel paths to get there, took his show back out on the road, where its spirit was needed.

PART TWO

FOLLOW THAT DREAM

Here comes a banker, here comes
    a businessman
Here comes a kid with a guitar
    in his hand
Dreamin' of his record in the
    number one spot
Everybody wants to be the
    man at the top
            —"MAN AT THE TOP"

Some of the many happy people who have learned more from three-minute records than they ever did in school . . .

Jon Landau in Dublin, 1985

Chuck Plotkin

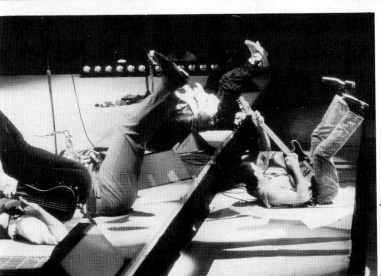

"I know your mama don't like me 'cause I play in a rock and roll band . . ."

With Patti Scialfa

"*I danced 'til quarter to three . . .*"

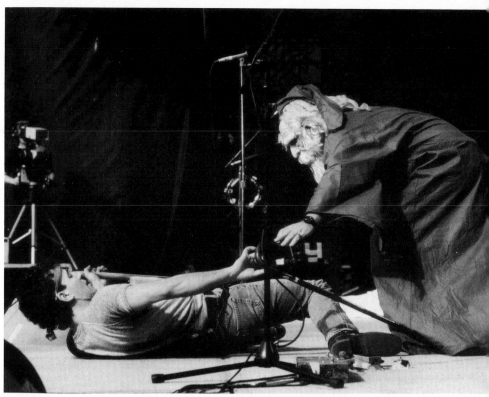

Not even middle-aged rock stars can always resist the tug of time. Here, a noted example goes willingly.

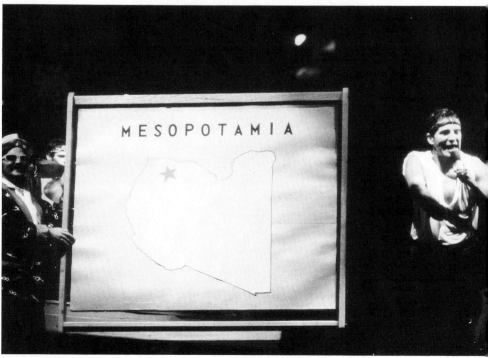

In search of ''Paradise by the 'C' ''

The world's only saxophone-playing Santa discovers a long-lost guitar-crazy elf.

With his sister, Pam, after dancing in the dark at the Los Angeles Sports Arena, 1984

Cadillac fantasy

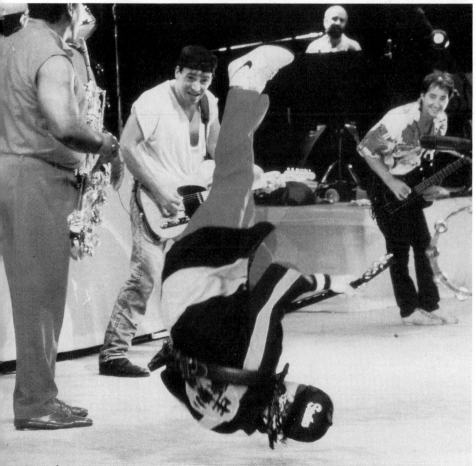

lose call for Nils

got this guitar and I learned how to make it talk . . .''

"... but it wouldn't shut up, so I tried to strangle it."

10 NATIONWIDE

Nobody give me trouble 'cause they know I got it made
Baby I'm bad! Baby I'm nationwide!

—ZZ TOP

B ruce, photographer Annie Leibovitz, and art director Andrea Klein spent months working on a cover concept for the album. They were trying to find an illustration that conveyed the loving but critical picture of contemporary America *Born in the U.S.A.* created and yet remain distant from the rampant chauvinism frothing so heavily in the year of an American-based Olympics and the electoral coronation of Ronald Reagan. Jon Landau at one time thought of using a Jasper Johns flag painting because Johns' paintings had just the right combination of distance and respect to undercut the superficial patriotism of Bruce's title. Although that thought was never developed, it suggests what they had in mind.

Somewhere along the line, Springsteen had acquired a gigantic United States flag, and the best shots came from posing him in front of it, sometimes in action, sometimes stock still. Springsteen and Leibovitz, formerly *Rolling Stone*'s principal photographer and a veteran of many such projects, did five or six sessions, but Bruce was uncomfortable with the result—the images were all too huge, excessively mythic. He must have understood the risk in linking his most commercial and accessible album to patriotic iconography; he needed something that worked against the mood of jingoism created in the Carter and Reagan years but didn't push him into anything superficially "rebellious."

In the end, he and Klein settled on a picture Leibovitz disparaged as "a grab shot": Springsteen, wearing a white shirt and faded jeans with a hole in one back pocket and a red baseball cap hanging out of the other, stood with his back to the camera, his arms hanging loosely and his right leg set slightly forward, as if he were actually walking into the flag. Close cropping focused attention on Springsteen's back and, most of all, his jeans-clad ass, which had the Johns-like effect of reducing the flag to a design element. But it was still unmistakably the flag, especially with the album title spelled out in blue at the top of the frame. And somehow, even though you couldn't see his face, Springsteen was immediately recognizable, just from his posture.

That the picture effectively created the necessary distance from American chauvinism was proved by a rumor that circulated just after the album came out. Springsteen, it claimed, was pissing on the flag. "No, no," Springsteen told *Rolling Stone*'s Kurt Loder, who asked him about it. "We took a lot of different types of pictures, and in the end, the picture of my *ass* looked better than the picture of my *face*, so that's what went on the cover. I didn't have any secret message. I don't do that very much. We had the flag on the cover because the first song was called 'Born in the U.S.A.,' and the theme of the record kind of follows from the themes I've been writing about for at least the last six or seven years. But the flag is a powerful image, and when you set that stuff loose, you don't know what's gonna be done with it." Bruce was a long way from throwing caution to the wind, but his ability to live with the wide-open possibility of misinterpretation was another signal that he'd relaxed his need to rigidly control every nuance of his work and image.

Leibovitz's frustration was easier to understand when you saw the remarkable sleeve for the "Dancing in the Dark" single. It showed Springsteen in a leather jacket and black jeans, leaping in the air with his heels kicked up, a look of intense concentration on his face.

The shot was grabbed on an April evening in an impromptu session in the basement of the house Springsteen had finally bought, a huge white-columned center hall colonial with a healthy six-figure price tag, which Springsteen referred to as "the mansion on the hill . . . the kind of place I told myself I'd never live in." It was located in Rumson, an extremely posh Monmouth County suburb, the kind of town Bruce always swore he'd never live in. He'd moved there for the obvious reason: The kind of house he wanted and needed and could afford wasn't readily available anywhere else in central New Jersey.

Leibovitz had just finished a photo session there that April evening with the E Street Band, including already-departed member Steve Van Zandt. At the end of the day, Springsteen brought out a tape of the just-completed "Dancing in the Dark."

"It was great," remembered Leibovitz. "It was the first time we heard it and it was *just great!* We had worked all day long with the band and everything, and everyone had left. We were the last people there and I said, 'Look, I just want to try one more thing. Come into the basement.' And he put on that song and he started dancing, and it was like *magic!* It was really like time stood still."

It was an ironic ending to the original version of the E Street Band, Springsteen dancing by himself to the tune of the loneliest song he'd ever written and looking locked into focus. He had to be, because there wasn't time for slacking off; the band had to be reconstituted before the concert tour could begin. Bruce could and did easily handle all the guitar parts in the studio—Van Zandt's most prominent solo on *any* Springsteen record is that brief mandolin bit on "Glory Days"—but onstage a second guitarist was essential, both to fill out the sound and because there were songs where Bruce needed complete mobility.

Springsteen had several guitarists in mind as potential replacements for Steve Van Zandt. Most of them were local people with whom he'd jammed in Asbury Park bars. He was also giving some thought to adding a woman to the group, to expand its emotional and mythic range. But the name that kept rising to the top was more surprising: Nils Lofgren, the veteran guitarist and songwriter, who had made nine albums, first as leader of the band Grin and then under his own name.

Springsteen and Lofgren had known each other since 1969,

when Bruce's band Steel Mill auditioned for Bill Graham at
Fillmore West on the same night as Grin. After the *Born to Run*
period, which also was the height of Lofgren's solo career, Bruce
and Nils became more friendly, and for the past few years
Springsteen had sat in with Lofgren whenever Nils played Jersey
clubs, as he'd done several times in 1983 and 1984.

In the spring of '84, Lofgren didn't have a steady band and
was without an American label, although he was on the verge of a
record contract with the English label Towerbelle. Nils was a
virtuoso guitarist and a more than able keyboardist, a skillful
songwriter, and an effective if limited singer. But he'd never had
a hit, and in the Eighties, without hits you were dead to the
recording industry. (Typically, Gary Bonds was immediately
dropped by EMI-America when his Springsteen-produced second
album flopped.) All that notwithstanding, Lofgren and Springsteen grew more friendly as their circumstances diverged. As
Bruce said, "I had spent some time with him, and I knew that he
thought and felt about music and rock and roll the way that I
did."

That spring Lofgren called Bruce, said he'd heard that Steve
Van Zandt had left the E Street Band, and offered Bruce his
services "if you ever need a guitar player." From Lofgren's own
point of view, there was nothing shocking about the idea. He'd
first come to prominence as a guitar and keyboard sideman with
Neil Young soon after that Fillmore audition, and he'd played off
and on with Young's groups ever since. But Bruce rarely formed
any lasting bonds with musicians or celebrities outside his New
Jersey network. Moreover, he and Nils had been perceived as
rivals in the mid-Seventies because of the many similarities in
the songs they wrote. It just didn't seem likely Springsteen would
replace his long-time sidekick with somebody *famous*. But when
you got right down to it, Nils Lofgren was the only sensible
choice, because his musical skills were perfect for the job and
because he had experience on superstar tours—whatever happened, he could keep it all in proportion.

In May Springsteen called Lofgren in Maryland, where Nils
was staying with his parents. Bruce asked if he would come up to
Big Man's West in Red Bank, where the E Street Band rehearsed,

to jam with the group. Bruce wasn't proposing anything permanent but, Lofgren said, "I treated it like an audition."

"We jammed together for a couple days, and it felt good to Bruce and the guys in the band and they asked me to join," Lofgren recalled. "It was about four and a half weeks until the first show, so it was like a crash course. I basically put a ban on all music—I didn't listen to anything except Bruce's music day and night." During the weeks before the tour, he studied the band's huge repertoire with the aid of Bruce and bassist Garry Tallent, and because there were so many tunes to learn—more than forty floated in and out of the set—he kept up his studies during the first few weeks on the road.

But first he flew back to D.C. to settle his affairs. "The day that I was asked to join the band was a fantastic emotional day for me," he later recalled. "I was in New Jersey and I flew right home. And I had so much work to do, but just for that day I got my car and I just drove around town really feeling great, playing 'Dancing in the Dark' over and over again."

Lofgren was an ideal choice for many reasons, but the keys were his experience, professionalism, and virtuosity. Before inserting his own ideas, he devoted an incredible amount of time and concentration to simply mastering the parts Miami Steve had played. Even though Nils was an artist in his own right, his work with Neil Young meant he knew exactly the role to play. As far as he was concerned, he hadn't signed up to do a tour—he'd joined the band. "When Bruce needs me, I'm there. And when he's not working, I'll continue to do my own shows and records."

Lofgren proved to be much more than a guitar player. He even managed to fill Miami's shoes as onstage sidekick, becoming a "waifish little brother," as critic Joyce Millman put it. On "Cadillac Ranch" he took a careening solo while wearing a huge foam rubber cowboy hat with "HOBOKEN" felt-tipped on the side, indulging in leaps and flips learned during his years as a student gymnast. For a time "Rosalita" featured Lofgren doing a trampoline flip while playing his guitar.

Lofgren also helped steady the E Street Band's mix of personalities, partly just through his complete respect for them: "They needed all that time, ten or fifteen years, to all progress to this stage. To walk into the band at this moment is just fantastic."

Most of all, Lofgren fit in because of his empathy with Bruce's goals. "I was very surprised when he called me to come up and jam, but I definitely *wanted* the job," he said. "I've known Bruce, we're the same age, we grew up with the same music. I've always loved his music and, you know, saw his shows whenever I could, and it's just . . . it's osmosis. . . . With Bruce you wind up treating those four hours [of the show] as if someone said, 'You've got four hours left on earth. What are you going to do with them?' "

For Bruce, seeing Nils fit in so skillfully must have been a relief and a joy. However much he missed Steve—and that was a lot, as all those dedications of "No Surrender" to his departed sidekick testify—Lofgren earned his highest praise: "He really brought an emotional thing to the band. At this point I think that the band is the only thing that counts. It's the emotional commitment you gotta have to get on that stage."

Nils Lofgren had it. Playing alongside the rest of the E Street Band, he helped increase it. Steve Van Zandt was never an especially eager guitarist; he was always most comfortable lying back in the shadows, playing rhythm. Nils Lofgren, a born guitar virtuoso, stepped forward to create high-profile parts, which proved particularly important on the sketchy mood pieces from *Nebraska*. That's not to make an invidious comparison. Lofgren simply brought different skills to the task than Van Zandt. But that difference was one of the determining musical factors in what the *Born in the U.S.A.* tour became.

"The best thing for me in the beginning was to play the lines that Bruce and Steve had written. And I continued to do that up until about the twentieth show," Nils explained. "The band made me feel comfortable emotionally right from the start, but musically I was uncomfortable as far as what I was contributing. But there's no short cuts—I had to go through that period. I was building toward the first of the ten shows at the Meadowlands. I knew the press was gonna be out to make their inevitably stupid comparisons between me and Steve, whom I respect and admire. And what I wanted to do was walk out onstage and feel—no matter what anyone thought or said—that I was definitely gonna be able to be great and be real happy with what I played, and feel like I belonged. And I did."

After that, he recalled, he was "able to shift the lines around. There are still a couple of lines I play the same every night, but each show I add a little bit of a fingerpick here or there, a little more of my own style. Now, even though it is very subtle, everything I play is definitely my own." This culminated in the guitar parts so central to the two new songs added late in the tour: "Seeds" and "War."

Nils was also the band member who best expressed the reason for the abnormally disciplined backstage and offstage scene around the biggest tour of the Eighties. Some—even Pete Townshend, when he visited backstage in 1981—had criticized the Springsteen concert hall environment as too sterile, not sufficiently rowdy and sleazy for rock and roll. "Depends on what you consider is a rock 'n' roll atmosphere," said Lofgren. "The reason we tour is to do these shows. If you see it as a fairy tale rock and roll existence, you might get through two or three weeks, but you couldn't play a hundred and sixty shows over a year and a half. I won't beat around the bush. Offstage we're a boring band— normal, nice guys. If we weren't, it'd hurt the show."

As the tour progressed and Bossmania swept the land, out of all the band members it was Nils who best kept perspective, because he'd been there before, with Young in the early Seventies. Lofgren, whose parallel career gave him most reason for envying Bruce, assessed the situation without rancor, out of friendship and understanding. "Right now you've got seven or eight million people that are fanatic fans. Two years ago five or six million of them didn't know who Bruce was. There's electricity that won't ever quite be exactly like this," he said. "Nobody's happier about Bruce's success than me. I'm the guitar player in the band and we both know that and I'm happy with that. I'll just work my thing around whenever he needs me. The way it is now, it couldn't be much better."

There couldn't have been a better replacement for Miami Steve.

■

As the mixing and mastering sessions for the *Born in the U.S.A.* album wound down, Bruce became more visible on the New Jersey club scene. Clarence was finishing a tour with his group, the Red Bank Rockers, and in April Springsteen sat in with them several times. He also played in Asbury Park with Cats on a Smooth Surface. In early May Bruce went to San Francisco to see his parents for a few days before the tour started. While there he slipped unrecognized into Elvis Costello's show at the Fox Warfield Theatre.

As news leaked out that the Springsteen crew was finishing an album, the rumor mill began churning. Its best product was unquestionably columnist Herb Caen's February report in the *San Francisco Chronicle* that Bruce was the father of Natassja Kinski's child. Springsteen and Kinski had never met.

Such outlandish tales were created because of public fascination with Springsteen's mystique, which was enhanced by his aloofness from conventional publicity machinery. CBS could never have engineered stories that preposterous, even if it had had Landau and Springsteen's encouragement. But the label had known that a blockbuster album was on its way since January, when Landau had talked with CBS Records executive vice-president Al Teller. "Al called up to see how we were doing, just a checking-in type call," Landau recalled. "We were already mixing at that point. Generally, our relationship with CBS is such that, for the most part, they show interest in what he's doing, but there's just no pressure from them. They accept the fact that Bruce is not a guy who's going to make records on a schedule. And that's great.

"Generally, for peace of mind, our approach is to do things and tell people about them when we're done. Otherwise expectations get built up and then they get knocked down. It's just more civilized to wait until the end. But at this point I had the degree of confidence to let it go.

"So Al was taken by surprise because I started to tell him, 'This is how it's starting to shape up. Funny you called, because I'm ready to talk.' "

Springsteen had released commercially successful records before, but Landau already had the feeling that this album could be something much bigger. "I had a sense that certainly this was the most explosive record we would be putting out since *Born to Run*. I'm not talking about necessarily best or not best, but I just knew what its impact was likely to be. And I felt in particular that we were going to have some hit singles to a degree that we'd never had happen before. And I knew that the song "Born in the U.S.A." was something that was just . . . there was nothing like it. From the night that that song was cut, no matter what happened, sometimes at some fairly low moments where I just didn't know where the record was going, I knew that that was there.

"In other words, I knew that there was a single type thing ["Dancing in the Dark"], and then I knew that there was another song, that we didn't know if it was going to ever be a single, particularly . . . I didn't care. I knew what it was going to mean, and it was going to mean something special."

Weeks after Landau and Teller spoke in January, however, CBS still hadn't heard a note of music. The two men spoke again in March, the morning after the "Dancing in the Dark" session. Jon was so charged up he was practically floating.

"Well, we cut a hot one last night, buddy," Landau enthused.

"What's it called?" Teller asked.

"It's called the first single."

"Yeah, but what's its name?"

"Well, you're gonna tell me when you hear the album."

A couple of weeks later, when Springsteen and Landau played the album for Teller and Walter Yetnikoff for the first time, Teller grew excited at the first track, "Born in the U.S.A.," but reined himself in. Landau had said this one was a surefire hit. "Born in the U.S.A." was a strong possibility, but it wasn't what Teller was looking for. A couple of more times—with "Cover Me," "I'm on Fire," "Bobby Jean"—he leaned forward with a gleam in his eye.

"Dancing in the Dark" is buried, the eleventh song on a twelve-song album, which is not where you're supposed to hide the first single, but the instant Teller heard it, he knew not only that this was a strong album with a surefire first hit, but a record with the potential as one of the biggest-selling ever released.

The multiple single possibilities on *Born in the U.S.A.* took advantage of new developments in Top Forty radio programming. Until the advent of the "contemporary hit radio" format in the early Eighties, there was almost no possibility of squeezing more than two or three hits out of even the most popular LP. Contemporary programmers, however, had decided that it was safer to program the fourth or fifth most popular track from a best-selling album than to take a risk on an altogether unknown quantity. In a time when most successful albums sold fewer copies than they would have in the Seventies, a few blockbuster LPs could break all previous sales barriers. It took at least one big single to take an album to the gold record threshold (sales of 500,000 copies) and two or three to take it to the platinum plateau (sales of a million or more copies). If you could get three or four (or more) singles, the possibilities were stratospheric: You could expect sales of more than 5 million copies, and by then, with all costs amortized, the profit percentage was extraordinarily high. The mid-Eighties saw a series of such blockbusters, spearheaded by Michael Jackson's *Thriller,* which had seven Top Ten singles and sold 38 million copies, and including Madonna's *Like a Virgin,* Cyndi Lauper's *She's So Unusual,* Prince's *Purple Rain* soundtrack, and *Born in the U.S.A.,* the second best-selling album, with eventual worldwide sales around 18 million units.

In addition to their abundance of Top Forty hits, these records, and the performers who made them, shared several features. Each skillfully used music video (and/or the movies) to build a broad but clearly defined image, each worked variations on older styles of rock and soul, each managed to make his or her sexuality simultaneously provocative and reassuring. (On this last count, Springsteen might barely seem to fit, being commonly considered just another all-American. But scruffy outcasts have never been that welcome when you bring them home for dinner, and beyond that there was a running element of male bonding so powerful that its homoerotic undercurrent was undeniable. And, of course, there was that soul kiss with Clarence at the end of "Thunder Road." It wasn't the outrageousness of Prince or Madonna but it fit the bill.)

Finally, all of them recorded for either CBS or Warner Communications, which each controlled about twenty-five percent of the American and worldwide record markets. Making the right kind of music was the irreducible base for blockbuster success, but after that you needed a marketing and merchandising and promotion army to get the records into the stores and on the radio. The result was both the greatest degree of hegemony in popular music history and also the most exciting Top Forty radio in more than a decade.

Obviously, that hegemony wasn't spontaneously generated. Bruce Springsteen didn't flog his records as hard as he could have, but he no longer stood in the way of his record company's marketing plans. Whereas Bruce had attempted to convince CBS that there should be no advertising at all for *Darkness on the Edge of Town,* he was willing to see the label roll out its big guns for *Born in the U.S.A.* The label may have felt constrained, because the Springsteen campaign still had to live up to the standards of a "class act," but within those boundaries CBS was free to market its heart out.

The plan was to release "Dancing in the Dark" on May 9, a month in advance of *Born in the U.S.A.* That would not only build anticipation for the much more profitable album, it would focus radio station attention and prevent having the airplay split among other tracks even at the AOR level, ensuring that "Dancing in the Dark" would get the concentrated attention needed to fuel it up the charts. Columbia Records simultaneously began an "awareness" campaign aimed at retail stores. On May 1 the label sent its sales and radio promotion men field kits containing a facsimile of the album cover and an announcement of the promotion campaign, emphasizing the company's heavy commitment to this project. T-shirts emblazoned *Born in the U.S.A. 6/84* were handed out to disc jockeys and record store clerks. Each CBS distribution branch got giant three-by-three foot blowups of the LP cover for display in its record store accounts. Later in the month, as "Dancing in the Dark" swept up the charts, the distributors held advance listening parties for chain buyers and key radio programmers in eleven markets. The result was a boom in advance orders for the new album and a resurgence in sales of Bruce's back catalog.

According to Jack Rovner, Springsteen's Columbia product manager, the campaign was "designed to give rock radio stations and record stores an equal chance to climb on the Springsteen bandwagon." In fact, it was designed to make sure that nobody forgot there was a bandwagon to leap aboard.

CBS didn't do this for every album, and the plan didn't always work when it was tried. But *Born in the U.S.A.* had the goods: pop appeal, depth for serious listeners, and the mystique of Bruce Springsteen.

In the late Sixties and early Seventies, when FM rock stations were considered "underground," it was commonplace for new albums by superstars—the Beatles, Dylan, the Stones—to leak unauthorized onto the radio several days, maybe even weeks before their official release. Except for the Beatles, Top Forty radio had almost never indulged in any such practice. In the Eighties, FM rock stations proliferated and became more competitive and cautious; album marketing strategies became more sophisticated and closely tied to the disc's availability in stores, so advance airplay all but ceased. Leaks were no longer arranged by zealous promotion men; radio stations were more likely to wait and see what happened than to offer sneak previews.

But in the case of "Dancing in the Dark," key radio stations all around the country jumped the gun. First on the air, on Saturday, May 7, was New York's Z100 (WHTZ), the highest rated Top Forty (CHR) station in the country. The city's top-rated AOR outlet, WNEW-FM, started playing its copy before Z100's had finished spinning. Both continued until Columbia's legal department sent them a "cease and desist" order by telegram. By then—it was Sunday—the record had leaked out to other stations around the country, more telegrams were sent, and the *Born in the U.S.A.* boom was off to a healthy prerelease start. Columbia wasn't heard complaining very loudly.

"All we had to do was make people aware that Bruce Springsteen is coming out with a new album," Rovner told the *Wall Street Journal*. But Columbia didn't just keep up the heat, it fanned the flames. Norman Hunter, buyer for the Carolina-based Record Bar chain, called it "the most expensive, best organized prerelease campaign I've ever seen." And Hunter was a doubter, certain that *Victory*, the album by the Jacksons (Michael and his brothers) that CBS was preparing for release later in the summer, was "going to be five times bigger and last ten times longer."

(Despite a similar prediction by *New York Times* critic Robert Palmer, *Victory* sold only about 2.5 million copies and was a spent force by Labor Day. Nobody ever claimed much for it artistically.)

By May 18 record stores were loaded with posters, displays, reproductions of the record cover ("album flats"), and huge banners ("Gigant-O-Grams") announcing the album release date. On Memorial Day weekend, just five days before the album was to hit the stores, the three-by-three-foot slick of the album cover was plastered circus poster–style on walls and on hoardings in New York, Los Angeles, Chicago, Washington, Philadelphia, Cleveland, Detroit, Atlanta, Boston, Dallas, and San Francisco. The nine-and-a-half-minute "Rosalita" clip, which had never been seen in its entirety in the United States, was released to MTV, "Entertainment Tonight," and other shows, while an MTV ad campaign also started. And on Monday, June 4, 1.25 million copies of the album were sent into the nation's record stores. Three days later, CBS had reorders for 300,000 more. *Born in the U.S.A.* entered the *Billboard* chart at Number Nine, the highest position reached by any new album upon release in two years. The next week it hit Number One. The album stayed in the Top Five for a year and in the Top Ten for several months more.

"Dancing in the Dark" faced much stiffer chart competition. It quickly climbed to Number Two but was blocked from the top spot by "When Doves Cry," the amazing first single from Prince's *Purple Rain,* a left-field movie hit. "When Doves Cry" and *Purple Rain* were the hegemonic blockbusters of the moment, newer, fresher, more revolutionary. Springsteen had reached the Top Ten with his last four albums; Prince had been there only once before. And while *Born in the U.S.A.* and "Dancing in the Dark" represented a striking evolution in Springsteen's personal style, Prince heralded a revolution (or at least a trend), leading a wave of Minneapolis-based black rockers that was still going strong three years later and paving the way for the resurgence of "black rock," like the heavy metal rap hits of Run-D.M.C.

Although it was easy to miss the resemblance, music's central heroes of 1984 also shared a lot. Among other things, both Prince and Springsteen were the product of regional isolation—practi-

cally and metaphorically, central New Jersey is as far from the
media centers as Minneapolis—and both were especially interested in the collapse of domestic values.

As it happened, *Born in the U.S.A.* also became identified
with a trend: the so-called American rock renaissance. In 1983 a
"second British Invasion" had been ballyhooed. Now, with
Springsteen, Prince, Jackson, Madonna, Lauper, Tina Turner,
Huey Lewis, ZZ Top, and Van Halen crowding the top of the
charts, the trend had turned the other way. It was probably
inevitable that such a trend would develop that year, given the
chauvinistic frenzy into which the country was whipped, first by
the Los Angeles Olympics and then by the elections. Certainly,
many performers—not only in music—exploited this mood, and
Born in the U.S.A., however critical its contents may have been,
was helped along by the patriotic hysteria. The irony is that the
so-called "heartland rockers" with whom Springsteen did share a
great deal thematically and stylistically—Bob Seger, John Mellencamp, Tom Petty—were mostly absent from the '84 scene.

So maybe it was appropriate that the *Born in the U.S.A.*
concert tour opened in St. Paul, just across the river from the
town Prince called home.

■

Bruce himself remained abstracted from the hoopla. As his
record became an epicenter of pop, he simply went about his
business. On May 19 he appeared at the Stone Pony in Asbury
Park, where he sang "Fire," Wilson Pickett's "In the Midnight
Hour," and Little Richard's "Lucille" with Clarence Clemons and
the Red Bank Rockers. They topped the evening off with "Twist
and Shout." That was the last show the Red Bank Rockers ever
played. The next week Bruce and the E Streeters went into
rehearsals at shuttered Big Man's West just up the coast in Red
Bank.

A week later, on May 26, Bruce appeared with a group called
Bystander at Club Xanadu in Asbury Park and sang "Dancing in
the Dark" onstage for the first time. He played a lot in the shore
clubs throughout the late spring weeks, as if to get his fill of the
local night life he'd be missing through the months of touring

ahead. On June 1 he sat in with John Eddie and the Front Street Runners (two years away from their own Columbia debut album), performing "Dancing in the Dark," ZZ Top's "I'm Bad, I'm Nationwide," Creedence's "Proud Mary," and Chuck Berry's "Oh Carol."

As the Big Man's West rehearsals progressed, so did some of the important auxiliary activities of the tour. Art director Andrea Klein and Winterland Promotions created a series of t-shirts, sweatshirts, and other "tour merchandise," including an elaborately illustrated and annotated program, all of which had to meet Bruce's approval before going into production. Bruce had accepted the need for selling his concertgoers some sort of merchandise, noting the demand of his audience for even the low-grade junk sold in the streets around his shows by "t-shirt bootleggers," unauthorized merchants preying upon rock star images. Anyway, however superfluous such stuff might be, Bruce was at least avoiding the tug of an even more trivializing force, corporate sponsorship of rock tours, a system by which rock stars were paid to perform under the banner of consumer products (beer, cars, cologne, jeans).

Sponsorship was an issue Springsteen understood especially well, because friends like Bonds and Southside Johnny, all but ignored by radio and the record industry, had received their only recent paychecks from singing in beer commercials. Their acquiescence in Madison Avenue's post–*Big Chill* discovery of the power of rock and roll was understandable. But, as Springsteen must have known, a star who wanted to say something serious couldn't simultaneously present himself as a vehicle for flogging products or trumpeting the chimerical superiority of one brand over another.

"We get approached by corporations," Bruce later commented, beginning with a classic bit of understatement. Companies like Coca-Cola and Chrysler besieged Landau's office, proferring sums ranging from $5 to $10 million (as openers!) for the opportunity to snatch a piece of the all-American rock and roller. How much even Bruce knew about that was anybody's guess, because his instructions were that Landau's office convey a blanket "not available."

"It's just not something that struck me as the thing that I wanted to do. Independence is nice. That's why I started this— for the independence. I'm telling my story out there. I'm not telling somebody else's. I'm saying what I want to say. That's the only thing I'm selling. I had a few small jobs before I started playing, but when I picked up that guitar, that was when I could walk down my own path. That's just the way I like it. It's a lucky feeling, you know, because how many people get to set their own standards and kind of run their own circus?" He wasn't making even an implicit criticism of anybody else. Not collaborating with a tour sponsor was simply a reflection of Bruce's understanding of the luxury afforded by his own good fortune and of how that luxury ought to be used.

So the work continued as Bruce Springsteen's work, without much outside intrusion. Klein and photographer David Gahr appeared at one rehearsal for a photo session that included the shots of Bruce and the band grouped around the Sixties Chevy convertible "Dedication," a gift from Gary Bonds. Meanwhile, Nils Lofgren was living with Bruce at the Rumson house, and they studied the songs late into the night. Landau and Spring-steen held frequent meetings, planning the DePalma video, discussing various aspects of the tour, coordinating the assembly of crew and management personnel with tour director George Travis. But Bruce also had time to relax, journeying into Manhat-tan one evening to have dinner with author Stephen King, for instance.

On Friday, June 8, the Stone Pony marquee again read "John Eddie and the Front Street Runners." Inside, the scheduled opening act, Eddie Testa and the Cruisers, became upset when told they were being replaced, although they'd still be paid. But Testa and his band were more forgiving when they learned why: John Eddie's show was to be followed by a full-scale set by Springsteen and the E Street Band, their first public appearance since 1981 and their first ever with Nils Lofgren.

The weeks after Memorial Day are the season in Asbury Park, so the Stone Pony probably would have been packed that Friday night to its full 1,000-customer capacity anyway. The club actually felt even more crowded. The temperature broke a hundred degrees, because one of the air conditioning compressors malfunctioned. But as the night went on, nobody left. In fact, the lines at the telephone lengthened as one patron after another, spotting Clarence Clemons' bright brass tenor sax on the stage or catching a glimpse of Lofgren in the crowd, went to let a friend in on the open secret.

At 1:45 Bruce and the gang slammed into "Thunder Road," quickly following with "Out in the Street," "Prove It All Night," and "Glory Days," their first number from the just-issued new album. They paused to catch their breath and wipe the sweat from their eyes. "Man," Bruce gasped, "I hope I can remember the words to this song; it's been a while," then dedicated the next number, "The River," to Testa and the Cruisers.

They kicked back in with hard rockers: "Darlington County," "Dancing in the Dark," and "Promised Land." At quarter to three, the doors closed because of the liquor law curfew. "Who's here from North Jersey? Who's here from Central Jersey?" Bruce inquired. "Me too . . . This song is a way of reminding me where I come from." They played "My Hometown" to thunderous approval and quickly followed it with "Born in the U.S.A." before closing with "Badlands." Inevitably called back for an encore with chants of "Brooooce . . . Broooooce," Springsteen responded with the equally inevitable "Born to Run."

That was it for the night, but on Sunday Bruce and Nils came back to play with Cats, doing "Gloria," John Lee Hooker's "Boom Boom," the Animals' "We Gotta Get Out of This Place," the Stones' "The Last Time," and "Rocking All Over the World."

A few days later they were in Lititz, Pennsylvania, doing full dress rehearsals with full sound and lights on the specially built stage with which they'd tour. Later in the week they blocked out moves for the "Dancing in the Dark" video under Brian DePalma's direction. On June 21 the band took over the Village bar in nearby Lancaster for a final warm-up set, playing "Out in the Street," "Prove It All Night," "Glory Days," "Hungry Heart," "Dancing in the Dark," and concluding with "Rosalita."

Tickets had been going on sale in cities around the nation and selling out in record time. The measure of popularity for Bruce's shows was no longer whether they would sell out or how many dates he could play in a given town. The story was the pace at which the seats were gobbled up. In most places the answer was a few hours. By the end of May, tickets for twenty-nine shows had gone on sale; every available seat was immediately snapped up at $15 to $16 apiece, and that included 201,000 seats for a remarkable ten-date stand scheduled for late August at the Brendan Byrne Arena in New Jersey's Meadowlands Sports Complex, the same arena Bruce had opened with five shows in 1981.

The Meadowlands tickets were gobbled up by a fanatic East Coast audience in a bare twenty-eight hours on June 19 and 20. It took that long only because Ticketron and Teletron couldn't spit them out any faster. Meadowlands general manager Loris Smith estimated that demand was sufficient to have sold out thirty such shows. The $3.2 million gross, the 16,000 seats sold in the first hour of sales, and the 29,000 seats sold by Teletron, the over-the-phone ticket agent, in the first day were all records. (Teletron's first-day sale broke its record for any previous *week*.) On June 19 New Jersey Bell registered 120,000 extra calls per hour through its central station in Hackensack, an overload foreshadowing things to come. On a slightly smaller scale, the same story was repeated over and over in St. Paul, Cincinnati, Hartford, Philadelphia, and other cities.

The Springsteen tickets were sold with amazingly few glitches—despite complaints by rabid fans about ticket scalping, such problems were far better controlled than in 1978 or 1981. This was in stark contrast to the other gigantic summer tour of 1984, the one starring Michael Jackson and his brothers. Promoted by figures from the sports world, sponsored by Pepsi-Cola, and playing the biggest football stadiums available with truck-loads of special effects gimmickery and a huge stage that killed thousands of seats—and with a $30 ticket price—the so-called Victory tour was a public relations disaster and a financial debacle for principal promoter Chuck Sullivan, whose family wound up putting its New England–based National Football League franchise on the market to make up its multi-million dollar losses. Part of what made Victory look so bad was the efficiency with which George Travis and the Springsteen crew ran their shows, but equally remarked on in the dozens of reviews comparing the two tours was the disparity between Michael Jackson's rote performance and Springsteen's searching one.

Bruce seemed impervious to comparison, whether it was to punks and New Wavers, to the so-called "heartland rockers," or most persistently during 1984, to Michael Jackson and Prince. Springsteen saw the Jacksons late in the summer at Philadelphia's Veterans Stadium and was impressed by what he heard. "I thought it was really a great show," he told *Rolling Stone*'s Kurt Loder. "Real different from what I do, but the night I saw 'em, I thought they were really, really good. Michael was unbelievable—I mean, *unbelievable*. He's a real gentleman, and he's real communicative . . . and he's *tall*, which I don't know if most people realize." As for Prince, Bruce was simply a stone fan, comparing the critically disparaged *Purple Rain* to "a real good early Elvis movie" and gushing over the live gigs he'd seen. "He is one of the best live performers I've ever seen in my whole life. His show was funny; it had a lot of humor in it. He had the bed that came up out of the stage—it was great, you know? I think him and Steve, right now, are my favorite performers."

Bruce was having second thoughts about the configuration of his own band. Not that there were any regrets about Nils Lofgren, but Bruce still hoped to expand the band's musical and emotional range. In the past he had occasionally performed (once done a whole tour) with a horn section, dubbed the Miami Horns as a result of Steve Van Zandt's tutelage, which later became La Bamba and the Hubcaps under the direction of trombonist Richie "La Bamba" Rosenberg. Bruce had become friendly with one of the group's singers, a redheaded Irish/Italian-American from Asbury Park named Patti Scialfa. Scialfa had auditioned for one of Bruce's Asbury groups while she was still in high school, but he'd turned her down then because she was still too young. Later Scialfa toured with Southside Johnny and the Jukes, who also used La Bamba's horn section. Earlier in the spring of 1984 she'd auditioned for Bruce again, but he'd never called back.

On the Sunday night before the band left for St. Paul, Bruce finally called Scialfa and asked if she'd like to join the tour as a background vocalist. "I wanted to tell him that I had to wash my

hair, that I didn't have enough time to get ready," Patti told Steve
Pond. It was virtually true—she had four days to pack and learn
the show. But she said yes anyway. It wasn't the kind of
opportunity a person could resist. "See," she later cracked, "you
can meet a nice guy in a bar."

Bruce also seemed well satisfied, even though it would take
some weeks to fully work Scialfa into the show musically. "It's
real nice having her in the band," he told Don McLeese of the
Chicago Sun-Times after the first St. Paul show. "It's kinda like,
'Yeah, everybody join in.' She's a local person, and it just feels
like a bunch of people up there. It has a little of that community
thing to it." Now, his tableaus of male bonding would acquire a
different dimension.

■

At 8:37 P.M. on June 29, 1984, Bruce Springsteen and the
new, expanded E Street Band raced onstage at the St. Paul Civic
Center and launched into "Thunder Road." In only a few seconds, it felt just like old times as 17,500 voices joined Bruce's to
complete the second verse:

> Show a little faith, there's magic in the night
> You ain't a beauty but hey you're all right
> Oh and that's all right with me

The song galloped to a close, and Bruce gasped, "Missed ya!"
before snapping right into "Prove It All Night," which slid into
"Out in the Street," Patti Scialfa picking up Little Steven's duet
lines and standing in for 10,000 female fantasies.

Bruce wore a blue shirt open to the neck and greasy jeans,
the kind of uniform he'd always chosen. But the resemblance to
tours past ended there. The most immediately noticeable change
was in his arms—always muscular, they'd become huge, "biceps
that would reduce Popeye to tears," as Joyce Millman wrote. His
legs, neck, and chest had also grown to what seemed like NFL
proportions.

In 1983 Bruce had begun attending a gym in Red Bank
owned by physical therapist Phil Dunphy. Although Bruce

claimed he'd "never exercised before in my whole life," he had always done a few things (notably, surfing) which kept him in decent physical condition. He'd never have made it through his own sweat-soaked concert marathons otherwise. On the other hand, the lingering effects of the leg injury from his high school motorcycle accident kept him limping and required frequent treatment, particularly after he was reinjured in a three-wheeler accident in 1979.

Springsteen had always been an extremely physical person; one of the things that "Dancing in the Dark" captures is how repressed he felt while sitting on his ass in a recording studio. So it made sense that he responded avidly to Dunphy's fitness regimen. Soon Bruce was doing strength and weight training and running six miles a day. He also radically altered his eating habits. ("All I knew was fast, fast food. That's all I had the dough for.") The result was a measurable increase in stamina as well as physique and a degree of dedication that included bringing Dunphy on the road as his personal trainer. As Bruce later told Chet Flippo, "It's really helped on the road. Before, I would come out the first night, and I'd almost die, wanna throw up, gaspin' for air." He was giddy and dizzy by the middle of that first night's set, but that was from the surge of adrenaline and the accelerated pace the band took in its initial excitement.

"Here we are!" Springsteen shouted after "Out in the Street." "It only took me three years. I should write, right?" Then he pulled the set back down with the first of the night's songs from *Nebraska*, "Johnny 99," performed with just drums, harp, guitar, and Clarence Clemons on pensive tambourine, following it with "Atlantic City" in a full band arrangement, with bagpipe effects reminiscent of the Celtic rock pioneered by U2 and Big Country, and a ghostly "Mansion on the Hill," introduced with words that emphasized its autobiographical nature: "This is a song about when I was a kid. My father was always transfixed by money. He used to drive out of town and look at this big white house. It became a kinda touchstone for me. Now, when I dream, sometimes I'm on the outside looking in—and sometimes I'm the man on the inside."

So the show oscillated, old songs ("The River"), new rockers

("No Surrender," "Glory Days"), and *Nebraska* numbers alternately presented as fictional ("Highway Patrolman") and as a species of autobiography ("Used Cars"). The show didn't really have a structure yet—or at least it was hard to follow the logic with which it was constructed, to fathom how each song was supposed to set up the next. (The sequencing had been the most original and unsettling quality of previous Springsteen shows.) But that wasn't surprising, because this tour presented an enormous amount of new material, far too much to digest immediately, even for someone as adept and instinctive as Bruce Springsteen. Between *Nebraska* and *Born in the U.S.A.*, there were twenty-two new songs to integrate. The band had two new players whose skills needed to be weighed and balanced with the others'. Beyond this, there were many technical differences. Everyone in the band except Tallent had the added mobility of playing with wireless amplification (and Garry would soon surrender his guitar cord, too), while Roy Bittan now played as much synthesizer as grand piano. There was a new lighting designer, Jeff Ravitz. The stage had a subtly different configuration than the one used on past tours. Bruce could hardly have known what his own new physique was really capable of. And of course, above all else, there was the altered content of all those new songs, which pushed the meaning of the show in unexpected directions—directions that often ran directly counter to the enthusiasms of the audience.

The day before, Brian DePalma had taken Bruce and the band through their paces, working with three cameras through eleven setups and several hours of repetitious shooting and posing, then polishing off the afternoon of lip-syncing with a live version of the "Detriot Medley," a sequence of Mitch Ryder and Little Richard hits. Bruce stayed cheerful and high-spirited through all that, but during the first night's show he seemed about as vulnerable and introspective as a pop star could be, struggling to find a structure for the show. The only time he projected a clear ebullience was for "Dancing in the Dark," which he ran through twice for DePalma's cameras. Although it surely had its exciting high points, moments of sheer fun, more than anything the first show of the *Born in the U.S.A.* tour was a struggle. Bruce did five songs from *Nebraska,* eight from *Born in the U.S.A.* For the most part, their purpose in the context of this performance was unfocused, cloudy, and uncertain.

Even so, there were galvanizing song sequences that came together in a radiant exemplification of what Bruce had been through and what he was pushing for. "Bobby Jean" was open, spacious, driving, *modern,* and it set up the wordless moans of "Backstreets" exquisitely. In introducing "My Hometown," Bruce put his finger on a lot of what he was fumbling to say elsewhere: "When I started playing guitar I had a couple of ideas in mind. One was to avoid all responsibility as much as I could for the rest of my life. We used to sit in bars and say, 'If I could just get this down.' The other idea was to get girls.

"Well, that idea didn't work out. Seems as you get older, you just can't get outta the way . . . I thought I was writing this song about the town I grew up in, but it turned out to be about responsibility. Whether it's done here or thousands of miles away, it's done in your name, and you share the shame and the glory." He followed that song with "Born in the U.S.A." and then, with his teeth gritted hard and staring straight into hot white spotlights, brought the first set to a brilliant, bitter close with "Badlands."

He brought the message back one more time, during the first encores, saying simply, "When I grew up, rock and roll was delivering a simple message: 'Let freedom ring!' But remember, you gotta fight for it!" then launching into a medley of "Born to Run" and "Street Fighting Man." Singing "What can a poor boy do/'Cept sing in a rock and roll band?", he emptied the question of Mick Jagger's cynical irony and brought it back home with bite.

Springsteen's reasons for choosing that song said a lot about what the show had to be and what he hoped to accomplish with it. "I just picked it out of the air a few days ago during rehearsal," he said. "It seems to fit in with the whole thing, for some reason. You come crashing down—it has that edge-of-the-cliff thing when you hit it. And it's funny; it's got humor to it.

"That's just me kinda being a fan. But that song did seem to fit in with the whole thing—with the whole feeling of the show and where it was kinda going. That one line, 'What can a poor boy do but sing in a rock and roll band?' is one of the greatest rock and roll lines of all time. It just seemed right for me to do it. In that spot of the night it just fits in there. It's just so driving, man. After 'Born to Run,' we got to go up. That's the trick. 'Cause it's hard to find songs for our encore. You gotta go up, and then you gotta go up again."

But then again, the other encores were some of the longest songs in his repertoire: the Detroit medley, "Rosalita," "Jungleland," great in themselves perhaps, but dissolving as much focus as they created. Did they take the show up? Yes, but in the end the encores became a parable of exhaustion, too damn much of a good thing.

However much instinct Bruce brought to the enterprise of each concert tour, he was clearly going to have to work hard to make this new set of circumstances reach the heights of his previous tours. To any random observer, the first show in St. Paul, so typical of the run of shows in the first few weeks of the tour, was nothing but excellent. But to the seasoned eye, it lacked the seamless, almost effortless quality of construction that earlier Springsteen concerts possessed.

You could almost imagine that Bruce wanted it that way. The show was no different than his current attitude about recordings and merchandising and publicity. All indicated that Springsteen wanted to *try things*. Control remained the central issue of his approach to his work, but now he was ready to try controlling less regimented situations; he wanted to take bolder risks.

The same day that the tour began, Columbia issued a "dance mix" of "Dancing in the Dark" on a twelve-inch disc. "Dancing in the Dark" was already getting mixed reactions from the hard-core Springsteen aficionados, many of whom disdained its more limber and modern rhythms. The fact that "Dancing in the Dark" expanded Springsteen's appeal might have been just the problem from their point of view. But the dance mix, concocted by producer Arthur Baker, spun hard-core Springsteen buffs to a frenzy. As Bruce put it, "People kind of get a rigid view of certain things."

Springsteen's Columbia A&R man, Joe McEwen, himself a

former critic and deejay, was eager to have Baker rework the song, as he'd already done successfully with Cyndi Lauper's "Girls Just Want to Have Fun."

Baker and Springsteen were at once a perfect and a perfectly unlikely match. Baker grew up in Boston and went to school in one of that city's few integrated high schools. There he acquired an expertise in dance-floor beats totally belied by his beefy, long-haired appearance. Baker revolutionized dance music when he moved to New York and began producing records—"Looking for the Perfect Beat" and "Planet Rock" by Afrika Bambaataa and the Soul Sonic Force and I.O.U.'s "Freez" and Planet Patrol's "Play at Your Own Risk"—ushering in an era of electronic beats and computer effects over hard-edged street raps.

Beginning with the Lauper record in 1984, Baker and his partner John Robie began remixing pop hits, radically restructuring each composition at the studio console, dismantling some sections of a song to its skeleton, doubling other parts, stretching and extending and bending the record into a danceable commentary upon itself. The result was almost a kind of computer-based rock criticism. It was also startling and a hell of a lot of fun.

Hearing what Baker was up to, Springsteen wanted in on it. "The entire thing is Arthur Baker. He's really an artist," he said. "It was fun to just give him a song and see what his interpretation of it would be. I was always so protective of my music that I was hesitant to do much with it at all. Now I feel my stuff isn't as fragile as I thought."

Springsteen wasn't dropping out of the process, though. He made sure that he was present for Baker's remix session. "Arthur's a character, a great guy. He had another fellow [Robie] with him, and they were really pretty wild. They'd get on that mixing board and just crank them knobs, you know. The meters were goin' wild. His overdubs were kind of connected to my songs. He would put in something that sounded like a glock or a twangy guitar. When I heard it, I just thought it was fun. This was kind of wild, man—this guy, he's got an unchained imagination. I thought it was real creative. You've gotta do different things and try stuff." Added Chuck Plotkin, "Some of the things that Arthur did on it we could very well have incorporated into the album version, and would have been glad to."

Baker was equally eager to work on the song. "First time I heard it, it freaked me out, because I could relate to the lyrics, and I just heard in my head all these parts that seemed to be missing." He took the master into the Power Station and rethought the song with Bruce looking on. Working with John Robie, engineer Chris Lord-Alge, and an electronic percussion team called the Latin Rascals (Albert Cabrera and Tony Moran), he overdubbed "tom-toms, dulcimer, glockenspiel, background vocals, sort of a bass synth part, a horn synthesizer part, and also some gunshots."

There was more than one purpose to creating such a melange around *Born in the U.S.A.*'s most apposite, modern, and catchy track. As Baker pointed out, "The one last frontier Bruce has is obviously black people. I heard someone say that he had more black people onstage than in his audience." The exaggeration was very slight. Baker felt he not only knew the reason, he had the cure. "It's not like these people will come out in droves and flocks and be into Bruce, but he should realize that all these people are missing what he has to say because they can't relate to the music. Prince and all these other acts that are black but are doing rock and roll, they just know that they can relate to everybody. It isn't even a matter of selling more records, because once you're selling five million, what's the difference? It's just that it would be cool if black people knew Springsteen like white people know Prince."

As a good American populist, Springsteen was sensitive to the issue; it was disturbing, not ironic, to see exclusively white faces at a concert that was so concerned with injustice and inequity in America (a nation more than a third black and Hispanic). But populism by itself provided no solution, especially given the basic economic inequality that made even the Jacksons' tour—which presented itself as a triumph for black Americans, in that one of their own had become the world's single most popular entertainer—play to a crowd about ninety percent white.

But it wasn't just high ticket prices and low minority incomes that kept blacks away from Bruce Springsteen's shows and prevented that community from exhibiting much interest in his records. Nor was it skin color per se: Daryl Hall and John Oates, Boy George of Culture Club, and many other white singers were extremely popular with black audiences. The real dividing line was Springsteen's nervous aversion to syncopation, which he conscientiously avoided. It was hard to figure out why—whether Bruce feared some innate lack of ability in dealing with rhythmic nuance beyond a basic backbeat or whether years of trying to whip a band of white boys into shape to play with some semblance of soul had simply led him astray. If Springsteen had been more of a typical singer-songwriter, if the root of his music had been commercial folk music or even British rock, the lack of appeal would have been no surprise. But the basis of his music was soul, and in spirit, it was meant to be all-encompassing, so the lily white composition of his crowd was a little frustrating and embarrassing.

Baker alleviated those problems with a radical restructuring of "Dancing in the Dark" that kept its darkness of mood while making the music lighter on its feet. The twelve-inch contained three versions of his work: a full-length (6:09) "Blaster Mix," a "radio" edit (4:50), and a "dub" with much of the vocal dropped out (which clocked in at five and a half minutes). The result, wrote *Newsweek*'s Jim Miller, "recasts the song as a rock and roll symphony in the spirit of 'Born to Run.' " Others compared it to the Phil Spector records on which "Born to Run" was based.

And no wonder. Springsteen now sang against an electronic background of voices and drums that exploded in the spacious mix like a bomb, with glockenspiel synthesizer effects shattering like glass against sharp guitar, his key lines—"You sit around getting older"; "Heeeey, baby!"; "This gun's for hire"—doubled, echoed, isolated, broken down to syllables, and reinforced by choral repetition. By the time he got to the last verse—"Stay on the streets of this town/And they'll be carvin' you up all right . . ."—Springsteen sounded even lonelier and more vulnerable than he did on the original track. Now when he cried, "There's somethin' happenin' somewhere . . ." there was no reassuring "baby, I just know there is" tagged on. If you listened closely enough, you found that Baker had stripped the smiling face from "Dancing in the Dark" and revealed a death's head lurking beneath, and did it in a way that pulled you from your seat to dance until breath ran out.

It was a monumental achievement, making a great record even greater. It even sold fairly well, although it won Bruce no visible long-term allegiance from the black pop audience, even after Baker did similar (and in some ways, even more striking) remixes of "Cover Me" and "Born in the U.S.A." Again, the primary reason was probably musical—in the strict sense, Springsteen's basic approach remained adamantly unswinging.

The sad part was that the Springsteen cult—by now beginning to resent its stature as a diminishing proportion of his audience anyway—liked it even less than the original. This left Arthur Baker annoyed, even angry. "I got really offended. What is so different? It has a fucking glockenspiel, which Bruce has used before, background vocals . . . it's no different. See, if any of those mixes had come out before, with no one knowing the other version, no one would have said a word. Even Bruce says it."

What Bruce actually said was predictably more measured and conciliatory. "I figured that a lot of people would like it and that the people that didn't like it would get over it. My audience is not that fragile, you know. They can take it," he said, then shifted gears to discuss what was really on his mind—his own altered approach. "I'm just into seeing some different things. I could easily go out and do just what I did before. But now we're playing outdoors on this tour, which I hadn't done before. And we did the blaster thing and the video thing. I want to learn it myself. I want to just step out and see what works. If something doesn't work, that's okay, and if something does, great. In ten years I've built up a relationship with my audience." Unfortunately, during this period of tremendous artistic and personal growth, as he stepped forward to take on challenges and responsibilities on which every rock great before him had choked, Bruce was opposed almost every step of the way by the very cult that proposed to protect the integrity of his work.

Bruce ignored the claims of his retrograde older fans; that doesn't mean he was unaware of what they thought or insensitive to their attitudes. He told Chet Flippo that songs like "Born to Run" and "Thunder Road" were among "the most emotional moments of the night" because "I can see all those people and that song to them is like—that's their song, man. A lot of times they mean so much to me now because they mean so much to the audience. They just take over. And that's where it becomes more powerful. They're like little touchstones for the people. And that's a great compliment. I like it when the lights are up, because you can see so much from people's faces. That's what it's about."

Right then, however, he was more concerned with fashioning new meaning from the old structure of his concerts, with exploring new recording possibilities, with speaking to the vast young video audience, fixed on getting over to ever larger groups of people without losing the essence of his message or, by the same token, leaving people stranded on the path that he had previously taken to the despairing outer darkness of *Nebraska*. That is, he wanted to communicate a remarkably idealistic sense of possibility balanced by a very worldly knowledge of restriction, and nobody and nothing would hold him back from expressing either side of the equation.

11 GROWIN' UP

66"This is for all the *old* fans out there," says Bruce with a grin. He isn't thinking of age; he's referring to the hundreds or maybe thousands of fans out there who are attending their third or tenth or fortieth Springsteen show, the hard core who've followed him since *Greetings from Asbury Park*, or *Born to Run*, or at least *Darkness on the Edge of Town*.

There's no way to tell how many of the 100,000 spread out before him in the Coliseum are veteran concertgoers. Certainly it is proportionately far fewer than in the arena shows of 1984, when (especially in New Jersey and California) it sometimes seemed that the tiny turnover in the crowd from night to night gave Bruce an audience as predictable and homogenous as the one that attends an urban parish's 6:00 A.M. mass. The arena shows of 1984 sold out so rapidly in part because the cult was now large enough to fill a substantial portion of an arena and wanted to come back night after night; the same number of cultists in a stadium soaked up a far smaller percentage of the tickets.

One reason for making the move to stadium shows was Springsteen's need to keep from being strangled creatively by this cult (big as it is, there's no other term that accurately describes it in the mass context). He needed the artistic challenge the vast spaces of the football fields afforded, but he also had to open the gates to begin to preach beyond the converted. Many cultists had taken Springsteen's resistance to each move in scale up the concert ladder, balking at the transition from clubs and theaters to sports arenas as much as he'd hesitated before taking the stadium plunge, as an ideological standard. When new conditions encouraged him to try an all-stadium tour, these fans felt some degree of betrayal, accusing him of abandoning the pledge of audience intimacy that had always been the key to his appeal.

Instead, the result has been a newer, fresher relationship between Bruce and his listeners, without altering the meaning of the show very much. You might even argue that the infusion of new and less attentive blood has enhanced the concerts, simply by forcing Springsteen to struggle to make sure he gets across with the darker parts of the program. The arena gigs could have been done on autopilot, and it says something about the cult that it didn't notice this. The old fans come to see the enactment of a ritual and feel threatened when it changes. In this case, however, the creator of the ritual is aware that not to change is to watch the spirit behind it die.

But even among the new, expanded audience, the level of Boss recidivism is high, judging from the wave of applause and cheers that greets Bruce's dedication to the "old fans." Those who know only *Born in the U. S. A.* must be mystified by a great deal of this show (where have all these songs been hidden?), but even those who've traced the story back as far as *Born to Run* will be unfamiliar with the song the band now begins.

"Growin' Up" is a song from Bruce's first album, and like so much of *Greetings from Asbury Park,* you can't tell much about it from the half-hearted recording. It seems just a jumble of images more or less pertaining to the fantasies of youth, with a single gem that leaps out as a kind of Springsteenian signature: "I swear I found the key to the universe in the engine of an old parked car."

But live, in a full band arrangement that ranges from tinkling to thunderous, the song gains a life. It's only when the power of the music is enhanced, buttressed by big drums and crashing guitars, underpinned by glockenspiel and trebly grand piano, that the lyrics snap into focus and the fantasy of the lyrics suddenly seems pointed. This is Bruce Springsteen's story, announced in a whisper and quickly rising to a roar, and if you know a little about what he's been through—that his presence in school was welcomed by neither nuns nor fellow students, that things weren't much friendlier at home—you can hear it as a kind of secret autobiography, written before he had a grip on the real thing. It may not have been his alone—"I combed my hair 'til it looked just right" is a sentiment not unfamiliar even to the likes of Rod Stewart—but it was certainly his in particular:

> I hid in the clouded wrath of the crowd
> When they said, 'Come down,' I threw up

"On my school shoes!" Springsteen interjects with a shout, spun away in the ecstasy of the moment. But when the first verse ends, he brings the music down. Now only the glock and piano continue behind him, repeating their little melodic riffs over and over again.

Veterans know what's coming as soon as the opening notes are heard. Over the years, Springsteen has opened the song up with a legendary series of shaggy dog monologues ranging from episodic stories of parental conflict to an actual encounter with God (who explained that Moses forgot the Eleventh Commandment: "Let it rock"). But mostly these tales concern the myth of how Bruce the Loser discovered rock and roll magic—and his true identity. There have been various vehicles toward this realization, including wild bears, gypsy fortune-tellers, and drag-racing UFOs. (God was not such a vehicle; he just told Bruce that he was on the right track.) On this tour, "Growin' Up" has evolved into a skit, with assorted crew members in the cast.

In the age of high tech rock extravaganzas, when it's hard to find an indoor show without lasers and computerized sets, Springsteen's skit is striking for its amateurishness. The couple of costumes used are rented or homemade; there are no sets; the visual effects come from the show's regular lighting rig; the few

props are not even electric, much less electronic. It's just the
same Boss and his buddies, hamming it up like any high school
talent night. The comedy is broad: Bruce and Clarence now
appear less as Huck and Jim than as Laurel and Hardy or, from
time to time, Fred Flintstone and Barney Rubble, though there's
some Ralph Kramden and Ed Norton and even some Yogi Bear
and Booboo in there, too. The sketch works off joking asides to
the audience and a "this'll get 'em" attitude. Springsteen is no
more reluctant to go for the obvious here than in his rock and roll
songs. And that's why it works.

With the piano and glockenspiel ticking away measure after
measure, Springsteen begins to speak.

"Now *there I was*. I was still in high school, but I wasn't doin'
too good. I was doin' bad in my studies, and they sent me down to
see the guidance counselor. I walked in and he said [*in a
threatening voice*], 'Mr. Springsteen, what seems to be your
problem?' So I said, 'Well, sir, it's like, you see, I don't have any
interest in anything. I don't know what I want to do with myself. I
don't care what's going on around me. I ain't got any faith, I don't
have any hope in anything; I don't have any *close interpersonal
relationship with a member of the opposite SEX*. I don't have,
uh . . . " He pauses, scratches his cheek, rubs his hair. "He said,
'No, that's too big a problem. You better go home and talk to your
folks about it.'

"So I went home and I went in the kitchen, and my pop was in
there and I said, 'Pop, man, I got sent home from school. I been
in a lotta trouble lately. I really gotta talk to you about something.
I don't know what's gonna happen with me. I don't have any
interest in anything. I daydream in class alla time, and I don't
have any faith in anything—in myself. I don't have any hope in
anything.' And he said, 'Willya get me another beer outta the ice
box?'

"So that was it," he says, picking up the microphone and
walking off to his left a couple of paces. "I decided I was gonna
do myself in. I was gonna *end it all*. I was gonna say, 'Goodbye,
cruel world!' Yeah!

"So I got out and I hitchhiked down to Asbury Park. I was
gonna drown myself. I was gonna jump in the ocean and drown

myself." He sits at the edge of the stage. "I was sittin' there on the boardwalk, contemplatin' the water temperature, when all of a sudden, in the distance, this big, handsome dude came walkin' by." Into the spotlight strolls Clarence Clemons, derelict beefcake personified in white shirt and slacks with a white cap askew on his head. Bruce cracks up at the sight. Clarence sits down.

"He kinda sat down next to me; I started sayin' my prayers. But we kinda got talkin'. I was tellin' him all about my problems. Then he started tellin' me all about his problems. Then we cried on each other's shoulders for a while." They do that, mugging shamelessly. "But we decided we'd make a good team and we became partners."

"That's right, that's right, that's right," they tell one another, vigorously shaking hands.

"And Clarence, he said that he knew a gypsy lady that could help us out with our troubles. So over to the gypsy we went," Bruce continues. He rises and walks to his right, over past Danny Federici's keyboards, where sits a gypsy lady (Landau's managerial associate Barbara Carr, togged in a gold turban and flowered print dress), seated at a table, waving her hands over an illuminated crystal ball.

"It was late at night; the boardwalk was deserted. We walked in, we paid our two-fifty each—I had to loan Clarence his two-fifty—and she looked into the crystal ball and she said, 'You guys are in a lotta trouble.' " The gypsy nods wisely. "Paid another two-fifty—I didn't get it back yet either—and she looked into the crystal ball, and then she said, 'You boys are gonna go on a real long trip. You're gonna seek out new forms of life. You're gonna explore new worlds. You're gonna go where no men have ever gone before . . . and stay twice as long. And have a lotta fun doin' it, too.' And she gave us a map to the secret of the world, and she said if we followed that map at midnight, we'd find the answer to all our troubles."

Clarence tucks the map into his shirt, and they return to center stage.

"So that night we got into Clarence's Oldsmobile and we started drivin' south down Route Nine. South through the rain. Down through *Lake*wood, down through *Free*hold, down through

Tom's River. And a hurricane hit! And then a tor-nah-do blew across the highway. And then a blizzard hit. And then a heat wave broke. And then the roof flew off the car; and then we got two flat tires; and then the fenders flew off; and then the engine block cracked; and then the carburetor went; and then the windows blew out. And then . . . and then . . . and then! THE RADIO BROKE!"

They shout this final disaster in unison and fall flat on their faces, pounding their heads. Spasm completed, they slowly rise to their knees. "You know what that's like," says Bruce.

"But there we were—on the side of this dark dirt road. And according to the map, what we were looking for was just on the other side of those woods." He points to his left, and he and Clarence reluctantly get back on their feet and move in the direction of a huge tree (Clarence's personal assistant, Terry Magovern).

"So into the forest we went. It was spooky in there," Bruce stage-whispers in mock-terrified tones that wouldn't frighten a three-year-old. "There were sounds comin' from all over the place." The audience picks up the cue and makes pseudospooky noises. "Sounded like werewolves." From the audience, somewhat sinister snarls. "Sounded like homicidal cows." The crowd obliges with massive mooing. "Sounded like mad dogs barkin'." The fans approximate barking. "Sounded like the JERSEY DEVIL out there!" At the mention of this mythical creature from the South Jersey swamps, the crowd ditches pretense and simply hollers its lungs out.

Meanwhile Clarence is cringing behind Bruce, who with back bent in an exploratory posture, slowly creeps across the stage. He addresses Clarence as he stalks.

"Now, Big Man, I ain't never heard of no killer beasts like in New Jersey or nothin'. Did you? No? I hearda killer hamburgers but no killer beasts." He straightens up some, and they totter back toward stage right.

"I think we're safe out here, don't you?" Clarence denies this by vigorously shaking his head. From behind them, two bears appear (Bruce's aide, Jim McDuffie, and soundman Tom "Midget" Foelinger). The larger bear, a bit shorter than Bruce, wears a battered beige fishing hat. The smaller bear, diminutive next to Clarence, wears a blue LAPD baseball cap.

"I think I heard something behind us," says Bruce, and he and Clarence turn together to look over their left shoulders. The bears follow suit and therefore theoretically remain unseen. "I think I heard something behind us," Bruce says again, and again the quartet turns in unison.

"I think I heard something," Bruce whispers a third time, and now he and Clarence begin to whimper, Springsteen sounding just like Stan Laurel in his most fretful scenes. He grimaces piteously for the video screens. Suddenly Bruce and Clarence wheel about. The bears are caught by surprise, but it's the Boss and the Big Man who are startled. "Whoa!" they holler; the bears and Clarence scatter to the corners of the stage. Bruce barely holds his ground.

"And all of a sudden," he continues, "up behind us came these two big, man-eatin' bears. But instead of jumpin' on us and making us their dinner, they were actin' kinda friendly." The bears make anthropomorphic gestures of affection, the larger one petting and stroking Bruce's arm and shoulder.

"And they said that they weren't mean but that they were just lonely, and that they'd been out in the woods for a long time by themselves, after they escaped from the circus, 'cause they got tired of livin' in them cages. And they said that if we'd be their friends, they'd help us find what we were lookin' for." Together the foursome begins to stalk the stage.

"And so back into the forest we went. And all of a sudden the clouds pulled away from the moon, and there in a clearing we saw the answer to our quest."

A pair of pinpoint white spots hit Bruce's guitar and Clarence's sax. The bears retrieve this equipment, the big bear bringing Bruce the horn and the little one carrying the guitar over to Clarence. Bruce puts the sax strap over his shoulder and tries to strum it. Clarence blows into the neck of the guitar. Nothing. They look at one another and exchange instruments.

Bruce walks back to center stage, strapping on his guitar. He looks lovingly at the instrument, as if it really is the answer to his prayers (as, of course, it really was). For the first time since the story began, he replaces the microphone in its stand.

"And then we said goodbye to the bears, for the last time." He turns and hugs the big bear, then the smaller one. "And as we stood there in the moonlight, we knew that everything was gonna be all right. Because . . . because . . . when we touched"—he and Clarence stretch to tap their fingertips against one another, and lights and music explode and the song romps to its conclusion, Bruce concluding (as he always must) by interpolating a line from Chuck Berry and John Lennon: "And it was bye-bye New Jersey, we were *air*borne."

The song complete, he stands bathed once more in sweat. Then he looks out into the dark and a huge silly smile breaks across his face.

"And here we are tonight," he says, portentously as a five-year-old at the conclusion of a Christmas pageant, then twirls to count off the next number.

12 MONEY CHANGES EVERYTHING

"No substantial problem of art is soluble by art alone."
—HAROLD ROSENBERG

T he most significant change in performance Springsteen made during the early weeks of the *Born in the U.S.A.* tour was almost overlooked. He'd ended his long holdout against playing outdoors. (He'd first been approached about playing stadiums in 1976 by Philadelphia promoter Larry Magid.) But it was a tentative move at first. Bruce was fearful of a loss of control as well as about a lack of intimacy, doubtful about the havoc that those wide open spaces might wreak on his sound, and wary of the problems of communicating with audiences more than a hundred yards away.

Of course, he'd adopted exactly the same attitude about playing indoor sports arenas (and with good reason, since his initial foray into those venues, when he'd served as an opening act for Chicago in 1973, was the one disastrous tour of his career). But there were some precedents for succeeding in indoor arenas; *nobody* had ever created a satisfying outdoor rock and roll show. So the tour still ducked the massive football and baseball stadiums that other acts who'd reached Springsteen's level played exclusively. But an expanded audience and the threat of arena stagnation meant it was time to try something.

During the first month of the tour he played three open-air

facilities, the "sheds," as they're known in the concert business, at Alpine Valley, Wisconsin, and Saratoga, New York, which each drew an average of 25,000 for one-nighters, and Toronto's CNE Grandstand, a 22,000-seater across the street from the ball park housing the baseball Blue Jays. (Springsteen did three shows in Toronto—and no wonder, since *Born in the U.S.A.* was, if anything, more popular in Canada than the United States, eventually becoming the Northland sales equivalent of *Thriller*.)

Springsteen had played a "shed" on the 1981 homecoming tour: Denver's Red Rocks, a beautiful natural amphitheater in the Rockies, although he'd agreed to do that show only after weeks of cajoling by Landau and booking agents Frank Barsalona and Barry Bell. It rained that night, and Springsteen tried to talk the audience out of continuing, vowing to return the next night when the weather was better. But the proposition was shouted down in a voice vote, and the show continued in an off-and-on downpour.

It poured at Saratoga, too. The site's second biggest crowd in history no more wanted to stop than the Colorado fans had. Alpine Valley went fine, but Bruce found even good weather less than prepossessing in Toronto. The Grandstand seating was configured like a fairgrounds, so that the crowd was spread out before him broader than deep, which created weird sight angles and strange sound trajectories for both audience and performer. When the tour rolled into Detroit, its next stop, to play the Joe Louis Arena, Springsteen was relieved. "Man, it's great to be back inside again," he exulted backstage. And that feeling was confirmed by the shows, which were among the first in which the set really gelled, helped along a lot by the fact that "Born in the U.S.A." had finally asserted itself as the permanent set opener.

Those shows *had* to gel, because they were the prelude to the ten-night stand at the Byrne Meadowlands Arena in New Jersey. The incredible demand that created this unparalleled stand— Bruce would play to 210,000 customers over two weeks— symptomized the reasons that larger facilities (which only existed outdoors) had to be considered. The Meadowlands gigs were oversubscribed by a factor of ten, meaning that had they decided to fulfill the entire demand, the E Street Band would have been

stuck in that one town—albeit their home turf—for several
months. Something had to give.

Nevertheless, the Jersey stand was a love-in rivaled only by
the M.U.S.E. concerts and the Meadowlands shows of 1981.
Each night, ticket holders came out hours early to hang out in the
parking lot, where they barbecued, sunbathed, threw Frisbees,
squared off in touch football matches, and played Springsteen
tapes through their car and portable stereo systems. By showtime
the house seemed ready to implode, and when Bruce snapped off
the tight-jawed cadence count for "Born in the U.S.A.," the roar
of adulation seemed sure to be heard clear to Camden.

"At first, watching Bruce Springsteen vault into the raging
closing verse to 'The Promised Land' . . . I thought the band's
supporting harmonies sounded uncommonly forcible—something
like the roar of orchestrated thunder," wrote Mikal Gilmore.
"Then, after a few moments, I realized that vocal blare wasn't
issuing from on stage, but rather from above and below and
beside and around me: from 20,000 young rock fans (many
decked out in red, white and blue, to honor the hard-bitten
Americana that Bruce's new music espouses), gathered here in
New Jersey's Meadowlands to celebrate the public return of a
regional hero."

And each night, after the audience soloed on "its" verse of
"Hungry Heart," Bruce reciprocated. "That's *my people!*" he
would exult. He had good reason: As Robert Christgau pointed
out in the *Village Voice,* "the fans . . . sang not just refrains but
whole verses back to the stage whenever their spokesman gave
them an opening, which couldn't have happened if hundreds or
even thousands weren't singing along at almost every moment."

Springsteen gave these crucial shows a sense of event, helped
along by special guests, including Gary Bonds, Southside
Johnny, the Who's John Entwistle, and, on the final evening,
Little Steven Van Zandt and the Miami Horns. Little Steven's
return, even in a cameo role, was possible so soon after he'd quit
the band only because Lofgren fit in so well that it was clear his
appearance didn't signal any change of heart. When Steve and
Bruce rejoined their voices for duets on "Two Hearts" and a
hastily arranged, raw but moving rendition of Dobie Gray's "Drift
Away," the full story of their comradeship was obvious to every-

one in ways that neither "Bobby Jean" nor "No Surrender" could ever tell. Dobie Gray's anthem spoke for both of them: "Thanks for the joy that you've given me/I want you to know I believe in your song."

For newcomer Nils Lofgren, the Meadowlands shows were both acid test and revelation. "It was very intense, certainly the most intense run of shows in one place I've ever been involved with—really intense and rewarding," Nils told Bud Scoppa and Don Perretta. "I remember it being *terrible* at the time—the worst hotel on the whole tour, and we were there for a month! But it was a special time for me, because it was so important to the tour. I mean, every show is important, but those ten! And then the last show—Steven came to the show and jammed, which was really nice. Made me feel good. It was good to see him out there.

"Usually after a show you feel really good until you go to sleep; you enjoy it, and then it's on to the next show. But I remember after that show we were up all night long, and I got on the first plane home because the next show was in Washington, D.C., where I live. I'm used to getting up at that time of day and starting work—learning different songs and getting on with my work—but that morning I felt so good. For the first time, instead of worrying about practicing, I could just relax. That was a real big turning point for me."

Lofgren had put his finger on a nerve. The lengthy run at the Meadowlands was in some senses as stultifying as it was rewarding; part of the idea of touring with a rock band is its hit-and-run quality, the constant moving from town to town, barnstorming 'round the planet, not settling in for Broadway-length stays. As Bruce put it, "To me, the idea is you get a band, write some songs, and go out to people's towns. It's my favorite thing; it's like a circus. You just kind of roll on, walk into somebody's town and bang! It's heart to heart. Something can happen to you; something can happen to them." The fact that dispensing music this way in an age of instantaneous electronic access is a complete anachronism is beside the point. Moving on is what touring is about; staying in one place for so long violates the concept. Although maybe that meant a new concept was necessary—something that lingered longer.

Anyway, anyone who experienced the full complement of

Meadowlands shows was as likely to be enervated as energized. The shows were epic in length and the crowds were ecstatic, but that only emphasized the way in which Bruce had to struggle to make them meaningful, to undercut the predictability of ritual and get *his* meaning across.

You could argue, as Mikal Gilmore did, that "the real glory of Springsteen's rise became increasingly apparent in the living drama of his 1984 nationwide tour, in which he . . . bound mass audiences together into an emboldened community that eventually took on a character and zeal all its own." But what made the process dramatic was that it was such a near thing. For Gilmore, seeing Springsteen perform "Born in the U.S.A." before those Jersey crowds meant witnessing "a segment of America coming face to face with the acerbic realities and undisguised goodness and hope that bind together the colors these fans waved." But that omitted several crucial facts. Many of those rock fans "decked out in red, white, and blue" weren't dressed up "to honor the hard-bitten Americana that Bruce's new music espouses," but to purvey the same sense of jingoism Gilmore decried when it dominated that summer's other events: the Los Angeles Olympics, the desperate Democrats' Ellis Island histrionics, and the orgy of pseudopatriotism with which the Republicans moved to deify Ronald Reagan at the ballot box.

None of this was Bruce Springsteen's fault exactly. He was doing what he'd always done. But that didn't really address the new context his greater success created. Springsteen was pouring his heart out, at least the part of his heart that he dared to show and the audience deigned to notice, but it wasn't always clear where the process was leading. It was hard to see these shows as creative activity in the way that previous Springsteen tours had been; instead, they were celebrations of previous events or dramatizations of public assent in the star-making process.

Such problems are easier to spot retrospectively. During those months in 1984, Bruce Springsteen's across-the-board stardom was blossoming; for the first time his image blasted past the bounds of rock and roll into mainstream attention. It wasn't just New Jersey; across America "Bossmania" ruled the airwaves and print media, and, as *Purple Rain* began to flag, dominated record store attention, too. Suddenly it wasn't just a mammoth cult of postadolescents and young adults who hummed Springsteen songs on their way to work. It was Mom and Pop and teens and grade school kids who found "Dancing in the Dark" and its Top Ten successor, "Cover Me," irresistible.

In a way, Bruce Springsteen was no different than Elvis Presley, Bing Crosby, Michael Jackson, or Paul McCartney. He made concessions for a run at the top. Except Springsteen, so deeply imbued with a sense of tradition that he was in a sense the direct inheritor of each of those precursors, was more aware that what he was doing was compromising.

The compromises didn't involve music so much as media. Springsteen still did the show that he'd always done, give or take the new material and a slight unbending in order to ride out the mania that couldn't control itself—he hadn't previously faced an audience composed purely of screaming teenagers, but that kind of adulation was now a nightly factor. Still, what remained remarkable about Bruce's performances was their constancy— his ability to continue eschewing high-tech geegaws and his earnest efforts to undercut hero worship with dark mood pieces and pessimistic philosophizing. It was, in the main, a triumphant show and one that cashed in on a promise that many thought no longer a possibility. As Christgau wrote, "It seems a simple thing—articulating the contradictions of freedom and powerlessness in America for both teenagers who still believe they're born to run and adults who know where they end up. But though many have set out to do it, nobody else has succeeded before cynicism and foolishness struck. And without doubt it's Bruce's passion for maintaining contact with his fans, his people, that has made the difference, to him and to them."

In media relations, however, Springsteen had begun to cut a few corners. "No, your eyes are not deceiving you," wrote Patrick Goldstein of the *Los Angeles Times* just after the Meadowlands run. "That *was* Bruce Springsteen on the cover of *People* magazine . . . and being interviewed on 'Entertainment Tonight' . . . and yes, believe it or not, on MTV, promising that some lucky fan will get to win a week on tour as a roadie 'if you earn it!' "

That Springsteen was expected to be above such crass

attention seeking was a little silly. After all, he *was* a rock and roll star, and anyway, it's not like there was a lot of alternative: Since *The River*, the already wobbly rock press had further deteriorated. Yet Goldstein had a point. Bruce's stature as the most insightful rock interview subject since Pete Townshend was partly based on being interviewed by like-minded reporters and critics. Although he'd spoken briefly to a good one, Don McLeese of the *Chicago Sun-Times*, in St. Paul, there simply weren't that many of the old crowd still working the beat. Besides, Bruce simply didn't have that much energy for interviews. That being the case, both his management and CBS were steering him toward mass circulation enterprises: MTV, *USA Today*, "Entertainment Tonight," *People*. Springsteen himself felt too preoccupied to handle a full-scale *Rolling Stone* interview, which remained the vehicle best suited for elaborating on his musical ideas.

The mass media interest in Springsteen coincided with his obvious interest in making music that reached beyond his hardcore rock audience, but that didn't mean that he had a very good idea of how to communicate what made him special to the newcomers—or that the mass media themselves had much idea what to do with such an odd fellow. His ambivalence about celebrity was legendary: "It's the old story of getting elected to a club you may not want to be a member of. But you are anyway. You're just another trivia question on 'Jeopardy' or something." From time to time he seemed to view every aspect of fame as the nastiest trap of all. "Celebrity. That's a distraction. It's false. That's the false image," he told Kit Rachlis in 1981.

Bruce dwelt heavily on the topic that summer of 1984 during an interview with British disc jockey Roger Scott. "One of the problems is that the audience and the performer have got to leave some room for each other to be human, or else they don't really deserve each other in a funny kinda way," he said. "I think the position you get in is unrealistic to begin with, 'cause you're just basically a guy. You know, you play the guitar and you do that good, and that's great, that's nice. If you do your job well, people like it and admire you for it or respect you for it or something; that's a plus. But . . . the idealizing of performers or politicians doesn't seem to make much sense. It's based on an image, and an image is always basically limiting and only a portion—and only the public portion—of that individual's personality. Which is not to say that it's necessarily false; it's just not complete.

"The thing is, the inspiration comes from the music. And the performer, he's the guy that's doin' the music, but he's not the thing itself. The thing itself is in the music—that's where the spirit of the thing is.

"I guess I basically feel it's like Elvis. People say they got disillusioned or something. Well, I don't feel that Elvis let anybody down. Personally, I don't think he owed anything to anybody. I think that, as it was, he did more for most people than they'll ever have done for them in their lives. The trouble that he ran into, that's the trouble that you run into. It's hard to keep your head above the water, but sometimes it's not right for people to judge the way that they do."

On the other hand, he set a higher standard for himself. "I feel that the night you look into your audience and you don't see yourself, and the night the audience looks at you and they don't see themselves, that's when it's all over, you know?

"I don't feel that people 'sold out.' I don't think Elvis sold out when he lived in Graceland—people never sold out by *buying* something. It wasn't ever something they bought; it was something they *thought* that changed. . . .

"My audience, I always hoped, would be all sorts of people— rich and poor, middle-class people; I don't feel like I'm singing to any one group of people. I don't want to put up those sort of walls. That's not really what our band is about."

Bruce might get away with such complex and relatively long-winded expositions on album-oriented radio and in the rock press. In the mass circulation magazines and on television, however, his philosophical bent and skill as a raconteur undercut him. Bruce tended to warm up to interviews slowly and to express himself verbally only in roundabout ways, often through painstaking and indirect parables. He needed a great deal of time and space to express himself correctly, and he simply wasn't given that in the quickie spaces provided by the mass media, who had to move on to the next celebrity.

Moreover, the people who were doing the interviews weren't especially interested in pursuing ideas or helping anybody—Springsteen or their audience—think things through. Barbara Howar of "Entertainment Tonight" knew nothing about rock and roll except the questions someone had written for her. While *USA Today* gave rock writer Bruce Pollock plenty of space, he presented only the most predictable quotes and commentary. *People* sent former *Rolling Stone* staff writer Chet Flippo, who did a fine interview (later printed in full in the rock magazine *Musician*), but the copy published in *People* was restricted to that magazine's personality gloss-over format. MTV's Mark Goodman was a professionally shallow boob who seemed most concerned that he look as hip as possible while also asking questions prepared by others; by the time Bruce's answers were cut up into the cable system's predigested bites, their substance was sucked dry. Worse, the "The Boss" contest, by trading on Springsteen's overused nickname, managed to trivialize the very idea of labor that Bruce's shows worked so hard to dignify.

But whatever the limitations of those entertainment business interviewers, the ultimate problem was Bruce's. It was exacerbated by his tremendous detachment from the ordinary processes and even desires of celebrities. As Landau said, "I don't think Bruce has ever identified with the conventional idea of success. And for that reason, he hasn't been overly affected by it." Every achievement of his career was predicated on doing things his way, which often meant outside the bounds of show business (or even rock and roll) convention. He got over in arenas, when so few others had, by transferring his show almost unchanged from theaters and clubs; he made hit records by ignoring trends if not technology; he'd reached Europeans by speaking to them as straight-from-the-shoulder as he did to Americans.

Furthermore, Bruce Springsteen maintained an extraordinary detachment from the ordinary pop celebrity's goals and values. He wasn't especially interested in great wealth, although he was surely glad not to have to worry about the rent; he did not confuse size with quality (otherwise he'd never have released *Nebraska*). If anything, he was concerned with being *too big*, because that implied a loss of control and a restriction of mobility that was foreign to his nature. Had he been in less of a risk-taking mood, who knows if he'd ever have released an album like *Born in the U.S.A.* The album most pop musicians would have struggled all their careers to create was for him an affordable luxury.

Springsteen hadn't done things his way simply out of pop star perversity. He'd moved at odd angles to stardom and skewed show business procedure out of a deep need to secure and maintain the integrity of his life and work. If he couldn't do something similar now, his rise to superstardom would prove a net loss. But almost everyone who had ever risen to these precincts of fame was overwhelmed by them, forced into going along with the game. There were no road maps to show him how to avoid the pitfalls of celebrity rigamarole and still maintain access to a mass audience. If he was looking for new adventures, this was one that really counted.

That story was being played out as a private, almost secret drama, behind the scenes of Bruce's near-canonization as the All-American Rock and Roll Star. However much the mass media may have misapprehended what he was really about, they very much wanted a slice of his success because it was so palatable on their terms. Here was a performer who refuted the idea of the rock star as an outlaw, whose earnestness was beyond question, whose humility seemed complete, who was without visible vices—didn't smoke, drink, dope, or womanize to excess—whose dress was ragged but comfortably familiar, who spoke of America at a time when the country was enduring a festival of Americana. Any editor or news director with a pulse had to want in on this story. So they all checked in, from the lowliest dailies and weeklies on up to the network news. And if what Bruce Springsteen was about had been misinterpreted before, the story of his life and career and success was now butchered beyond all belief.

On September 12, 1984, the "CBS Evening News" ran a two-minute piece by correspondent Bernard Goldberg about the Springsteen phenomenon. "Bruce Springsteen sings about Americans—blue-collar Americans trapped and suffocating in old broken down, small towns," Goldberg declared. "His songs are about working-class people, desperate people hanging on to the

American dream by a thread." So far, so good, and as the piece continued, playing fragments of "My Hometown" and "Dancing in the Dark," all was well . . . until his conclusion. Trying to summarize what it all meant, Goldberg stumbled and in the process twisted Springsteen's message into just another aspect of the country's free enterprise juggernaut: "He touches his fans and they touch him. His shows are like old-time revivals with the same old-time message: If they work hard enough and long enough, like Springsteen himself, they can also make it to the promised land."

Ironically, *Born to Run*, even *Darkness on the Edge of Town* and *The River*, might fairly have been interpreted in that way. But *Born in the U.S.A.* took pains to talk about the ways in which hard work was *not* enough, the ways in which the game was rigged to make honest effort and good intentions inadequate. In his shows, Springsteen did his best to make this clear. But if the ways in which his shows were being interpreted was any indication, it wasn't good enough.

Bernard Goldberg's piece was filed from Largo, Maryland, at the Capitol Center between Washington, D.C., and Baltimore, where four shows were scheduled for August 25, 26, 28, and 29, immediately after the Jersey run. Sadly, he wasn't the only political journalist to attend those shows and misunderstand them.

■

> When you start to get real popular, you have to be careful that there isn't a dilution into some very simplistic terms of what you're doing. There are times when you have to get up and say, 'Wait a minute, this isn't right. This is it: This is the way I feel.'
> —SPRINGSTEEN TO JOHN HAMMOND, 1984

Max Weinberg's wife, Becky, a high school history teacher, watched "This Week with David Brinkley" faithfully each Sunday morning. She was a fan especially of the prime antagonists on the program's roundtable D.C. gabfest, liberal reporter Sam Donaldson and conservative pundit George Will. "So for the last three years we've been watching and saying, 'Gee, we should invite them when we come to Washington. Maybe they'd be interested in seeing rock and roll,' " Weinberg later told Craig Hankin and John Ebersberger in an interview for Baltimore's *City Paper*. As the Capitol Center dates approached, the Weinbergs had a mutual friend call Will and ask if he'd like to attend. (Donaldson either never got invited or declined.)

"And he said, 'Yeah, great, I'd love to see it,' " Weinberg said. "He was really excited—he'd never been to a rock and roll show. It was funny. He called me up and asked, 'What should I dress like?' So he came in his bow tie, of course, but he wore a sport jacket and slacks rather than a suit. That was casual. He really enjoyed the show. He got it. Unfortunately, he had just returned from the convention in Dallas and had to get up early to do 'This Week,' so he left before the show was over."

Since Will left the sweltering auditorium, bow tie unknotted but otherwise unchanged, during "Cadillac Ranch," just two songs into the second set (that is, two songs after the intermission, when he'd been ushered backstage to meet Weinberg and Springsteen), there was plenty of reason to wonder how much "he got it" even while there.

But Will must have had some sort of vision that Saturday night. He saw, at least, a golden opportunity for Ronald Reagan to pick up more of the youth vote in the November election. After the concert, Will, who sometimes served as an unpaid Reagan campaign adviser, relayed the idea of Springsteen's endorsing Reagan to the White House, most likely through reelection staffer Morgan Mason (the young son of actor James Mason) who had originally come to prominence as the go-between in the Alfred Bloomingdale–Vicki Morgan sex scandal.

Mason played an important role in the reelection committee's attempt to create an image of broad-based unity around Ronald Reagan, attempting in particular to woo all sectors of show business for the actor-turned-President. He'd gone after rock star John Mellencamp in an attempt to recruit Mellencamp's "Pink Houses" as a campaign theme song. (A year after the election Mason married Belinda Carlisle, the former lead singer of the Go-Gos.) Similarly, the White House arranged an election year visit by Michael Jackson, who posed with Reagan as part of an anti–drunk driving campaign; Billy Joel was also invited to dinner that year (a Democrat, he declined). Reagan attended a Grand Ole Opry salute to venerable country star (and sometime Republican candidate for Tennessee state office) Roy Acuff, at which Lee Greenwood agreed to sing "Proud to Be an American"—after Barbara Mandrell declined. The reelection committee's wildest move was attempting to associate ZZ Top guitarist Billy Gibbons (he of the Rip Van Winkle beard and hair) with the campaign because of the tangential fact that Gibbons' parents, prominent figures in the Houston classical music world, were close friends of Vice-President George Bush.

Eventually Will's plan for a Reagan–Springsteen linkage filtered through to presidential adviser and political fixer Michael Deaver's office. There it was duly noted that the President was scheduled to make a campaign stop in Hammonton, New Jersey, on September 19. Springsteen's popularity in his home state was enormous, and a Springsteen endorsement of Reagan would swing a lot of votes.

Deaver's staff knew no one in the Springsteen camp, but they did have an ally in the Virginia offices of Cellar Door Productions, the company that promoted the Capitol Center shows. Cellar Door contacted agent Barry Bell with a proposal that Bruce appear with Reagan in Hammonton. Bell politely declined, saying that Springsteen was unavailable for any outside appearances during the tour, which was true. Even so, he relayed the information to Springsteen and Landau, who took it as just another example of the weirdness associated with both Washington and the uproar over *Born in the U.S.A.* They'd deflected similar proposals in the past from politicians trying to glom a little pop star glamor.

On September 13 Will's syndicated column was published under the headline "A Yankee Doodle Springsteen." Will's chosen label for his own political and cultural philosophy was "Tory," with all its implications of aristocratic conservatism and highbrow elitism, but from time to time, lest he register as a complete wimp, he liked to slum, usually abusing baseball in the process. In Springsteen Will found (or so he thought) an equally perfect icon, one that spoke explicitly to the antipopulism he wished to encourage.

"There is not a smidgen of androgyny in Springsteen who, rocketing around the stage in a t-shirt and headband, resembles Robert DeNiro in the combat scenes of *The Deerhunter*. This is rock for the United Steelworkers . . *?*" wrote Will. "Today, 'values' are all the rage. Springsteen's fans say his message affirms the right values. Certainly his manner does.

"Springsteen, a product of industrial New Jersey, is called the 'blue-collar troubadour.' But if this is the class struggle, its anthem—its 'Internationale'—is the song that provides the title for his 18-month, worldwide tour: 'Born in the U.S.A.'

"I have not got a clue about Springsteen's politics, if any, but flags get waved at his concerts while he sings songs about hard times. . . ."

Will was not the first conservative to attend Springsteen's shows and become confused about the message. For instance, Barbara Carr's father, an oil executive, came away with the impression that Springsteen was implicitly proposing a national reorientation best realized through the "Reagan-Bush program." But George Will had quite a bit less excuse, for if he had listened more closely—or less selectively—that Saturday night, he would have heard Springsteen introduce "Nebraska" by saying, "It seems like one of the big problems we've got in the country today is people feeling isolated from their jobs, or from their friends, from their government. You get a sense of powerlessness some-times and . . . uh . . . some people just explode." This was not the optimistic, hard-working patriotism Will wanted to purvey, so the columnist simply ignored it (presuming he was still there to hear it).

"An evening with Springsteen tends to wash over into the A.M., the concerts lasting four hours," the column continued, though the author was hardly in a position to know. "Backstage there hovers the odor of Ben-Gay: Springsteen is an athlete draining himself for every audience.

"But, then, consider Max Weinberg's bandaged fingers. The rigors of drumming have led to five tendonitis operations. He soaks his hands in hot water before a concert, in ice afterward, and sleeps with tight gloves on. Yes, of course, the whole E Street Band is making enough money to ease the pain. But they are not charging as much as they could, and the customers are happy. How many American businesses can say that?

"If all Americans—in labor and management, who make steel or cars or shoes or textiles—made their products with as much energy and confidence as Springsteen and his merry band make music, there would be no need for Congress to be thinking about protectionism. No 'domestic content' legislation is needed in the music industry. The British and other invasions have been met and matched."

Since the politicians Will most avidly supported had done their best to deny adequate compensation and health care for workers who were not "making enough money to ease the pain," or simply denied the existence of such diseases as black lung and asbestosis, the column ended in even deeper smarm and hypocrisy than it began. George Will had never held a job in which his hands were more than metaphorically dirtied and was proud of it. The notion of his lecturing on the joys and rewards of labor to steelworkers who risked their lives in filthy, unsafe mills every day was such a perversion of what Springsteen was trying to communicate that it constituted an obscenity. Yet the column was well received.

Released as it was in a time of chauvinism masquerading as patriotism, it was inevitable that "Born in the U.S.A." would be misinterpreted, that the eponymous album would be heard as a celebration of "basic values," no matter how hard Springsteen pushed his side of the tale. (In 1986 Jackson Browne's much more explicit "For America" met the same fate, despite its being surrounded by a group of songs that attacked U.S. foreign policy in the most explicit terms.) Certainly, any popular song that honored the American Vietnam veteran in the age of Reagan and *Rambo* was going to be misconstrued as celebrating the war. Issued in the teeth of a presidential election being sold as a plebiscite on national virtue, such a song could expect to be misappropriated. Surrounding that song with others that presented equally mordant views of the country was no help: Irony had all but been abolished.

Like any hit record, *Born in the U.S.A.* is very much of its times, and in the autumn of 1984 the country was giddy from the

Olympics and gearing up to salute a Reagan "landslide" whose preordained meaning was patriotism personified. What was one more distortion in all of that?

Again, Springsteen just shrugged it off. Will's opportunism was as overripe and obvious as his prose; it wasn't likely to fool anyone who mattered. Bruce wasn't in the habit of making public statements to refute the mistaken ideas of newspaper columnists.

A week later Ronald Reagan made two campaign stops in the Northeast. At Waterbury, Connecticut, which John Kennedy had visited during the 1960 campaign, Reagan specifically identified himself with JFK. "Over there, on the balcony of the Elton [Hotel] one night in 1960, young John Kennedy stood in the darkness. He was exhausted, but the night was bright with lights and they lit the faces of the tens of thousands of people below . . . He smiled in the glow. And even though it was the fall, it seemed like springtime, those days," said Reagan, who had supported Nixon in the 1960 election.

"I see our country today and I think it is springtime for America once again. And I think John Kennedy would be proud of you and the things you believe in."

It was two weeks into the fall campaign, and Reagan had backed off from earlier comments exalting the interrelationship of politics and religion, which had proved controversial, in favor of optimistic themes "designed to identify himself with positive developments ranging from rising college entrance test scores to Olympic victory," as Francis X. Clines noted in the *New York Times*. "When America goes for the gold nothing can hold her back," Reagan enthused after noting a four-point rise in the national average SAT results. He was hunting Democratic crossover votes—and the youth vote, even though, if reelected, he would be the oldest chief executive in U.S. history.

Later the same day, the campaign plane moved on to Hammonton, New Jersey, a town of 13,000 located in the rural southern part of the state. There Reagan appeared before a select audience. As at Waterbury, the event was a pure campaign stop, the audience brought out by the local campaign staff for the sole purpose of showering the President with affection, just part of the day's arrangements to ensure favorable attention on the evening news with its important national audience. Reagan spoke on essentially the same themes he'd touched on in Waterbury, but this time he added, "America's future rests in a thousand dreams inside your hearts; it rests in the message of hope in songs so many young Americans admire: New Jersey's own Bruce Springsteen. And helping you make those dreams come true is what this job of mine is all about."

As the *Christian Science Monitor* later commented, Springsteen thus became "the first popular singer to be recruited by a President of the United States as a character reference." It was hard to see the Reagan remarks as anything but the crudest sort of exploitation, especially since the campaign staff was unable to answer the obvious follow-up question: What was the President's favorite Springsteen song? (By the next day the answer was "Born to Run," but, as Johnny Carson remarked in his "Tonight Show" monologue, "If you believe that, I've got a couple of tickets to the Mondale-Ferraro inaugural ball I'd like to sell you.")

Well, Bruce Springsteen must have felt as John Mellencamp had: "I didn't know whether to be embarrassed for me or for the President." Still, it didn't seem necessary to do anything. "It just seemed like the same kind of thing the President did all the time, only this time he was doing it to me," Bruce said a couple of days later. His initial reaction was to treat the whole idea of a relationship between himself and the President—*any* president—as a preposterous joke. Springsteen may not have been an outlaw, but he'd grown up in the era of outlaw rock and roll, when the notion of any public official endorsing a rock star in the midst of an election campaign would have been a ludicrous impossibility.

In fact, there were certain similarities between Ronald Reagan and Bruce Springsteen, although these had little or nothing to do with a shared perspective on the problems facing America, as Reagan and Will and their ideological cohorts implied. What they shared was an unflappable attitude, a tremendous conviction of being the right person for the job at hand and a deep belief in their own authenticity. This was easy to define. As early as 1975 Martin Nolan of the *Boston Globe* wrote, "Ronald Reagan may be the Bruce Springsteen of politics. And Bruce Springsteen may be the Ronald Reagan of rock," in an article that attempted to fathom how either man had ever wound up with simultaneous cover stories in *Time* and *Newsweek*. The common element has to do with what in Reagan's case has been called his "Teflon" quality but which in Springsteen has usually been appreciated as a survival instinct. Both men know almost automatically when to attack and when to back off; neither seems much troubled by existential doubt in the validity of his own enterprise. Examples pertaining to Reagan are an overfamiliar legion, although the quick shift in emphasis in his campaign, as reflected in the Hammonton and Waterbury speeches, is a particularly good example.

In Springsteen's case, the best example might be his reaction to Reagan's endorsement by imperial fiat. Bruce didn't respond quickly. Reagan made his speech on a day off for the tour, which had just finished a four-night run at the Philadelphia Spectrum. Bruce's initial reaction was a kind of shocked amusement, and since he wasn't the kind of performer who issued press releases, he simply said nothing, figuring the issue would blow over. Only the growing awareness that many in his audience—and in the press—who loathed Reagan and had faith in him expected some sort of reply forced him to react at all.

There are several obvious reasons why Bruce was slower to react than another performer might have been. In his own mind, he was utterly certain that Reagan had misinterpreted him. As Jon Landau pointed out, "Bruce has never thought the message or the lesson of his personal success was 'Hey, be like me, you can do it, too.' " To Bruce, this was obvious from all the songs he had ever written. He took it for granted that everyone interested knew all his work, not just *Born in the U.S.A.* Only when it was pointed out that this was an impossibility, since sales of *Born in the U.S.A.* were already over 5 million copies, more than twice as many as *The River* or *Born to Run* and about five times as many as his other albums, did he begin to feel differently.

But Springsteen was also extremely reluctant to speak in specifically political terms because he feared his own lack of expertise would prove embarrassing. He certainly had principles that he adhered to and tried to foster, and he also had a method of communicating those principles. Telling stories was a part of that method; making speeches wasn't. Even when he played the M.U.S.E. shows, which involved taking a stand against the proliferation of nuclear power plants, he was the only artist who declined to make a statement on the issue in the tour program. His position was that his music spoke for him. But as he tackled more concrete issues and situations in his songs, that position began to prove inadequate. It risked his work being made subject to all sorts of expropriation and dangerous misreadings, not only by opportunistic politicians but by his everyday listeners, too.

Like Reagan, Springsteen was also blessed with a larger than ordinary ration of good luck. As he was getting ready for a gig in Pittsburgh, perhaps the major city most devastated by Reaganomics, it became obvious that he would have to make some sort of disavowal of the President's endorsement. He had been asked to meet briefly that evening with Ron Weisen, president of United Steelworkers of America Local 1397, located in Homestead, Pennsylvania, legendary for decades as an outpost of union militancy and under Weisen's recent leadership the most vocally dissident local within the USWA, consistently opposing "concessions" (givebacks of rights and wages) that both company management and the international union leadership insisted were necessary.

Springsteen was canny enough to know that a frontal attack on Ronald Reagan would never work. Reagan was the most popular President since Franklin Roosevelt and all direct assaults somehow redounded to his credit; denigrating the President would only make Springsteen seem an ungrateful hothead. Reagan's particular brand of Teflon was characterized by the ability to turn any awkward or unseemly situation into a positive advantage. Anyway, Bruce continued to abhor negativity. And talking with Weisen that evening must have helped him focus on what he needed to do, which was distance himself from the President and his policies by linking himself to their polar opposite: the disenfranchised workers exemplified by the men of Local 1397, who had, among other things, banded together to form the most thriving union food bank in the country, which aided hundreds of their laid-off brethren monthly. (This didn't stop the Pittsburgh area from having the highest suicide rate in the nation, but not much could have.)

In the midst of his first set on September 22, Springsteen made his statement. Finishing "Atlantic City," he said bitterly, "The President was mentioning my name the other day, and I kinda got to wondering what his favorite album musta been. I don't think it was the *Nebraska* album. I don't think he's been listening to this one." And he played a scorching "Johnny 99."

Before playing "My Hometown" at concerts, Bruce frequently told a story about growing up in Freehold and playing "out behind the Monument." He was in high school, he said, before he realized that the Monument was dedicated to the Battle of Monmouth in the American Revolution; the battle had been fought in Freehold. That night in Pittsburgh he described going to Washington, D.C., before the current tour began and making a "long walk" from the Lincoln Memorial to the Vietnam Veterans Memorial and he concluded by saying, "It's a long walk from a government that's supposed to represent all of the people to where we are today. It seems like something's wrong out there when there's a lotta stuff being taken away from a lot of people that shouldn't have it taken away from [them]. And sometimes it's hard to remember that this place belongs to us—that this is our hometown."

Those were bold words to come from someone with so little political experience or self-confidence. And it was a smart tactic, tackling exactly the issues that Reagan's "springtime" speeches evaded. Landau made sure that Springsteen's comments were relayed to interested journalists and by Monday, three days later, several influential newspapers ran follow-up stories on the rock star's reaction to the President's rock criticism.

But if it was not Springsteen's style to make speeches or set himself up as a political expert, it was even more unlike him to let such a traumatic incident pass by with a single gesture. His commitment was not a one-night stand. So he came back at his second Pittsburgh show, after the brief meeting with Weisen the night before, with much stronger and clearer remarks that amounted to a bill of particulars against the devastating winter that Ronald Reagan's administration had helped create in the real America.

"There's something really dangerous happening to us out there," he said. "We're slowly getting split up into two different

Americas. Things are gettin' taken away from people that need them and given to people that don't need them, and there's a promise getting broken. In the beginning the idea was that we all live here a little bit like a family, where the strong can help the weak ones, the rich can help the poor ones. I don't think the American dream was that everybody was going to make it or that everybody was going to make a billion dollars, but it was that everybody was going to have an opportunity and the chance to live a life with some decency and some dignity and a chance for some self-respect. So I know you gotta be feelin' the pinch down here where the rivers meet." The sharp opening harmonica blasts of "The River" cut through the dead stillness his speech had created, and the crowd erupted. After the song was finished, he said simply, "That was for Local 1397, rank and file."

The next night the tour party moved on to Buffalo, another ravaged industrial city. There Bruce turned thirty-six, with a party at a local roller skating rink, and treated himself to a rare drunken night out. But he was fully recovered for the first of the two shows at the Buffalo War Memorial. There Bruce said things from the stage that showed he had turned a corner. He wasn't just reacting against Ronald Reagan, he was reasserting the importance of his own more positive vision.

"I dreamed something and I was lucky. A large part of it came true," he said just before singing "Born to Run." "But it's not just for one; it's gotta be for everyone, and you've gotta fight for it every day." It was the ghost of "Street Fighting Man" again, only this time Bruce was much more inextricably linked with that poor boy with nothing to do but sing his heart out.

In all this Springsteen was careful not to hamstring himself by giving an endorsement to the Democratic ticket. The lack of a significant difference was brought home in the days after the Pittsburgh show when Democratic presidential nominee Walter Mondale told a press conference, "Bruce Springsteen may have been born to run but he wasn't born yesterday" and then claimed to have received a letter from Springsteen endorsing his candidacy. Landau's office denied that any such letter had been sent, and the next day Mondale was forced to the excuse that he had been "misinformed" by his staff.

Springsteen kept his distance from both the Democratic and the Republican parties. (He'd only recently registered to vote, and then as an independent.) "I don't generally think along those lines," he told Kurt Loder. "I find it very difficult to relate to the whole electoral system as it stands." (Election night would find him onstage in Los Angeles.)

Bruce's political goal wasn't to elect candidates; it was much more basic. He meant to link his wealth and fame with the sort of people who were living in the circumstances in which he'd originated. By late 1984 there were millions of such people, thrown out of work permanently or reduced to menial, minimum-wage jobs without even such basic fringe benefits as health care, while industrial capital took flight from the United States and corporate profits were spent in a round of mergers and acquisitions that spiraled into outright scandal by the end of 1986. Springsteen operated from the understanding that his sympathies belonged with "my people." (The politicians' response to this was another matter. Mikal Gilmore guessed that Reagan probably dismissed this sort of concern "with his characteristic shrug of contempt," and after November 4 nobody cared what Mondale thought about anything.)

Bruce told *Rolling Stone*'s Loder, "I want to try and just work more directly with people, try to find some way that my band can tie into the communities that we come into. I guess that's a political action, a way to just bypass that whole electoral thing—human politics. I think that people on their own can do a lot. I guess that's what I'm tryin' to figure out now: Where do the esthetic issues that you write about intersect with some sort of concrete action, some direct involvement in the communities that your audience comes from? It seems to be an inevitable progression of what our band has been doin', of the idea that we got into this for. We wanted to play because we wanted to meet girls, we wanted to make a ton of dough, and we wanted to change the world a little bit, you know?" He still hadn't fully learned his lesson, obviously, since the implications of *laissez faire*—"people on their own can do a lot"—were exactly what misled Reagan and Will in the first place. Nevertheless, this was the dawning of something better than a candidate endorsement—it was the awakening of an actual political program independent of any candidate.

The Buffalo show ended the first leg of the *Born in the U.S.A.* tour. Everyone flew home for three weeks of rest and recuperation. Springsteen spent part of his time off planning a new course of action with Landau and Barbara Carr, who began researching groups around the country that worked with the hungry, the homeless, and the unemployed. Meanwhile, Bruce decided to make a $10,000 donation to the Local 1397 food bank. And he wanted to make similar contacts in every tour stop from then onward.

■

The Reagan episode was a watershed, first of all because it unlocked Bruce Springsteen as a conscious political actor, by forcing him to see that he had to speak explicitly if he wanted to retain the right to choose his metaphors, but equally important, because it demarcated the *Born in the U.S.A* tour. Now Bruce reasserted his previous style. No restrictions were placed on CBS's full-tilt record marketing, but Bruce regained his more personal and reserved focus. He canned plans for interviews in the mass circulation media and began preparing for a *Rolling Stone* interview with the excellent Kurt Loder. Although "Cover Me" had come and gone in the Top Ten with no video at all, Bruce was still attentive to the potential video presented. However, he wanted to pull back from the slickness of the "Dancing in the Dark" clip. Director John Sayles, who had made several significant films on funky budgets, was hired to direct a bare-bones live performance clip of "Born in the U.S.A.," the album's third single, during upcoming shows at the Los Angeles Sports Arena.

The only public announcement of Springsteen's plans came when Columbia Records issued a late autumn press release headlined: "Bruce Springsteen Announces New Tour Dates in Twelve Cities; Local Community Organizations Benefit from Tour Support; 'Born in the U.S.A.' Is Third Single, As LP Sales Top Four Million." Announcing a swing to begin on the West Coast and move through the South before winding up in the Northeast, the release also stated that Springsteen would henceforth be meeting local groups in each town he played, to express his "concern for depressed conditions in various communities."

The result was an active enhancement of Springsteen's prestige in many quarters. Meanwhile, growling back at the President had done nothing to slow down album sales. *Born in the U.S.A* had now spent four months as the nation's Number Two bestselling album, and the title single entered the *Billboard* Hot 100 at Fifty-two, took a ten-point jump its second week, and eventually made the bottom rung of the Top Ten. By Christmas, sales had leaped over 5 million copies in the United States, were nearly double that worldwide, and showed no sign of slacking.

"Born in the U.S.A." wasn't selected as the third single in order to capitalize upon the Reagan endorsement or to correct it. It wasn't even the top choice of the CBS promotion department, which would have preferred the softer, more surefire "I'm on Fire." But Al Teller, with Landau's concurrence, saw "Born in the U.S.A." as an ideal "image single," one that might not sell as well or receive quite as much airplay as a more obvious pop song but would lock in on exactly what Springsteen and his latest album were all about. It was a good call. During the ten weeks that "Born in the U.S.A." spent on the singles charts, albums sold at a meteoric clip.

Bruce continued to work with Arthur Baker, whose controversial remix of "Dancing in the Dark" had been followed by a restructuring of "Cover Me" that even involved cutting a new bass line. (Because it was only meant as a demo, the song had been recorded in such haste that Garry Tallent had never had a chance to cut a proper track.) Baker also rescued an unused but outstanding background vocal sung by the well-known session singer Jocelyn Brown. His "undercover mix" drew the song's groove close to reggae and its density close to dub, a transformation so great that Bruce, who'd been reluctant to sing the song live at all, adopted several elements of the remix and began opening the second set with it, which also gave Patti Scialfa her only solo spot.

But Arthur Baker really outdid himself with his "freedom mix" of "Born in the U.S.A." If there was any lingering confusion about what the song said, the "freedom mix" dispelled it forever by enhancing every mournful accent Baker could find in the track. Baker also stripped the song, isolating synthesizer, drums, and voice in order to condense the E Street Band's brutally hard rock into electronic dance music played off against a martial snare. In a way, by featuring glockenspiel and synthesizer and deemphasizing guitar, Baker made the song prettier—as eerily beautiful as tracer fire. The effect is stark and scary. At the end of the second verse, Bruce's voice is simply overwhelmed, and for several minutes it jumps and skitters, fighting to be heard above the insistent rhythm. In the background, echoed and multiplied, one phrase rings time and again, like a Morse distress signal: "U.S.A.—U.S.—U.S.—U.S.A."

In the remix, parts all but hidden in the original are pulled into prominence: an acoustic guitar, a single zooming bass chord, Springsteen muttering "Oh my God, no." These things have been there all along, just waiting to be discovered, and Baker makes like Ali Baba. Finally, rather than the concert ending of the original, there's a violent finale, first the music and then Bruce's voice declaring "I'm a cool rockin' daddy in the U.S.A. now" sliced off. The last sound is the noise of a tape clipped to a halt, cruel as a last heartbeat.

The starkness of the "freedom mix" was matched by the 45's previously unreleased B side. "Shut Out the Light" is a song from Bruce's Los Angeles home studio; its musical atmosphere couldn't be farther from Baker's crashing electronics. It's just a guitar, a tambourine, a little synthesizer, and Eric Weissberg's fiddle. This time Springsteen sings a folkish melody as though telling a ghost story, his voice doubled an octave higher to sing harmony with itself on the chorus.

The lyrics are incredibly detailed and exceptionally brief. Vietnam is unmentioned but omnipresent, looming over each verse. The story is "Born in the U.S.A." set back ten years, to the evening of the protagonist's homecoming. His plane lands; he takes a taxi to a bar; he remeets his family and his wife, who love him utterly and think of the future. He cannot connect—or maybe he can't disconnect. It's more or less the Vietnam veteran's cliché but rendered with such passionate simplicity that it's as if you've never heard it before.

What's new is Springsteen's treatment of the presence of the war in these lives. It's like some mysterious disease in which part of the contagion is an inability to speak or think clearly. No one talks about it, because nobody understands it, least of all Johnson Linnier himself, who simply lies awake at night and cries a helpless prayer:

> Mama, mama, mama, come quick
> I've got the shakes and I'm gonna be sick
> Throw your arms around me in the cold dark night
> Hey now, mama, don't you shut out the light

. . . and then the harmonica and the fiddle, harmonizing as perfectly as bile and bitter tears. "Born in the U.S.A." is the Vietnam story as carried forward in one heroic life, but "Shut Out the Light" is something much more frightening: the dank after-taste the war left in the mouth of the nations it poisoned.

■

Springsteen's interest in working with community groups wasn't just a refutation of Ronald Reagan. He had spoken to Steve Van Zandt during *The River* tour about doing "something that would leave something behind" in the cities through which they barnstormed. He had mentioned similar ideas to Barbara Carr after the Vietnam Veterans benefit and during the album-making months. Landau also remembered talking with Bruce before the tour started about trying to "get into some kind of program on a sustained basis." There's plenty of reason to believe that Springsteen meant from the outset to do such things on the *Born in the U.S.A.* tour but then had simply become so wrapped up in his own phenomenon that he'd never started. The confrontation with the President was the catalyst, and it couldn't have come at a more opportune time.

Jon Landau points out that Springsteen's response was a typical example of his turning a negative into a positive. "He said, 'Okay, let's get our thoughts together on what we're doing and let's get a plan together. Now's the right time to start. Because rather than reacting to somebody else, this is the best way for me to get across my ideas about things in general.' "

"If I'm going around this country, I want to know what's going on where I'm playing, and I want to leave something positive behind," he told Landau. Perhaps there was a selfish motive, but it was not the crass need for a benevolent image—he already had that. Rather, Springsteen wanted to assuage his fear of becoming a star who lived cut off from "real life." But like any performer who had reached superstardom, Springsteen *was* now cut off from much information about the everyday world. Even in his ascetic backstage, the people who turned up were purely show biz types, and if he met someone when he went for a walk, everything they said was most likely filtered through the knowledge of who he was. Anyway, trying to establish this kind of contact on a one-to-one basis was too haphazard.

"We talked and I said, 'How should we do this?' " remembered Landau. " 'I mean, what type of thing are we interested in?' " If Bruce simply wanted to do charity work, there were dozens of worthy diseases and causes. But he was moved by the hungry and homeless of America, in no small part because he could easily imagine himself and his family among them. "For him this was the most personalized thing, and so this is where we channeled our efforts; this was our focus point. Things that you could say were having an effect on people that Bruce identified with, he feels close to, because they're the kind of people he grew up with.

"In other words, it is not merely about a quantity of money. It was not about that. It could be very helpful in that local area, but in terms of the needs of the situation, on a relative scale it was more symbolic than truly problem-solving." Instead, the contributions (which averaged $10,000 a night during the arena portion of the tour, $25,000 nightly when the shows moved outdoors in the summer) would symbolize commitment and solidarity and perhaps serve as an inspiration to his fans. "Since his father was an unemployed blue-collar worker, he's naturally most concerned with groups like food banks for unemployed union members and groups that deal with environmental responsibility," Barbara Carr told the rock magazine *BAM*.

Carr did the advance work, identifying the one or two organizations in each city with ongoing programs that put them in direct contact with people in need. In the main, this meant food banks, some of them established by trade unions, some by churches, some by the food industry itself (the "Second Harvest" network). Occasionally Springsteen worked with citizens action groups that targeted specific issues—usually environmental—in their area. In Philadelphia, in the summer of 1985, they linked up with Chris Sprowal and the Committee for Fairness and Dignity for the Homeless, which spawned the National Union for the Homeless, the first organization to work for the empowerment of the homeless themselves.

Springsteen processed the information he received as an artist, not a politician. In all his meetings, he felt that he received at least as much from the community group as he gave to them. What was most remarkable wasn't his ability to remember names and figures and spiel them out to a crowd (that was just a basic show biz skill at work) or even his plain courage and refusal to back off from supporting those shunned by society (that might even have been a good career move, since it preserved his image of unshakable integrity), but rather the way in which his community contact was integrated into the bedrock of his performances. Springsteen was integrating a new, unambiguous social vision into work still rich in metaphor. If forced to choose, he might have selected art over politics, but typically, he refused to make such a false choice and did his best to crowd his plate with both. The result was an exceptionally powerful combination, especially since it meant he was able to champion radical causes and working class dreams without ever losing his grip on a huge audience or the respect of the creative community.

And Springsteen's popularity continued to grow. By Christmas he'd have performed eighty shows before an audience of 1.3 million. "Whose nickname is 'The Boss'?" asked the network game show "Trivia Trap," in reasonable expectation that contestants would have the answer. The Pennsylvania House unanimously adopted a resolution proclaiming Bruce "the Boss of rock 'n' roll," further bringing attention to a nickname that Springsteen didn't much like. (As Bob Dylan said, "What is it with this name, Boss? You know, that used to be a negative term. They used to hate bosses. The boss was somebody you used to have to go punch your timeclock to." And yet Dylan, never known as a generous competitor, also said he loved *Nebraska* and "Racing in the Street.")

For an All-American boy, the greatest mock honor was yet to come. In early October director Bob Giraldi chose "My Hometown" as the theme music to introduce the two-minute vignette he produced as a lead-in to the World Series telecasts—all seven games. Bruce probably didn't get to see it much, though, because it was during the Series, on October 15, that the next leg of the tour began with a show in Vancouver, British Columbia.

The show was as high-spirited as ever. During "Rosalita" Nils Lofgren brought out his minitrampoline and essayed his nightly flip (complete with guitar). He missed on five straight attempts; Bruce finally just laughed, "Fuck it," and moved on to the climactic introduction of Clarence Clemons as "the king o' the world . . . the master of disaster . . ." "Rosalita" was the warhorse of warhorses; it had ended every Springsteen show since 1973, when Bruce wrote it. Sometimes it seemed that he did the entire show merely as an excuse to reach this epic, comic quarter-hour of rock star bluster, cartoon poses, athletic leaps, and slapstick introductions—"Now you see him, now you don't . . . Phantom Dan Federici"; "The only member of the band with a high school diploma . . . Professor Roy Bittan." But "Rosalita" was also a ponderous pile, a somewhat bloated compendium of musical notions that had long since had its vital juices drained. Placed elsewhere in the set, that might not have mattered so much, but as the final pre-encore number, it had begun to drag somewhere around 1980. Yet it remained embedded in place, symptomizing Springsteen's root conservatism.

The tour moved on to Tacoma for two nights at the 25,000-seat indoor Tacoma Dome. The second date had to be pushed back a night when Bruce came down with a terrible case of food poisoning—or maybe it was the flu, though it could just have been the "Tacoma aroma" (the local euphemism for the stench coming from the lumber mills), or even the proximity of a toxic waste site to the hotel. Nobody in the tour party felt very well, but Bruce literally fell into the van after the first show and barely made it back to the hotel. Tour manager Travis and the hotel doctor insisted he stay in bed for a solid day. (Ticket holders were

offered refunds if they didn't want to wait out the postponement;
only three asked for their money back.)

Before each Tacoma show Bruce met in his dressing room
with community representatives. The first night he saw people
from Washington Fair Share, a two-year-old "nonpartisan coali-
tion of church, labor, and community organizations" with a total
membership of more than 15,000. Fair Share had helped pass a
state "right to know" bill informing workers when they worked
with hazardous substances (information companies ordinarily try
to hide), worked to keep phone rates down after the AT&T bust-
up and to tighten toxic disposal laws, fought unsuccessfully
together with steelworkers to keep area mills from closing, helped
close dangerous toxic chemical plants in the Puget Sound area,
and tried to stop cuts in Social Security benefits. The second
night leaders of the Northwest Harvest Food Bank came along.
Carr met briefly with the representatives, introduced them to
Bruce (who had already read the literature about their work that
they'd sent beforehand), then left them alone to talk. When they
emerged ten minutes later, enthusiastic about Springsteen's
intense interest, she requested that they meet her backstage
again at the break.

The Tacoma shows opened the same way those on the first leg
of the tour had, but toward the end of the first set Bruce paused
and launched nervously into a new rap, one that seemed less
prepared than his usual narratives. He spoke for a couple of
minutes about Fair Share, about the danger of "blind faith—
whether it's in your girlfriend or the government. This is 1984
and people seem to be searchin' for something." He praised Fair
Share, saying, "They think that people should come before profit
and the community before the corporation," and opened the
encores by reminding his listeners, "Remember Fair Share—this
is *your* hometown."

The next night was Northwest Harvest's turn. "This is a song,
it's kinda about sharing some of the responsibility for the place
that you live," he said, then hesitated. "Sometimes . . . I know
when I was a kid I used to have a real love/hate relationship with
the place I grew up. I felt like I didn't wanna . . . I didn't wanna
belong. I guess I was afraid to belong to somethin'.

"But right here in your town there's an organization called

Northwest Harvest. What they do is, they do somethin' real simple: They feed people—people that have been cut out by some of the injustices of our social system or by the economic policies of the current administration. There's people out there that are just hungry; they need something to eat. The name of the organization is Northwest Harvest, and they can use . . . ya got extra food, you got anything that you can give them, their number's gonna be out at the concession stands during the break. They're here in your town trying to make it a more decent place to live. If you get a chance, check 'em out and help 'em out—'cause this is your hometown."

Springsteen's very awkwardness helped him get over with a speech many might otherwise have found heavy-handed or inappropriate to "entertainment." Furthermore, his hesitancy and lack of polish worked toward establishing the kind of character who might tell a story like the one in "My Hometown." Over the next few months, various versions of this rap, elaborated and edited, became the prelude to the final section of the first set: "My Hometown" leading up to the explosion of "Thunder Road," with its last line, "This is a town full of losers / I'm pullin' outta here to win." Inexorably, the kid who ran away from home was reining domesticity back into his orbit and doing it through the vehicle of joining the rock and roll circus.

Backstage during the break Barbara Carr again met with the community group representatives. Without any advance notice, she presented them with a check, again signed by George Travis on the Thrill Hill Productions tour account. In this case, because two groups were involved, each received $5,000. The money wouldn't go far, given the scale of poverty, but Springsteen's onstage rap would be reported in all the reviews, and a press conference could be held the next day, announcing the donation and soliciting both more funds and greater community involvement.

But it was the end of the second night's show that really threw the old fans. As mordant organ and piano chords brought "Backstreets" to an end, veteran Springsteen concertgoers braced themselves for the "Rosalita" finale. But that night, for the first time in eleven years, the song that poured out next was

not "Rosalita" but "Born to Run." And the old-guard Bossma-
niacs were stunned.

Wrote Charles Cross, editor of the Seattle-based Springsteen
fanzine *Backstreets*, "It was a version of 'Born to Run' that
sounded like a Thompson machine gun gone mad. But 'Born to
Run' is an encore song, a song the crowd (and the band) expected
to be played after everything else had been pulled out, as a final
aperitif [*sic*] to the Bruce Springsteen experience. This is a very
different setting for 'Born to Run' and consequently it was a very
different song. . . . stuck back into the set, back into the light of
day, it came to life and once again had the great rush of
innocence it had when first played in 1975. The song ended,
Bruce said thank you, and the band left the stage.

"The crowd of twenty thousand was speechless, dazed, frozen
in their places. Was the show over? Where was 'Rosalita'? As far
as I can remember, ever since Springsteen wrote 'Rosalita,' he's
ended every show with it—it was the great punctuation point to
his body of work."

Even beyond the obvious fanzine hyperbole, it's hard to
imagine that very many imaginations were as frozen as Cross
suggests. But if all Springsteen had done was disrupt the ritual
expectations of the fanatic fans Cross represented, he'd done
himself a service, establishing through a burst of creativity just
who *was* boss. And he'd done more than that—he'd liberated the
show from an albatross, a song that was too long and had long
since stopped breathing. Refreshed, the band, as if working off
excess energy, came back for an unusually lengthy and diverse
group of encore numbers, including "I'm a Rocker," "Wooly
Bully," the "Detroit Medley," the medley of "Twist and Shout"
and "Do You Love Me," and finally—as Bruce shouted (probably
telling the truth), "I can't go on. I'm *ill!*"—"Santa Claus Is
Coming to Town."

After two shows at the Oakland Coliseum, marred only by
promoter Bill Graham's inability to control ticket scalping, the
tour moved on to a seven-night stand at the Los Angeles Sports
Arena. The show was evolving but it hadn't lost its high spirits.
The final night of the Los Angeles run was Halloween, and Bruce
entered like Screamin' Jay Hawkins, lying upon a black cof-

finlike box amidst billows of dry-ice smoke and spooky music. Flat on his back, Springsteen told the story of a Dr. Frankensteen who couldn't wake up. "They tried music," he intoned, as Clarence held a boom box playing "Louie Louie" to his ear. "They tried sex," he said, as Scialfa, outfitted in a nurse's uniform, bent close. Then Jim McDuffie came out and presented him with a guitar, and Bruce leaped off the box and cranked into Jerry Lee Lewis's "High School Confidential."

Just before showtime Springsteen informed the crew that in honor of Danny Federici's fifteen-year tenure in his bands, it would be appropriate to present him with a gift. A washing machine would be a good idea, he suggested. But it was too late in the day to buy one. Instead, stage manager Bob Thrasher and several other crewmen went to Bruce's L.A. house during intermission and dismantled the washer there. (Because it would otherwise be too heavy to lift onstage, they had to remove the motor.) When they hauled it out in TV game show style, Federici smiled serenely; the audience went nuts.

But the shows were made more meaningful not only because Bruce had restructured their endings—now "Racing in the Streets," "Born to Run," or "Backstreets" closed the set; "Rosalita" usually didn't appear at all, and the ponderous "Jungleland" and unwieldy "Detroit Medley" were swept out of the encores—but because he had enhanced his community support.

Springsteen wasn't looking for any publicity for himself, although working with local groups did help to take some of the media pressure off. Since he wasn't doing any interviews (the *Rolling Stone* story with Kurt Loder, who finally got Bruce to sit down in Los Angeles, was the last of the tour), his support for the food banks and other community groups gave the media something else to cover. The only restriction placed on what the groups did with Bruce's support was that they wait until after the first night's show to do it. Asked by the press why Springsteen didn't make a statement explaining his actions, Barbara Carr simply replied, "This *is* his statement," and that threw the reporters right back into the arms of the community groups, who wanted and needed the extra attention.

It worked, too. In Memphis food bank director Virginia

Dunaway found herself interviewed on the local rock station; the next month the station did a series on hunger issues. In Oakland Bruce worked with the Berkeley Emergency Food Project, whose manager, Becky Aiello, remarked, "No one knew we existed until the Boss said this is a good thing to contribute to. After that, even high school students came in to volunteer." A year later some were still helping out.

Even if Arthur Baker couldn't give Springsteen an audience among the dispossessed, who remain disproportionately black and Hispanic, Bruce's music already had a grip on many white community activists who worked with them. For instance, Dwight Pelz, executive director of Washington Fair Share, waited in line five hours for Tacoma Dome tickets; when a phone message came through from Jon Landau Management in New York, one of the Fair Share staffers recognized Landau's name from Springsteen liner notes. As a result, the dressing room meetings with activists didn't have the tone of politicos addressing a celebrity or of a media aristocrat deigning to notice representatives of the plebians. They had the quality of a respected leader encountering peers. "I spent a night in jail in Wildwood [at the Jersey shore] when I was sixteen," said Pelz to break the ice. "Everybody did," Springsteen replied.

Additionally, the food bank directors were precisely the right people to help translate Springsteen's ideas to the media. Even their skepticism was useful. "We asked him quite candidly why he was doing this, and he said, 'Rock stars come into a community and leave,' " said Gene Hanlon of the Omaha Area Food Bank. "This was his way of coming into a community, thanking the community, and leaving something behind."

Many other performers made charitable gestures part of their shows by collecting canned goods or writing a check. Springsteen's approach was different. He plugged into ongoing processes. He carefully combed through the research Carr gave him; nearly every food bank director who met him was impressed with his command of the facts. He not only wrote a check, he made a speech placing local problems in a national context and prodded his listeners to do something themselves. Often, those things were worth more than the check.

As Bruce gained more experience, his confidence rose, and rather than worrying about the things he didn't know, he gave his audience as much as he could about what he did understand. Springsteen recited the appalling statistics of hunger in the richest, most agriculturally productive country in the world, noting the tons of food that rotted each year, the thousands of undernourished children. And at each stop he'd stick his neck out a little farther. "There are a lot of people out of work, seniors whose Social Security doesn't get them through the month, kids who don't have enough to eat," he'd say, adding, "and they ain't gettin' caught in no safety net." He talked about fighting for your community, about the importance of a hometown, about the ways in which joblessness robbed people not only of subsistence but of their human dignity. And he signed off with a slogan that was also a pledge: "Remember, nobody wins unless everybody wins." There were those on the left who'd argue that this was "just charity," but in fact, by asserting the reality of impoverishment for so many Americans (whose existence both political parties tried to downplay or deny), he forced the well-off customers at his concerts to face serious questions about their own lives.

In Los Angeles, his second hometown, Springsteen worked with the Steelworkers–Old Timers Food Bank, based in Maywood, one of the string of working-class towns in the southeastern section of sprawling Los Angeles County. Following the Local 1397 example, this food bank had been established by out-of-work steelworkers from the defunct Bethlehem mill in Vernon, under the leadership of USWA Local 1845 president George Cole. By the end of 1984, it was feeding 5,000 families a month, almost 100,000 meals.

Like the Vietnam Veterans of America in 1981, the food bank was almost broke when Springsteen came to town. By the time he left, it had begun to thrive, building on his contribution, the first media attention it had ever received and new initiatives of its own. For instance, in Tacoma and Oakland the community groups had merely set out posters at the refreshment and merchandising stands. George Cole and his staff proposed setting up tables at which literature could be distributed and donations received, giving Bruce's audience an immediate opportunity to match his generosity and offering that much more opportunity to involve concertgoers in the groups' ongoing work.

Over the seven-night stand, and counting checks that poured in after the E Streeters left town, the audience contributed about $20,000, doubling Springsteen's contribution. Cole exulted that the donations would allow the Steelworkers–Old Timers group to buy "literally tons of food," but he also knew that it would be hard to keep up the pressure. Yet as he acknowledged, "Over the course of a week, [Bruce has] focused people's attention on organizations like ours. A lot more people are now aware that there's more to Los Angeles than Hollywood glamor and good times."

Furthermore, Springsteen and Cole struck up a friendship. Thereafter, whenever Bruce was in California, George was one of the people he stayed in contact with. Following the Los Angeles shows, it was Cole and his staff who persuaded Springsteen to work with Dr. Jorge O'Leary's People's Clinic in the destitute mining town of Clifton, Arizona, where striking copper workers had been bankrupted by the strike-busting tactics of Phelps-Dodge and the lethargy of the United Steelworkers international leadership. The clinic, located in a converted feed store, was only days from closing. The $10,000 Springsteen contributed, supplemented by more than $2,000 in audience donations, enabled O'Leary to move to better facilities in a mobile home and kept the clinic, which had become the center of resistance to Phelps-Dodge, alive for many additional months.

More importantly, there was an entire organization around the food bank in Los Angeles County. Even after the Bethlehem mill folded, Cole had managed to hold Local 1845 together, and he'd managed to get elected to the city council of Bell, another of the towns near the mill. (In 1985 Cole was elected mayor of Bell.) Included were dozens of different people, not just steelworkers but textile workers, machinists, and other unionists, many of them Hispanic or black, perhaps a majority over forty.

On one of his off-days in Los Angeles Springsteen drove down to the hall and met with a group of steelworkers. Most were only vaguely aware of who he was and they greeted him, Ann Japenga wrote in a *Los Angeles Times* story that appeared after Bruce had left town, "not as a rock star but simply as a generous man who cared enough to donate ten thousand dollars. . . ."

Springsteen donned a Local 1845 cap and joined the theater workshop organized by actress Susan Franklin Tanner. Tanner read some lyrics from "Downbound Train," and Springsteen participated in an exercise in which each participant imagined himself to be some sort of work tool. ("I'm a guitar," Bruce said without hesitation.) Many of the workers had seen the show; like other food banks, the steelworkers received six tickets for each evening's show and food bank volunteers could swap between seats and the donation tables in the course of the long night.

One who attended the shows and the workshop was Luis Rodriguez, a laid-off steelworker from the East Los Angeles barrio. Prompted by participation in Tanner's workshop, he wrote a brilliant poem, "Bethlehem No More," which recounted his experiences amid the ugly and dangerous conditions of life in the mill, evoking also the tremendous affection the workers developed for each other and for the steel with which they did nightly combat.

Like Rodriguez, the other laid-off steelworkers had little idea of their artistic abilities until they began meeting to swap stories and trade experiences. Out of such dialogue Tanner was helping the workers develop a play entitled *Lady Beth*, which had been their nickname for the mill. (In 1985 Springsteen went to see *Lady Beth* several times and participated in the final act, which was a discussion with the audience. He later sponsored and helped to fund a national tour by the Theater Workers Project.)

"The guys all asked, 'Why did you come?' " George Cole said. " 'Why did Bruce Springsteen take four hours out of his life to spend with us?' He said one of the things that he wanted to make sure he did was stay in touch with the real people in the U.S.A."

"He said one of the things that happens when you get in the position he's in is you cut yourself off from the real people of the world," another food bank worker told Japenga. "You end up in a limo with a big house on the hill and a big wall around it. That's all you live in—that limo, that house, that recording studio. He didn't want that to happen to him. He felt the strength of his music is how it connects with the real people in the world." Never had the lessons of *Nebraska* been better articulated.

"Bruce is at a crossroads now," a "Springsteen associate" told Robert Hilburn in Oakland. "He's thinking about the connection between what he writes and the world. I think what you're seeing in these shows is him trying to find a way to make that connection in a way that's comfortable for him. . . . Rather than getting embroiled with personalities and endorsing candidates, the thing that seems to make the most sense to him is to keep it more personal."

What was really great, though, was that keeping it personal meant working with exactly the people whose lives and work had most often been robbed of the chance to establish personality. As a result, Springsteen's legend grew—and it cast a long shadow for those who desperately needed some shade.

The tour moved onward, through the heartland. Bruce played Ames, Iowa, and talked about the demise of the family farmers, then sang a revitalized "Sugarland," ending with a rare image of rebellion:

> Well if land prices don't get no higher
> I'll fill this duster with gas and set these fields on fire
> Sit up on the ridge where the bluebirds fly
> And watch the flames rise up against this Sugarland sky

The next night they moved on to Lincoln, Nebraska, where Bruce sang of Charles Starkweather. Then they crossed over to Kansas City, heading south into Texas and Louisiana, Alabama, Florida, Kentucky, Tennessee, and Georgia. In Memphis Little Steven turned up for the encores. In Atlanta they wound up the second leg of the tour with "Santa Claus Is Coming to Town." They'd played eighty shows in six months and only had about a hundred left to do.

■

After a two-week Christmas break the tour reassembled in Columbia, South Carolina, swinging straight up the East Coast, from good weather into bad. By now the tour had its own momentum and, in a sense, its own life. While the outside world

celebrated Springsteen as a superstar and hero of the underprivi-
leged, the internal story was simpler—and maybe sweeter. With
the changes he'd made in the ending of the show, Bruce had
trimmed the event to a more livable pace and the result was some
of the finest performances he'd ever given. Moving outside major
media markets, the show became looser and freer.

In the outside world the legend simply grew. It was only
marginally helped along by Bruce's second video. "Born in the
U.S.A.," shot rough by John Sayles, had the kind of dark-tinged
performance footage you'd expect from a grab-shot documentary
or a low-budget heavy metal band. Bruce wore layers of sweatshirts and jackets, a headband, and several days' growth of
stubble. (Because of the video shoot, the band had to wear the
same stage clothes every night of the Sports Arena stand, and
Bruce's beard had to be trimmed by hand each afternoon). Sayles
took a crew to various locations in New Jersey—most notably a
Veterans of Foreign Wars hall—and came away with interesting
cutaways that enhanced the message of the music. The problem
was that the video had to be out before the single's run up the
charts was finished. There wasn't time to do the painstaking
mixing necessary to use the live soundtrack, and after "Dancing
in the Dark" Bruce absolutely refused to lip-sync. The result was
a hodgepodge: The documentary effect was undercut by the lack
of live sound, and any inherent artfulness was dispelled because
the sound didn't match Bruce's lip movements. (The effect was
even odder because the live "Born in the U.S.A." Sayles filmed
was played a little slower than the record.)

Nevertheless, the video increased recognition of Springsteen's face in the unlikeliest ways. While Christmas shopping
with his mother in a San Francisco department store, Bruce felt
his coattail tugged and turned to find a three-year-old looking up
at him: "I know you. You're Bruce. I saw you on TV."

He'd become one of those one-name Eighties media stars—
like Michael and Mick, Tina and Barbra, Ronnie and "heeere's
Johnny"—but unlike the others, he didn't do regular press
conferences or stage media stunts. The papers and television and
radio worked twenty-four hours a day; their need for celebrity
copy was insatiable, and stories about food banks and union halls
could substitute only so far. So they planned scams.

The greatest of these by far was the disinformation campaign run by Houston radio station KKBQ during the first leg of the tour. Through CBS the station had received concert tickets to give away. Its morning show, "The Q-Zoo," directed by John Lander—one of the country's original "morning zoo" formats—featured parodies of Springsteen songs and live "begging and pleading" by ticketless listeners hoping to have their desires fulfilled. On opening night KKBQ broadcast live from the Summit arena—a privilege frequently granted important local rock stations along the tour route—although they were permitted only a few minutes actual coverage each hour, with the music dinning in the background, not to broadcast the concert itself.

The next morning KKBQ outdid itself. "When Q-Zoo came on the air Friday morning at 6 A.M., reports began coming in that the Bruce Springsteen concert from the night before was still going strong," wrote *Performance* magazine. "Apparently Bruce hadn't been fooling around when he said earlier he would 'Prove It All Night.' As patrons were leaving the Summit following Bruce's third encore, KKBQ disc jockey Archer, who had stayed all night, reported, 'The Boss felt the need to express himself further and came back on stage. He's still on stage.' "

Archer's reports continued throughout the morning. "The Boss is doing yet another rendition of 'Dancing in the Dark' and has just pulled the two-hundred-thirty-fifth girl from the audience," he exclaimed. Throughout the morning he continued his "live" account of the frenzy at the Summit.

Across town, KRBE, another Houston rock outlet, picked up the scam and they soon had one of their own celebrity deejays on the scene, attempting to "get backstage" for an interview with the Boss and being foiled by Summit security. Meanwhile KSRR, Houston's third CHR station, was flooded with calls demanding to know why it wasn't keeping up with the concert reports. The KSRR jocks denied the stories and denounced the competition, but no one believed them. Impossible as the Q-Zoo scenario was, the myth of the Springsteen concert marathon made people want to believe, so they did.

By six fifteen the Summit's night security man began getting calls: "Is it true?" "Won't he be too tired to play tonight?" When the Summit's management staff got to work at seven thirty they found their night watchman trying to persuade the public that the concert was really over and by nine A.M., when the arena switchboard opened, some callers were sounding desperate: "Is it true?" "How can I get in?" "If I had a ticket to last night's show, can I come back?" A Beaumont, Texas, radio station contacted the Summit's marketing director, wanting permission to come to Houston immediately to do a live report on the concert marathon.

After ten, when the morning shows ended, the calls subsided, but a steady stream of inquiries flooded in throughout the day. And the scenario repeated when other stations around the country, notably Z-100 in New Jersey, repeated the ploy over the next few months—Springsteen's image as the hardest-working man in show business was that well fixed.

Springsteen's aloofness from the media was relaxed only twice in this period. In Greensboro he allowed a crew from the ABC show "20/20" to film the portions of the set in which he addressed the food bank issue for a story they were doing on the growing hunger pangs of American workers and the resurgence of activism among unemployed unionists. (Springsteen didn't do an interview for the show, but he did have a brief off-camera meeting with Hugh Downs, whose sons had made him a fan.) And the *Rolling Stone* interview with Kurt Loder appeared, in two parts— one in early December and the second (presented as a separate story but based on unused quotes and material from the first) in mid-February as part of the magazine's annual awards issue. (Bruce, the E Street Band, and the *Born in the U.S.A.* album and singles made a clean sweep of those.)

Loder's interviews were by far the most interesting and challenging Springsteen did in the entire *Born in the U.S.A.* period. Loder was particularly good at probing Springsteen's politics, probably because his questions were gently phrased and didn't scare Bruce by backing him into the limits of his knowledge of specifics. But Springsteen himself was also much clearer about his ideas. In 1981 he'd told his last *Rolling Stone* interviewer, Fred Schruers, "There's too much greed, too much carelessness. I don't believe that was ever the idea of capitalism. It's just gotta be voices heard from all places, that's my main concern," adding only that for him, the American dream "ain't about two cars in the garage. It's about people living and working together without steppin' on each other." With Loder he was much more concrete.

"I think what's happening now is people want to forget," he said about his reading of the country's mood. "There was Vietnam, there was Watergate, there was Iran—we were beaten, we were hustled, and then we were humiliated. And I think people have a need to feel good about the country they live in. But what's happening, I think, is that that need, which is a good thing, is gettin' manipulated and exploited. And you see the Reagan reelection ads on TV—you know, 'It's morning in America'—and you say, Well, it's not morning in Pittsburgh. It's not morning above 125th Street in New York. It's midnight and, like, there's a bad moon risin'. And that's why when Reagan mentioned my name in New Jersey, I felt it was another manipulation and I had to disassociate myself from the President's kind words."

In 1980, in an interview for *Musician* magazine, Springsteen had used the hustler image but had specifically resisted having the conclusions he'd drawn from that analysis applied as an answer to the reasons for his involvement in the anti-nuclear movement, reducing his perception to just another genre image: "It's just the whole thing; it's the *whole* thing. It's terrible, it's horrible. Somewhere along the way, the idea, which I think was initially to get some fair transaction between people, went out the window. And what came in was, the most you can get." He'd stopped and laughed, perhaps at his own audacity in presuming to tackle such an important idea. "The most you can get and the least you can give. That's why cars are the way they are today. It's just an erosion of all the things that were true and right about the original idea."

If one thing was clear from Springsteen's life and career, it was that he was far too cautious to put himself in a position of responsibility for things he didn't understand. Now, though, he seemed to have decided that he was ready to speak as if his ideas about the world counted in the most particular ways. He was by no means a politician; he wasn't even necessarily a "political" artist, if that meant that he had to stop singing and start campaigning. But if others were going to interpret his work in that way, then he'd make damn sure that his own interpretation was on the record—and that it was solidly grounded.

For the first and last time he specifically addressed his reaction to the President's endorsement-by-fiat. And he very typically did it by reducing the question to its most personal elements, disassociating himself from Reagan and Reaganism much more firmly than he could have done with political rhetoric or name-calling. "Well, I don't *know* him. But I think he presents a very mythic, very seductive image, and it's an image that people want to believe in. I think there's always been a nostalgia for a mythical America, for some period in the past when everything was just right. And I think the President is the embodiment of that for a lot of people. He has a very mythical presidency. I don't know if he's a bad man. But I think there's a large group of people in this country whose dreams don't mean that much to him, that just get indiscriminately swept aside.

"I guess my view of America is of a real big-hearted country, real compassionate. But the difficult thing out here right now is that the social consciousness that was a part of the Sixties has become, like, old-fashioned or something. You go out, you get your job, and you try to make as much money as you can and have a good time on the weekend. And that's considered okay."

■

Swinging back into the frigid, winter-desolate Northeast, Springsteen was still having a good time, but he was also wrestling with a complex situation. Because he'd become so much more popular, the demand for his concert tickets had risen to ridiculous levels. The current tour ended with two shows at the 38,000-seat Carrier Dome in Syracuse, New York. After a few weeks break, he would spend the spring doing his first shows ever in Australia and Japan, then tour Europe in the summer months. Tickets in both Pacific basin countries had sold out in record-shattering time.

In Australia as well as Europe there were logistical reasons obliging Springsteen to play outdoor stadiums. Neither continent contained the number and quality of indoor facilities to make it feasible to play arenas. If Bruce had insisted on not playing stadiums, he would have had to commit himself to spending months in just a few cities in order to fulfill the demand even fractionally. So he agreed to do both tours on the only practical terms.

Another decision needed to be reached as well. After Europe some sort of homecoming tour would be desirable. But the demand in most American markets now made the very idea of playing indoors out of the question—even ten more Meadowlands shows wouldn't begin to slake the thirst of "my people" to see the Springsteen show. And that demand might well grow. *Born in the U.S.A.* was still Number Two; it had cracked the 5 million sales barrier, and one of the album's most surefire hit singles, "I'm on Fire," was in the wings. If Bruce wanted to do another American tour in the summer of 1985, there wouldn't be any way to avoid playing stadiums.

Bruce wasn't sure he was willing to take that step. But for the first time since Philadelphia promoter Larry Magid had offered him a shot at 100,000-seat JFK Stadium in 1976, he wasn't sure that he didn't, either. Neither Jon Landau nor George Travis saw any creative or production problems with taking the show outside. Frank Barsalona and Barry Bell of Premier Talent, which had enormous experience with outdoor concerts, predating even Woodstock, were both certain that the shows would translate and that Bruce would satisfy far more of his audience than would be annoyed by the prospect of sitting farther away. Most significantly, Springsteen himself had sat in the crowd at the Who's final American shows in Los Angeles back in 1982, and he'd not only had a good time, he'd been inspired to think about how he'd perform in a similar situation.

The arena shows he was doing were unquestionably great, but they'd about run their course. In the States, he'd been playing arena-size buildings for the most part since 1978, a total of four swings around the nation. He now knew almost exactly what would happen each night; so did the audience. Since he wasn't prepared to radically change the show, maybe the venue ought to be altered. That would open Bruce up to a new challenge, it would invite some new blood aboard (and give it a place to sit down), and it would make a strong statement about his inclusive artistic and political priorities. Presuming that the hard core would still want to go to every show, they would occupy a far smaller percentage of the total number of seats each night. Stadium gigs might even cut into the booming scalpers market, since that much more of the demand would be filled legitimately.

But it was the creative challenge that made Springsteen take the prospect of a stadium tour so seriously. He was always looking for a way to find out new things from his shows. He was at every one of those arena shows; he knew all their flaws as well as their glories. And he knew it was time to make a move.

"We build up so much horsepower that by the time we got out of the arenas, the band was tugging at the reins," he said. "From the beginning, my music fits a big place—it's big, it's a loud noise. And I sing at the top of my lungs. It works in a big place like that. I didn't think that the thing to do was to get overconcerned about it. Even with all those people out there, you're still in business that night to initiate some sort of one-on-one contact. So all you need is one person. And if there happen to be sixty thousand out there, they're all individuals. I'm basically trying to reach as many of them as I can, in as personal a fashion as I can. That's how I think in my head, anyway.

"That was the whole point from the very beginning, when there really were more people in the band than in the audience. And we had good nights, nights that were fine. We had a good time, the people that were there had a great time. I guess for me that was the important idea. It's not that big a deal, it's just something that just felt natural to me. It wasn't a plan or anything, it's just that that's the way we've always done it."

He'd resisted the move from club to arena, then, because it seemed possible that making that alteration would sacrifice that crucial idea. What he found out was that the opposite was true.

"Those places are great because, first of all, they have a roof, and the roof bottles in so much energy," he said. "And you get a band like ours and look out! It's like shakin' up a pop bottle. What we tend to do is, I wait until I have that feeling, that we *are* gonna blow the roof of this place, you know. And I wait until I feel that we have so much muscle behind us on that stage that like, hey, bring on what's next. We'd played every city twice, six nights or however we did it. When we were in clubs we did it—

we'd play five or six nights in a club before we'd go into a theater. Played in a theater, we played five or six nights in a theater before we'd go into an arena. In the arena, we'd play five or six nights in the arena. Because I wanted to feel the tension, I wanted to feel before we went on, just for my own comfort or sense that it was time *to;* I wanted to feel that tenseness, like the place was just gonna explode. Like the band was carrying so much muscle, and it was so high-powered that it couldn't be contained here anymore."

Furthermore, the changes in Bruce's own personality made the transition easier to make. "I changed in a way that change became easier for me. It wasn't as difficult. I'm sure I agonized tremendously over it when we were moving from theaters; I can remember talking about it.

"So this time out, we planned from the beginning, before the tour started, that we'd end up in the stadiums. And at this point, it just seemed like that was the only thing to do."

The Australian and European shows made certain of that. The question was whether he and the band had the stamina and interest to come back and do the same thing in the States that summer. The answer, whatever it was, wouldn't be couched in theoretical resistance, just based on fact and feeling. But as always, Bruce left the actual decision up to the last minute.

Outside the small world of the tour, the Syracuse Carrier Dome gigs looked like nothing less than a final cash-in—the gross for the two shows was more than $1.3 million—in a little-played part of Springsteen's prime Northeastern market. But in the final moments of the sound check before the first show there, on January 26, you could feel the added tension. The Carrier Dome shows were also a dry run in which the larger stage and runways, lights, and sound—even the digital delay lines and video screens that cut down the distance outdoors—would be put through their paces so that Bruce could get a feel for them. And Bruce appeared to have every intention to push these shows as far as he could, to find out if he really could communicate in such a vast space. At that sound check, as Springsteen played "Working on the Highway" in the emptiest space he'd ever faced, he was greeted in part by a huge burst of feedback, a voluminous warning signal.

For the first time on this tour (give or take Pittsburgh after the Reagan incident), there was *really* something at stake. The Meadowlands dates were a longer version of the inaugural run in that building three summers before; any performer's mettle is tested in a city like Los Angeles, but Bruce had safely passed that test long before; and although integrating the community groups into the rap preceding "My Hometown" was a delicate artistic maneuver, Springsteen had long found ways to shoehorn the unlikeliest of topics into his songs and shows.

If the stadium venture didn't work, however, he was going to be stuck. There was not much thrill left in the arenas, and no real challenge—in most places he'd gotten over the moment he took the stage. If he tried and failed in the stadiums, then Springsteen would have suffered the first blow to his image of integrity, the most precious commodity he possessed. He knew by now that site selection on ideological grounds wasn't worthwhile—there was no principle standing between him and the larger venues, even if others thought there was. He figured he could do it, but he had to be absolutely certain before committing.

In St. Paul, at the very beginning of the tour, songs like "Atlantic City" and "Reason to Believe" had occupied too much of the show, and as a result, there he *was* blowing it in a way—but the band pulled the performance along so that it was hard to tell or to find the space where telling could be done. Now Bruce had cleared that space for himself, and he set out to push and test the limits of this new kind of venue.

As always, they came out smokin' in Syracuse, but Springsteen soon pulled the show back inward, spewing out songs in an unusual configuration. The sequence of "Johnny 99," "Atlantic City," "Reason to Believe," "Shut Out the Light," and "Bye Bye Johnny" was probably the longest set of somber songs he'd allowed himself since St. Paul. And given the mood that those established, even the anthemic songs that followed—"Glory Days," "Promised Land," "My Hometown," and "Trapped"—took on a darker cast, which was enhanced when he ended the first set without the ritualistic "Thunder Road." (It popped up in the encores.)

To watch that show, especially the first set, was to be mesmerized. Here was Springsteen, acclaimed as the greatest performer in the world even by doubters, in a situation where he lacked his usual total confidence, especially his complete assurance that he would get across to the audience. You could feel that he didn't know. The moment when he had come down on Ronald Reagan in Pittsburgh was nothing next to this, for that night he'd been sure of having the crowd on his side. He'd learned since then the difference between making statements anyone can hear and saying things that were too unambiguous to be misunderstood. So he played a stadium; so he played the most acoustic/soft stuff he'd ever done. And in a sense, he confirmed his genius in the process, because he played the stadium with a show that had evolved in the arenas, and it translated perfectly. Old-timers might complain about the vastness, but then old-time Boss fans always assumed that *they* would never be without one of the limited numbers of tickets.

That didn't mean there weren't problems. The sound wasn't great, but then there was so much of it (it was the same system that had carried the three-day US Festival) that it had to be hard to control. "Glory Days" became terribly distorted as the high end blew out, but not any worse than could have happened in a 10,000-seater. And when Springsteen came out alone to sing "No Surrender" or to do the soft-spoken introduction to "Racing in the Street," there was a sense of intimacy as great as any in the smaller building. And as for the rockers . . . forget it. Like all party songs, they just sounded better when more people crammed the room. The essence of that show translated perfectly, and it became even clearer just what magic Bruce Springsteen could wring out of cheesy rock and roll chords and the trashy images of cars 'n' girls. As on any night when his show clicked, you could see the bones behind it all. Whether he was goofing on Clarence and himself getting old in "Glory Days" or honoring the arrival of Jon Landau's first child, Kate, with a rousing "Promised Land," Bruce brought his listeners into contact with their own mortality in the hardest and the kindest way. From such a show you emerged quickened to every breath you take.

If there had been any doubt about the feeling onstage, it was dispelled when Clarence Clemons exulted to George Travis at the break before the first encore, "Me and the Boss are havin' fun up there!"

The second show was the mirror image of the first. Not only did Bruce know that he could make his more ponderous and difficult ideas work in such a venue, but this was the last night of the American tour. It was a night to pull out all the stops, to see how much fun you could have in a breakneck rock and roll show. He omitted nothing, including one of the hardest-hitting "My Hometown" intros he'd yet attempted. "The economic recovery isn't reaching down to the people at the bottom," he said. "It's something that if the government don't do it, the people ought to do it. We've got fifteen percent of the population in this country below the poverty level. We've got old people who've worked their whole lives whose Social Security checks won't get 'em through the month. Just remember: Nobody wins unless everybody wins." He even extended himself to ask if someone out there could donate a forklift truck to the new Food Bank of Central New York (and a week or so later, somebody did).

As rock critic S. K. List wrote of that second Carrier Dome show, "In the first set Sunday night, the band barely stopped to draw breath, where the night before they'd been almost contemplative. . . . From the hurricane finish to 'Born in the U.S.A.,' they went straight into the weighty compulsion of 'Prove It All Night' in place of Saturday's giddy romping with 'Out in the Street.' Likewise, the Sunday crowd seemed much hotter, although the synergistic relationship between Springsteen, the band and their audiences is so close and co-ordinated that it's hard sometimes to tell who's giving (or taking) the cues."

Bruce still hadn't told Landau or Barsalona or the band and crew whether they'd be working in America the next summer. He'd decided to end the show by crashing through John Fogerty's "Rockin' All Over the World," but that wasn't a clue, since they'd be playing Japan and Australia and Europe for the next few months no matter what. And who knows when he made his choice. Maybe it was the consonance between himself and one of the wildest crowds he'd ever played for that forced his hand. At any rate, as he slammed that last song to a halt, Bruce shook off his joyous sweat and shouted above the cheers, "That's it! Thanks for comin' down to the show. And we'll be seeing you next summer."

13 PINK CADILLAC

Bruce strides to center stage and stands, legs spread, behind the microphone and begins to deliver an oration in the fashion of his favorite television evangelist, the Reverend Jimmy Lee Swaggert of Ferriday, Louisiana, cousin of Jerry Lee Lewis and no mean player of honky-tonk gospel piano himself. Since Bruce's accents have always had a slightly Southern tang—the result of his youth in Freehold's "Texas," no doubt—the effect is extraordinarily convincing.

"Now *this* is a song about the *con*flict between worldly things and spiritual health," he declaims, his strange stresses and odd shifts in tempo perfectly evangelical, "between desires of the flesh and spiritual ecstasy.

"Now, where did this conflict begin? Well, it began in the beginning—in a place called the Garden of Eden." From the wings Jim McDuffie wheels out a blackboard-style map board.

"Now the Garden of Eden was originally believed to have been located in Mesopotamia," says Reverend Springsteen, using a long pointer to direct his congregation's attention to the proper area on the map. "But the latest theological studies have found out that its actual location was ten miles south of Jersey City, off the New Jersey Turnpike." McDuffie turns the map around, revealing a map of New Jersey with a small star at Trenton, the capital, and a larger star in the area Springsteen has just indicated. The pointer clacks down on the map. "That's why they call it *the Garden State*," Springsteen declares.

"Now, understand, in the Garden of Eden there were none of the accoutrements of modern living. I mean, there weren't any houses and there weren't, like, any laundromats you could go down to and do your clothes. There wasn't no *toasters*—you couldn't pop no *Pop Tarts* in that little toaster at night and go watch *Johnny Carson*. You couldn't go out on the highway and buy a *cheeseburger* if you wanted one.

"In the Garden of Eden, there was no sin, there was no sex," he says, in an urgently revelatory tone. "Man lived in a state of innocence." A Jack Benny pause, a brief glance downward, a quick running of fingers through tousled hair. "Now, when it comes to no sex, I prefer the state of guilt that I live in. But before the tour started, I decided to go on a spiritual journey to the location of the Garden of Eden to find out the answer to some of these mysteries—to what temptation is about, to why my body pulls to that spot, and I found out that it's now occupied by Happy Dan's Celebrity Used Car Lot.

"So I walked in. The man looked at me. He said, 'Son, you need a [*Bruce speaks incredibly rapidly*] yellow-convertible-four-door-DeVille with wire-chrome-wheels-air-conditioning-automatic-heat with a-fold-out-bed-in-your-back-seat, eight-track tape deck, TV, and a phone [*he slows so that each syllable is lasciviously distinct*] so you can speak to your baby when you're driving *alone*.

"And I said, 'I'll take two.' " Bruce pauses, then draws out the sense of tormented mystery.

"But I said, 'Dan, now, that's not the reason I really came. What I want to know is, what's the answer to these mysteries? Why do I feel so . . . so torn apart by this conflict all the time?'

"And he said [*Bruce becomes Cal Worthington, a late-night television used car evangelist*], 'Well, son, that's easy. Because right here at the beginning of time, on these ten beautiful, industrially zoned acres was the sweetest little paradise that man has ever seen. [*Now he speaks softly, swiftly, sensuously.*] And in the Garden of Eden there were many wondrous things. There was the Tree of Life. There was the Tree of Knowledge of Good and Evil. There was a man—Adam. There was a woman—Eve. And she looked fine. And when Adam kissed her, it was the first time that a man had ever kissed a woman. And she had legs that were long and pale. And when Adam touched her, it was the first time that a man had ever touched a woman. And then they lay down in the green grass, and when Adam . . . well, it was the first time."

The preacher returns: "But, son, somethin' else was in the Garden of Eden that day. *Satan* came slitherin' up on his belly! And somehow he turned their love into a betrayal and sent them running down into the darkness below."

Now it's Cal again, full tilt, making that last push to nail down the sale.

"But right here on this back lot—for ninety-nine ninety-five and no money down—I've got their getaway car. And if you've got *the nerve to ride!* son, I've got the keys . . . to the first . . . pink Cadillac!"

A rockabilly rhythm begins.

14 STRANGER IN TOWN

"Well, I'm no hero, that's understood . . ."
—"Thunder Road"

Bruce left Syracuse on a charter jet and arrived back in New Jersey around 3:00 A.M. He got up the next afternoon and drove to Newark Airport for a flight to Los Angeles, where he was scheduled to perform at the U.S.A. for Africa recording session that evening.

Even as Springsteen was creating his links with economically disenfranchised Americans, British rock star Bob Geldof began a move to involve pop musicians in feeding the starving in Africa. Spurred by a BBC news report on famine in Ethiopia, Geldof, leader of the Irish-originated band the Boomtown Rats, wrote a song he titled "Do They Know It's Christmas?" and recruited more than two dozen British pop stars to make a charity record. "Do They Know It's Christmas?" featured such noteworthy pop personalities as Boy George of Culture Club, U2's Bono, Phil Collins of Genesis, the Police's Sting, and parts of the black American group Kool and the Gang. Geldof dubbed the group Band-Aid; proceeds from sale of the disc were assigned to the Band Aid Trust, whose mission was to spend the money quickly and wisely to allay the immediate effects of the famine that raged not only in Ethiopia but throughout the sub-Saharan region of Africa.

"Do They Know It's Christmas?" became the biggest-selling 45 in British history, and it enjoyed similar success around the world. Geldof, who had planned on making a healthy donation to Save the Children, suddenly found himself with close to $20 million in the kitty and a full-time commitment on his hands. Over the next year he jetted into Africa and organized an even more profitable second event, the worldwide broadcast concert Live Aid, did thousands of interviews, and cajoled and hectored entertainers and governments into putting bread into the mouths of ravaged Africans. He was dubbed St. Bob by England's tabloid press, made a knight by Queen Elizabeth, and given serious consideration for the Nobel Peace Prize. Geldof resisted all attempts to make his work explicitly political (which left him free to make alliances with Western politicians) and in the process inspired dozens of other entertainers to make similar stands.

In America, after "Do They Know It's Christmas?" appeared, folk singer Harry Belafonte took notice and decided it was ridiculous that American performers weren't doing something similar. Several days before Christmas, Belafonte called talent manager Ken Kragen, a veteran from the folk music period who now handled such stars as Lionel Richie and Kenny Rogers. Kragen had managed the late singer-songwriter Harry Chapin, who had made ending world hunger a personal crusade, establishing in 1975 the World Hunger Year organization. Kragen explained that planning, financing, and running such a show was a long cumbersome process; it would be logistically simpler to do a record.

Right after Christmas Kragen went to work. "Basically, I started at the top of the record charts and began making phone calls." He already held an ace: Lionel Richie was at the peak of his commercial and artistic influence, and Richie's commitment, given early, validated the record idea and helped persuade such other early participants as Michael Jackson and Quincy Jones. Ray Charles, Paul Simon, Willie Nelson, Bette Midler, and Smokey Robinson. Among the first to join was Bruce Springsteen.

"The turning point was Bruce Springsteen's commitment," said Kragen. "That legitimized the project in the eyes of the rock community." Most of the other acts that signed on early were black or middle-of-the-road stars. In order to have the greatest impact, though, some rock and roll stars were needed. Springsteen's credibility was now enormous and his credentials were unquestionable. By Christmas he'd already donated $225,000 to American groups working with the hungry. Once Kragen could tell other artists that Bruce was in, offers to sing on the disc proliferated so much that the organizers wound up having to turn some down. (Bruce's importance was ironic since, according to Jones, Springsteen's first reaction to the project was: "You sure you really want me to do this?")

The session was set for January 28 at the A&M Records studio, located on the old Charlie Chaplin studio right on Sunset Strip. Richie and Jackson wrote the song "We Are the World" about two weeks earlier, Lionel helping to polish the basic structure and lyrics that Michael provided. Richie, Jackson, Jones, and Stevie Wonder recorded the basic instrumental track and guide vocals over which the superstar choir would sing. The groundwork for a media extravaganza was already being laid: A video crew caught everything that went on throughout the session.

The first stars arrived by limousine, each attended by a small entourage, and all were quickly ushered inside, away from the crowd of star-spotters that had gathered outside. Jones had taped a handwritten sign on the studio entrance: "Please check your egos at the door."

Springsteen landed at Los Angeles International and picked up a rented Corvette, which he drove to a parking lot across the street that George Travis had told him would be a suitable place to leave the car. It wasn't exactly a Hollywood arrival. "I swear I walked out to the gate just as he was coming in," said an amazed Ken Kragen. "I was looking to see if there were any hangups out there, and in walked Bruce . . . by himself. He walked across the street away from the crowd and said, 'What do you want me to do?' "

It was still a night of hurry up and wait. Although vocal arranger Tom Bahler had come up with a brilliant and intricate scheme for recording both group and solo singing, the process couldn't begin until everyone turned up. In the control room Bruce found the Pointer Sisters, whom he knew slightly because they'd had a hit with his song "Fire," and more familiar acquaintances Bob Dylan and Billy Joel.

Control rooms are cramped quarters, and Bruce and the Pointers wound up sitting on each other's laps as they waited for the rest of the team to arrive. By ten thirty everyone was there, the cameras were rolling (they shot fifty hours of raw footage and boiled it down to a one-hour videocassette), and Jones was ready to begin. First they would record the chorus, then individual solos. The performers then heard from Bob Geldof, who talked about the horrifying things he'd seen in Ethiopia (not failing to score a few points against the lavish buffet—"whole *bowls* of caviar"—laid out for the performers). Stevie Wonder then presented a pair of women from Ethiopia who tearfully expressed their thanks that people were helping.

The session had a dissonant beginning. At first the chorus was pitched far too high for most of the male singers. Springsteen, Dylan, and a couple of others just laid out, but so many others didn't that Jones had to bring the first take to a screeching halt and eventually lower the register. When they finally got rolling again, Jones noticed a strange, jangling noise coming through the mikes. It was caused by Cyndi Lauper's jewelry. She removed it and they got on with the show.

Springsteen must have been beat, but he wasn't the only one. Paul Simon had just finished an all-night recording session, and Hall and Oates also arrived late from the East, where they'd been delayed by a snowstorm. But Bruce had a second problem. He never sang more than two nights running, because his concerts simply took too much out of him to do more. The two shows in Syracuse were more strenuous than average, and on this, the third night in a row, his voice was so raw it sounded as if someone had taken a rasp to his throat.

Nevertheless, Springsteen had been selected as a soloist, and it was clearly not going to be a short night.

The song opened with Richie, Wonder, Simon, Kenny Rogers, James Ingram, Tina Turner, and Joel singing the first verse, then Diana Ross and Michael Jackson completing the first chorus together. The second verse started with Dionne Warwick's perfect plum tones shading off into Willie Nelson's scratchy purple sage, the record's most unlikely transition (and because it sounded effortless, the finest tribute to vocal arranger Bahler's acuity). Al Jarreau was to complete the second verse, while Springsteen kicked off the second chorus. The third verse was sung by Kenny Loggins, Perry, Daryl Hall, Jackson again, Huey Lewis, Lauper, and Kim Carnes. The record ended with legends shouting the full chorus: Bob Dylan, Ray Charles, then a final duet between Stevie Wonder and Springsteen. Charles and Ingram shouted out tag lines like preachers bringing the congregation to the altar.

By the time they got to Bruce's spot it was half past five in the morning. "You sounded fantastic, Dylan," he called to the man who'd just finished, then stepped to the mike. Dylan, Bette Midler, and a few others remained to watch him work.

Springsteen wanted direction. "It's like being a cheerleader of the chorus," Quincy Jones told him. "I'll give it a shot," replied Springsteen, sticking his sheet music in his back pocket. Bruce didn't have much voice but he pushed through the ache with a shattering bellow. He sang a mawkish line—"We are the world, we are the children"—but to the cliché he added rocks and gravel (the only material he had available) and blew everyone away. In effect, he stiffened the song for its final takeoff. Later, with Bruce's voice dubbed into a duet with Wonder's, the same line provided the single's climax.

Finishing that first take, Springsteen looked up shyly. "Something like that?" he asked.

Quincy Jones had to laugh. "*Exactly* like that," he said.

Springsteen left about dawn, drained by the events of the last few days but feeling good at all he'd achieved, too. As Bruce walked through the A&M gates toward his car, an A&M security guard asked if he wanted an escort. Springsteen just smiled. "No, thanks. I can make it on my own."

■

In rock circles "We Are the World" was widely despised for what it was not: a rock record, a critique of the political policies that created the famine, a way of finding out how and why such famines occur, an all-inclusive representation of the entire worldwide spectrum of post-Presley popular music. Some of these criticisms were just; some were silly; none mattered much against what the record actually represented, which wasn't even the $40 to $50 million it raised for hunger relief. Sentimental as it might have been, "We Are the World" was a grand pop event with serious political overtones. While it was true that it barely challenged the political process by which food was produced and hunger created, it did a great deal to subvert the political process by which music and meaning are made. That is, "We Are the World" obliterated the often arbitrary stylistic boundaries set up in broadcast centers and by record companies and showed that musicians of diverse styles—and races—could work together creatively and productively. U.S.A. for Africa was an important element in the "crossover" boom of the mid-Eighties, which saw great numbers of black artists once again entering the pop music mainstream; by showing the interconnectedness of old and young artists, it helped create a sense of continuity amidst the endless newness of the Top Forty. Both had a value beyond charity.

It was just such undercurrents that made the record thrilling, despite the rather maudlin, sentimental song with its blissfully half-baked lyrics. The best elements of "We Are the World" were torn straight from gospel, and the best performances went to those who testified. With James Ingram and Ray Charles tearing it up to the very last note, "We Are the World" became the world's least likely choir hit, though its most salient highlights were the series of vocal solos. Half a dozen singers went straight over the top, reaching in a few notes pinnacles that were the equal of their own best records. Newcomers like Cyndi Lauper and Huey Lewis stood right alongside veterans like Dionne Warwick and Bob Dylan, and each served not only as a distilled essence of him- or herself, but also as a link in a chain. So even though "We Are the World" was by no means a great song, it *was* a great record.

Everything came to a head in the final duet between Stevie Wonder and Bruce Springsteen. In the contrast and connections between Wonder's still-boyish purity and the leather-lunged shout that was all Bruce had to offer this night lay the whole story of rock and roll. Wonder was the only other performer present who'd gone out on a limb politically in recent years, single-handedly rescuing the Martin Luther King birthday holiday from Ronald Reagan's red-baiting dismissal, so teaming him with Springsteen offered a definition of the different ways in which hope might take shape.

Bruce Springsteen and Stevie Wonder are almost exactly the same age, but their experiences were radically different: one black, one white; one a child star in the greatest musical factory mankind has ever known, the other a product of Jersey isolation. Wonder is a composer with aspirations to the kind of quasiclassical stature Duke Ellington possessed; Springsteen is content to tread the paths worn by Chuck Berry and Elvis. Stevie is physically locked up by his blindness; Springsteen is the apotheosis of the artist-athlete. Yet it now became clear that what they shared was more important. Out of the poverty of their origins, each had created magnificent music; each had torn his songs from deep emotional wellsprings and sung them in kind; both had refused to turn their backs upon their roots. Simply by bringing them together, "We Are the World" made an important statement.

The record was marketed with all the muscle CBS could put behind it, and with such low overhead that almost every penny went into the U.S.A. for Africa coffers. It was an easy Number One straight into the airplay charts, and sales didn't take long to catch up. Within the first month it had sold 4 million copies (sales of more than half a million singles represent a massive hit). It also spawned a hit videocassette documentary and a multi-platinum album (whose most widely aired track was Bruce's "Trapped," recorded live at the Meadowlands the previous summer). All told, U.S.A. for Africa raised about $200 million, a drop in the bucket but far more than any of the world's wealthiest governments provided in so short a span.

Why did it all happen? Bruce Springsteen best placed the artists' role in perspective. "Anytime someone asks you to take one night of your time to help people who are starving to death, it's pretty hard to say no. I think hunger all around the world—in the United States as well—is such an abstraction to most people

No point in even *tryin'* to tear this sucker off the wall. London, 1985.

A stadium-sized "Hungry Heart" sing-a-long

The stage in the cow pasture below Slane Castle, outside Dublin, where the 1985 tour of Europe began

Independence Day

Little Steven and Bruce rejoined on the runway at Leeds, ready to close out the '85 tour of Europe

"And a freight train runnin' through the middle of my head . . ."

(NEAL PRESTO

"Ten years burnin' down the road..."   (NEAL PRES

uce teams up with *(from left)* Karen Adams and George Cole, co-directors of the Steelworkers dtimers Foundation; and Albert Turner, Lawrence Woffard, and Geri Silva of the Equal Rights ngress.

With the cast and crew of *Lady Beth*

At the Oldtimers Food Bank in Los Angeles, October 1984

ris Sprowal, president of the National Homeless Union, Bob Brown, president of the United
ctrical Workers UE District One, and Leona Smith, director of the Philadelphia Dignity Shelter,
th the check that Bruce presented to the Committee for Dignity and Fairness for the Homeless
a concert the evening before in Philadelphia.

Jon Landau appears onstage wearing Bruce's guitar and Jimmy McDuffie's jacket for a final "Traveling Band" at the Los Angeles Coliseum, 1985.

"You know all my dreams come true/When I'm walking down the street with you . . ."

that trying to bring it closer, to make it more real, is something that has to happen.

"It's unbelievable that with the amount of wealth we have here in this country, people are still hungry. Part of it, like I said, is that it's so abstract to people. It's very difficult if you're sitting in front of your TV in Iowa or New Jersey, seeing hungry people; nothing you see on TV is really real. Unless something touches people directly, they don't react to it. But when we get all of these [artists] together like this, in the same room, you don't turn away. I think that's what everybody was trying to say that night."

It was still true that his music spoke for itself; but the maker of the songs was learning to speak his piece pretty well, too.

■

One reason Springsteen hadn't minded flying straight to California was that his new girlfriend, actress Julianne Philips, was living there. Philips, a twenty-five-year-old actress, grew up in the suburbs of Portland, Oregon, and modelled in Manhattan before moving to Los Angeles, where she'd appeared as the girl of .38 Special's dreams in a rock video, which led to starring roles in two television movies: *Summer Fantasy*, in which she played a lifeguard; *His Mistress*, in which she played the title role, with Robert Urich; and in Blake Edwards' 1985 film, *A Fine Mess*, a comedy with Ted Danson. She met Springsteen through his old friend and booking agent Barry Bell. Bell knew Philips through acquaintances at the Elite Modeling Agency and because they both hung out at the same New York restaurant, Cafe Central.

Bell got them together for dinner after one of the Sports Arena shows (he characterizes it as "a good booking"), and they'd been seeing each other steadily ever since. Julie came to New Jersey for the holidays and flew to North Carolina to surprise Bruce, sticking around through the end of the tour in Syracuse. In February they'd even visited Julie's parents, Bill and Ann, when the latter were vacationing in Palm Springs. When Springsteen went to the Grammys (where *Born in the U.S.A.* had many nominations but won only an off-camera award for best male rock album), Philips sat by his side in the front row.

It was extremely obvious during the American tour that Springsteen, without a serious girlfriend for the past couple of years, was dealing with some intense emotional conflicts. In fact, it was obvious even before that—back in the Asbury clubs when he was making *Born in the U.S.A.* and singing a new song called "On the Prowl":

> Well, night after lonely night
> My head don't touch the bed
> I'm on a 2-lane blacktop
>   cruisin' in my rocket sled. . . .
> They got a name for Dracula
>   and Frankenstein's son
> They ain't got no name, now, mister
> For this monster I've become
> I'm on the prowl, I'm on the prowl
> I'm lookin' for a gal, gal, gal
> Hey, hey, hey, I'm on the prowl

Similar thoughts could be heard in the introductions to "I'm on Fire," "Pink Cadillac," and "I'm Goin' Down"—and in the songs themselves—as well as in Bruce's frequent references to his youthful "lack of a close interpersonal relationship with a person of the *opposite sex!*"

Sexual frustration has always been a central theme in rock and roll, and Springsteen frequently dealt with it onstage, usually comically (as in his hilarious spoofs of "Fire"), but sometimes more poignantly, as he looked back on a life in which he had by no means always been a matinee idol. In a way, even the roiling conflicts of *Nebraska* weren't unrelated to this pent-up heat.

When he wasn't joking, Springsteen was ambiguous; when he sang about itching with a "bad desire" in "I'm on Fire," you had to wonder when he'd ever defined *any* carnal desire as good. (In that respect, it's emblematic that "I'm Goin' Down," a song of sexual frustration, made the album while "Pink Cadillac," which celebrated sexual expression, didn't.) But of course Springsteen wasn't just singing about getting laid but about having that "close interpersonal relationship." And here was a greater, weightier, far more troublesome problem, and one with even fewer ready-made solutions, because that all boiled down to the perpetual American artist's conflict between individual freedom and domesticity.

"I never wrote romantic songs," he said around the time of *The River*. "That was what everybody else did. . . . The romantic songs that I did write I tended to give away, like 'Because the Night' and 'Fire.' " Bruce felt he'd changed, and in some ways he had—that album contained a number of songs reconciled to at least the dream of domesticity (most obviously "I Wanna Marry You"). On the other hand, its biggest hit began: "I got a wife and kids in Baltimore, Jack/Went out for a ride and never came back." Introducing "Two Hearts," Bruce often talked a lot about hearing Marvin Gaye and Kim Weston's "It Takes Two" at the wedding of lighting designer Marc Brickman and how much the song meant to him. He also talked about what the rabbi performing the ceremony had said: "When you're alone, without anybody, your dreams and fantasies are all of what you got, and when you get married, when you get together with someone, that is the first step toward making those dreams and hopes a reality."

"Boy, that really got to me. I wrote a lot of songs after that," he said with a laugh when he told Kit Rachlis the same story in a 1980 interview. But Bruce quickly depersonalized the message, just as he did onstage. "It was like you can write a song up in your room by yourself, but it don't mean a damn thing unless people hear it." Similarly, the songs in which marriage features on *The River*—and on *Nebraska*—mostly present it as a state of disaster: "The River," "Stolen Car," "Jackson Cage."

Springsteen's diffident attitude towards marriage and domesticity had deep roots. "I couldn't bring up kids," he told *Melody Maker*'s Ray Coleman in 1975. "I couldn't handle it. I mean, it's too heavy, it's too much. A kid—like you better be ready for them. I'm so far off that track. I'm so far out of line that it would be disastrous. I don't understand it. I just don't see why people get married. It's so strange. I guess it's a nice track, but not for me." Earlier he'd said he wasn't "ready to write married music yet."

By 1980 he'd modified his hard-line attitude somewhat, but he still talked about his work as if it were family. "To me, the type of things that people do that make their lives heroic are a lot of times very small, little things—little things that happen in a kitchen or something, or between a husband and a wife, or between them and their kids. It's a grand experience, but it's not always big. There's plenty of room for those kinds of victories, and I think the records have that."

More recently, however, Springsteen had begun to reassess. In North Carolina the previous December, doing an interview for a book Robert Hilburn of the *Los Angeles Times* was writing about him, Bruce showed himself clearly bending.

"I don't think I felt I was making any sacrifices until I was older—until probably relatively recently," he said, acknowledging that getting older and watching almost all his friends marry and settle into domestic routines and begin raising kids made a lot of difference. "I guess relationships have been [hard for me] just because I've traveled for my whole adult life, and it was difficult to settle into something and make those types of sacrifices," he said. ". . . I guess the most precious thing anybody has in the end is their time. That's what you can't bargain with quite a bit. It's not a question of wanting to do less. It's just more a question of wanting to round out your life." And that's when he also admitted, "To blame something on your job is an excuse, no matter what it is. It can make it difficult, no doubt about it. But in the end you do what you want to do. That's what I basically believe. All the rest is excuses."

This marked an alteration in attitude even from what he'd told Kurt Loder in the *Rolling Stone* interview. When Loder asked if Springsteen ever would marry, Bruce first tried to make it a joke: "I got an Italian *grand*mother, and that's all she asks me. She speaks half Italian and half English, and every time I go over it's 'Where's you girlfriend? When are you gonna get married?' "

Then he became a little defensive, before admitting that he harbored some desires along those lines. "I've had steady girlfriends in the past. I went out with a girl I met at Clarence's club. I'm just not really lookin' to get married at this point. I've made a commitment to doin' my job right now, and that's basically what I do. *Someday*, I'd like to have the whole nine yards—the wife, the kids."

It's romantic to believe that getting to know Julianne Philips, which is what happened between those two interviews, had caused Springsteen to begin to speak of marriage in more concrete terms. But it's not necessarily unreasonable to see it just that way. After all, as Springsteen told *USA Today* the previous summer, "I don't rule out marriage. If it's the right moment, the right relationship, the right person, maybe you'll change the way you do the job. I love women. I love kids. I've been with my sister and her kids and see where certain feelings they have match the intensity that I get onstage. It's a different type of experience, and it's not something I want to miss out on."

So maybe he saw the moment not at hand but on the horizon.

And maybe he didn't. His other project while in Los Angeles during the break between the U.S. tour and leaving for the Orient was shooting a video for "I'm on Fire," John Sayles once more directing. The song was scheduled to be the fourth *Born in the U.S.A.* single, and this time Springsteen was determined to have a first-rate video to go with it, something that worked at an angle to what the song said, not just a performance piece.

So he and Sayles concocted a story line. Springsteen is an auto mechanic. A well-to-do woman (all we see of her are Cybill Shepherd legs and hem) brings her vintage Thunderbird into his garage for service, although it can't really need service, because he's only recently worked it over. She leaves him the keys . . . and innuendo. He tunes up the car and drives to her huge house, parking in front and walking slowly up the steps. Bruce reaches out his finger to push her doorbell, then thinks better of it. He smiles wistfully to himself, walks back down the steps and off toward the lights of the city below.

It was a terrific way to extend the meaning of "I'm on Fire" without rupturing its fragile allusiveness, but it didn't exactly strike anybody as the product of somebody getting ready to be hitched.

■

The second week in March, Springsteen and the entire band flew to Honolulu for two days, a useful intermediate stop on their journey to Australia that also gave Bruce a chance to make a nonperforming stop at the CBS Records convention being held at the Kahala Hilton on the fifteenth. Just to get everybody back in shape, they rehearsed on the sixteenth and seventeenth, then flew to Sydney, Australia, where they arrived late Tuesday morning, March 18, two days before the first of five shows there. All 60,000 seats had sold out in just six hours when they went on sale the previous month, even though the ticket price ($27, Australian) was one of the highest Australia had ever seen.

Bossmania was the order of the day through the Antipodes. Bruce had agreed to play outdoor dates in Melbourne, at the 45,000 capacity Royal Agricultural Showground and in Brisbane at Queen Elizabeth Park, which held 37,000. In Melbourne the first show sold out in two hours, and promoter Kevin Jacobsen immediately announced a second, which also sold out by the end of the day. Meanwhile the political opportunism associated with the tour continued. Mick Young, "special federal minister of state," tried to "lobby" Jacobsen to add a date in Adelaide. Of course, the tour dates had been fixed well in advance, but the noise generated in the press no doubt ensured that Jacobsen would unload the 2,000 tickets set aside for those willing to travel the 600 miles between Melbourne and Adelaide.

Dominated by the sleazy tabloids of Rupert Murdoch, the Australian press can whip itself into a frenzy over far less than a Springsteen tour. Literally from the moment that Bruce left his plane at Sydney Airport, reporters were on his case. About 200 fans, attended by the press, were at the gates. Rather than attempt to negotiate a way straight through the mob, Springsteen's security chief, Bob Wein, naturally preferred to escort Bruce through a side exit to the waiting hotel van, but airport officials refused to allow that and the band had to push their way through. Murdoch's *Sun* managed to get a picture of Bob Wein and McDuffie escorting Bruce from the airport. BOSSY! screamed the tabloid's headline, as if Springsteen, simply by taking the most ordinary of safety precautions, had breached his populist image. (Wein and McDuffie later wore t-shirts emblazoned with that front page.)

"Police and private bodyguards using fists, elbows, shoulders and knees formed a flying wedge at Sydney Airport today to give

singer Bruce Springsteen his first on-ground look at Sydney,"
wrote the *Daily Mirror* the next day. Its animus became obvious
two paragraphs into the story: "Springsteen, renowned for refusing to acknowledge the press, kept his record intact. In the hurly
burly and jostle from gateway 3A across the terminal foyer to his
waiting vehicle thirty metres away he refused to turn for photographs and would not answer questions."

Throughout the band's stay in Sydney, the papers fanned the
flames. When the Springsteen tour management denied access to
Jacobsen's so-called "ticket club," a device by which the promoter sold privileged clients good tickets at a premium, the New
South Wales consumer affairs minister misinterpreted this as a
ban on *credit cards*, and the press had a field day, running
hysterical banner headlines:

PUBLIC TREATED LIKE A "BUNCH OF HILLBILLIES"
ROCK STAR CONCERT TICKET CHAOS

Meanwhile, reports of fictitious interviews proliferated. "During your concert, it's been reported that you give a long kiss to
your black (male) drummer," one interviewer claimed to have
inquired. "Is this a political symbol?" Bruce's every real-life
move was also spotted and noted. He swam at Bondi beach, took
a harbor cruise, and dropped into Paddington pub "for a Fosters
and some pool," and each "event" made the front pages. So did
his appearance with Nils Lofgren at Neil Young's final Sydney
concert (sandwiched between Bruce's first two shows). During the
encore Bruce sang with Young on a twenty-minute "Down by the
River"; Nils made several appearances during the show, playing
piano on "Tell Me Why" and accordion during "Comes a Time."

The start of Bruce's own first show at the Sydney Entertainment Center was delayed for half an hour due to electrical
problems, but "Born in the U.S.A." was greeted with New Jersey-
level pandemonium. (Australia, after all, was the country second
most responsible for prosecuting the war in Vietnam, and it
hadn't treated its vets much better than America treated hers.)
Bruce pushed some of his grimmest material that night, including
the same five-song *Nebraska* sequence that he'd sung in Syra-

cuse, and closed with "Racing in the Street." But in between it was a show typical of those he'd most recently done in the States. As in Europe, Springsteen seemed determined to bring his show intact to foreign lands, making changes mostly for the sake of local color—"even Mad Max in that black Trans-Am," he sang in "Cadillac Ranch." Through the tour he performed a few relatively rare numbers ("Wreck on the Highway," "Santa Claus Is Coming to Town") but nothing he might not have done during a similar string of shows in the States. And the response was just as he must have hoped and imagined it. However idiotic the local papers, Australian rock fans were up to par.

And they bought records in serious quantities, too: *Born in the U.S.A.* sold over 100,000 copies in Australia, the equivalent of going platinum five times back in the States. During the tour the album returned to Number One in the charts, and three singles from it were simultaneously in the Top Twenty.

Bruce shared the wealth by making donations to three Australian charities: the Childrens Hospital/Youth Ward '85 fund in Sydney; the Prince Alexander Hospital Transplant Trust Fund in Brisbane; the Vietnam Veterans Association of Australia in Melbourne. He met with representatives of each of these groups as he'd done in the States, but the community connections weren't nearly as specific, largely because time was short and the terrain was so unfamiliar. As it was, Bruce just managed dedications of "Born in the U.S.A." and "Shut Out the Light" to the Australian vets and spoke only briefly about the others.

Naturally, it rained during his first ever stadium show, at Queen Elizabeth Park, a racetrack, but not long and not hard. In fact, the drizzle let up altogether after Springsteen played "Who'll Stop the Rain." (In fact, over the next six months only two other shows were rained out.) The Melbourne and Brisbane dates also featured festival seating—nothing reserved anywhere in the stadium—which was regarded as risky since the death of eleven young people at a Cincinnati Who concert in late 1980. The reason for playing without reserved seats was simple: The Australian tour had to be brief and the demand was incredible. In the end, the audience response was so overwhelming that Springsteen found his dislike of the open-air format turning to enthusiasm.

The final Melbourne show wasn't especially long; there was an eleven P.M. curfew, and the band had to jet to Tokyo later that night.

■

The Australian tour wasn't much different than the American one—the gap in cultures wasn't that marked. Despite enormous geographical distance and many distinctive local elements, the atmosphere was essentially Anglo-American. Sydney, where the band spent most of its time, was like an odd combination of London and Los Angeles.

Japan was strikingly different in every way. Even in cosmopolitan Tokyo, the contrasts were immediate and unmistakable. Although the promoter, Seijuro Udo, was the most impeccable and generous host imaginable, in Japan it simply wasn't possible to put on a typical Springsteen show.

To begin with, because of curfews the shows were scheduled to start at six P.M. Japan has strict regulations that insist on clearing most public events by nine P.M. This was extended to ten P.M., but that still meant the band had to be offstage by nine thirty. As a result, the Japanese shows were trimmed back to about two and a half hours plus intermission.

The Japanese venues were the smallest of the entire tour. The five Tokyo concerts were held at the 12,000-seat Yoyogi Olympic Pool (a covered swimming pool built for the 1964 Olympics) in the week between April 10 and 16. The facility was extremely modern and rarely used, but in advancing the tour, George Travis found it far preferable to the Budokan (where most such shows were held), with its odd sight lines. In Kyoto Springsteen played 5,000-seat Kyoto Gymnasium, the smallest place in which he'd done an official show since 1978. The tour finished up with two nights at 10,000-seat Osaka Castle Hall on April 22 and 23. Bruce might have been big enough to play stadiums on his first Japanese tour, but he wasn't eager to do so. The Japanese tour, with its frequent days off, was reminiscent of the 1981 European tour.

Because Springsteen was playing at closer quarters than usual, it was reasonable to expect he'd put on some of his most intimate shows. And beginning with the opening night, he certainly tried. When he burst onstage at Yoyogi to open his first show, he shouted, *"Konbanwa Tokyo!"* ("Hello, Tokyo") then ripped into "Born in the U.S.A." with the huge U.S. flag from the album cover displayed behind him. The roars were tremendous; the reviews the next day said what they said everywhere else— that there had never been a crowd response quite like this.

But Springsteen's more venturesome moves simply fell flat. When he introduced "Atlantic City" by making reference to growing up in New Jersey, there was no response to indicate that the words—guaranteed to prompt a roar anywhere in the West— registered at all. Bruce followed with "The River," offering a rap in which he talked about the song's relationship to the future, then spun off to reminiscences of school and cars in his own life, concluding with a summary of his devotion to the old haunts at the Jersey shore, "because they seem more like my hometown than my own home does. 'Cause everybody needs someplace to go to when they can't go home." Again, no response . . . until the song began. Then the house came down. The energy stayed high through "Glory Days," bisected by Bruce's story of being a lousy baseball player (which got over a little bit) and "Prove It All Night."

Bruce brought it back down for "My Hometown," which he prefaced with a long talk including several Japanese phrases. He bent and picked up the set list from the stage floor next to the microphone and explained what he had to say, haltingly reading the phonetic words he'd scribbled at the side of the page: *"Watashino foodoo sato cara meanasan no ko koro eh"* ("This song is from my hometown to your hometown"). With that the kids went crazy, but they quickly settled back politely for the song that followed.

They were out of their chairs for "Badlands," and then Bruce brought it all home with "Thunder Road," on which many of the kids were sufficiently savvy to sing along with the line, "You ain't a beauty but hey! you're all right." No audiences sang sweeter than the Japanese, although whether that was because they had better pitch or just enough sense to shut up if they couldn't carry a tune is anybody's guess. Saying *"Sugu modorimasu,"* Springsteen informed the crowd that the band would be right back and left to thunderous applause.

The second set went much the same. The girl Bruce selected from the audience for "Dancing in the Dark" seemed startled and embarrassed, almost reluctant to have him put his arms around her. On "Hungry Heart," not many sang along, although the song itself got the best reaction of the set. But when Bruce tried his pent-up intro to "I'm on Fire," it never crossed the language barrier. And when he did his Jerry Falwell turn on "Pink Cadillac," it became obvious that the barrier was composed of more than just language. "There was temptation," said Bruce, giving the crowd the Japanese word, "there was sin (*sumi*), there was an apple"—here, he said the word in Japanese and faked a bite—"and then there was a *pink Cadillac*." Except for the odd American serviceman, nobody in the crowd had any idea what the hell he was talking about.

They closed with a rave-up "Bobby Jean," then did his increasingly contemplative "Racing in the Street." The former worked, the latter didn't; none of it mattered much when he hit the encores, which were as jam-packed with funny, danceable energy as ever. If you'd come for a rock and roll show, you went home fulfilled. But if you wanted concrete evidence of the difference between America and Japan, all you had to do was watch as the crowd, rather than flooding the exits at the end of the show, was dismissed by having its row numbers called out from the stage—the sort of orderly departure impossible even in U.S. junior high schools.

Springsteen intended to bring a lot more than a superlative rock and roll show, but in the Japanese context it just wasn't possible. In the first place, he spoke no Japanese and the audience understood only a smattering of English. More important, rock and roll existed in a different cultural dimension in Japan than it did in the United States. In America Springsteen was able to attach tremendous political significance to many of his gestures because of the specific context in which rock and roll had originated: among blacks, poor white Southerners, their transplanted brethren in Rust Belt factory towns and, to some extent, working class ethnics in the Northeast.

All this gave American rock and roll a tradition not only of rebellion but of connection to the lives of its audience. In Japan this wasn't necessarily the case. There rock and roll was an import in every sense, and while it might signify a kind of rebellion, it doesn't seem likely that very many people used it to make sense of their lives. Japanese audiences responded avidly to rhythm, melody, and emotion but the other cultural traditions Bruce evoked generally weren't accessible in this way. Such discrepancies could be felt even in Western Europe, but they were much more total in Japan. There simply wasn't any tradition of Pentecostal preaching in the Swaggart style, so "Pink Cadillac" had no hope of having the same meaning. It could be fun, and an intellectual segment of the audience might apprehend some larger philosophical issues at stake, but there was little or no overall social impact at work.

In a sense, this was reflected most strongly in Springsteen's inability to find a community group to support. Given Japan's very different sense of social organization, nothing like a public food bank existed. After a long quest, Barbara Carr finally found an organization that did need help: The title didn't really translate, but the concept was to help the unmarriageable widows of men who had died in traffic accidents.

Springsteen remained unfazed; he just altered the shape of the show, talking much less and (after the first two shows) ending with the easier-to-grasp ecstasies of "Rosalita." On the other hand, he never abandoned his darker, more reflective material. For instance, there were two or three songs from *Nebraska* every night, and he talked a little bit in front of "My Hometown" in each show. He also kept the old-age skit in "Glory Days," and during that song he worked out with the crowd on some nonsense syllables in a "What'd I Say" style, but mostly Bruce devoted himself to rocking out, accepting what he couldn't conquer.

As a reward, he got the Kyoto show, which was like the old days of barnstorming clubs and theaters. Instead of fifty yards, the back of the room was perhaps fifty feet from the front of the stage, and the result was, among other things, breathtakingly loud, perfect for the kind of show Bruce was now doing. He opened with "Born in the U.S.A.," "Badlands," and "Out in the Street," slowed down just long enough so that Max Weinberg's hands could survive, and then pumped it up again, shooting off three- and four-song rock sequences like automatic weapons fire.

Not only was the singing sweet on "Thunder Road," the kids also formed a ghostly echo to Bruce's acoustic "No Surrender" as if Bruce's memories were singing back to him, trying to soothe his cares.

"It felt like New Jersey," someone later told *Newsweek,* but it felt like Jersey in the Seventies, when everything was up for grabs and half the audience was discovering new horizons every night. When Bruce finished the show by hollering *"Aishite-matsu!"* ("I love you!"), what came roaring back was simple affirmation. He'd gotten over in Tokyo, as he would get over in Osaka—he really was running the rock and roll tour all but guaranteed not to fail. But only in Kyoto did the audience finally crack through to the band, and that made it one of the most special events of the entire tour.

Julianne Philips arrived in Tokyo on April 15. Philips and Springsteen spent the rest of the Japanese tour together, seeing the sights in Kyoto and visiting the A-bomb memorials at Hiroshima during the stay in Osaka, then returning to Tokyo for a one-day shopping excursion and a party hosted by CBS/Sony Records in honor of the tour and *Born in the U.S.A.*'s double-platinum status in that territory. On April 25 Julie and Bruce flew to Maui for a brief Hawaiian vacation.

15 U.S. MALE

Where's everybody running?
Look at everybody go
Somebody please tell me, what's all the fuss
I'm gonna tell you: Babalu's getting married
—THE ETERNALS, "Babalu's Wedding Day"

What the hell did Julianne Philips and Bruce Springsteen have in common?

After all, not only was Julie ten years younger than Bruce, she'd lived what one high school friend called "a charmed life." Growing up as the youngest of an insurance broker's six kids (four boys, two girls) in the comfortable Portland suburb of Lake Oswego, her biggest trauma supposedly was having to wear braces. A representative of the Elite Modeling Agency in New York, which represented her in 1982, described her as "a perfect ten package" who could earn as much as $2,000 a day. Then she'd thrown that career over and moved to Los Angeles, where she had some success as an actress.

But they did have things in common. Julie Philips only looked like a cheerleader; she was really an athlete who worked out intensely and race-walked several miles every day. Bruce Springsteen may have been a scruffy rock and roller, but he kept himself in physical trim. One of the first things they did together was visit Julianne's Los Angeles health club, Matrix One; when Philips came east, Bruce took her to Phil Dunphy's New Jersey workout spot.

Bruce said he could remember "lying in bed and thinking

about getting married and knowing that whoever's sittin' in that seat, it's not going to be the easiest place to sit in the whole world." Julianne seemed to fit the bill—in part, he thought, because "she was just tough; she had confidence and resilience and she wasn't afraid to confront facts or their implications." A second advantage was that Julie was "well versed musically," meaning that she was exceptionally familiar with "all the great older records," so that Bruce "never sensed or felt the age difference."

Besides, Springsteen was an eccentric rock star in part because he wasn't interested in being eccentric—all these years he'd been working hard to *fit in*. Conversely, even if Julie Philips lived a "charmed life," she'd found reason enough to leave Oregon and attempt to build a different kind of life. So at least they shared a certain level of ambition.

At any rate, it seems safe to say that if Springsteen was capable of using rock and roll individualism as a way of creating some kind of community, he was certainly capable of setting up shop with a beautiful actress-model who happened to have a completely different class and social background. (It sure didn't hurt that both were Catholics, although Julie practiced far more often than Bruce.) And for that matter, who'd ever led a life more charmed than Bruce Springsteen's? What was its climax supposed to be—marrying Rosie the Riveter?

Trying to account for the reasons anybody is attracted to anybody is risky business and thankless to boot. Most of us, fortunately, don't have to explain our loves. In the case of Springsteen and Philips it's mostly the overreaction of the world outside their little love nest that makes the question worth exploring.

It was during their Hawaiian holiday that the prospect of getting hitched first arose, although they didn't say yes to each other until they'd been back in California a few days. Bruce told friends at the time that he'd decided to take the plunge because "it just didn't feel right" to introduce Julie Philips as his girlfriend. As reasons go, that's not bad, but of course it's no more (or less) rational than any other he might have found.

They didn't tell anyone else until Sunday, May 5, when they

went out to dinner with Bruce's parents and his sister Pam to celebrate both Mrs. Springsteen's birthday, which had been the day before, and Julie's, which was coming up on Monday. Bruce's family was surprised—and pleased. (The reaction of his Italian grandmother is not recorded, but it probably had something to do with grandchildren.)

When they got back home, they made a few phone calls—to Julie's folks in Oregon, to Bruce's sister Ginny in New Jersey, to Jon Landau and Barry Bell in New York. All the folks back east were contacted after midnight, but nobody complained.

Now that they were engaged, they wanted to be married quickly, before Bruce's European tour began on June 1. The quickest and simplest means of getting married would be a Los Angeles civil ceremony; a wedding reception could be held later wherever they chose. But they preferred to be married in church and feared that a church wedding in Los Angeles or New Jersey would too easily become a media circus. Billy Joel and Christie Brinkley hadn't had much privacy even though they had gone out into New York Harbor on a boat to say their vows; Keith Richard and Patti Hansen had been plagued by reporters even though they had wed at the tip of Baja California in Mexico. It seemed logical to go to the Philipses' family parish church near Portland. The wedding was set for Wednesday, May 15, at Our Lady of the Lakes in Lake Oswego. Who'd be looking for a rock star wedding there?

As public relations miscalculations go, this was a doozy. True, nobody was looking for Bruce Springsteen to turn up in the Portland suburbs. But in order to have a wedding you have to get a license, and that's a matter of public record. In order to plan a church wedding, you have to do business with florists and caterers, arrange for music, and rent a hall for the reception. With all those businesses in the know, it obviously didn't take long for word to leak out, and when it did Bruce and Julie were sitting ducks in her parents' living room. Portland hadn't seen a story this good since Mt. St. Helen's had erupted. (*People* claimed it was the biggest news in Oregon since Lewis and Clark.) Paparazzi flooded in from all over the world, and there was nowhere to run, nowhere to hide.

Bruce's family understood his penchant for strict privacy as well as his business associates did. Throughout their son's twelve-year career, neither Doug nor Adele Springsteen, nor either of his sisters, had ever given a reporter so much as a one-line quote about him. It certainly was no accident that his closest advisers—starting with Jon Landau—also liked playing it close to the vest. In fact, Springsteen had been able to lead his personal life more privately than any other American celebrity of similar stature in the Eighties, largely because those around him worked overtime to shelter his life from prying eyes. It wasn't even something Bruce demanded, although he clearly preferred a modest approach to publicity, but you didn't have to know him long to understand that he needed a great degree of isolation.

Certainly, that secretive atmosphere added impact to his mystique. Anything he did publicly was an event: releasing an album, going on tour, making donations, participating in "We Are the World." But if Springsteen had harbored any desire to expose his private life, the aura wouldn't have lasted. No one with enough ego to become a star could have maintained such a lock on exposure if keeping out of the limelight hadn't fulfilled personal needs, too.

By now it was the conditioned response of everyone who worked with Bruce to stonewall all personal probing—not only because of Springsteen's personality but because of their own as well. Only people as concerned with control as Bruce himself could have worked with him successfully, and the first principle of control is to keep the spread of information within the tightest limits possible. Once information is widely shared, particularly once the public has access to information, control seeps away. And after the near-debacle with Reagan, Springsteen, Landau, and their associates were more than ever devoted to complete control of his life, work, and image.

Julianne Philips understood this very well. She was herself a minor celebrity and had the performer's natural instinct for self-preservation. But her family wasn't show biz savvy, and they were eager to announce their daughter's engagement, as any proud parents would be. They knew reaction might be intense, but they never saw what was coming until it was too late.

The Philipses didn't have any reason for such an understanding. As they began planning the wedding, rehearsal dinner, and reception, rumors naturally began circulating in the Portland area. And when a local radio station, working on a hot tip from a florist, called on Thursday, the ninth, to confirm them, Bill and Ann Philips told the truth. Pandora's box flew open.

Naturally, Columbia Records and Jon Landau Management tried to put the lid back on. "We checked with his management, and they say it's not true," Columbia's Marilyn Laverty told reporters. "We haven't heard anything," Barbara Carr was heard to say from the offices of Jon Landau Management. "We haven't heard a thing about it. As far as we're concerned, there's no wedding," said Barry Bell for Premier Talent.

It wasn't that Bruce Springsteen didn't want the world to know that he'd decided to marry; it was the attendant hoopla that he wished to avoid, the media circus that could trample and trivialize one of the most important days of his life.

From New York, Landau and Carr tried to explain the situation, and Bill and Ann Philips listened and did their best to comply with what must have seemed the odd request that they make no further comments. But they didn't seem to grasp the idea that not talking about the wedding meant saying *absolutely* nothing—even one sentence could become a quote, and a quote could be inflated into a story, a story into a headline, and a headline into more disruption than any wedding could handle. Media professionals like Carr and Laverty could easily stonewall the story for as long as it took—at least long enough for the wedding to take place unburdened by paparazzi. But when the Philipses looked out to their front lawn and saw reporters camped there, or when their listed phone rang with solicitous queries about the big event, they didn't see an enemy force besieging them. In fact, it struck them as absolutely rude not to answer the reporters' simple questions. One night Bill Philips even brought out pizza and beer for them.

For the next week it was hilarious to watch the Springsteen camp try to hold onto the threads of the wedding story, only to have them unravel in their hands. Time and again over the next interminable week they'd think they had the situation in command, and then it would erupt all over again on the heels of some new minor tidbit blown out of scale by the supposed importance of this rock star wedding.

And the stories were coming now, thick and fast. Robert Hilburn called it one of rock and roll's "hottest pieces of gossip since the 'Paul is dead' rumors in the Sixties." Bruce Springsteen's star was peaking: *Good Housekeeping* had just named Bruce one of its fifty most eligible bachelors, and Columbia Records had just announced that sales of *Born in the U.S.A.* had surpassed 6.5 million, making it the largest-selling album in the label's history.

Springsteen's media aloofness made any information about him newsworthy, and a wedding—a *church* wedding—for the Boss, Mr. All-American Rock and Roll Star, was the kind of thing that the tabloids and the TV shows, the gossip columnists and their electronic counterparts, could really sink their teeth into. They'd been trying to corner him for months, in some cases years, and when they did pin him down, all *he* wanted to talk about was rock music and spiritual values and the plight of the unemployed. At least now they had a story that made sense for kerchiefed housewives at the checkout stand, that played without comment—well, maybe a leer or two—on the six o'clock news.

Headlines about the Rock Star and the Beauty Queen immediately proliferated. In New Jersey the news was greeted with shock. "Reports of Springsteen Wedding Breaking Fans' Hearts," headlined the *Asbury Park Press*, adding, "You could almost hear the sound of hearts breaking all along the Jersey shore."

Bruce Springsteen had always done his best to live a normal life, which was abnormal only because he was a pop star. He avoided photographers, mostly by never going to paparazzi haunts, but when they snatched his picture he never made a fuss. He disdained gossip columns, but when they ran an item about him, no matter how outrageous (such as that linking him and Nastassja Kinski), he never asked for a correction. Now the Associated Press was running an interview with the Reverend Richard Parr, the seventy-two-year-old Nebraska priest who'd been asked to officiate. (Parr said he had the flu and couldn't make it.)

If the situation looked fouled-up from New York, where Springsteen's damage control unit still sat, it was even hairier on the spot. Besides the media camped out in the Philipses' driveway, there were excited fans, some of whom had driven long distances. Reporters claiming they represented *Rolling Stone* and *People* knocked on the door, were fobbed off with a couple of sentences, and went off to file stories in the sleazier tabloids. One local radio station set up a "Springsteen rumor hotline" and had no lack of callers.

All that was happening even before Bruce and Julie hit town; when the protagonists of the great event arrived, the proceedings just got sillier. A neighborhood teenager sneaked his camera into the back yard next door and snapped blurry photographs from over the fence, which were later published in the tabloids. Reporters and fans continued to jam the driveway. It was soon arranged for Jim McDuffie to come and run interference, advising the Philips family on media and security matters and assisting in getting the wedding license and other details in order. Springsteen had asked three of his closest friends to serve as best men: Jon Landau, Steve Van Zandt, and Clarence Clemons. Clarence came out early and brought with him his assistant, Terry Magovern, whose complete cool (and experience in barroom security) proved immediately useful.

Bruce and Julie weren't completely trapped. They were able to sneak out through a neighbor's back yard. On Friday Bruce and the Philips men went to a local bar and grill, where they shot pool and ate pizza. Nobody recognized Springsteen even when "Dancing in the Dark" played on the jukebox.

Meanwhile Jon Landau and Bruce were spending hours on the phone, plotting their way out of the mess. Finally, late Friday evening, they decided they might as well call Ringling Brothers as wait until Wednesday. Given five more days of this kind of coverage, such a horde of fans and reporters could be expected that it would create an enormous diversion outside the church and possibly even disrupt the ceremony itself. Nobody wanted that sort of wedding. Oregon has a forty-eight-hour waiting period before a marriage license becomes effective; that meant the wedding could take place any time after midnight Sunday— 12:01 A.M. Monday.

Bruce had already notified the band and several of his East Coast friends of the Wednesday wedding ceremony; he notified as few as possible of the change in date. Those who got the word rushed to the airport; Landau himself didn't arrive until early Sunday evening. Ann Philips contacted Father Paul Peri at Our Lady of the Lakes, who agreed to open the church at midnight and perform the ceremony as soon as all the guests had arrived.

Around eleven o'clock Sunday night, Bill Philips took out the trash, rattling the cans loudly as he did so. He went back in the house and turned off the lights. The assembled reporters took that as a signal and went home for the night. "We were having fun," Bill Philips later said. "It was like a cat-and-mouse game."

Most of Bruce's guests were staying at a downtown Portland hotel—except his parents, who were also staying at the Philips home. At about eleven fifteen, Terry Magovern rounded them up and put them in two vans, which were driven to the parking lot of the Lake Oswego high school. It was a warm, starry night and when the vans pulled up to wait for several carloads of local guests, everyone got out to stretch their legs; they talked in low voices about the entire comical affair. By about ten minutes after twelve, all of the fifty-odd guests were present, and the caravan made its way to the church with a police escort.

All the lights in the church parking lot were off; a local police patrol car hovered outside, just in case word had leaked out and interlopers needed to be turned away. Inside, the church, a brick building with a low, modern altar arrangement, was lit only with candles. Guests stumbled into pews, barely recognizing friends in the dimness.

At about twelve thirty, the lights in the chapel came up full. After everyone's eyes had adjusted, organ music began to play and the procession down the aisle began. Bruce entered first, with his parents, one on each arm. He was wearing a blue silk suit but still proceeding casually—on his way to the altar he even said hello to a friend he hadn't expected to be present.

At the altar Bruce was joined by his best men. Julianne began her careful walk down the aisle, escorted by her parents. She wore an off-white, antique lace dress, with ankle-high boots and a waist-length veil borrowed from her friend Ann Stucky Bickford, who had flown in from Alaska to serve as a maid of honor (along with Julie's sister Mary and Bruce's sister Pam) even though she was eight months pregnant.

There had been no time for a rehearsal, and there was a brief mixup during the ring ceremony, because the best men had lined up on the wrong side. Bruce made light of the error, but when he and Julie stepped forward alone to kneel at the altar to begin the ceremony, he was all seriousness. It was a typical Catholic ceremony, including Bible readings by two of Julianne's brothers and a brief sermon, but mass was not served.

By twenty minutes to one the wedding was complete. Bruce and Julianne grabbed a long kiss and then proceeded back down the aisle to the applause of their family and friends. Everyone milled around the chapel for another hour or so, taking pictures and relaxing; there was no champagne, but a couple of pints were passed around.

At about two A.M. Landau and Carr were talking back at their hotel, trying to decide when it would be appropriate to wake up Marilyn Laverty in New York so she could release a statement to the press. They finally decided that it could all wait until morning and went to bed, feeling relieved that at least the wedding itself had been pulled off without an untoward media crush. But although they didn't know it, the Portland radio stations had already been notified, and the next morning they were awakened by calls seeking to confirm the news.

Bruce and Julie had already left for a couple of days in a cabin in the Oregon woods.

The press felt trumped, but there was little they could do. Most of the reporters packed their bags and headed for the next scene of celebrity non-news. Bill Philips more or less apologized for being so sneaky, while the tabloids kept on sneaking, the *National Enquirer* even managing to snatch pictures from the Tuesday night country club reception that had originally been planned as a rehearsal dinner. *New York Daily News* gossip monger Suzy got a front-page headline for her report that the midnight wedding was just a tale, a swindle perpetrated by Jon Landau Management in order to clear the way for the originally planned Wednesday ceremony. The filing of the marriage certificate with the Portland civil records registrar shut her up.

A bigger reception, at which the full E Street Band and a few dozen additional guests would be present, was scheduled for Wednesday afternoon at a house in rural Tualatin, from which Mt. Hood and the entire Willamette Valley were visible. Security was again tight, but word again leaked out and the occasion was badly marred by the presence of several news helicopters, which buzzed continually, drowning out conversation. A few paparazzi even managed to set up their gear in the yard next door; one snapped shots of Bruce and Julie as they walked and spooned in the fields, and these were later sold to the same Rupert Murdoch press organization that had plagued "the Boss's minders" in Australia. (Murdoch's *Chicago Sun-Times* deemed the wedding so important that it ran an editorial saluting it.)

The helicopters were the last straw, flying so low that the Federal Aviation Administration was eventually called and the pilots were ordered either to desist or maintain a much higher altitude. Late in the afternoon a beleagured and exhausted Bruce Springsteen flopped on a couch and looked up at two of his friends. "I do not believe or comprehend the world that I live in," he said.

16 IT'S TOO LATE TO STOP NOW

I don't like the word "dream." I don't even want to specify it as American. What I'm beginning to understand is there's a human possibility. That's where all the excitement is. If you can be part of that, you're aware and alive. It's not a dream, it's possible. It's everyday stuff.

—"Blue-collar housewife" to Studs Turkel,
American Dreams: Lost and Found

Columbia Records scheduled the release of "Glory Days" as the fifth single from *Born in the U.S.A.* for May 31, the day before the European leg of the tour began. The single had the usual unreleased B side, a little rocker called "Stand on It," which would be featured as the final encore later in the summer.

Bruce also wanted this single to have a video. Most rock performers made their videos all at once, before their album was released and touring began. That way the record label could distribute the appropriate video as each single was issued; later all of them could be packaged—together with some not-too-probing interview footage—as an "MTV Special" or even as a commercial videotape. But Bruce only dealt with one thing at a time. That meant he was constantly playing video catch-up. Of the five *Born in the U.S.A.* singles, only the last, "My Hometown," had a simultaneously released video.

Rather than lack of forethought, this reflected Springsteen's wariness about form. "The main thing with my songs right now is that I write them to be complete things, and they're filled with a lot of geographical detail and a lot of detail about what people are wearing, where they live," he said. "The thing about a video is that you only really have a few choices about what you can do. Either you illustrate a song, which in my case I can't do—because it's like you're gonna paint a mustache on it or something. Or you create another story to go over the song, and that's kinda silly, because there's a story already there. That's the story I wanted to tell, so to create another story to go along with it, that doesn't make sense either.

"I've spent twenty years learning how to write so that when you hear a song you get the information you need—you get the experience and the emotion that you need. I write with a lot of detail, and I'm proud of doing it and I think that I do it well. And so I'm hesitant to mess with that. You've gotta respect the integrity of the song a little bit."

Springsteen was also wary of video, perhaps because the audience for it was so young—too young, in many cases, to have any hope of grasping the broader implications of his music. "The main audience video seems to be real important to is the little kids, from about six, seven—real young—up to like pre-concert-going age, where they can't go out yet. It's taken the place of cartoons, I think, actually, for kids," he told the BBC's David Hepworth. "Every house I go in, the kids are glued to it; they know all the bands. So there is a completely different audience out there."

Springsteen still hadn't written the medium off. "I don't know exactly what I'm gonna do," he told Hepworth. "I'd like to do something with it because it is a powerful tool. It is something that can reach a lot of people, and different types of people."

As an inveterate moviegoer, Bruce's most agreeable vision of video was seeing it as a way of exploring his cinematic ideas, but he was aware that its accessibility also concealed certain pitfalls.

"I always loved the movies. And, after all, music is evocative. That's the beauty of it. Which is also the danger of video. The tools can be great there, and obviously it can be used real well. But it can also be used badly because it's an inanimate thing in and of itself. The thing about a good song is its evocative power. What does it evoke in the listener?

"A song like 'Mansion on the Hill'—it's different to everybody. It's in people's lives, in that sense. That's what I always want my songs to do: to kind of just pan out and be very cinematic. The *Nebraska* record had that cinematic quality, where you get in there and you get the feel of life—just some of the grit and some of the beauty. I was thinking in a way of *To Kill a Mockingbird,* because in that movie there was a child's-eye view. And *Night of the Hunter* also had that—I'm not sure if *surrealistic* is the right word. But that was poetic when the little girl was running through the woods. I was thinking of scenes like that."

But after gaining some experience in video, he was less sanguine; the frustrations overwhelmed the potential. Most of all, video seemed an extraordinarily difficult thing to control. "It presents a set of unique problems which are very different from the way that I usually work," he told Hepworth. "One, it's very expensive most of the time, particularly since the production values of videos have gotten so high. And they're made very quickly, in a day or so; there's this enormous financial input and it's kind of a real roll of the dice.

"The way that I work is very different. I'll go in the studio and I'll spend a night, and if I don't like what I did, I throw it out. Basically, you can afford to do that. Plus, I work very slow; I don't work fast. I enjoy having the control over what I'm gonna say and what my work is. I work somewhat collaboratively but not near as much as, say, a video, with a director and all this other stuff. On my records I'm the director."

Film-making is such an elaborate art that control is far more diffused than it is even in a significantly collaborative medium like music. Though most successful films reflect a strong directorial personality, that's not always the case—great actors (particularly comedians) and writers and even cinematographers have sometimes had their say. Bruce didn't seem especially interested in becoming a director, but he had discernible talent as an actor—at least the camera loved him. (Film critic Andrew Sarris, who was not at all knowledgeable about rock and roll, had compared Bruce's turn in *No Nukes* to a John Garfield performance.) But in order to realize his ideas, Bruce needed to find compatible people to work with, just as he'd done in record-making.

In John Sayles he had found an ideal creative partner. John and Bruce were almost exactly the same age. Sayles grew up in a working-class neighborhood in Schenectady, New York, essentially a General Electric company town. Although he got a degree from Williams College (a "Little Ivy" institution), Sayles, like Springsteen, had never abandoned his ties to working-class culture. After writing three novels—the best of which, *Union Dues* (1977), Bruce read and liked—and a number of profoundly trashy screenplays (among them *Piranha, The Howling,* and *Alligator*), Sayles began making films on shoestring budgets. His first, *Return of the Secaucus Seven* (1980), was best-known for its $60,000 budget (about one percent of what it would have cost in Hollywood), but what was really remarkable was its acute look at the lives of Sixties radicals nearing middle age. (Its plot was swiped and trivialized three years later for Lawrence Kasdan's odious *The Big Chill*.)

In 1983 Sayles made his only studio picture, *Baby It's You,* for Paramount. The story of a mid-Sixties high school romance between a middle-class girl and a working-class boy, it featured an outstanding period rock and roll score. Sayles approached Landau about using Springsteen songs as more contemporary themes for the boy. Springsteen had never before allowed any of his songs to be used in movies—he just didn't want them exploited that way—but he approved *Baby It's You* because he trusted Sayles. The film used four Springsteen songs, most memorably "It's Hard to Be a Saint in the City" in a high school lunchroom and "Adam Raised a Cain" as a travelogue that climaxed with an overhead shot of the Statue of Liberty.

However, Sayles and Springsteen did not meet until the spring of 1984. The night after they mastered *Born in the U.S.A.* Chuck Plotkin, Springsteen, and several other friends had dinner at the Hoboken home of Sayles and his producer, Maggie Renzi. (Among those present was Renzi's sister, Marta, a choreographer who'd created a dance piece based on Springsteen songs, "You Little Wild Heart," for PBS in 1982.) John and Bruce proved to be as personally compatible as the similarity of their work suggested they would be. But Bruce went on tour, and they didn't speak again until he called to ask if Sayles would direct the "Born in the U.S.A." video.

Sayles wasn't interested in music video formally or as a career move. He had already established his credentials as an independent film-maker; he'd learned from *Baby It's You* that studio productions weren't really his metier. While he hadn't struck it rich, his screenplays and a so-called "genius grant" from the MacArthur Foundation supported him well enough so that he could later donate his $10,000 fee from directing "I'm on Fire" to a fund that sent ambulances to Nicaragua. Like Springsteen, Sayles was more interested in doing good work and keeping control of it than in wealth and glory. He was interested in making a music video with Bruce because their work had such strong stylistic affinities and because Springsteen was one of America's great undeveloped moving picture possibilities.

Bruce's proposal also came at a good time for Sayles. He'd finished his latest feature, *Brother from Another Planet,* and was in the midst of the arduous process of raising independent financing for *Matewan,* based on a segment of *Union Dues* that took place in the West Virginia coal fields during a strike in the early Twenties.

So Sayles agreed to make the "Born in the U.S.A." video, even though Bruce imposed severe restrictions on the shooting. Sayles was widely criticized for that clip's lack of lip-syncing, but the decision was entirely due to Bruce's dissatisfaction with the lip-syncing in "Dancing in the Dark." ("Lip-syncing is one of those things—it's easy to do, but you wonder about the *worth* of doing it," Bruce told Kurt Loder.)

"I'm on Fire" was much more a joint effort, but still it was shot and edited in haste, against the tight deadline of the single's chart life and Bruce's impending departure for Australia and Japan. Sayles was able to give Springsteen his first speaking lines, and Bruce pulled them off with aplomb; the look of mingled innocence and awareness that fills his face when his customer asks him to drop the T-bird off at her place is terrific.

"Glory Days" was also a collaborative venture, inasmuch as Springsteen and Sayles cooked up the story line together. This time they had the luxury of a three-day shoot (May 24, 27, and 28) spread over four North Jersey locations: a construction site and a decrepit baseball stadium in West New York; the Secaucus house of a bar owner Sayles knew; and Maxwell's, a Hoboken bar ordinarily the habitat of avant-garde rock and rollers but converted for this occasion into a sweaty working-class hangout. The video didn't exactly have a plot, but it was several minutes longer than the song; Bruce again spoke a few lines. It had a cast of four (Bruce's sons were played by Barbara Carr's nephews, eleven-year-old Jason Fisher and three-year-old James "Lucky" Dunning, and his wife by Julianne Philips), plus about fifty extras for the barroom sequence.

In the "Glory Days" video Springsteen plays a construction worker with two kids who harbors big league baseball fantasies. He's seen at work, munching an apple while sitting atop a crane; at home watching Dwight Gooden on TV; contemplatively oiling his own glove; being awakened by his son, who smacks him with a plastic bat; and at the ball field, standing alone on the pitcher's mound throwing at a piece of board. (Sportswriter Shelby Strother of the *Detroit News*, a fan, commented that Bruce "throws a baseball like a man with a torn rotator cuff.")

In the barroom scene Springsteen leads the E Street Band, with Little Steven Van Zandt returned for the occasion to mug and play his mandolin solo. Although the story never spells it out, the singer/guitarist in the bar band and the baseball addict are probably meant to be separate but equivalent identities—two guys who work day jobs and find fulfillment at night by sticking with things that they loved as children. (Baseball looks like hard work, while the shots of the bar band are radiant, a discrepancy surely not intentional.)

The energy and excitement of seeing the E Street Band live came across in a Springsteen video for the first time. The pained and scruffy poses of "Born in the U.S.A." were almost as artificial as the exuberant and manicured stances of "Dancing in the Dark." (Bruce performed solo—and only a little—in "I'm on Fire.") But with "Glory Days" Sayles was given much more independence and Springsteen wasn't trying to alter his own pop star image; they worked together to burnish that image, and in deepening its sheen they finally got it right. This isn't what a "real" Bruce Springsteen song looks like onstage, but it's exactly what it feels like.

The family scenes establish a Springsteen persona that steps outside rock and roll's myth of eternal youth. It's hard to think of another music video in which a star functions comfortably—and as an adult—in the interior of a nuclear family. The identity of most rock stars would explode in any version of this situation. But it enriched Springsteen's image and allowed the video to burrow much closer to the heart of the song, which is just as crucial to the *Born in the U.S.A.* album as "Dancing in the Dark," "My Hometown," and "Born in the U.S.A." but more easily missed because it doesn't sound as big.

"Glory Days" is about rock and roll's promise of eternal youth and the reality of aging. The music, which marries rinky-dink organ, honky-tonk piano, and garage-band guitar kicked along by an explosive tom-tom pattern, suggests a joke. Springsteen sings most of the song in a comic tone; when they get to the bridge he gleefully whoops and exhorts the group through its paces.

But "Glory Days" isn't really optimistic; behind its glee are some sad stories—the baseball pitcher who never topped his high school heroics, the good ol' girl whose marriage fell apart, the rock and roll singer who's embarrassed by his own fixation on the past. All are wasting away for the same reason, which isn't that they're living in the past but that they're missing the moment. The song's energy really comes from the contradictory atmosphere of the music, because it's the kind of trash—updated frat rock, archaic dance music—whose prime purpose is to propel you into the here and now.

Somehow its first verse defines "Glory Days" as a rock and roll song about baseball, an idea reinforced by the video and Bruce's comic onstage raps about his preteen athletic ineptitude. In fact, the song says nothing much about the game; the singer just encounters the high school ballplayer who "could throw that speedball by ya/Make you look like a fool" but has now become a bar-hopping fool himself.

There's another reason baseball seems important to understanding "Glory Days," though. Rock and roll and baseball, despite the radical difference in the way they're paced—the former galloping, the latter ambling—share a common trait: In each of them, what seems so simple and easy when played by children becomes deeper and more complex when played by adults. There's nothing to that home run swing when you're twelve; those songs are just three chords and a lot of attitude when you're sixteen. But as time goes by, both the sport and the music grow richer. Suddenly Chuck Berry isn't just outlining the ideal teenage life-style but illuminating the bitterness of a black man mocking everything he can't have; watching Ozzie Smith throw to first from deep in the hole, we realize the subtleties of positioning as a concomitant of grace. The blood squeezed from Pete Townshend's fingertips and the tears that fell from Wade Boggs's eyes have a lot in common.

In the last verse of "Glory Days" Springsteen prays to be released from his own obsession with the past and then laughs mockingly at the very idea, spitting in the eye of the idea that rock and roll is a toy for tots. "Well, but time slips away and leaves you with nothing, mister, but boring stories of . . ." he yelps, but the band won't let him stop. And when he whips the band onward in the final seconds—"All right, boys! We gonna go home now!"—he echoes Van Morrison, the most reluctant rock and roller of all: "It's too late to stop now."

Bruce had long been determined to find out what rock and roll became when it wasn't "youth culture" anymore. "Glory Days," in which he mocked his own nostalgia into proportion, is the first step in searching out a livable answer, which is why it's the perfect lead-in to "Dancing in the Dark," where Springsteen finally stops "sittin' around thinkin' about it" and starts moving on. "Dancing in the Dark" boils "Glory Days" down to two lines—"You sit around gettin' older/There's a joke here somewhere and it's on me"—and passes to a place where its author could face an interviewer in the fall of 1984 and say without sounding fatuous, "Maybe you can't dream the same dreams when you're thirty-four that you did when you were twenty-four, you know, but you can still dream something." And he told another, "After I wrote the *Nebraska* record, I said, 'Well, gee, I wonder what it'll be like when I sing "Born to Run." Do I still believe these songs?' And when I thought about it, I wasn't sure. But when I sang it, I knew that I did. It's just all different parts of life, you know. It's just all a different part of life."

In concert "Glory Days" grew further. Wrote Joyce Millman of his Boston show, "Springsteen led off 'Glory Days' with a hilarious rant about the bad old times, skittering around like Richard Pryor, with his mouth scrunched up, his eyes bugging out, and his hands up in the air: 'I *hated* high school! I had a terrible time in high school! When fall comes around, I'm *still* glad I don't have to go *back* to high school!' Still, his ending shout of 'I can hear the clock ticking. It says, "Boss, you're 30–31–32–33–34 . . ."' was ironic because, watching him hop around the stage in a loony kick-line . . . it seemed impossible that Springsteen will ever be too old for rock and roll. How can he ever look undignified or foolish when he's always been willing to risk looking undignified or foolish if the mood dictates? As he teetered on one clunky biker boot, then the other, swinging his guitar back and forth, with a gloriously spaced-out smile on his face, he made a convincing picture of both a tot and a dreamy old codger." Bruce put a finer point on it during his Ames, Iowa, show when, Steve Perry reported, he halted the band and screamed, "I don't EVER wanna die!"

After that shout, Perry added, Springsteen looked startled, and that makes sense, for he'd just broken a mighty taboo or two. Humans are aware of their own death, but it's something they're supposed to contemplate only alone. Rock stars have it worse; for them age is a constant, early arriving spectre, but you're not supposed to admit that you crank up the amps in order to cheat the reaper—or at least to console yourself against his approach.

Rock and roll has been portrayed for so long as a child's game, and the facts that disprove the proposition are so rarely uttered that even most dedicated fans don't know that Chuck Berry was married and the father of two kids when he wrote all the hits that defined the first generation's glory days. "I was thirty-one years old, but I could *remember*," Berry told Bill Flanagan in *Written in My Soul*. But Berry didn't escape the fear that plagued everybody from Elvis to Pete Townshend to Elvis Costello. "I remember the first time I heard a kid say, 'Thirty-five years old! He's as old as my father!' I went, 'Oh, shit.'" And it wasn't just Chuck Berry: Fats Domino, Elvis Presley, Carl Perkins, Ray Charles, and John Lennon were all adults when they laid the ground Bruce Springsteen and his peers walk upon.

All of rock's other great performers felt they had to turn away from the essence of the music in order to be grown-ups. But there's more than one mythology of rock and roll. One of its more disabling spectres is self-parody, in which the greatest, most experienced performers are paralyzed by the idea that what they're doing is a waste because they're no longer 'twixt twelve and twenty. (The audience also experiences this whenever some pompous ass asks a fan when he or she will "outgrow" such music or why he or she expects anything more than a hot time from it.) It seemed to happen to everybody: Chuck Berry and Mick Jagger got cynical; Little Richard and Carl Perkins got religion; Jerry Lee Lewis got drunk; Bob Dylan got lost; Elvis got confused; John Lennon got shot. For the Fifties rock stars, those who survived, there was the purgatory of the oldies circuit; for the Sixties stars, those who didn't overdose, there was the limbo of heartless craft. Seen in this light, "Glory Days" is a portrait of the rock star taking out the trash.

"I guess basically I always thought that I'd do it forever in some fashion," said Springsteen to an interviewer who asked how it felt to reach thirty-five. "I didn't think that you had to stop or that age was a factor. Age was just something to be dealt with— you grow into it. It just becomes a part of what you do. I mean, rock and roll anymore is not just somethin' for if you're seventeen. There'll always be fifteen-year-olds doin' it, but now there's gonna be forty-five-year-olds doin' it, too." He laughed; it's hard to say why.

Maybe even Bruce Springsteen felt the pressure not to "take it all too seriously." But most of his responses to such questions reflected how imperative answering them was. "You know, as you get older, the main thing that you gotta deal with is all the things you lose," he said, adding the even more heretical idea that aging could well be an advantage because it offers broader perspectives. "I guess basically as you get older your main battle is a battle to not give in to despair.

"Which is difficult," he laughed again. "It's difficult to do. And basically that's the fight most of my characters are fighting now in some fashion. Certainly the guy in 'Born in the U.S.A.,' his thing is just a survival thing. There's not the naïveness that there initially was in my earlier music. There's not a certain kind of youthful optimism—even though optimism may always be youthful in some sense. But it's not like you're gonna save the world. It's mainly people trying to find some place for themselves *in* the world—some place where they can live with some dignity and some decency, some sense of self-respect, to find some place in some community somewhere, to find some friends, to find a job, to be able to live with their wives or their kids, to make some sort of life for themselves."

And he not only knew that this was important, in the end he also knew why. "If you can deal with that, if you can deal with just that sense of leaving things behind . . . Or else you go crazy, you go crazy tryin' to hold on to the same dream you had when you were twenty-two."

The "Glory Days" video brought such ideas to life, in a far different way than a song could. Whether or not he ever made another great video, Bruce Springsteen had finally done one that lived up to the best parts of his music.

■

Making music about community was one thing; living as the biggest rock star in America was another. After the wedding, Springsteen's permanent celebrity was assured. *He* was famous, not his records or his shows, and that caused all kinds of craziness. Sometimes when Bruce pulled up to a Jersey stoplight, other drivers would recognize him and park, walk up to the window, and demand an autograph, creating a snarl by ignoring the light as it changed.

Nevertheless, the first day of the video shoot, at the construction site and the ball park, proceeded without incident. It was the beginning of Memorial Day weekend, but the traffic passing by never noticed the guy in the hard hat and sunglasses peeling an orange for the camera, and nobody in the neighborhood around the ball field guessed who was inside with the camera crew. (It was the same ball park where Bob Giraldi shot the sequences for the World Series vignettes that used "My Hometown.")

That was Friday night; by Monday, which was the holiday, word had leaked out that Charles Krajewski's house on Mill Ridge Road in Secaucus was being used for a Bruce Springsteen video. The *Secaucus Home News* sent a photographer, who hovered in the weeds outside the yard, periodically chased back by McDuffie. Meanwhile star-seeking, autograph-hunting neighbors and their kids filled the street and driveway around the two-family house. New Jersey Springsteen fans have a feeling of proprietorship about him; part of the peril of a populist image is continually having to measure the distance between the crowd's fantasies of access and the need for security. In Secaucus the situation stayed well in control.

The next day's shooting at Maxwell's, located in the center of Hoboken just down the block from the huge Maxwell House Coffee plant, commenced before nine A.M. The back barroom was rigged with a pool table, its walls covered with dozens of brewery logos. The band set up on a riser in the middle of the floor; it was bigger than the club's regular stage, but Roy Bittan's piano still had to be placed on the floor.

That back room had no windows, but Maxwell's, which usually opened only at night, was crowded front and back with crew and extras. Before noon word of what was going on inside had spread through the town, only a five-minute bus or subway ride from Manhattan. And this time the radio also broadcast the news. A crowd of fifty onlookers became a hundred, then two hundred. It was a hot, wet day, and it began to rain hard about the time that school let out. Even so the crowd doubled in size again before five. The onlookers, egged on by the presence of radio and television crews, heaved against the plate glass doors and windows. They sent up a demanding chant: "We want Bruce! We want Bruce!" The local cops, stationed inside and out, didn't seem especially concerned. "I don't blame them," said Officer Tommy Meehan to the *Daily News*. "It's not every day the Boss is in town."

Inside the band was having a good time. The extras included the band's wives and girlfriends, a dozen or so old friends, and friends of the directors and producers. During the lunch break or in long lags between shots, the atmosphere was that of a crowded, convivial party.

But outside, the crowding and the rain and the jostling for position and the whining of the television crews—one producer

complained it was easier to interview Cardinal John O'Connor—
continued through the heat and the drizzle. "We want Bruce! We
want Bruce!" the chant began, and it continued on and off until
shooting was complete, around five. Bruce wasn't about to make
even a token appearance for the media (although Hoboken's
mayor and a city councilman did badger their way in through the
cops to take a peek).

As the shooting drew to a close, it became obvious that it was
going to be a problem getting Bruce outside. If he went through
the front, the crowd was likely to surge against the doors and
windows so powerfully that the glass would shatter and someone
could get hurt. There was a back exit without windows, but the
crowd also swelled near that.

McDuffie, Magovern, and Springsteen strategized. They decided on a decoy. A crew member who was about the right size
grabbed a newspaper and held it up to his face as he was
escorted—well, shoved—through the front. The crowd stepped
back just enough to protect itself; the glass held. The waiters at
the back door moved to the front as Bruce slipped out through the
exit, wearing a Hoboken police cap and shades. Accompanied by
Julie, he hopped into a revved-up van. Only a few fans spotted
him; it was a clean getaway—and easy to laugh off the alarm of a
moment before. In fact, when one of the fans asked for a lift,
Bruce asked his destination and then said, "Sure, get in." They
dropped him off on the way back to Rumson.

■

Tickets for the European shows—eighteen dates, all outdoors—began going on sale the first week in May, only a month
before the first show, on June 1 at Slane Castle in Dublin. As the
cities were announced, one after another, many fell in the same
fashion as the American towns that preceded them; even though
capacities ranged between 50,000 and 100,000 (total attendance
was just short of a million), most shows sold out in a matter of
hours. In Gothenburg, Sweden, the only place Bruce was playing
in Scandinavia, two 60,000-seat shows sold out in ten minutes.
In Milan there were 250,000 applications for the only Italian
date. In England, where a mail-order system was used, there
were a million requests for only 300,000 seats.

As in Australia, the limited time available and the high demand required doing the largest outdoor facilities available; as in Japan, the shows started early—usually around four P.M., but at the beginning and end of the tour, at Slane and in Leeds, England, the concerts were set for one P.M. (There was no point waiting for full dark, which in the European summer comes only toward midnight.) In addition to Slane, Gothenburg, Milan, and Leeds, Bruce would play two nights in Newcastle and three at London's 70,000-seat Wembley Stadium, two shows in Rotterdam, two in Paris, and single dates at Frankfurt and Munich, West Germany, and Montpelier and St. Etienne in the French provinces.

Born in the U.S.A. was a massive hit in Europe. When first released, "Dancing in the Dark" had stiffed, as had all Bruce's previous European singles, but it was revived after a remarkable one-hour Springsteen special on the British television program *The Old Grey Whistle Test.* The show, later rebroadcast in many countries on the Continent, featured a sensitive and intelligent interview conducted by David Hepworth, extensive footage of fans before the previous autumn's shows in Philadelphia, and an amazing amount of concert footage. Not only did *OGWT* have access to the "Rosalita" clip, "Thunder Road" and "The River" from *No Nukes* and the "Dancing in the Dark" video, they were also able to film three complete numbers from the Spectrum: "Born in the U.S.A.," "Cover Me," and the "Detroit Medley" of Mitch Ryder hits.

The visceral excitement of this live footage spread the word about Springsteen as nothing else could have done. The interview also presold the show. Asked to define his ambitions for a concert, Springsteen gave a lengthy, seductive answer: "If it's a good night out, that's great—that's basically what it's meant to be. . . . I try to present a lotta different things so that it can be somethin'—I think you could come and maybe it'll change the way you think about something. Maybe about the way you think about your life or your job or your friends or . . . I think it can do that. We try to do it well enough so that it can do that. And at the same time, like I said, if it's a good date or somethin', that's good, too. Whatever people want—whatever they take from it— whatever they *need* at that moment is what I would hope that it would be." He hesitated, then plunged. "If you come and you need [*a heavy sigh*] some inspiration maybe, I would hope that you could find a little bit of it. But if you want to dance or if you wanna take your girl out—I'd hope it was a combination of all those things."

Springsteen explicitly offered an opportunity to have your life changed while you danced, yet his demeanor managed to make him seem modest while the concert footage more than backed up every word he said. Anybody who resisted wasn't capable of being interested.

That didn't mean that "Born in the U.S.A." was any better understood in Europe than it had been in the States. Although the live version shown on *OGWT* sounded mordant and mournful, Springsteen still had something of a reputation as a mere flag-waver. Steve Van Zandt, who had built a small but significant audience in Europe with his leftist rock and roll, found himself having to explain the bitter criticisms contained in the song's lyrics to left-wing journalists who grasped its intricacies no better than conservative American pundits.

Springsteen got his ideas across better in a three-hour show, of course, than in a sixty-minute television special that steered away from social issues; taken alone, none of his songs summarized his perspective. That was the point. Throughout the European tour there was an arresting contrast between Springsteen's songs of dreams and disillusion and the stars and stripes that almost always waved here and there amongst the crowd. Still, Bruce was sure of himself. When they ran into each other after the first Paris show, Robert Hilburn asked him if he wasn't surprised at the lack of an anti-American backlash. "Naw," Springsteen said. "Rock and roll has always been able to cut through all that. That's what's great about it; you don't have to intellectualize it. Everybody feels the same emotions. It's great out there when everyone sings 'Born in the U.S.A.' They put so much feeling into it that it's real for them, even if it's not technically true. They know what the song is about and they can relate to it. That's the real connection."

The biggest challenge of the European tour was the test of playing, for the first time, an entire tour outdoors in stadiums.

The smallest crowds numbered more than 50,000, the largest about double that. In that sense, Syracuse and even Australia were nothing more than dry runs. Furthermore, Springsteen was used to playing at night, with extremely dramatic stage lighting. The European shows were played in such strong daylight that lighting director Jeff Ravitz didn't even bother with the majority of his effects, using just white-hot television lights.

Syracuse and the Australian outdoor dates had gone well, even in bad weather, and Bruce was ready to tackle the new challenge, eager to learn the secrets playing to such a crowd had to teach him and confident that he'd succeed. Hepworth asked how he'd made the transition from clubs and theaters to arenas. "It wasn't that different," Bruce replied. "It was really much more of a mental thing, once you got the physical things taken care of, like the sound and lights." He was confident that Ravitz and long-time soundman Bruce Jackson were up to the job.

Additionally, tour manager George Travis had tracked down the best outdoor video system available, Panasonic's Diamond-vision, which was easy to view even in the brilliant daylight in which they'd mostly be playing. And he'd hired an outstanding director, Arthur Rosato, a rock and roll veteran who'd spent a long time working with Bob Dylan (among other things, he played drums on the tour following *Shot of Love*). Rosato's low-key, straightforward direction would be a key to effectively translating the visual side of Springsteen's show to audiences sometimes sitting more than a hundred yards away. As those fans learned, the cameras loved Bruce outside, too.

■

On May 30, Liverpool, England's reigning soccer champions, faced Italy's leading club, Juventus, in a European Cup match in Brussels. The match was televised live across Europe and in the United Kingdom. As millions watched, the Liverpool fans, who already had a reputation for rowdiness to the point of riot, attacked the Italian supporters and in the process, hundreds were trampled. Thirty-eight died; hundreds were treated for injuries. In the wake of the riot, England's soccer teams were indefinitely banned from participation in international soccer, and people all over Europe became wary of stadium events for the next few months.

The Springsteen tour suffered some peripheral consequences. One result was a slump in ticket sales in those few places that weren't already sold out. In Paris authorities created so many new security restrictions for playing the Stade de Colombes, a football field, that the concerts had to be moved to Parc de La Courneuve, in the northern suburbs.

In Dublin preparations had been underway all week for the Saturday concert. Slane Castle is located about thirty miles outside the city, in County Meath, just beyond an ordinarily sleepy village. The castle is the property of Lord Henry Mont-charles (who, like most Irish aristocrats, is British). Lord Hank, as Travis instructed his crew to call him, had converted a part of the castle to an inn; the previous winter, U2 had rented out several of the rooms and recorded *The Unforgettable Fire* there. For the past several summers, in order to help manage the expensive upkeep of the old monstrosity, Lord Hank had been staging rock concerts in the beautiful natural amphitheater (with a 65,000-person capacity) formed by the cow pasture just outside its walls.

Previous shows at Slane—by U2, David Bowie, and, in 1984, Bob Dylan—had proven so disruptive, with drunken kids litter-ing the streets, pissing in doorways, and trashing store windows and private lawns, that the townspeople had vowed, "Never again." But Belfast promoter Jim Aitken and George Travis, by starting to negotiate the previous October, were able to swing a deal. They promised sufficient sanitary facilities, large, colorful litter barrels, and security personnel to protect the town, and eventually the local residents association was convinced to allow the show, although it also insisted that it would be the last ever held there.

The scale of the preparations told the story of this massive undertaking. Aitken hired a security force of 800; they were supplemented by dozens of *gardai* (Irish national police). Five hundred telephone lines were installed at the site; the castle stables were converted into a field hospital staffed by doctors, nurses, and the Red Cross. "There is two hundred fifty thousand pounds invested on this site and it will all disappear overnight," Aitken told the press. (Bruce's guarantee was an estimated half million dollars.)

Bruce flew into Dublin at eight o'clock Friday morning, the day before the show. The Irish papers put his arrival on the front page, showing him arm in arm with Julie as they emerged from clearing customs. After resting up, Bruce and Julie left at six thirty for a seven thirty sound check and inspection of the site.

There was still plenty of light left as he walked through the tent city—with dressing rooms, hospitality tents, and eating facilities for the band and crew—like a general inspecting a battlefield. The tents were set up around a stream running perhaps twenty yards behind the stage—the River Boyne, trickling along about three miles from the spot where the Irish had lost the last vestiges of their independence to the British 300 years before in the Battle of the Boyne. (Kids without tickets would crowd the opposite banks the next day, as kayakers paddled past, getting a good listen.)

All around, assembly of the stage and sound system and barricades continued. The crew had even built a corduroy road leading to the stage from the dirt entrance road; it went off again to the security fence separating the crowd from the backstage. As Bruce traipsed into the field that spread out before the stage to listen from a fan's perspective, the ground was still muddy, although the heat of another day would firm it up.

Springsteen had hoped to see a demonstration of the Diamondvision screens, but they weren't ready to go yet and daylight was fading, however slowly. He took the stage and worked through a couple of numbers. "Born in the U.S.A." and "Dancing in the Dark" rang eerily through the beautiful and empty green hills, but not nearly as strangely as the final song Bruce pulled out of his hat, the Conway Twitty rockabilly arrangement of "Danny Boy." Roy Bittan made it seem as if those pipes acallin' had brought successive generations of Irish emigrants to America solely to learn to rock and roll.

At eight thirty there was still plenty of light, but it was becoming cold, so the band trooped into the castle's massive stone entranceway, which had been converted into a pub (closed for the evening). Equipment was set up in an anteroom for another hour's rehearsal. The band hadn't played together since Japan, and Bruce put them through almost a full hour's set before knocking off around nine thirty to head back to the Dublin hotel.

Saturday dawned bright and hot, by Irish standards, temperature peaking somewhere in the upper seventies. The *gardai* set up roadblocks on the two-lane highways that were the only way into Slane, and travelers had to show their tickets to get by, precautions designed to prevent another outbreak like the one that had marred the Dylan show. But thousands of kids had camped out overnight in the village or in the fields near the castle. Hundreds of fans had wandered the streets long past midnight, often drunk, carrying sleeping bags or just as likely wearing black plastic trash bags in which they'd flop to the ground for a few hours snockered rest. Many were up early to visit the hundreds of vans stretched along the final mile of road leading to the castle and offering fast food and bootleg t-shirts. Beer and hard liquor were also easy to find.

Slane was barricaded against the onslaught. The bank and other shops on its main street boarded up their windows just in case of trouble; home owners removed the plants from their front gardens so they couldn't be torn up.

Sixty-five thousand tickets had been sold; counterfeits had made an appearance in northern England; some level of gate-crashing could be expected. Police estimated the real size of the crowd at 100,000. The only road to the castle was narrow and winding, and Travis had already worked out a plan to alleviate the traffic jam. Although the tickets stated firmly that no one would be admitted until three P.M., the gates would in fact be opened at noon. (There were plans to open them as early as ten if the hordes had already arrived by then.) Bruce took the stage promptly at five.

Unfortunately, Bruce Springsteen and the E Street Band were only the day's main attraction, not its only one. Slane was the place to be that Saturday, whether you were a big Springsteen fan or not. Most were, but the hundreds who jostled closest to the stage included dozens of drunks whose enthusiasm was expressed primarily by shoving forward; on the fringes, but within Bruce's view, some got into fistfights. Jostling and jockeying for position in the front rows was to be expected, but this was nastier, a restless pushing back and forth in waves that sent weaker and smaller people to their knees or crushed them against the barricade before the stage. Several dozen in the audience, mostly young girls, fainted and had to be passed up over the barricade and into the infirmary area backstage. No one was badly injured; an officer of the St. Johns Ambulance Brigade reported that only twenty to twenty-five had even minor injuries, and some of them were just suffering from sunburn.

Wearing jeans and a maroon and white striped polo shirt, Bruce slammed through "Born in the U.S.A.," then "Badlands" and "Out in the Street" before pausing. Even on the video screen you could see distress and unease rush across his face. Maybe the danger wasn't real—"There is no built-in aggro, everybody there is a fan of one person," Jim Aitken told reporters who raised the spectre of the Brussels riot; Pete Townshend smiled at Springsteen's distress and commented, "But it's always like this when you play outdoors." But this shoving and mauling and milling around wasn't at all what a Bruce Springsteen show was supposed to be about. How could you sing about self-respect before an audience that threatened to become a mob? How did you readjust their focus and get them to listen?

"What you gotta do is stop that swaying back and forth, 'cause it's knocking people around, okay?" Bruce urged forcefully after "Out in the Street." "If anybody needs help to get out of there, raise your hand." He was probably a lot more freaked by the aggressive behavior than the crowd, but a look of fear could be seen in every band member's face, and on the ramp behind the stage, Jon Landau paced furiously, chewing his lip so powerfully it seemed he'd bite clear through.

Down in the pit between the barricade and the stage, crew members sprayed hoses on the crowd, to cool it off and perhaps help settle down some of the more drunken types. Julie Philips worked backstage with the first-aid crews, soothing the brows of the kids who'd fainted in the crush.

Bruce swung into the *Nebraska* portion of the set, which today amounted to only "Johnny 99" and "Atlantic City," then dedicated "The River" to "all of you who ever needed a place to go when you couldn't go home." On the video screens, the song was paired with a view of the placid River Boyne, an ironic contrast to the turbulence of the song (and a shot kept on tape that was used for the entire rest of the tour).

The pace became a bit rushed, and when Bruce tried to speak again before "The Promised Land," the fans were so loud he couldn't manage the tone at all. Still concerned about what he was seeing before him, he again suggested cutting each other some slack. But when he spoke again, before "My Hometown," he never mentioned the Simon Community, the Dublin organization for the homeless to which he was making a contribution, perhaps because by then he'd accepted that he wasn't being listened to. (In fact, those who sat well back in the crowd experienced no problem; the problem only existed where Bruce would be most aware of it.) When he finished "Thunder Road" in Clarence's arms, the band left the stage looking almost thankful in its relief.

Eight hundred guests of Lord Hank, including Irish politicians, Townshend and his family, all of Spandau Ballet, most of U2, and Elvis Costello dressed like a rabbi, watched the show from the castle, where they ate smoked salmon and drank champagne. A hundred eighty came for breakfast; two hundred stayed for dinner. All day long, helicopters zoomed overhead, flying in wealthy and famous observers. During the break, many members of the "regular" audience clambered over the green wire fence into the "VIP enclosure" (less like a cage than it sounds) in front of the castle. Some, but by no means all, were stopped by gray t-shirted security men and sent back into the mass below.

The second set opened as usual with "Cover Me" and "Dancing in the Dark." Bruce had come to terms with the circumstances, reassured that no one had been seriously hurt. Besides, the worst of the swaying was over; maybe the rowdiest drunks had simply exhausted themselves or lost their places going for more booze at the break. Even so, the crush remained strong and during "Dancing" Bruce chose Patti Scialfa as his partner, although he did spot an old friend near the front during "Hungry Heart" and brought her up to dance along the front of the stage for a moment. On "Pink Cadillac" he delivered his Jimmy Swaggart spiel ferociously, as if trying to exorcise a bad mood; it didn't make much difference, because Catholic Ireland had no more experience of television evangelism than Buddhist Japan, and even attentive listeners were somewhat mystified.

The second set ended with "Rosalita," Bruce saying that the band would be "pissed off" if he didn't introduce them, a remarkable comment since he rarely swore even offstage. "You can call me lieutenant, honey," he snarled in the course of the song, "but don't ever call me Boss."

He came back out for the first encore all alone, carrying an acoustic guitar, then sat down and played the Beach Boys' "When I Grow Up to Be a Man," his voice cracked and trembling. In that moment, he sounded as miserable as any misanthrope Elvis Costello had ever imagined. When the band came back on, he turned to them with a look almost of supplication, and in the next few minutes you could see what they were really worth to one another. He shouted for "Ramrod," and they hit it viciously, playing their hearts out inside that dinosaur beat. In the midst of the song, you could practically feel the band pick Bruce up and try to turn his mood around. They finished with an exuberant "Born to Run" and the medley of "Twist and Shout" and "Do You Love Me."

When it was over, the rest of the band and the part of the crew that didn't have to disassemble the show and get it to Newcastle dried off and repaired to the castle for a dinner the promoters had laid on. Bruce and Jon Landau, however, took the first chopper back to Dublin's Gresham Hotel, where they talked events over for the rest of the night.

Bruce had been making his adjustments all afternoon; he wasn't ready to make any radical alterations immediately. Landau was perhaps more worried than that. "I wouldn't say Bruce had a good time, but he was not feeling bad when the show was over," Landau said. "We had stuff to talk about, you know. . . . Let's put it this way, if that had been the third show instead of the first, it would have been a non-event. We got the wildest crowd in the first fifteen minutes of the tour. And the frightening thing was not what was happening here, but is it gonna be like this every night? Am I gonna have to go through six weeks of that, because that would have been a little difficult."

As it turned out, Slane was an anomaly in the course of the tour. George Travis had made one mistake, allowing the barricade in front of the stage to be laid out flat, rather than in a vee-shape (like a ship's prow), which would better disperse the crowding. Having made that alteration, the rest of the shows went relatively smoothly, although a few people were still hauled over the barricade each night because of the crush and some were savvy enough to see a way to get backstage. In fact, in Gothenburg, Springsteen had one of the fainters brought up onstage. She came to in his arms, then danced as if she'd died and gone to heaven.

Landau took a single additional precaution. He gave interviews in each of the remaining cities to stress the idea that the show was a Bruce Springsteen concert, *not* a rock festival. He also made sure that the promotion for the upcoming U.S. dates took the same tone.

As things turned out, the rest of the European tour was almost completely devoid of negative events. In most towns the arrival of the Springsteen tour was major news, worthy of headline coverage, but there was an utter lack of incidents. This was so even in Milan, and it's a rock and roll industry cliché that all Italian shows are accompanied by riots and customers without tickets breaking in. George Travis, determined that this would not occur during one of his shows, successfully defused the situation by placing extra video screens in the plaza outside San Siro Stadium. At dusk, just as the crowd was gathering itself for a rush at the gates, he switched the screens on. Since the music could be adequately heard coming over the roof of the stadium, that left nothing to riot *about*.

In fact, you couldn't have asked for smoother shows than those in Newcastle, the tour's second stop. Newcastle is a town of coal-miners and industrial workers, the British equivalent of Wheeling or Youngstown. Bruce pushed the possibilities in both shows, concluding the first with the somber "Racing in the Street" and filling out the second with quieter numbers like "Shut Out the Light" and "Can't Help Falling in Love." The weather had cooled and, with everyone's adjustments in place, the shows went smooth as a dream.

Springsteen was continuing his policy of working with community groups in each city that he visited, and in Newcastle he chose to work with the Durham Miners' Wives Support Group, the wives of men left destitute after losing a bitter strike against the British government, which had decided to bust the union by closing most of the state-owned coal mines and importing scabs to run those that were left.

This earned him an attack by right-wing Member of Parliament Piers Merchant, who wrote a letter and raised questions in Parliament about the donation. "I think he was badly advised about the coal strike and the issues involved; it was an ill-judged decision," Merchant told Gavin Martin of *New Musical Express*. "I don't think he supports violence. The money will be going to miners who've been sacked, and they've been guilty of violence and vandalism. It's a great shame because it was great to have him in Newcastle." It turned out that this British version of George Will had in the past been supported by the fascist-style British National Movement and that Merchant had refused to disavow such support.

The reaction of Anne Fiddick, the Miners Wives' representative with whom Springsteen met, was much more meaningful and symbolized the way in which Springsteen's "charity" work could have much broader political impact. Fiddick spoke of the group's amazement simply at being offered six tickets to the show. After all, once the Miner's Union declared the strike over, the majority of their media support had drifted away. (Gavin Martin and his colleague Cynthia Rose were significant exceptions.) "To me that was the *crème de la crème*," Fiddick said. "But when we were asked to bring information on the work we were doing now, I was taken totally by surprise.

"We met an incredible guy—he'd followed events on TV and in the press, and he wanted to know how we managed to live and organize the movement from within the communities so that it spread nationally. He told us about his own father, how being put out of work had drained his pride and spirit, and we explained how we were campaigning now to keep communities alive in places where pits are being closed down. His interest was obviously in the families and the communities.

"By doing this Bruce has become some sort of a symbol for the men up here. Since the strike ended they've become dejected and downcast. It seemed as if no one was interested and no one cared, with all the press campaigns dwindling. By proving he cares, Springsteen has reopened all the questions that have been left to die since the strike ended."

■

Meanwhile Bruce was evolving a slightly different format to suit the new facilities he was playing. In general, he spoke to the crowd much less; in Paris, Robert Hilburn reported, he basically talked only to introduce "My Hometown" and "I'm on Fire." Usually he dedicated "The River," as he'd done at Slane. "Glory Days," now an international hit, became a more elaborate skit, with Jim McDuffie appearing as Father Time and presenting Bruce with a cane. The song's sexual innuendos also grew, as Springsteen joked about "getting better at it" now that he was married and could "practice alla time."

Springsteen accepted a greater level of inattention at the stadium shows, as he'd had to accept an increase in distraction when he moved to arenas. "Hey, it's a rock and roll show," he said, shrugging off those who shouted and roamed during the slow songs. The nature of the event—outdoors, in a gathering more populous than Freehold, in the middle of the summer—didn't automatically grant the same ease of focus as indoor concerts. But that was part of the point; the adventure of these shows was figuring out how to center the crowd's attention and create a new kind of interaction.

In fact, Bruce changed the set very little. Basically, he stabilized the repertoire, making fewer changes each evening. This sort of thing had been a breaking point for every other rock act that reached stadium level; the vast audience came with its own expectations and the audience's sheer size gave its will enormous force. Mostly, a crowd of that size came to party more than listen, and to defy it risked not getting over at all.

Springsteen's show wasn't really an exception. It *was* measurably more difficult to pull off the slower, more thoughtful songs—the audience was restive through such quiet passages—but Bruce refused to back off. If he spoke less and relied more on a central core of songs on the Continent, it was probably because he was feeling the situation out, trying to sort out the songs that reached from those that didn't—not just which got the loudest cheers but which created the atmosphere that he wanted. In fact, without any production hardware to get in the way, Springsteen eventually found himself able to reach a level of interplay with this vast audience that was virtually identical with what he achieved in the clubs. It was an extraordinary act of will. Apparently he simply decided that he was going to do *his* show and left it at that. And it worked.

As in 1981, the European tour peaked with the shows at Wembley, but this time Bruce was playing the 70,000 capacity soccer stadium rather than the arena, which was barely a fifth that size. Little international media attention was focused on the Continental dates (although an ABC-Television crew had done a brief report on Slane for "Good Morning America"), but the shows in London were intensely watched, not only in England but back home, where the rumors of a forthcoming stadium tour were circulating widely. Furthermore, the middle night of the three was Fourth of July, which left Bruce to live up to the symbolism of playing the British capital on U.S. Independence Day.

The Wembley shows were packed with athletes and royalty, disc jockeys and movie and television stars, and such rock musicians as Wham's George Michael, Phil Collins, Sting, David Bowie, Pete Townshend and the other members of the disbanded Who, Mark Knopfler of Dire Straits (who were playing the Wembley Arena across the road), and Roger Taylor of Queen. Like all the other European shows, the seating was general admission, but the celebrities had access to the "royal box" and another section of preferred seating, where they could cluster with decent sight lines (about fifty yards from the stage) and be gaped at by the hoi polloi.

CBS Records' London branch worked itself into a low-key frenzy; the staff was actually given Independence Day (a date that is most certainly *not* celebrated in Great Britain) as a holiday. At

the stadium the company built a replica of a Fifties roadside
diner and hired twenty American waitresses to serve 800 VIPs a
day a menu consisting of approximations of such boardwalk
delicacies as hot dogs, hamburgers, french fries, and popcorn.
These concoctions were given what were presumably considered
quaint rock-ethnic names such as Bruceburgers, Clarence and
Nils fishburgers, Mainstreet dogs, and E Street cheesecake. The
bar was stocked with cola, Budweiser, and Colt .45, which came
out just right.

First night (or rather, afternoon—the shows started just after
six P.M. because of a local noise curfew) crowds in London hadn't
changed in four years. They were still stiff, although this time
there was no worry that industry guests would grab all the closest
seats. Within a few songs Springsteen had knit the crowd together
with their own mania. (When he'd first cracked Britain, he'd
cracked it big, and between the stories of his previous U.K.
shows and the success of "Dancing in the Dark," the crowd's
anticipatory energy was just about tangible.)

Four songs into the first set, Bruce pulled his first surprise.
Over a chunky boogie beat—like slowed-down ZZ Top—Bruce
shouted a stentorian introduction. Because he'd just finished the
hard opening push through "Born in the U.S.A.," "Badlands,"
and "Out in the Street," he was winded and almost panting. The
reckless energy with which he paced and hollered despite that
suggested anxiety, and his pauses appeared to be those of a man
having trouble suppressing his anger. If he was just acting, it was
the best job he'd ever done.

"When we were on the first part of our American tour, we
were down in Texas," he said and gulped for air. "Down there you
saw a lotta folks that had come down from up north—outta
Detroit, Pittsburgh. They'd gone down south lookin' for some
work in the oil field and on oil rigs, and when they got down there
the price of oil dropped. There wasn't no jobs.

"They'd end up sleepin' in tents out on the side of the
highway . . . sleepin' in their cars at night, with their wives and
their kids . . . with no work or no place to go [pause] and the cops
just tellin' 'em to move along. This is called 'Seeds.' "

The music lumbered into gear, a great roar of synthesized

brass and nasty guitar, as Springsteen spat out the lyrics in a leather-lunged voice:

> Parked in the lumberyard freezin' our asses off
> My kids in the backseat got a graveyard cough
> Well, I'm sleepin' in front with my wife
> Billyclub tappin' on the windshield in the middle of the night
> Says "Move along man,
> Move along."

This was a song of a man hurt to the quick, not the "wounded not even dead" of "Jungleland," but the discarded, left for dead of real life, and not just life in Houston, Pittsburgh, and Detroit, but all over. It was a song that would have been well understood in Newcastle or, for that matter, in Dublin and Milan, industrial cities that had also suffered the ravages of Seventies "recession" and the false prosperity of the Eighties.

The music had a spare, surging power that Springsteen had rarely commanded before, based in the blues, not soul. And what could be heard of the lyrics was as completely vernacular as anything he'd ever written. In words and music, Springsteen had become that freezing migratory worker and his onstage demeanor captured the restless, furious passion of a man cheated not just of a dream but of the very staples of life. He ended with a curse and a warning, vowing that if he "could spare the spit," he'd gob at every limousine that passed him by, suggesting that anybody tempted to follow in his footsteps was "better off buyin' a shotgun straight off the rack." When Springsteen shouted the final line—"Movin' on, movin' on/It's gone, gone, it's all gone"—he wasn't idly echoing fifty years of highway blues; this was "Johnny 99" for real.

The rest of the show went as usual, until the encores. Bruce had saved "Bobby Jean" until then, and when it finished he turned to the wings and called out Little Steven, who came aboard decked out in a pink shirt, mauve bandanna, and tiger-print tights. They shot into the song that stated their case best of all, "Two Hearts," and then wound the evening down with the medleys of "Street Fighting Man"/"Born to Run," and "Twist and

Shout"/"Do You Love Me." They'd exceeded the curfew by enough so that anxiety-stricken promoter Harvey Goldsmith looked ready for the cardiac ward, but they'd ended triumphantly.

Bruce took the stage almost half an hour late on the Fourth of July, arriving alone with just his acoustic guitar. His face was gigantic on the huge video screen, overlaid upon an American flag snapping in the breeze as he sang "Independence Day," a ten-minute ballad, all by himself to this massive crowd. At the end he was joined by the full band for the final chorus. Opening the show all but naked took great nerve, but the song was the least arrogant Bruce could have chosen—its metaphors of reconciliation served almost as well for Britain and America as for father and son or loner and society. It even modified the meaning of "Born in the U.S.A." and "Badlands," which followed.

If there'd been any doubt that Springsteen could do stadium shows as poignant as those he'd created indoors, this performance dispelled it once and for all. Springsteen struck every emotional note he'd ever reached in smaller halls, and he did it without once violating the context of the stadium show. The energy, supercharged by the thrill of those first few minutes, surged even when he slipped into sequences of songs from *Nebraska*.

Introducing "Highway Patrolman," a song which in the abstract seems impossibly fragile for such huge spaces, he said, "This is a song about, I guess, the conflict between what your heart tells you to do and what you do with it." And with those simple words, which might have applied to his decision to tackle the biggest challenges as well, the song came home.

This quiet story-song was given one of the biggest hands of the evening, indicating that when Bruce spoke, at least that night, he was *heard*. Even if that sort of song had flopped, Springsteen would have had his cake, since he'd dodged the sterility that was beginning to threaten his arena shows and had at last dared more than any other stadium rocker. Actually pulling the thing off meant that he got to eat it, too.

The final show of the European tour was something to savor from the very first notes, when Bruce, ready to kick off "Born in the U.S.A." shouted "One . . . two . . ." and the audience responded, "One, two, three, four!" in perfect cadence.

That show was held in Roundhay Park, which was (natives attest) the place to *park* in this Midlands city. Bruce was onstage by quarter past four, looking out at an audience that stretched beyond the open field spread out before the stage and spilled over into the trees nearly half a mile away. Eighty thousand tickets had been sold; there were at least another 10,000 counterfeits. When the temporary fencing was put up around the concert area, the joining bolts were left facing outward. They were easily unfastened by intermission, and then another 10,000 or so fans spilled through the gaps.

As with every other outdoor show Bruce had done in Europe, the weather was perfect—until the end of the day, when great black clouds began looming ominously overhead. As the band finished "Bobby Jean," Springsteen sat down and reached for a microphone. The air already felt damp as he began the story that led into "Racing in the Street," which would complete the second set in a somber mood.

It was another nervy move. Doing such a slow, sad narrative virtually invited any listener whose devotion was less than complete to rush for shelter or transport home. But as Bruce spoke and then sang, the crowd stayed almost completely still; there was no movement away from the stage. Bruce had transfixed them, held them in the palm of his hand, made them a part of the saga of his show as surely as if each had been able to look him in the eye.

17 SEEDS

As this show careens to its end, it's impossible not to be at least a little distracted by last-minute wishes and regrets. Springsteen takes so long between tours that the last night of every tour really seems to be *the* last. It's a feeling that grows stronger each time, not so much because he and the band are getting older but because the one constant in his work is change.

So even if your first thought on the first night of the whole tour was a cautionary reminder to wait, watch, and listen before judging, maybe you can't help anticipating the choices Bruce will make tonight. He's reached more than one pinnacle in the past eighteen months, and you figure the second set almost has to end giddy, with "Rosalita."

But if you're a fan, and not just someone who's along to take notes, then it's more than permissible to imagine another ending—another *kind* of ending, maybe another kind of triumph, less sweet but still worth savoring.

It's an ending Bruce has used recently and, in a way, it's the essence of the indefinable magic that he works in these dark evenings, because it explodes the bonds of genre—as song and as narrative. When they do it best, it goes something like this:

Roy Bittan begins to play an edgy, wistful synthesizer back-drop as Bruce walks to the edge of the stage, mike in hand, and sits down. It is so quiet onstage that you can hear every breath and holler in the crowd. Bruce puts the mike to his lips and begins speaking.

"It was around . . . it was around the end of summer, and I had this old convertible Camaro. I used to take it at night to this little place. There was this little strip off the river—I guess it was like a junkyard, where people from town would come down and they'd dump the things that they didn't want anymore and just leave 'em out there to rust.

"But there was this little spot where we'd all meet on Friday and Saturday, and that was the first place that I met her.

"And it was one of those . . . like, when you're first goin' out with somebody and everything's funny, it's easy—it's easy to be with somebody.

"But then time kinda passed, and I don't know what happened. It seemed like the things that made her happy once didn't make her happy anymore. And I was spendin' my time tryin' to figure out kinda what had happened, what I could do to make her happy again. And she got to where she didn't want to talk—she wanted to stay in at night. And she'd take my keys so I couldn't take the car out.

"And it was hard to get her to understand, and I *know* she knew because she remembered—she loved it once—that when I took the car out and when I won, that it was the only time that I really got to feelin' good about myself.

"And I don't know if people expect too much of each other sometimes—maybe they do. But to have just one thing—one thing in your whole life that you do, that you do good, that you feel proud of—that's not too much for anybody to ask."

The sound switches suddenly now, the synthesizer dying away as perfectly placed chords rise from the grand piano. It's the opening rhythm of "Racing in the Street," and the intro sustains through several repetitions before Springsteen rises and begins to sing:

> I got a '69 Chevy with a 396
> Fuelie heads and a Hurst on the floor
> She's waitin' tonight down at the parking lot
> Of the 7–11 store

This is the line of demarcation separating casual Springsteen fans from the fanatics. To those who keep their distance, it's an overblown metaphor, the Chuck Berry car song extended to the point of absurdity. For those who listen with their heart as much as their head, "Racing in the Street" is something else, maybe the best thing Bruce Springsteen has to give—it's the greatest imaginable subversion of the "Happy Days" illusions of rock and roll car songs; the genius bastard cousin of the ultimate automobile ballad, the Beach Boys' "Don't Worry Baby."

When Springsteen reaches the final lines, promising that tonight his baby and he will "ride to the sea and wash these sins off our hands," some shrug and walk away at this crazy guy's inflated notion of the importance of trash. Others stick around and hear something a lot better: a promise that if you let the little things add up, they count for more than all the monuments in the world.

By now, working off that opening story, Springsteen has added several layers of meaning to the song. He's made it a metaphor for his own life, an explanation of why he writes, sings, plays, tours. And in its junkyard images and allusions to the fact that we expect more from those we love than we do from life itself, he's created a description of why he has chosen the wretched and the despised as his allies.

Maybe—*maybe*—"Racing in the Street" was impossibly romantic in 1978, when it appeared on *Darkness on the Edge of Town*. But by now, in 1985, it has grown into the song that tells more about Bruce Springsteen and his accomplishments than any other, while still refusing to back off from its own romance. You can love it or hate it; you can love him or hate him. But the fact is that both the song and the singer speak the truth, in blind faith that someone will hear it. They reach and they connect, and sparks fly each time they do.

Bruce obviously can't let the story end with the simple absolution of guilt. At the end of the song Federici's organ and Bittan's piano and synthesizer rise together, not in combat but entwined in harmony, and the song bleeds through two or three more choruses as Bruce Springsteen sits back down and begins once more to speak, quietly and in a voice younger than you've heard all night.

"So that was the night that we left. Just packed up our bags. We still don't know where we're goin' yet, but I guess that'll come in time. As for this place, well, there's a lot here that we'll always remember. But sometimes it seems like time gets runnin' so short on ya that it's gonna run out. And so much gets lost and left behind that there's not much that you can do but to keep searchin' and to keep on goin', and to keep on goin', and to keep on goin', and to keep on goin', and to keep on goin', and to keep on goin' . . ."

Gently he lays the microphone on its stand and walks away, back toward the drums and the dark. As he does, the music rises once more, a solid wall of sound, the hearty wail of a dream being born out of one person's loneliness and pain. Born, rather than dying, because a single link is forged. And forged again, until it comes out right.

18 HOT FUN IN THE SUMMERTIME

Mama always told me not to look into the lights of the sun
Oh but mama that's where the fun is
—"Blinded by the Light"

After Leeds, the *Born in the U.S.A.* tour, about a year on the road, had played 128 shows with a total attendance of 2.9 million. The summer stadium tour of the United States would cover nine weeks, with twenty-eight dates in fourteen cities. Its total attendance would also be just over 2 million, an indication of how much more efficient stadium shows were. The tour was already huge: 3 million people was more than Springsteen had played for in the previous decade. Now it became gargantuan: The 5 million total attendance represents the largest live audience any rock act has ever reached in the course of a single tour. The tour grossed about $100 million from ticket sales alone, a sum greater than the annual gross national product of some countries, and that doesn't reflect revenue from records and concert merchandise, which might have come close to doubling tour income.

It was the summer of Bossmania. Columbia Records kept *Born in the U.S.A.* on the front burner; the album spent fifty-three weeks in the *Billboard* Top Five and remained in the Top Ten until the tour was over. Sales had passed 8 million copies in the United States; worldwide sales exceeded 12 million copies, and another Christmas shopping season was only a couple of months away. "Glory Days" was Bruce's biggest hit since "Dancing in the Dark," peaking at Number Five, and its humorous twists on nostalgia made it his most important image single since "Born in the U.S.A.," as well as perfect summertime blues. The video made Springsteen equally pervasive on rock and roll television. "Glory Days" was followed by "I'm Goin' Down," which became the sixth Top Ten hit taken from the album. (Only one LP in history—*Thriller*—had ever produced seven.)

Album and ticket sales weren't the only revenue source going through the roof. At each show vendors sold items ranging from buttons and programs to t-shirts and sweatshirts, at prices ranging up to $22. Don Hunter, head man at Winterland, the company owned by promoter Bill Graham and CBS which did Springsteen's concert merchandising, called the *Born in the U.S.A.* concerts "unquestionably the single largest merchandise grossing tour in the history of rock and roll."

Johnny Carson made Boss jokes—"Mick Jagger just had a baby boy; this kid has everything but he still can't get Bruce Springsteen tickets," he cracked one night. *Barrons* tried to divine the future of the stock market from the mood of *Born in the U.S.A.* Law firms around the country used Springsteen tickets as an enticement in recruiting desirable new law school graduates— according to *American Lawyer* magazine, one Cleveland firm had its staffers stand in line for six hours to buy seventy-two seats.

Magazines and newspapers ran lengthy articles by "serious" writers (meaning those who had no special knowledge of popular music) trying to assess what it all meant. Left *(In These Times,* the *Bay Guardian),* right (Leon Wieseltier in *The New Republic,* Norman Podhoretz in a column syndicated by Rupert Murdoch), and center (Jack Newfield in the *Village Voice,* Senator Bill Bradley in *USA Today)* all fumblingly tried to explain Springsteen's grip on the mass audience. None really succeeded because, of course, that grip derived its fundamental strength not from Springsteen's stand on the issues but from his perception of the importance of rock and roll music in the lives of his listeners and his ability to rock their butts off.

The previous summer's superstars—Michael Jackson and Prince—had faded from the front pages months before, each with his image sorely tarnished. In 1985 the only other pop stars the public found as fascinating as Springsteen were Sylvester Stallone, in his Rocky and Rambo incarnations, and Madonna.

Comparisons between Springsteen and Stallone were easy; they were bandied about everywhere, from casual conversations to the editorial page of the *Chicago Tribune*. The discrepancies were less instructive, given that Stallone's Rocky and Rambo were such obvious jingoistic stooges, with no depth, no humanity, and, in the end, a following that lasted only as long as the thrills were as fresh as the rivulets of stage blood that fueled them. If there was any purpose in comparing Springsteen to such brainless trash, it was primarily because *Rocky IV* and *Rambo* pointed up how completely the political and cultural right dominated all attempts to define "American" qualities, which suggests something of what Springsteen risked by daring to offer a separate vision.

Almost no one would have thought to compare Bruce Springsteen to Madonna. In fact, their images formed a fascinating polarity. Madonna's presence was as divisive as Bruce's was unifying. While both were noted for being physically fit, her reputation for sexual expressiveness made her seem tawdry; his legendary wholesomeness was in part a by-product of libidinal restraint (a topic explored in songs as various as "Cover Me," "Pink Cadillac," "I'm Goin' Down," and "Dancing in the Dark"). Madonna's music was purely the creation of the recording studio; her concerts were the most suspect element in her musical arsenal. She was eager for movie success and began making her first top-billed feature (*Desperately Seeking Susan*) even before her musical star had fully risen. Springsteen was obsessed with society; Madonna's public image was a testimonial to narcissism.

Even so, they had things in common. The most important was that both were levellers in their way: Springsteen's denim and cotton were the contemporary equivalent of homespun; Madonna's flaunting of lingerie and foundation garments as outerwear infuriated arbiters of fashion at the same time that it spurred a gaggle of imitators ("Madonna wanna-bes"). Furthermore, neither seemed willing to slip into a one-dimensional image and stay there. Far from remaining a dumb sexpot, Madonna pursued both

music and acting with serious purpose, and she exhibited genuine creative growth across her first three albums. Springsteen was
set up to be the perfect all-American boy, not only the darling of
presidential candidates but an absolute avatar of Horatio Alger
rags-to-riches success; he didn't just decline the honors, he
spurned the myth by bringing into focus the awful waste of human
life in the community from which he sprang.

No one is immune to the consequences of being publicly held
aloft for too long, particularly if disinclined to feed the media
mill. In Madonna's case the potshots succeeded at least in
driving her husband, Sean Penn, crazy. Springsteen seemed to
shrug the whole process off, but it was hard to imagine how long
he could keep it up. Later in the summer *Los Angeles Times*
columnist Patrick Goldstein, for one, wondered aloud about how
Springsteen might suffer, identifying a "backlash syndrome" that
had recently affected everyone from Boy George to the BeeGees
and inquiring of several industry figures what Bruce's eventual
fate might be. Goldstein wrote of "familiar warning signs: Paparazzi have snapped pics of him smooching with his new wife
. . . *Newsweek* put him on the cover even though he refused to
give the magazine an interview . . . Politicians are quoting his
lyrics, claiming to be lifelong fans . . . Just the other day, *People*
plugged him on its cover just so it could run three pages of photos
from his stadium tour and speculate about what turn his career
might take next . . . And *Time* ran 'the first-ever published
portrait' of Mr. & Mrs. Boss. Columbia's release of a sixth single
and plans to promote the album through Christmas increased the
risk."

"Sooner or later, it's inevitable," a "veteran industry publi-
cist" told Goldstein. "In a lot of ways, it's the media's fault, not
his. The media has become expert at building someone up to epic
proportions and then, just as quickly, tearing you down. It's hard
to imagine Springsteen getting caught up in the same process, but
he's being ballyhooed so much now that he may lose the mystique
that has always made him appear different from every other pop
star out there hawking themselves."

But Cliff Bernstein, manager of Def Leppard/Dokken, believed otherwise. "I think a sixth single is a little bit of overkill,

but his audience hasn't really changed. When you went to see Prince or Michael Jackson after they got hot, it was a different audience—a fickle pop audience—who come to see artists on a one-time basis. But Bruce isn't attracting fans who've just read about him in *Newsweek*. He's kept the ones who were there from the beginning."

In fact, Springsteen remained a center of fan fanaticism. In November 1984 Bert Epstein, a twenty-year-old Beverly Hills Bossmaniac, started a "Bruce Party Line" in Los Angeles. It offered a thirty-minute tape-recorded phone message on which fans could relay rumors, enthusiasms, and critiques of shows, records, and ticket-selling practices. It received more than a hundred calls weekly for more than two years and eventually expanded to a second line in New York. Sustaining that level of cultish addiction was unprecedented and the best evidence that Springsteen had more than maintained the loyalty of the majority of his old fans; new ones were often absorbed in the same kind of devotion.

"I'm Goin' Down" was a legitimate hit, reaching Number Nine in *Billboard*. And although Springsteen was easy to caricature—you just dragged out the headband, the torn jeans, and sweaty shirts, strapped on a guitar, adopted a scratchy Jersey accent, and mumbled street philosophy—he subverted both the pop star stereotype and the cartoon portrayal of the radical artist. He faced facts, but anger and frustration were never the core of his show, just the counterpoint to hard-rocking assent. He may have been the first left-wing star in show business history to make popular politics seem like a means of banishing drudgery. "Nobody wins unless everybody wins" is what he said, but "There ain't no party unless everybody's invited" is what he acted out. Since he also behaved as if he meant it, the only likely source of media burnout was the frustration of reporters, editors, and pundits trying to pigeonhole him.

■

Plans for the U.S. stadium tour weren't finalized until the last night at Wembley, when Jon Landau and Premier Talent's Frank Barsalona and Barry Bell sat down to hash out requirements and possibilities. Bell made a series of telephone calls when he returned to New York. A tour like this wasn't really negotiated, since promoters, agents, and artists all understood the business parameters—and the artist had all the leverage. Premier then mailed out contracts; when the signed documents were returned, tickets could go on sale.

This left only about two weeks in which to sell the tickets for the shows on the first half of the tour, but that seemed no special problem since demand for the arena shows had been at stadium-level just about everywhere on the previous year's itinerary.

The tour was scheduled to start August 5 with a single show at RFK Stadium in Washington, which held about 54,000. Since Bruce had sold 60,000 tickets at the nearby Capitol Center the previous summer, this hardly did much to service the expanded demand (although it did help some, since there were many repeaters at the Cap Center shows). Tickets didn't go on sale until July 22.

This was either a great logistical error—due to the decentralization of ticket sales through Ticketron and Telecharge, some people who'd camped out as long as four days in anticipation of the on-sale announcement were shut out—or accidentally a great piece of p.r. strategy. The show sold out in ninety minutes. Not only that, but between ten and eleven thirty on the morning of the twenty-second, the Bell system serving the District of Columbia, Virginia, and Maryland region registered more than 2 million calls—the previous Monday morning it had been used less than half as often. The difference was solely attributable to calls to Teletron for Springsteen tickets.

The flood of calls tied up the entire D.C. area phone system, affecting even the White House (but not the Oval Office) and systems as far north as New Jersey. This was worth national headlines, and it got 'em. And they repeated when phone systems also crashed in Pennsylvania, New York, and New Jersey as tickets went on sale for two Philadelphia shows, which sold out in six hours, and four shows at Giants Stadium in the Meadowlands. A couple of weeks later, when Chicago tickets went on sale, *Newsweek* reported, "Illinois Bell put on line a computer system that's usually used to control phone traffic on Mother's Day or to handle calls to towns hit by tornadoes."

In New York Ticketron sold 236,000 tickets for the shows at

70,000-seat Giants Stadium in one day, shattering their previous record. Ticketron officials estimated that the demand would have filled Giants Stadium more than twenty times. When dates in Boston fell through, two more Giants Stadium dates were added and the tickets for those were also gone in a day.

But it wasn't just New Jersey and the Northeast anymore; Springsteen was now an assured immediate sell-out throughout the country. Just as with the arena shows, the question became not whether he could sell out, but how many shows and how quickly. In Los Angeles he sold 340,000 tickets for four shows, "the biggest collective audience any single performer has drawn in this city's history," according to the *Los Angeles Herald Examiner,* and that wasn't untypical.

Once the tickets were sold, they were often avidly resold. In Toronto so many newspaper advertisements offered scalped Springsteen ducats that police began an investigation of promoter Michael Cohl and his staff (they were cleared). In Dallas scalpers paid homeless men and women up to $40 cash to stand in line and purchase tickets. In Philadelphia tickets went for $125 from scalpers; front row seats for as much as $400. Prices were similar elsewhere.

George Travis and his team had developed their own way of dealing with scalping. Besides doing their best to have any scalpers on the premises of a show arrested, they hoarded the extra seats made available by slight alterations in the production—moving the stage or sound and light mixing positions a few feet one way or another could open up a whole row. Those seats could amount to a couple of hundred additional tickets, which were put on sale just a few hours before showtime, either to fans already queuing outside the stadium or to fans notified by local radio stations, thus undercutting at least some of the scalpers. In Pittsburgh Travis's people were able to put 2,000 tickets on sale Saturday afternoon for a Sunday night show, which resulted in an attendance of 62,000 (the largest in Three Rivers Stadium history) and in tickets being scalped for as little as $5 two hours before showtime. "I'm getting stuck for sixty dollars, and I'm not the only one," moaned one scalper. "The professionals all thought they were going to make big bucks, and no one's making anything. I can't even give these tickets away."

In Chicago, where the show was announced several days before tickets went on sale, the promoters instituted a lottery that scrambled the sequence of those waiting in line. One reason was that ticket brokers (legal scalpers) were "paying people to stand in line. They were already taking orders for this show," according to promoter Jerry Mickelson. That show was also the only one on the tour to be held as a general admission event, and it sparked fears recalling the Who tragedy at Cincinnati and the Brussels soccer riot. In fact, it wasn't until the Jacksons tour of 1984 that anyone had ever played stadium shows with reserved seating; until the Jacksons tried it, it was believed that a stadium audience would simply trample over any temporary alignment of chairs set down on the field. Nothing of the sort happened with the Jacksons, and their experience was what encouraged Springsteen to run a real concert tour, not just a series of wildcat outdoor dates in which the event overwhelmed the music.

Nevertheless, the reason for playing with reserved seating was artistic control more than crowd control, and everybody knew it. When the *Chicago Sun-Times* asked Chicago Park District Superintendent Edmund L. Kelly whether Springsteen fans or Chicago Bears fans were more likely to misbehave, he instantly responded, "Oh, the Bears," and criticizing the Bears in Chicago is sacrilege. As it happened, the day of the show did produce a tragedy, but one that had nothing to do with the seating arrangement: A speeding bus ran over a car trying to enter the stadium, killing all seven of the Springsteen fans in it and injuring sixty bus passengers.

Ordinary Springsteen fans may have found the festival seating arrangement an inconvenient violation of protocol, but wealthy Bears fans weren't happy with Springsteen either. Springsteen's contract forbade their using their "sky boxes" for the shows, largely because piped-in sound and video would make bootlegging too easy. Bears general manager Mike McCaskey begged Springsteen and Soldiers Field authorities to reconsider, but no change was made.

A special area of reserved seating in the stands *was* provided for friends of the band and the promoters, which gave some well-connected Chicagoans a special vantage point. But in the end, its most fascinating by-product was a fistfight between former Bears

quarterback Bobby Douglass and George Cole of the Steelworkers–Old Timers Food Bank, who was in town for the founding
convention of the National Rank and File Against Concessions
(NRFAC). The Cole-Douglass bout was a draw, and Cole made a
bigger point that day by bringing with him members of union
locals from a variety of industries all over the country. One of the
food banks Springsteen supported that night was run by Steelworkers Local 1014 of Gary, Indiana, representing what was left
of U.S. Steel's once-massive Gary Works. The local, whose
3,500 still-employed workers were far outnumbered by the 5,500
who'd been laid off, was headed by Larry Regan, another key
player in NRFAC, who was able to discuss with Bruce the
problems faced by industrial workers in Gary and elsewhere and
what the most progressive local union leaders were doing about
them.

Indeed, it wasn't only politicians who found Springsteen's
hard-working, all-American image useful. Support of trade unions was so rare among celebrities that all of organized labor
seemed eager to canonize him. But the support Bruce offered was
not a blanket endorsement of American trade unionism; it would
have been as contradictory to accord blanket approval to the
AFL-CIO as to the Democratic and Republican parties. The
AFL-CIO, with the encouragement of its major member unions,
had avidly supported the war in Vietnam and, in the face of the
Eighties Depression, also turned its back on the jobless and the
homeless. The general principle of workers joining trade unions,
which so many Americans failed to understand, was of course
something that Springsteen endorsed. But he was careful to work
with the kind of productive militants typified by Ron Weisen,
whose USWA Local 1397 was (out of unfortunate necessity)
almost as combative in its posture toward the Steelworkers
International leadership as toward the steel companies.

Springsteen found Weisen and similarly minded local leaders
such as Cole and Regan among his most natural allies because
they were less concerned with abstract propositions about trade
union solidarity than with protecting the lives of the workers the
international unions often misrepresented. The best the AFL-CIO
could offer was Walter Mondale and a package of "domestic
content" legislation that was both rank protectionism and an

assault on the living standards of workers outside the United States. Such trade unions no more believed in the principle that "nobody wins unless everybody wins" than Ronald Reagan did.

For better or worse, Springsteen was never called upon to make such fine distinctions explicit. The closest he came to such controversy was just before his Cleveland Municipal Stadium show that August. There Chicago concessionaire Andry Frain was attempting to push the 350 ticket takers, ushers, and security guards represented by Local 85 of the Service Employees International Union (SEIU) into accepting wage cuts. Unlike the militants of NRFAC, Local 85 wasn't opposed to such concessions in principle, but they felt that Springsteen's reputation as a union sympathizer gave them additional bargaining leverage and threatened a strike for the day of the show. It's hard to know whether Springsteen would have crossed a picket line if one had been set up. Ultimately, it was in part the power of his image and the reluctance of both the union and promoter Mike Belkin to damage it that won SEIU a one-night contract—but with Belkin, not Frain—which assured them regular wages for the concert.

■

The stadium tour began at RFK Stadium for reasons that were practical rather than symbolic, but they couldn't have selected a better place to begin.

At most Washington shows the governmental elite are well provided with complimentary tickets or at least have special access to good seats. Springsteen's crew refused all requests, sending even the best-connected figures on Capitol Hill scurrying to the scalpers, which drove the prices way up.

The sole exception was New Jersey's Democratic senator Bill Bradley, who had been a fringe hanger-on in the Springsteen camp since visiting Bruce at the Power Station in 1980 during the making of *The River*. Bradley received tickets from Springsteen's crew and attended the show with Representative Thomas Downey, a Long Island Democrat (who headed the Congressional Arts Caucus, which provided for the special interests of so-called "serious" artists, writers, and musicians), and their wives.

Bill Bradley began running for President in 1963, when he

was an All-American basketball star at Princeton. Upon graduation in 1965 he accepted a Rhodes Scholarship to Oxford
University in England. There he organized pro–Lyndon Johnson
demonstrations, despite Johnson's prosecution of the war in
Vietnam. After returning to the United States, "Dollar Bill," as
he became known, was for several seasons a star forward with the
New York Knicks, NBA champions in 1970 and 1972. He first
ran for office in 1978 and was elected by a substantial margin to
the United States Senate from New Jersey.

Bradley's politics were definitively neo-liberal. The son of a
banker, he was fiscally conservative and supported most military
appropriations but tried to project himself as "young" and "hip,"
a pretty good feat for someone utterly lacking television presence.
Even though his favorite record in college was "You'll Never
Walk Alone," he tried to position himself as a rock and roll fan—
in New Jersey, where Bruce Springsteen's "Born to Run" was
named an anthem by the state legislature, liking rock music
meant votes. In his office, reported the *New York Times*, Bradley
kept a file on Springsteen between files labeled "South Africa"
and "Strategic Petroleum Reserves." One could only wonder
whether the senator made all of his file cabinets that easily
available to the press.

On the day of the RFK Stadium show, *USA Today* ran a page
one essay about Springsteen written by Bill Bradley. Had the
prose been less wooden, one might have suspected it was
composed by his staff. Bradley said that he wrote the article
"because [Springsteen] burst on my imagination, when I was kind
of reaching political maturity and trying to express the essence of
New Jersey, and as I looked into the songs, I kind of felt in a
funny way that we were trying to do the same thing."

If so, this was evident neither from Bradley's voting record
nor from his article. After misidentifying Bruce as "a product of
the New Jersey Shore," as though Freehold were a day at the
beach, Bradley described a late-night episode in which he and
his wife became fans after having their sleep disturbed by hearing
"Born to Run" played from a nearby seaside home. Bradley wrote
of Springsteen as if Bruce's subject were merely the landscape
between the George Washington Bridge and Cape May and not

America, or its working class, or the project of trying to become psychologically whole in a torn and bitter world. This parochialism was excusable, of course, since Bradley was for the most part writing as no more than a peculiarly elevated branch of the New Jersey Chamber of Commerce.

But Bradley then attempted to extend his vision of what Springsteen had to say, claiming that Springsteen's songs reflected Joseph Conrad's definition of work: "the sustaining illusion of an independent existence." Of itself this wasn't bad, but Bradley spent the rest of the article in barefaced contradiction of what Springsteen really had to say. "Bruce . . . doesn't delude himself with changing the world, or stopping war or creating a new consciousness. He simply isn't pretentious. He goes for the small, often sad, story, the insight into what makes us human. Above all, he goes for rock and roll." It was enough to make you wonder if Bradley had heard any of the songs Springsteen wrote *after* "Born to Run."

The senator concluded on an even more egregiously false note: "Forget that the factory closed or the marriage broke up. Forget—if just for a moment—and rock and roll. Remember the 'glory days.' Let the good times roll. The good and the bad, the highs and the lows—all part of a life, every life—and each life means as much as the next. Keep rocking, Bruce. Keep going. Let the good times roll." George Will and Ronald Reagan had practiced no greater distortion of what Bruce Springsteen's work was about. Yes, at the finest moments of a Bruce Springsteen show, listeners celebrated, but they never *ever* were left with the idea of fake "good times" that Bradley was trying to promulgate.

At the show that night Bruce Springsteen might have been directing himself straight at Bradley when he paused to introduce "My Hometown." Certainly what he chose to say was in part determined by an awareness of the many government employees in the crowd, as well as by the proximity of that scar in the earth that served as the unforgettable monument to Vietnam veterans.

Bruce never seemed very comfortable doing these introductions, partly because saying his piece this way was a little too close to actually making a speech and partly, no doubt, because a little uncertainty was what the part called for. That night he was unusually awkward. Still wearing his guitar, his black shirt sopping wet, he looked absolutely distressed at what was about to issue from his lips. As he spoke, he nervously scratched at his temple, and from time to time he'd bring himself up short. In closeup on the video screens, he was visibly upset.

"When I was about, I guess, fifteen—I was fifteen years old," he began, stumbling nervously, "and there were these two brothers in town. And one was a singer and one was a guitar player. And I guess they had the first really adventurous band in my little town. One was named Ray and one was named Walter.

"I remember Walter was the first guy I'd ever seen tuck his pants inside his boots," he said with a nervous little giggle. "That was revolutionary at the time. You know," he added with a slight pant, pulling the mood back into line, "he was real good, a real good singer. And he got drafted and went to Vietnam—I guess it was in sixty-six." He scratched at his sideburns, disturbed, and continued in a hoarser voice. "I remember when his mother got . . . got the word that he was missing in action. And Walter was the kind of guy, he didn't have the kind of talents that got ya . . . that kept you from gettin' killed in nineteen sixty-five and sixty-six. He just had a good voice and wasn't in college and . . ."

He looked down as the thought trailed off, as if summoning the strength for what came next.

"But, uh, I guess this next song is a song I wrote and after, quite a while after I wrote it, I guess I realized that what it was about was responsibility.

"And a lot of you young guys out there—and girls, too—the next time there's a little war, whether it's in Central America or wherever it might be, you're gonna be the ones that"—his voice sagged, hitting a sad note—"that they're gonna wanna go. And you're gonna need a lot more information than you get in the six o'clock news to know what to do."

Cheers stopped him. He reflected a second, then plunged on.

"And I guess, whether . . . whether we like it or not, it's our money that gets spent, either for makin' bombs, or it gets spent for feedin' people or it gets spent for wagin' little covert wars or for educatin' people. And we all get sucked into it, one way or another. There's no way around it." He said this as though describing a mountain he'd once explored, with a sense of painful assurance, in a tone that suggested how hard he'd looked to find such a path. And having no option, he continued.

"I guess a couple of years ago, I read a history book, *History of the United States*. I remember, when I was in school, I always hated history. But I read this book and I felt like I learned a lot about where we were comin' from, where we are today, and where we're goin'. And where we're goin' is pretty scary." He paused again and looked away. "Uhhhh . . ." he began, and broke again, as if unsure how to conclude or whether any conclusion at all was wise. He looked a little scared.

"So I guess all you really gotta do is take a walk from that Lincoln Memorial over to the Vietnam Veterans Memorial." Again cheers forced a pause, but this time he pushed through them to complete his thought. "Read. Read the names of the dead, and you get an idea of the stakes you're playing for in 1985"—he hesitated before making one last plunge—"when you were born in the U.S.A."

The cheers renewed, but Springsteen kept speaking, now as much to himself and the band as to the larger audience. "So this is your hometown, but you gotta put your stake in for it; you gotta make a claim for it." The cheers swelled again, but he still had a little left that he needed to get out. "Gotta find out what's going on around you," he muttered into the roar and turned to sing his song.

It was a beautiful moment, a revelation of Springsteen's gift as a story-teller as well as of his ability to recapitulate the most intimate occurrences in epic terms. It was, as well, a summary of the past five years of struggling to make sense of what he'd read in his history book, seen in his travels around the world, written in his songs, heard as an echo from the crowd, felt—and feared—in the depth of his soul. In a sense, you could say that story retraced the path from the ingenuous optimism of *Born to Run* to the unraveled pessimism of *Nebraska*, and, with that statement about what it means "when you were born in the U.S.A.," wound up in exactly the same place.

There were many national reviewers in attendance that night. Almost all of them made some reference to his powerful introduction, but none picked up on the crucial sentence in which Bruce Springsteen made his most ardent and loving assertion of his right to dictate the meaning of his own song.

That was too bad. The deliberate distortion practiced the next day by Senator Bradley on national television was something worse. In the course of a bumbling interview on the "CBS Morning News," in which both interviewer and interviewee revealed their complete ignorance of American popular music (Bradley referred to Bruce as an heir to "Buddy Holiday"), Phyllis George asked what Bradley thought of the anti-war sentiments Springsteen had expressed the night before.

"Well, I don't think he gave a lecture," Bradley claimed, backpedaling furiously. "I think he was simply saying that people should be aware of the world around them and inform themselves because there's a lot at stake. I think that's particularly true for all Americans. That's a positive message. That's a message of participation and involvement, and it's done with enthusiasm. I mean, Bruce Springsteen is an incredible talent, and there he is engaging you to be involved in the democratic process."

Did George Will practice any greater distortion? Had Ronald Reagan committed a greater perversion of Springsteen's words and actions? Well, if perhaps they had—and the point is arguable—certainly they didn't do so by speaking on network television in the assumed voice of a crony. Bruce Springsteen was talking about choice, all right, but he was also talking about situations in which there was only one correct selection to be made.

As it developed, Springsteen found an even clearer and louder way in which to voice his loathing of American foreign policy and what it had done to his bandmates. Bill Bradley also found a clearer way of saying what he really thought. In 1986 he voted twice to send military aid to the counterrevolutionary Nicaraguan *contras*.

In 1985 liberals moved to appropriate Bruce Springsteen's image and work just as conservatives had tried to do the previous year. Despite the myth, most leftists are uncomfortable around rock and roll; they prefer folk music—in particular the pseudo-folk produced by white, urban acoustic writer-performers of topical songs, the preferred musicians of the New Left as well as of the old. Liberal pundit Jack Newfield, for instance, who wrote articles for the *Village Voice*, *Playboy*, and even *ASCAP in Action*, had an extremely difficult time coping with Springsteen's esthetic. In a *Voice* article he described Elvis Presley as "a negative role model" and claimed that Springsteen's "canon of socially important songs numbers only twelve or fifteen at this point," as if the explicitly polemical utility of his works was their only salient characteristic (which is not true politically, much less artistically). It was feeling himself roped in by such agit-prop demagoguery that had driven Bob Dylan away from leftists in 1965.

Springsteen's activities also left left-wing pundits politically confused. Newfield could find no one better to compare Springsteen with than Robert Kennedy, a rather lame selection, given that Bruce is identified in the same passage as "neither a liberal nor a Democrat." David Corn, of the prominent socialist newspaper *In These Times*, referred to him as "the Mario Cuomo of pop music," which is *really* praising with faint damns.

Springsteen, it seemed, needed to exercise as much caution when dealing with leftists and liberals as with the right. Once absorbed into the cultural mainstream, most performers willingly surrender their "radicalism," since it is, after all, not much more than a gimmick. Springsteen's was more organic; he could no more give it up than turn in his fingers and stop playing guitar. As it was, leftists and liberals were as isolated from the homeless and the hungry as the right. It was in his alliances with the dispossessed, not with the politicos of whatever stripe, that Springsteen found a clear space in which his ideas could fight their way free.

So he carried on, doing the best he could, which was a hell of a lot better than anybody could have expected or would have dared to imagine.

◼

Springsteen debuted a "new" song at the Washington show—"Man at the Top," another *Born in the U.S.A.* leftover. Although Bruce had sung it once or twice on the 1984 U.S. tour, at RFK

Stadium it was a lot more site-specific. It had a light Ricky
Nelson pulse, and Bruce sang it a little bit as Nelson might have,
as a kind of quiet rockabilly. The lyrics inverted Randy New-
man's mocking "Lonely at the Top":

> Man at the top says it's lonely up there
> If it is, man, I don't care
> From the big white house to the parking lot
> Everybody wants to be the man at the top

If Bruce was feeling the strain of being America's favorite
son, that was as close as he came to showing it. Otherwise he
treated the stadium shows as he would have treated performances
in clubs or theaters or arenas, as occasions for hard work and
dancing, spiritual probing and near-orgasmic release.

The national reviewers who attended the D.C. concert arrived
skeptical that even Bruce Springsteen could pull off a meaningful
show in such vast spaces. For the most part, they left convinced
that he had managed to do exactly that.

"The size of the crowd seemed to intensify the music's impact
rather than diminish it," wrote Don McLeese of the *Chicago Sun-
Times*. "A Springsteen concert generally creates a sense of
community; here the community was larger than ever.

"Even so, part of Springsteen's instinctive brilliance as a
performer has been his ability to make his darker, more brooding
and painful material as powerful in concert as his full-throttle
rockers. At RFK, he was far less successful at running the gamut
of emotion within his performance than previously. Later in the
evening, some of Springsteen's extended introductions were
impossible to hear from certain sections of the stadium. The
crowd was filled with younger fans who know Springsteen primarily from his recent string of hits; many of them became restless
and impatient during the quieter, less familiar material."

All this was certainly true, as it would have been true
wherever Springsteen played, now that he'd reached an audience
too big to maintain cult purity. As David Hinckley of the *New
York Daily News* wrote, "Fortified with stage sets that make MGM
musicals look like a vacant lot, and speakers that make subway

stations sound like the meditation room at a convent, [previous stadium] rockers have made large amounts of money. What they haven't made is anywhere near their best music.

"Maybe Springsteen won't, either. But he's got to try." It seemed to be the consensus that the slightly streamlined show—the RFK concert lasted three and a half hours (counting the forty-minute intermission), which was at least half an hour less than the show had run the previous summer—worked well and that the mountainous sound system and the huge video screens did much to knit the audiences together.

But Hinckley, too, noted the rowdy, more easily distracted element in the audience. "Ironically, however, the factor he cannot control is his fans. As he gets more and more of them, and as the new ones get the idea they are supposed to stand up, yell, wave their arms, clap and sing along, Springsteen loses some of his control over the show no matter where it's held. And that may be the most important factor his next time out."

As he became more experienced in outdoor touring, Springsteen picked up some tricks. From time to time, particularly during the skits accompanying songs like "Pink Cadillac" and "Growin' Up," he played to the cameras, a useful change since the majority of the audience could see him clearly only on the video screens. And he was careful to rein in the energy as he prepared to speak. Mainly, though, Springsteen seemed looser, more exploratory. He never seemed regretful about what had been left behind in smaller venues, only eager to find out what could be learned in the new ones. And it was his very directness and enthusiasm that transformed the stadiums from spaces of mass isolation to the temporary but thrilling condition of community. When Springsteen reared back during each night's encores and asked, "Do You Love Me?" the assent that came roaring back was enough to make you feel goofy and dizzy. The exhilarated eruption seemed to be the crowd's way of saying, "Yes, that's just what's on our minds." Whatever risks success of such scale posed, Bruce seemed unfazed by them, just eager to keep on pushin'.

He was able to continue performing such a straight-ahead show in part because his set lacked the lasers and other gim-

micks on which other outdoor acts relied. This hardly made the
stadium tour a small production—the stage, sound, and light
gear traveled in a total of fifteen thirty-foot tractor trailer trucks,
and there were a few more for the video equipment. It took a
hundred stagehands to rig the 18,000 pounds of lights, mount the
sixty-foot stage, and assemble the 400 speakers over three layers
of scaffolding. Load-in lasted close to two days, and it took
another day to pack all the stuff up and put it back on the
highway again.

By the time they got to Philadelphia in late August, the
temperature was sweltering; an official 98 degrees increased to
over 110 on the Astroturf-covered field and went way beyond that
under the hot lights onstage. "I need some *air-conditioning*,"
Bruce moaned on opening night. He wasn't kidding. By the next
evening Bob Thrasher had rigged up an air-cooling unit that
blasted straight up at Springsteen's face through the monitor
speaker grilles in the stage floor, a device that continued in use
for the rest of the tour. (It was hot *all the time* onstage, where the
lights added about twenty degrees to the normal air temperature.
As Nils Lofgren pointed out, Bruce didn't have the luxury of
stepping into the shadows the way the rest of the group could.)

The only person who remained undeterred by the temperature
was Chris Sprowal, head of the Committee for Dignity and
Fairness to the Homeless, who was there to meet with Bruce and
receive a donation. "I spent eighteen months living on the street,"
Sprowal remarked, "and after that it took me another six months
to get warm. It'll *never* get too hot for me again." Sprowal was (and
is) unique among leaders of the homeless because he had been
homeless himself. He started the Committee and later the National Union of the Homeless (NUH) with other homeless people
as a way of fighting for basic rights; the central premise of both
groups was to provide homeless people a means of battling for
themselves instead of relying on more affluent surrogates. The
Committee had won homeless Philadelphians the right to vote
and to welfare. (They had previously been disenfranchised and
disqualified from governmental aid because they lacked addresses.)

With the $10,000 Springsteen gave it, the Coalition was able to expand its activities from Philadelphia to Camden, across the river in New Jersey, renovating a house there, and to train organizers for the NUH in five additional cities.

Sprowal, a black man in his mid-forties, came to the show (with Bob Brown of the United Electrical Workers, another NRFAC partisan, who'd made the contact) expecting nothing more than a useful handout. By intermission he was raving, especially about "Seeds," which the NUH adopted as its unofficial theme song, and about what Springsteen had said before "My Hometown": "The Committee was started by homeless people who try to let other homeless people be productive members of society. Right now they need all the help they can get. The things I'm singing about in my songs are things happening in your everyday life. In a country as rich as ours, it's a shame that fifteen percent of the population lives below the poverty level. There's absolutely no reason for it, but it affects all of us."

Sprowal was also impressed by his conversation with Springsteen. "He talked to us about how he hopes his music will bring to the attention of Americans the poverty and misery in this country," Sprowal said. In the end, the homeless leader felt, "the money is not that important. But Springsteen, by singling our group out, has raised the issue of homelessness before the whole country."

Springsteen's reputation as an ally of the poor was growing not only in the media but among the destitute themselves. "When we played the Cotton Bowl, I got a call in the hotel from a woman with a Spanish accent," remembered Barbara Carr. "She started to tell me all these terrible problems, and I was thinking, 'Oh no, she'll want Bruce to give her money; that's what this is leading up to.' But then she just asked me to thank him—for bringing the food bank to her attention. She had already phoned them up and received help." As well as being a pathetic comment on the inability of the American poor to receive even the most minimal information about where to receive assistance, that story also suggests the real potential for increased activity among the disenfranchised themselves when given even a minimum of information.

As it was, a call from the Springsteen organization had

become the community organizer's version of a visit from television's mythical Michael Anthony of "The Millionaire." And the shrewder organizations continued to line up many new donors and volunteers via the resulting publicity. Unfortunately, taking donations at the shows had to be discontinued when in several cities members of the Hare Krishna sect were discovered to be soliciting donations fraudulently in the name of the legitimate food banks and homeless organizations. Bruce actually had to warn people from the stage that anybody taking money in the halls at intermission was a crook. Even so, and despite skeptics left and right, every food bank or homeless union organizer the tour worked with in 1984 testified that the attention Springsteen had focused on the shameful problems they were working to address had carried over into the next year, and the effect of his work during the stadium shows was equally long-lasting.

The point, of course, is not that Springsteen was doing something saintly but that he was once more forming a substantial set of ties with the people to and for whom he most wanted to speak. Since it was unlikely that many of them could afford concert tickets, this was the only way of reaching out he had. For Bruce it was a two-way street; he felt he left each city a little more aware of what was really going on, which had always been part of his purpose in touring. People talked about running him for office, but no campaign he could have run would have been as effective as this one. When Springsteen's show came to town the hungry and homeless made headlines, and that was a step in the right direction. In the best cases—in cities like Pittsburgh, Gary, Los Angeles, and Philadelphia—the battle waged by the unemployed and discarded on their own behalf ceased being invisible and received a blast of fresh energy. As the flyer handed out by the Steelworkers–Old Timers group at the Los Angeles Coliseum shows put it, "Bruce Has Set the Tone."

■

In New Jersey people just went nuts. Cops were accused of ticket scalping in more than one community; New Jersey Bell suspended five employees for illicitly commandeering access to the Ticketron lines; the governor, the attorney general, the state's police superintendent, and the state consumer affairs director announced a crackdown on scalping, alleging that tickets with a face value of $18.50 were going as high as $300 for the front rows. Officials at the Meadowlands pledged to double security and set up patrols by undercover state police in order to quell scalping.

Governor Tom Kean, a conservative Republican, issued a flatulent proclamation of Springsteen's virtues in *Rolling Stone* (he was running for President, too). "During his latest concert tour, Bruce's support for regional food banks and other organizations to help the unemployed made a lot of people think about those problems for the first time," Kean wrote in unctuous agreement, but driving through Newark or Red Bank or Camden, you had to wonder how much thought the governor himself was giving to those problems.

In Freehold Mayor Mike Wilson and four other members of the town council boasted to the *New York Times* of attending high school with Bruce (nobody in Jersey knew he had a last name). Wilson, who'd been in a band, The Legends, which shared manager Tex Vinyard with Springsteen's Castiles, wanted to place a plaque on the Springsteen "homestead" or rename South Street Springsteen Boulevard. (The move was headed off by its subject's noticeable lack of enthusiasm and a realization that the signs were certain to be stolen as collector's items the moment they were put up, as the town councils of Liverpool and Memphis had already learned.)

Every reporter on the East Coast wanted a Springsteen story as the Giants Stadium dates approached, but neither Bruce nor the E Street Band were giving interviews. So camera crews and reporters flooded into Asbury Park and Freehold, digging for background and local color. Former sidemen, acquaintances from school, Asbury bartenders and club regulars spent most of August with notepads, cameras, and microphones shoved in their faces. The fact that none of them had much to say didn't matter. For the moment they were good copy because they were the only copy available.

The Giants Stadium stands were choked with such celebrities as Raquel Welch, Yankees star Don Mattingly, former Steelers quarterback Terry Bradshaw, and such politicians as Kean and New York Mayor Ed Koch, but Bruce maintained his focus on smaller kinds of heroism. His remarks were often intimate, even familial. The first night, he dedicated "The River" to his sister Virginia and her husband, Mickey, just as he had at the Madison Square Garden "No Nukes" shows (the first time he'd ever performed the song live). Later he cracked, "It's family night. All my relatives are here to see if I'm behaving myself." Before another song he shouted, "All *my people* out there! How have things been here in New Jersey?"

But when it came time to sing "My Hometown" each night, Bruce offered not a sentimental reminiscence of Freehold but hard facts. "In every state people are going to bed hungry. A lot of people are falling through to the bottom. They ain't getting caught in no safety net. They're hurting and they need some help. Remember, New York and New Jersey: This is your hometown."

The tour went up to Toronto for a few days, then came straight back to play Giants Stadium again on August 30 and 31—these were the extra shows that replaced the Boston dates. On the afternoon of the thirtieth the weather was growing bad, but so far the tour hadn't been rained upon once since Australia; the near-perfect conditions were an inside joke among the crew, a sign of the luck that blessed the whole tour. But that Friday night's forecast was for severe thundershowers, and that meant lightning, a hazard among all that equipment and scaffolding. At six o'clock, an hour and a half before showtime, George Travis made one last call to the weather bureau at nearby Teterboro Airport. Then he grabbed Jon Landau, and they went into Bruce's dressing room, where they decided to postpone the show until Sunday, September first.

Many of the nearly 70,000 ticket holders were already in the stadium parking lot; almost all the rest were on their way. Traffic snarled in the lots and on the highways as thousands of cars turned around and headed home. To top it off, it barely rained a drop, and aside from an occasional flash of heat lightning, there was no electricity in the air.

In less charmed circumstances this might have been an omen. As it happened, it was just somebody else's turn to be fortunate.

For several months Little Steven Van Zandt had been working on a song he'd written after returning the previous fall from a "fact-finding" trip to South Africa. Steven was appalled by everything he saw there, especially the so-called "homelands," a variation on the United States government's reservation system, which had all but destroyed unity and community among American Indians. Van Zandt understood the parallel quite well. He was particularly horrified at the way one such homeland, the so-called independent state of Bophuthatswana, had been transformed into an African Las Vegas, complete with pop music concerts that were used to legitimize both apartheid and its homelands system.

The song he wrote as a reaction, "Sun City," was an infuriated mixture of American black dance music, a few African inflections, and kick-ass rock and soul. Its lyrics denounced the homelands fraud and lambasted the apartheid regime, the American government's hypocritical policy of "constructive engagement," and the spectacle of international performers playing a resort surrounded by such total oppression and misery. This rock and roller was not for sale, Van Zandt declared. In a classic rock and roll stammer, he took a solemn oath: "I . . . I . . . I . . . ain't gonna play Sun City."

Little Steven made a demo of the song early that summer. When Arthur Baker heard it, he was so excited that he proposed they produce the record together at his Shakedown Sound studio. Journalist Danny Schechter, who heard a second demo featuring vocalist Will Downing, pushed them toward making "Sun City" into a more political "We Are the World" type of production, using a broader cross-section of pop musicians, including many who wouldn't have been deemed big enough for the U.S.A. for Africa supersessions.

So they began to assemble a series of sessions, spending their own time and money. (Steve was between record deals.) First they called upon New York rappers and old friends: rappers Afrika Bambaataa, Melle Mel, Duke Bootee, and Run-D.M.C.; Darlene Love, the veteran great of Phil Spector sessions; *salsa*'s Ruben Blades and Ray Barretto; Peter Wolf, late of the J. Geils Band; reggae singers Big Youth and Jimmy Cliff; punk godfather Joey Ramone; demi-monde giant Lou Reed. But as more artists found out about "Sun City," they clamored to be a part of the project. Soon Jackson Browne had a separate set of master tapes in Los Angeles, where he recorded himself, Daryl Hannah, and Bob Dylan. Meanwhile such impressive names as Miles Davis, Herbie Hancock, Bono of U2, and Peter Gabriel were among those who visited Shakedown Sound in New York to add their voices to the "Sun City" tracks. In July Van Zandt flew to London, where he recorded Pete Townshend, Ringo Starr, Bob Geldof, dub poet Linton Kwesi Johnson, and several others.

At this point Bruce Springsteen was just about the only pop star with progressive sympathies who *wasn't* involved in "Sun City." Steve Van Zandt was one of his best friends, but that meant, among other things, that Steve was sensitive to exploiting Bruce. Additionally, Steve undoubtedly felt some need to achieve a hit on his own. Also, Bruce was busy on the road; he didn't really have time to make a record date. So Van Zandt didn't say a word to Springsteen about it; Bruce heard the demo and received further word of the sessions through mutual friends (including Clarence Clemons, who also appeared on it).

Once aware of the project, Bruce was naturally enthusiastic. "Sun City" represented not only a significant political gesture but a huge musical leap for his friend. Still, it didn't seem likely that he would have time to appear on the record—and then the Giants Stadium gig was postponed. After the traffic cleared on the evening of the thirtieth, Bruce drove into New York City and met Steve at Shakedown Sound to review the tracks.

"I knew of Steve's involvement during the past couple of years, and that he'd been down [to South Africa] and back a couple of times," Bruce told the "Sun City" video crew. "I don't think I could just sit back and watch what was going on without feeling that I had to say something about it. The funny thing about it is that [racism] is so out in the open down there, but I was hoping that by helping bring attention to what's going on in South Africa it'd also make us look in our own back yards, at the terrible problems we have with racism right here in this country right now. So when Steve said, 'Come on,' I said, 'Sure.' "

Bruce quickly added in his part. The approach taken on this recording was completely opposite to that Quincy Jones had taken with "We Are the World." Because the sessions were catch-as-catch-can, Steve had each singer separately perform the entire song (five verses); then he selected key lines to mix together into a composite version. On the finished record, Bruce completes the second line, bouncing off Eddie Kendricks of the Temptations to sing, "We're stabbin' our brothers and sisters in the back." In the award-winning "Sun City" video, made later, Springsteen appears paired with Kendricks and fellow Temptation David Ruffin.

"Sun City" was not the international multi-platinum smash that the Band Aid and U.S.A. for Africa records were, but that's not surprising, for it was musically and politically much more adventuresome. The record was a substantial hit in England and Holland, got significant attention in many other European nations, and, of course, had the honor of being immediately banned in South Africa. In the United States it cracked the Top Forty and sold several hundred thousand copies, and the video opened MTV to integrated music almost for the first time, testimony to the way its message came back home, just as Bruce—and Steven, who had expressed similar sentiments—hoped it would.

On Sunday evening, in closing out the postponed Giants Stadium show, Bruce brought Little Steven onstage to sing "Two Hearts." "Two hearts are better than one," they sang, shouting with one voice into the mike. "Two hearts get the job done."

■

From there on it was just another roller-coaster rock tour, moving through Detroit and Indianapolis to Miami and Dallas. The band traveled by charter airplane now, which allowed them to base themselves at home, except in towns where there was more than one show. Staying in hotels hardly allowed any real local contact, anyway, although Springsteen managed reasonably well through his nightly meetings with community organizers.

After the mid-September shows at the Cotton Bowl in Dallas, the band based itself at the Sunset Marquis in Los Angeles, flying charters to the two remaining tour cities, Oakland and Denver, both short hops.

The Oakland shows went off without incident. But September 22/23 was late in the season for a pair of shows at Denver's Mile

High Stadium and they paid the price: Freezing rain fell on Mile High all morning on Sunday, the twenty-second; the temperature at Stapleton International Airport dropped from 58 to 44 degrees in fifteen minutes and sank into the low thirties for the rest of the day; 25-mile-an-hour winds rattled the stage lights. The National Weather Service, issuing a "special weather forecast for the Bruce Springsteen Concert," predicted even icier temperatures, accompanied by snow flurries. Although the tickets guaranteed a show "rain, snow or shine," it was decided to postpone the performance. The announcement was made at two fifteen that afternoon; Springsteen and the band never left Los Angeles that day.

Postponing the Sunday show until Tuesday, the twenty-fourth, also meant pushing the first Los Angeles date back and ending the tour on October 2 rather than September 30. But that was no big deal, since that show still had a couple thousand unsold seats; making it the final night would make being in those last few rows a lot more special.

But it was one thing to shuffle August dates in New Jersey, where few fans drove more than a couple hours to get to the show—and at a time of year when school was still out. Denver had been chosen partly because it was a regional center for the entire Plains and Rocky Mountain area, and fans had driven in from all parts of the West and Southwest: Nebraska, Wyoming, New Mexico, Arizona. Some of them had driven hundreds of miles, planning to drive straight back; they had no place to spend the night, let alone two nights. Furthermore, Tuesday was Yom Kippur, which meant that every Jewish fan was faced with an impossible choice. The situation posed a dilemma no indoor show had ever presented, but there really wasn't much choice. Forget about whether the audience was willing to listen in such conditions—who wanted to play in them? For that matter, given that fingers had to be nimble and legs limber, who could?

Almost as soon as he hit the stage both Monday and Tuesday, Bruce apologized profusely for Sunday's inconvenience. That was all the amends he could make. In fact, the weather during the shows he did play wasn't much better than Sunday's—Monday the sky was clear, but by the time the show ended temperatures were back in the low thirties; Tuesday they played in a chill downpour that made everything so slick that Bruce had to quit playing his acoustic guitar at one point because it was too slippery to pick up. To top it all off, the charter flight back to Los Angeles on Tuesday night, which carried Clarence, Nils, Barbara Carr, and George Travis, lost its electrical power and had to execute a blind landing in California.

It was a hell of a way for Bruce Springsteen to spend his thirty-sixth birthday, although, all things considered, it was a big improvement on the year before, when he had been single and alone and was still under presidential siege.

■

> And I said, 'Hey, gunner man, that's quicksand; that's quicksand, that ain't mud
> Have you thrown your senses to the war or did you lose them in the flood'
> —"Lost in the Flood" (1972)

In Los Angeles, on one of the last days off before the Coliseum shows, Jon Landau and Bruce Springsteen went for a drive through the canyons above Hollywood. In the course of their conversation they discussed how to approach the Coliseum dates. "It seemed like, Los Angeles is the last show; this is a unique event and we need to personalize it in some fashion," said Bruce. Landau mentioned the idea of doing Edwin Starr's "War," and Bruce said he'd thought about the same thing.

"It was funny," Bruce said, "because it was a song that Jon suggested maybe a year before. And we just couldn't get it down—it seemed too hard to play or we didn't have the patience at the time. Or at the moment it didn't make enough sense. And then we just tried 'War' one afternoon and we just got it fine. So I taped the words to my arm and we did it."

"War" was an extremely bold choice, though. Starr's original made Number One in 1970, and in retrospect it served as a signal. The song began with an unforgettable gravel-voiced shout: "WAR! What is it good for?/Absolutely nothin'! Huh!" It made Number One legitimately—by never backing off from its opening premise and backing its ideas up with equally tough and funky music. If ultraconservative Motown was willing to go that far, then Vietnam had to be coming to a conclusion (though it took four more terrible years to do so).

It was quite a different thing to sing "War" in 1985, when America was not at war but behaving so belligerently around the world that war seemed imminent in various places from the Middle East to Central America. It meant taking a stride beyond what Bruce had written in "Born in the U.S.A.," or even what he'd said at RFK Stadium. "War" was the one song that could make every implication of U.S. policy unmistakably explicit.

Obviously, as a devotee of complexity, Bruce Springsteen couldn't just leave it at that. Constructing the previous shows on the stadium tour had been a fairly simple matter of juggling the well-established set pieces of the arena show; the alterations were so minimal they were almost invisible. Simply adding "War" without other adjustments would disrupt the show's balance. It had to be surrounded with just the right blend of prefatory explanations and opportunity for release.

On earlier tours Springsteen had rehearsed the band rigorously through hours of daily sound checks. For a variety of reasons, those rituals had been trimmed down until, by the end of the 1985 dates, they were sometimes skipping the sound check altogether. Bruce had begun doing such rigorous sound checks because he placed an extremely high value on consistency. "We've got the best equipment, the best people, and it got to the point where some of the things I'd been doing became purely ceremonial, you know. It was a half hour or forty minutes where I'd come out and say, 'Hi, how's it going?' and we'd take a little walk," Bruce said. Both the E Street Band and sound mixer Bruce Jackson had long ago proved their mettle; driving them through several hours work before the four-hour show even began could actually result in leaving the best music of the night in the sound check, which wasn't the idea at all. After all, not even Springsteen found the sound checks fun, and on the stadium tour there was no way to improve the band's playing.

The ritual persisted as long as it did because it had another value. "In the end, what I was really doing was just familiarizing myself with where we were going to be working that night. Going out there, seeing the place, talking with a few people—personalizing it. That's pretty important. That was part of the job. Part of the job was to personalize that event, that night, that evening. What makes those people in Cleveland different from people in Chicago? You've gotta look to see what that is."

That part of the ritual was a valuable and healthy sign of commitment, and adding "War" to the set caused it to be revived for the Los Angeles stand. When it was, everyone from band to crew responded heartily, as if at the end of this cycle of shows as well as at the beginning, all concerned welcomed the opportunity to reaffirm their devotion to high standards. And the results were certainly worthwhile: a hard-rock arrangement of "War," whipped together in a couple of afternoons, that couldn't have sounded any more powerful if a battlefield had been brought to the stage.

The shows opened just before dark; the stage was framed within the Coliseum's beautiful synthesis of Californian and Grecian architecture so that the day's last rays glinted off it as off a devotional object. The concert opened with a triad of rockers—"Born in the U.S.A.," "Badlands," and then either "Darlington County" or "Out in the Street"—slammed out hard and fast, one after the other, without pause for breath or comment. The tone darkened with "Johnny 99," just as it had in all the other shows on the tour. But then out rumbled the bluesy grunge of "Seeds," a clatter of guitar and synthesizer introduced with almost exactly the same words Bruce had used in London, only with a few more American specifics.

"We were down in Texas on the first part of our American tour," Bruce said, still panting from his earlier exertions. "We were down around Houston. We saw a lotta folks down there from the Northeast—outta Pittsburgh, the Monongahela Valley, out of Gary, Indiana, outta Youngstown, outta De-troit—who'd moved South lookin' for work on the oil rigs, in the oil fields. And when they got down there the price of oil dropped and there wasn't any jobs. They'd be there with their wives and kids, with nothin' to do, no place to go. You'd see 'em sleepin' in tents out on the side of the highway or in their cars at night with nothin' to do but move on. This is called 'Seeds.' "

As "Seeds" ended, the Dylanesque chords of "Darkness on

the Edge of Town" arose, a perfect segue from rampant rage to suppressed fury. "Darkness" had expanded in meaning and contracted in girth since its incarnation on LP. The song was a tough little rocker now, which only made what it had to say about how hard Bruce was willing to fight for breathing space—and how hard anybody had to—that much more pungent.

The stage went black, then a single spot illuminated Nils Lofgren as he strummed a folkish melody; Roy Bittan swirled reedy synthesizer over it. After a few bars Bruce strode forward, wearing a black leather jacket over a couple of sweaty shirts. As he stood up to the mike, he gazed into the darkness, as if contemplating the wistful music.

"How ya doin' out there tonight?" he asked with a shy smile, his voice surprisingly loud against the softness of the playing. Anyone who'd ever attended a concert had heard the question asked, but even if you'd been to a thousand, this might be the first time the answer seemed to matter.

The answer swept back over him in a wave.

"That's good," Bruce said. "That's good." As he began to speak again, the music rose a bit, creating a backdrop for the story he would tell.

"When I was growin' up, me and my dad we used to go at it all the time. It seemed like it was over anything. But, uh, I used to have really long hair, like way down to my shoulders." He gestured broadly, holding his hands six inches away from his head and well below his shoulders. "When I was seventeen or eighteen, oh man, he used to hate it. He used to hate it so much that he used to wait for me at night in the house.

"It got to where we were fightin' so much that I'd stay outta the house a lot. In the summertime it wasn't so bad, but when the winter came . . ." He paused to button his jacket and cross his arms, left over right, a posture he held. He shivered a little, or maybe it was just a tremble—it's colder in L.A. after the sun's gone down, but not that much.

"I remember bein' downtown and it would get so cold. And when the wind would blow I used to have this phone booth that I used to stand in. I used to stand there and call my girl and get her to call me back," he said with a short, nervous laugh, "and then talk to her for hours at a time, all night." He hesitated a beat, to let the squeals die down.

"Finally, when I'd get my nerve up to go home, I'd stand in the driveway and he'd be waitin' there in the kitchen. I'd tuck my hair down so he couldn't tell how long it was, and I'd get up on the porch and I'd get into the kitchen and he'd always want me to sit down and talk to him. And he'd sit there with all the lights out and I could never see him. And he'd always ask me the same question—what I thought I was *doin'* with myself. And the worst part about it was that I could never explain it to him.

"I can remember one time I had an accident—motorcycle accident. I was laid up in bed and he had a barber come in and cut my hair when I couldn't walk. I can remember tellin' him that I hated him. I told him that I hated him and that I would never, ever forget."

Another beat; he shifted his arm. The left still held the right, which was now aimed straight ahead, rigid yet shaking.

"He used to tell me, 'Man, I can't wait 'til the Army gets you. Man, when the Army gets you, they're gonna make a man outta ya. They're gonna cut all that hair off, and they'll finally make a man outta ya.'

"I remember the day I got my draft notice in the mail, I hid it from my folks. Then, three days before I was supposed to go up for my physical, me and my buddies went out and we stayed up all night.

"I remember when we got in the bus that mornin', we were so scared. 'Cause it was in sixty . . . sixty-eight, and the Vietnam War was goin' on. There was a lot of guys leavin' town that didn't never come back, and there were guys that came back that just weren't the same no more. And we were so scared goin' up on that bus. And we went up and we took the physical and I failed." He laughed, a couple of nervous barks, then quickly admonished, "It's nothin' to applaud about.

"But I can remember comin' home—comin' home, walkin' in the kitchen . . . and my mom and pop sittin' there. And they asked me, 'Where you been for three days.' And I said, 'I had to take my physical.' And my dad said, 'What happened?' And I said, 'I failed.' And he said, 'That's good.' " The cheers rose almost to a scream, but Bruce said nothing, just uncradled the microphone and blasted into it with a harmonica wail so sharp it felt like a knife.

"The River" poured out of him, and old fans caught their breath as he sang. In a single tale Bruce had combined and resolved themes he'd been exercising for years. That short story, built on the framework of the raps Bruce had used to introduce "It's My Life" and "Independence Day," not only brought them up to date but uncovered their secret heart. And this song rocked harder than ever; it felt unhinged, cut free.

As it finished Bruce stepped out of the spotlight and the stage went black again. A diffused red spot caught Nils Lofgren, who picked up a new riff, threatening and bluesy. After a moment Bruce stepped back to the mike, his jacket off, his shirtsleeves rolled above his massive biceps. He closed in tight, head turned slightly to the right. He moved little more than his lips as he spoke. His right hand held the mike hard, like a tool or a weapon. His voice was steely, even though he was slightly breathless from the exertions of "The River."

"I want to do this next song for all the young people out there tonight," he said sternly. "When you grew up in the Sixties, you grew up with war that your country was involved in every night on television. And, uh, I remember . . . I remember a friend of mine, the drummer in my first band, comin' over to my house with his Marine uniform on, sayin' that he was goin' to Vietnam and that he didn't know where it was. And kinda laughin' about it.

"I'd like to do this song for you, 'cause if you're seventeen or you're eighteen out there, the next time, the next time they're gonna be lookin' at you. And you're gonna need a lot more information before you're gonna be able to make a decision about what's right for you to do. Because in 1985, blind faith in *anything*—your leaders—will get you killed."

He picked up the mike, took a couple of steps to his left, then turned. "Because what I'm talkin' about here is"—suddenly he was screaming as the lights exploded to full brightness—*"WAR!!!"*

The song erupted into action; the lights flashed bright as Bruce sang, referring from time to time to the handwritten lyrics that he'd taped to his left wrist. He mostly matched Edwin Starr lick for lick, "Good God, y'all" for "Good God, y'all." But Max Weinberg was delivering a sledgehammer beat, not funk, and as Bruce cracked down hard on each line, the words were as sundered from their original musical context as they were from Motown's political meaning. When Bruce sang, "They say we must fight to keep our freedom/But Lord there's got to be a better way," he found irony—and discarded it.

The song came to a halt on another blast of "*WAR!*" this time swamped in reverb and echo. The band shifted into "Working on the Highway" so suddenly that it was as if Bruce were deliberately deflecting the audience response (which was extremely intense), turning it aside as he'd finally reached the point in that long dialogue where he wanted to say, "I don't know what you think; it doesn't really matter right now. But this is what I think."

Bruce Springsteen sang those songs that way for four nights running, and in the process he recast his show. Packaging the new version of "The River" so tightly with "Seeds" and "War" and "Born in the U.S.A." did what Bruce's shows had always aimed for and promised: It knit together the threads of many years, so that each song knew its own heart and read new meanings into the hearts of the others, opening itself to all who were willing to listen. It was tempting to construe this suite of songs as "political," but that was too narrow an interpretation. The point wasn't that Springsteen had finally found a way to speak his mind in a fashion that couldn't be co-opted. It was that he was finally sure enough to speak with all the talent and power he commanded. What made "War" so ferocious was not just its appropriateness to the occasion—after all, anyone could have sung the song—but the utterly personal way in which Bruce put it across, so that its rage took on a dimension that went far beyond melodrama.

Toward the end of each of those four nights, Bruce sang "Twist and Shout," the lights flooding the entire stadium as he threw back his head and looked up, circling the building with his finger to acknowledge each section. And he crooned, "Do you love me?" It was another lost Motown classic, a silly song by the Contours. But those nights it never seemed silly. And the answer was right at hand.

The last two nights Bruce invited Jon Landau onstage to play guitar on "Travelin' Band," a resurrected Creedence Clearwater song. On the last night, just before he collapsed to one knee, he turned back to his manager and friend and shouted gleefully, "Hey, Jonny, it's too late to stop now!"

19 FORTUNATE SON

After "Rosalita" the band goes backstage and towels down, but everybody knows they're not going anywhere. This is a rock and roll encore—a necessary part of the show, an especially important moment in the Springsteen liturgy because it's traditionally the part where all debts have been paid and you're free to bop 'til you drop.

Tonight Bruce retakes the stage by himself, harp rack 'round his neck, an acoustic guitar in his hand. He does this sometimes as a kind of final "balance due" notice—there are some dues no one ever stops paying.

The nervousness Bruce occasionally shows when he's about to talk, rather than play or sing, is completely absent. He speaks confidently but with an air of fatigue, staring into the middle distance, thinking through the topics he needs to cover.

"I guess I'd like to take a minute and thank people who don't get thanked very much. I guess first and foremost is my crew and all the people who work behind the scenes at my show." The crowd cheers; a smile blossoms on his face. "Yeah!" he says, pumping his fist in the air. "Right! let 'em hear it!" Then, more soberly, "We've traveled all year; they've put this show up in the cold, they've put it up in the rain, they've put it up when it's ninety-nine degrees and ninety percent humidity. And they've just done the best job that's ever been done.

"Now I'd like to thank . . . uh, I'd like to thank all you guys for comin' down to the show tonight. And I guess I'd especially like to take the chance to thank all my fans for all the years of support that they've given me and the band. This has been the greatest year of my life"—he pauses to blink—"and I wanna thank yas for makin' me feel like the luckiest man in the world.

"And, uh, I'd like to do this song for yas," he says, and now the fatigue really shows. But it's not the weariness of having performed for so long; it's the kind of tired a man feels when he's butted his head against a wall. "This is, I guess, the greatest song that's ever been written about America. It's by Woody Guthrie and it gets right to the heart of the promise of what our country was supposed to be about. And, as we sit here tonight, that's a promise that is eroding for many of our fellow citizens every day, with thirty-three million livin' at or below the poverty line.

"I guess I'd just like to do this for ya tonight, askin' you to be vigilant, because with countries, just like with people, it's easy to let the best of yourself slip away."

Bruce begins "This Land Is Your Land," not the melodic rendition he first uncovered in 1981 or the cheerleading version used at gatherings of patriots and protesters. He sings the song as a stark and somber confession of beauties and indignities seen and unseen; the equation of individual lives with whole societies that he's made in the introduction is carried through into the music. Tonight Bruce Springsteen sings the song that ideologues of any stripe will never get—the part that's alive and still changing fifty years after the writing, the part that's so fragile any reasonable person never stops marveling that it survives, but so strong that it requickens each time someone comes along who's strong enough to pick it up. You might call it blues. Whatever it is, it's about the saddest damn thing you've ever heard.

As he sings it, someone sitting alone in the dark may be remembering what Bruce said earlier that evening as he introduced "My Hometown." That was so long ago; the show has pushed its way through so much that it's a little hard to believe it's all one thing. But it is, and in thinking back the connections are tangible.

"I remember when I was a kid, I walked to school in the morning, it used to seem like the loneliest walk in the world," Bruce says, standing alone in the spotlight, holding his guitar, without even the harp rack for armor. "And I remember the first thing we'd do when we'd get into class is, we'd . . . you know, they get you all standin' there and you'd say the Pledge of Allegiance. You know how it goes." He executes an extremely rapid mumble of the Pledge. "The one thing I always remembered from when I was young, that if somebody asked me what the flag meant . . . I guess even when I was a kid, I used to think, well, it meant fairness—that this was a place where the fair thing was supposed to happen. And we've been all over this year— we've been just about all throughout the States—and I've gotta say I've learned some things that have given me a lotta hope, and I've learned some things that have made me sad. I guess the fair America was not the one that I found there often enough for most people.

"I guess I'm bringin' it up tonight because I guess I think we all got—have—a chance and a responsibility to do something about it. And tonight in the audience there's some folks from the Community Food Resource Center of Los Angeles. That's a food bank, and they're connected to food banks in Long Beach, in Orange County and Riverside and San Diego. And there's some folks from the Steelworkers–Old Timers Food Bank in East Los Angeles, who we worked with the last time we were out here—"

He breaks off, then resumes speaking suddenly, as if something important has just occurred to him.

"And one thing I *have* found out over this year is that *every* place you go, no matter where it is, when you mention the name of that place people go *nuts*. Like, we'll give it a try here for a minute. Los Angeles [*monotone—eight-second cheer*]. That happens every place you go. And I finally figured it out that that happens because people are proud of where they come from. And if you're proud of where you come from, [think about] the folks from these food banks that are out there every day takin' some of these ideas that I'm singin' about up here tonight and tryin' to make 'em a reality in people's lives. They're tryin' to make Los Angeles and the whole surroundin' area a better and fairer place to live for all of its citizens. Without them, what I'm doin' up here tonight don't amount to much more than words."

If you're looking for answers, there are some here. He sang these songs, it seems, in order to fit one life into many, in order to feel that he's accomplished something—when he looks back over his shoulder the world has to be a different place because of it. Tonight is a night for such glances, some hasty, some lingering. And if the task for an attentive listener when this tour started way back in Minnesota was to hold back judgment, things have now come full circle: Now's the time to weigh events and find out if they balance.

"From the redwood forest to the Gulf Stream waters," Bruce Springsteen sings. "Yeah, this land was made for you and me." He sounds so lonesome he could cry, and the song trails off.

Then in the next moment all is transformed with a simple shout of "ONE . . . TWO . . ." The band kicks in, and Springsteen, no longer alone, can shout out the story's other side. It begins in a rush:

> In the day we sweat it out on the streets of a runaway
>   American dream
> At night, we ride through mansions of glory in suicide
>   machines

Where it ends, nobody yet knows. But the stadium lights have turned night into day, and all around, 85,000 fists punch the air and 85,000 voices chant the words, the multitude ready to come along.

20 NO SURRENDER

I can recall a time when I wasn't afraid to reach out to a
    friend
Now I think I've got a lot more than my toys to lend. . . .
A little bit of courage is all we lack
So catch me if you can, I'm goin' back
                                    —THE BYRDS, "Goin' Back"

The *Born in the U.S.A.* tour ended just after midnight on
October third with a last, rapturous rendition of "Glory
Days." Still toweling themselves dry, Bruce and the E
Street Band immediately dove into vans and were driven
to their West Hollywood hotel, the Sunset Marquis. Rather than
staying at his house, Bruce had rented a large suite there for the
evening, the better to accommodate the end-of-tour party.

The ritual festivities at the end of a tour are usually mildly
uproarious, featuring hard dancing to tapes of British Invasion
and soul hits and large quantities of a Kahuna punch concocted
by Clarence Clemons. At the end of *The River* tour, in Cincinnati,
Springsteen danced fifty people into the ground and everybody
stumbled aboard the next morning's plane looking happily ravaged.

But the *Born in the U.S.A.* tour party was subdued. Music
played but there was little dancing; Clarence made up his
mixture, but most contented themselves with sipping beer or
wine. Band, crew, and a scattering of friends talked quietly in
small knots. The evening still bore a glow, but it stemmed from
simple satisfaction. The tour had been a herculean undertaking
and they'd pulled it off all but flawlessly.

The air was also melancholy. Off the road these people often didn't see each other for long stretches, and after so many months together their partings were reluctant and regretful. For that matter, it wasn't only a question of the tour coming to an end— what about everything else that *Born in the U.S.A.* had stirred up? Did that just stop, too? No one knew and Bruce wasn't offering any clues.

But Springsteen had more than clues about how he felt about what they'd just accomplished. It was no mystery at all.

"Basically, by the time that we got on the road, things were real relaxed, and everybody was experienced and older, so everything was a lot more stable. And we were enjoying what we were doin' more than we ever had. The *Born in the U.S.A.* songs were a lotta fun to play live. And eventually, once again, the whole thing was more focused; I had a better idea what I wanted to do. And then when we started to get involved in different local organizations, I felt that that was really the first step in really beginning to reattach the thing to the different communities that you would play in. Once again, if you want to personalize the event, you have to constantly find some way to do that. You gotta work at doing it. That's why doing something different in every town was important because you got to meet with people from that town. You know—what's their story and what's going on? And it was a way of dealing with any impersonalness that could creep into a show of that size.

"This particular tour, everything seemed pretty clear to me. And not only did it seem clear to me, but it seemed clear to other people. I remember there was a year-end *People* magazine where they had one page on the tour, and it was about things that we did—it was about the work we were doing. And I said, Gee if that weird light of celebrity or whatever you want to call it [can be focused in that way], I felt that we'd done a good thing. On that particular page, that was what it was about. It was about what we were doing, what we'd done over that year. I said, Well, if it was gonna get lost, what we were trying to do would get lost here. But I felt that we'd kept the focus on the important stuff, and the superfluous stuff that attracts a lot of attention was minimized for the most part—and that I was pretty comfortable in the shoes I was in."

Bruce stayed in his Los Angeles house for a while after the tour's close, getting reacclimated to life without a next show in front of him, sorting out a domestic routine with Julie. The couple weren't doing anything in particular, so the following Tuesday, when Bruce was invited to see a production of *Lady Beth,* the play written by the theater project at the Steelworkers–Old Timers Food Bank, they went.

In the year since Bruce had visited with the former steelworkers, they'd developed a two-act presentation. The first act of *Lady Beth* presented the workers reciting reminiscences of lives surrounded and engulfed by the steel mill and relating what happened to those lives when the mill ceased to exist. (The Vernon Bethlehem steel mill lay idle for four years and then was dismantled and its machinery sent to Japan, where it was melted down and sold as scrap.)

The second act was an audience participation discussion, in which the steelworkers and their audiences confronted the myths and attitudes on both sides of the stage. At its best, that act could be as revealing and legitimately theatrical as the first. Springsteen, whose own approach to involving an audience was equally direct, loved what happened.

That night's audience was especially good. In addition to Bruce and Julianne, George Cole and the staff of both the union local and the food bank, those in attendance included the legendary Alabama civil rights activist Albert Turner.

Turner, the father of the Selma march, the man on whose living room floor the 1965 Voting Rights Act was first drafted, and Martin Luther King's chief Alabama organizer, was in Los Angeles on a fund-raising mission. He and twenty other west Alabama civil rights veterans had been indicted by federal authorities for so-called "vote fraud," which really meant so efficiently organizing their heavily black counties that it threatened white power all the way to Washington. He and his wife, the first to be indicted and tried, had already been found innocent, but their house was fire-bombed the night they were acquitted. In the end, the government was able to secure only one minor conviction out of more than two hundred charges brought, and the federal prosecutor in these cases, Jefferson Sessions, became the first nominee for a federal judgeship to be rejected by the Senate in decades. But for Bruce, who had just sung on "Sun City" for the purpose of bringing the fight against racism back home, the connection couldn't have been clearer.

Turner's comments following *Lady Beth* reflected the decade he'd spent at Martin Luther King's side, and the rest of the discussion was almost as stirring. Afterward, everyone repaired to a nearby restaurant, the Guadalajara Inn, where they ate and drank and hung around for several hours more. "We had a great time," said Cole, when the *Los Angeles Herald Examiner* asked him about it. "We had a little trouble getting the dancing going, even after we moved the tables to one side. But then we got 'Glory Days' on the jukebox and turned it up real loud and everyone was up on their feet."

There were those who found it perplexing that a wealthy celebrity who had married an actress-model and drove a Corvette felt so easy with such a crowd, but what made Bruce Springsteen's relationship with organizations like the Steelworkers–Old Timers Food Bank a matter of equality rather than charity was that they also had something *he* needed. In addition to pink Cadillacs and the adulation of millions, what rock and roll had promised Bruce Springsteen was that he would find a community where his loner heart fit in.

■

Back east again, Bruce and Julianne spent the majority of their time in Rumson but made frequent forays into New York City, where they eventually bought an apartment. There was even a spot of work for Bruce to do. "I'm Goin' Down" was completing its chart run, and with Christmas again on the horizon, it was time for one last single (the album's seventh). The choice was "My Hometown," a song with heavy resonance during the holidays.

Putting out another single didn't require much from Bruce besides assent. But by now it was expected that each of his singles would have a flip-side not taken from the album—there was hardly anything left on the album that hadn't been released as a single or given saturation AOR radio play—and there was also the question of video.

The first idea was to make the B side a live take of "War" from the Coliseum shows. But when Jon Landau went back and listened to the Coliseum shows, something bigger leaped out. Rather than sending Bruce "War" in isolation, he sent a tape that included four songs in sequence: "Born in the U.S.A.," "Seeds," "The River," and "War." Strung together like that, with their spoken introductions intact, the songs owned a startling unity.

Landau was already thinking about a live album. Bruce was a lot less certain. In fact, when they'd discussed the possibility just after the tour ended, he'd simply said no.

"I was against it," he said. "I never listened to any live tapes, really, and it just seemed like you were rehashing things. Maybe I was superstitious about it. But he sent me down that tape, and that was when I started to think that maybe there was something to it."

In any event, "War" was clearly too powerful to toss off as a B side. Instead, they used "Santa Claus Is Coming to Town," a live recording made in 1975 at C. W. Post College on Long Island. The song had appeared on the 1981 children's album *In Harmony 2,* and it was already a rock radio holiday staple. But most fans didn't own it.

Bruce wasn't interested in jumping right back into harness to make a conceptual video. He'd had "fun" working with John Sayles but said his interest then was primarily that "it was a new thing. It was just something different and I wanted to learn a little bit about it."

He had little interest in continuing to pursue video for its own ends. "Basically, it's a whole other form of expression, 'cause it's based around artifice, it seems to me. It's essentially cool, and its coolness is the problem for me," he said. "But I think that at this point I don't have any need to do any particular thing just for the sake of doing it. Basically, I think my main thing is that I set out to have a life as a musician and to explore what those particular possibilities were—as a musician, a guy with a rock band. That's where I want to focus my energy."

That didn't mean the video audience had to be abandoned. Arthur Rosato, who was video director of the live shows, was already sequestered in an editing room at the Cherry Hill studios of NFL Films, cataloguing all the footage from the tour for future reference. Rosato quickly put together a video of "My Hometown" based on Bruce's live performance; it was released to MTV on November 19, 1985, two days before the single came out. It was Bruce's most modest video; the song spoke in the quiet, simple voice it had found onstage.

"My Hometown" took off commercially, becoming *Born in the U.S.A.*'s seventh Top Ten hit, matching the record set by *Thriller*. *Born in the U.S.A.* sold like a blockbuster for a second Christmas season. Its sales topped 18 million worldwide and 10 million in America, making it, according to *Billboard*, the fourth best-selling LP of the past decade (after *Thriller*, Fleetwood Mac's *Rumours*, and the *Saturday Night Fever* sound track). By Christmas *Born in the U.S.A.* had also surpassed *Thriller*'s seventy-eight weeks in the Top Ten of the LP charts. It didn't drop out until the chart of February 1, in its eighty-fifth week—the longest Top Ten chart run of any album since *The Sound of Music*. With "Sun City" also riding the charts, Bruce Springsteen still seemed almost as ubiquitous as he had while touring.

■

Bruce had hardly been back home for a week when events in his real hometown caught up with him. On October 17, 1985, Stanley Fischer, president of Oil, Chemical and Atomic Workers (OCAW) Local 8-760 wrote Bruce a letter outlining the plight of his 450 members, who operated a Minnesota Mining and Manufacturing (3M) professional audio and video tape plant in Freehold—3M had just notified OCAW that it would be shutting down the Freehold plant in 1986 because the facility wasn't worth modernizing.

"You wrote a song about your hometown and about a factory that was shut down and what it meant to the town. When we hear that song, it strikes a very painful chord," Fischer wrote. "It's painful because it's happening all over again . . ."

It was literally true; a number of the 3M workers had been employed at the A and M Karagheushian rug mill, "the textile plant across the railroad track" of the song, before that plant moved south in the Sixties.

But that wasn't the only similarity. The rug mill moved to an area with cheaper wages and lower taxes. 3M, a company with almost $8 billion in annual sales and profits of more than $700 million, claimed it was closing the Freehold plant "as part of a program to reduce costs and improve product efficiency." The company maintained it would cost $20 million to make the Freehold plant "competitive" with Japanese plants. It was cheaper, the company insisted, to use its more modern plants in Hutchinson, Minnesota, and Wahpeton, North Dakota, and cheaper was all that mattered. The company had an obligation to make money for its shareholders and none at all to the workers whose livelihoods it controlled six and seven days a week through compulsory overtime.

"This shutdown will really hurt us," Fischer wrote. "Fifteen to twenty percent of us are single parents. This is by far the best job we will ever find around here. Twenty-five percent of us are minorities. Our average wages are $20,000 per year. . . . We must be honest with you. Many of us feel like there is nothing we can really do. This is a big company and there are no laws to stop this kind of thing.

"But . . . we believe the company might respond to a positive public campaign that would encourage them to keep the plant open ('3M and Freehold . . . We Need Each Other'). . . . Because of your special connection to Freehold and the entertainment industry, we believe that an open letter to the 3M Company signed by the Freehold workers and by you would have a tremendous impact on this situation. . . . We are not looking for your financial support. What we need is to make a positive public statement that will cause the International Board of Directors of 3M to take notice of our hometown. . . ."

Since Springsteen's interest in working with the needy and disenfranchised had become apparent, the Jon Landau Management office was daily besieged with propositions from charities, union groups, and individuals who were broke or sick or both. It's a familiar accompaniment to celebrity, in Bruce's case intensified by the specific content of his songs and by the fact that he actually took corresponding initiatives through the tour and on records like "We Are the World" and "Sun City." All Landau's office could do was screen the requests; there were far too many for all to be answered.

When Bruce saw Fischer's letter, sent to Landau's office through Lee Ballinger, associate editor of the *Rock & Roll Confidential* newsletter, his interest was immediate. Not only was the tie-in with "My Hometown" obvious, but Bruce's father and grandfather had been among the laborers in that rug mill. His response was personal as well as political. A meeting with Fischer was soon arranged; Bruce and Julie drove to Freehold for a lasagna dinner with Stanley and his family, and the drive to keep the plant open began.

Country singer Willie Nelson had already agreed to sign a public appeal if Bruce would. So Fischer and Les Leopold of the Labor Institute in New York drafted an open letter to 3M. After some tinkering it became a two-part ad—the first part a letter to the company from the Local 8-760 workers, the second a shorter message to 3M from Springsteen and Nelson.

The ad appeared on December 4, 1985, in the *New York Times, Variety,* the *St. Paul Pioneer Press,* and the *Asbury Park Press* (Freehold doesn't have its own daily newspaper). "3M: Don't Abandon Our Hometown!" read the headline.

The workers' letter followed a quote from the "textile mill" verse of "My Hometown," using much the same language in Fischer's appeal to Bruce: "For 25 years we have produced professional quality video and audio tapes for the broadcast and entertainment industries. Our work allows performers to share their images, words and sounds with the world.

"But now you are shutting us down. For many of us, this is not our first plant shutdown. Some of us actually came to 3M from the textile plant shutdown that Bruce Springsteen refers to in his song 'My Hometown.' We can't just let this happen again and again."

The ad told of the local's efforts "to meet with management to find a way to keep the plant open" and reported 3M's rebuff: "This wasn't a labor issue. . . . it would be more cost efficient for 3M to move the work elsewhere." "But what about the costs to human dignity?" the letter asked.

The workers' letter praised 3M's donation of the tape on

which "We Are the World" was recorded, but pointed out, "Here is suffering that you and only you can alleviate. We are not asking for charity. All we want is the chance to work."

Appearing slightly below the OCAW plea, the second letter read: "On behalf of the working people, their families and the community of Freehold, New Jersey, we urge you to reconsider your decision to shut down the 3M video and audio tape facility.

"We know that these decisions are always difficult to make, but we believe that people of good will should be able to sit down and come up with a humane program that will keep those jobs and those workers in Freehold."

Springsteen and Nelson's signatures followed, along with an informal P.S.: "We ask that other entertainers voice their support and concern. . . ." More than a few did. A week later a similar ad appeared in *Variety*, signed by virtually the entire cast of "Hill Street Blues." On January 28, 1986, a third ad appeared, bearing the signatures of Springsteen, Nelson, the Hill Streeters, and a large group of entertainers ranging from actors Ed Asner and Robert Foxworth to musicians like John Mellencamp, Joan Jett, and the Blasters. It was headlined "3M: VIOLATING THE HUMAN RIGHTS OF OUR HOMETOWN" and proposed a "national bill of rights" for communities faced with plant shutdowns, including the right to rebuild careers through higher education, the right to full medical protection and income security, and the right to child care. Stanley Fischer undertook a national informational tour to present the workers' case.

To all this 3M responded with a stone wall of meaningless corporate clichés. "It was a difficult decision, but our analysis makes it clear that no alternative to consolidation is possible, and production must be moved now for 3M to remain competitive in this advanced technology market," said plant manager Kenneth R. Dishno. This boiled down to saying that the company was entitled to do whatever it wanted, employees be damned, an especially ironic position given that only a few weeks after the Freehold plant closed, 3M's professional tape production capacity was so diminished that it had to put its labels on tapes made by Sony.

The company wouldn't budge, but the workers kept fighting.

A benefit concert for the beleagured local was arranged for Sunday, January 19, at the Stone Pony in Asbury Park. Ten bands, mostly little-known local acts, were scheduled to play from two P.M. to two A.M.

Naturally, the event was jammed all day, as rumors circulated that Springsteen and the E Street Band would make their first post-tour appearance. Several E Streeters were visible early in the evening, but that didn't mean much since Garry Tallent had been involved with Jersey Artists for Mankind, the group putting on the show, and one of the acts on the bill was J. T. Bowen, formerly lead vocalist with the Red Bank Rockers. But just after eleven, Bruce himself turned up, and the club's phone lines were soon flooded as friends went to spread the word.

Bruce took the stage just after midnight, supported by Tallent, Clarence Clemons, Danny Federici, Max Weinberg, and Patti Scialfa. (Roy Bittan and Nils Lofgren were out of town.) Before beginning to play, Bruce calmed the crowd and spoke in a cold, angry voice.

"The marriage between a community and a company is a special thing that involves a special trust," he said. "What do you do after ten years or twenty years, you wake up in the morning and you see your livelihood sailing away from you, leaving you standing on the dock? What happens when the jobs go away and the people remain?

"What goes unmeasured is the price that unemployment inflicts on people's families, on their marriages, on the single mothers out there trying to raise their kids on their own."

Now he spoke with ice in his words. "The 3M company: It's their money, it's their plant. But it's the 3M workers' jobs. I'm here to say that I think that after twenty-five years of service from a community, there is a debt owed to the 3M workers and to my hometown."

Bruce said nothing more, just broke into the tautest "My Hometown" he'd ever played. Though his voice soon started to unravel, the band slugged through a set of anthems: "Promised Land," "Badlands," and "Darkness on the Edge of Town," the last dedicated to Fischer and the Local 8-760 membership. Springsteen was hoarse when he paused after that song. But instead of stopping he reversed the mood with a series of rockers—"Stand On It," "Ramrod," "Twist and Shout"—before calling it a night just before one A.M.

That was it. Over the next few months, 3M closed the Freehold plant in stages. By January 1987 only about a quarter of the workforce still held on to its jobs. (At least one of the dislocated workers got a job at a chemical plant further north in Sayreville, Stanley Fischer reported, but in less than six months, that plant, too, folded.) Stanley Fischer and the OCAW local fought for state legislation on plant closings and filed lawsuits against 3M, but to little avail. For the most part the dismissed 3M workers were consigned to the growing heap of discarded Americans. Corporate reputation might be affected by rock stars—3M was near the top of the *Fortune* magazine list of most admired corporations in 1985; in 1986 it didn't make the list—but not the process of dismantling the American worker's standard of living. That was inexorable.

■

Late in the year Bruce briefly visited California. During that trip he was surprised by an invitation from his father. Doug proposed spending a week fishing in Mexico. They didn't catch much, but the weather was fine and the pair enjoyed their time together immensely.

When Bruce returned to the East Coast, he and Jon began seriously talking about a live album for the first time since *Born to Run*. For just that long, fans and businessmen had campaigned for such an album, the former because they wanted a souvenir to take home, the latter because Springsteen's live-performance reputation would make it a guaranteed gold mine. Both points were underscored by the proliferation of "bootleg" live albums; according to record collectors, by 1985 Springsteen was the most bootlegged artist in history. Bootlegs—the term refers to music recorded and manufactured without the artist's permission—were difficult to find, extremely expensive (averaging about $20 per disc), usually poorly recorded, and haphazardly packaged. Yet hundreds, perhaps thousands of Springsteen buffs cherished bootlegs and clandestinely recorded tapes of his shows.

Springsteen made his disapproval clear by allowing CBS and the Recording Industry Association of America (RIAA), an industry trade group, to pursue bootleggers aggressively in his name. (A couple of them even went to jail.) Even prosecution didn't end the practice. It only slowed from a flood to a trickle.

Bruce's personal animus seemed to be simply artistic, not mercantile. "I guess nobody likes the feeling that they wrote a song and in some way the song is bein' stolen from them, or presented in a fashion they don't feel they'd want to present it in—the quality isn't good, and they're so expensive," he said to *Rolling Stone*'s Kurt Loder. "I always tell myself that some day I'm gonna put an album out with all this stuff on it that didn't fit in. I think there's some good material there that should come out. Maybe at some point, I'll do that." So when Springsteen spoke of bootlegs, he was thinking of surreptitiously taped live shows as much as of tapes containing unused or unfinished songs that had leaked out over the years from recording studios.

His reasons for not releasing a concert album were significantly different. "I never wanted to do just a live record," he told Robert Hilburn. "It wasn't ever interesting enough for me. What I was interested in was finding out what kind of songs I could write and finding my way around the studio to get some of the feeling that the band gets on stage. . . . I get interested in what I can do next; I get curious and anxious about writing more songs." In a way, then, Bruce's reluctance to satisfy the demand for live material was akin to his avoidance of hit singles, embedded in his general suspicion of things that came too easily.

David Hepworth confronted Bruce with the same question during the *Old Grey Whistle Test* interview in 1984 and got a different kind of answer.

"A lot of what we do at this point is about *being there*, which is why we haven't done much television or too much of the video thing," Bruce said. "A lot of the problem is that it allows too much distance. What our band is about is about breaking down distance, and I think it's important that people come out, they come down, they go some place where there's a bunch of other people.

"And then the other thing was, [on] a live record, a lotta times you're doing things that you've done already. I think it'd probably be a little boring to work on, maybe."

In this sense, then, Springsteen's avoidance of a live album stemmed from a feeling that concerts were a distinct medium, quite separate from the process of songwriting and album-making, that what was special and spontaneous onstage probably wouldn't translate into the careful and considered world of the recording studio. He was interested in going out and performing his songs night after night, but if he was going to spend all the time and energy it took to fix a song on tape, it seemed right to do it with new material.

However, he was starting to bend now, perhaps because some of his recorded songs—often the best ones—acquired a different and larger life onstage. "There are songs that I want to re-record, that I was unhappy with the original studio recordings of," he told Hepworth. "Mainly the *Darkness* album, which was a record that I thought had some of my best songs, but I always felt was a little dry recording-wise. I felt we kinda underplayed and oversang a little bit, you know. That stuff sounds quite a bit different in performance, and I'd be interested in getting different versions of some of those songs."

To those aware of previous Springsteen pronouncements on the subject, this was a fascinating change—not just another sign of his relaxation about the uses to which he could put his work but evidence that he was thinking seriously about something he'd previously dismissed. Still, it seemed likely that when it actually came time to make a new record, Bruce would want to cut new songs.

The tape Jon Landau sent Bruce changed that because it included both new songs ("Seeds," obviously; "War," too) and new ways of looking at old ones. "Born in the U.S.A.," taken slightly more slowly than in the studio, was much more emphatic in the verses, and that made the ironies of the chorus unmistakable. The stories Bruce told before "The River" and "War" were not only worthy of repeated listening (always the central problem with spoken material) but cast the music itself in a different light. As a piece of music, "War" had a brittle intensity that the band had never captured in a recording; as a public statement, it affirmed Bruce's beliefs more pungently than anything else he'd ever sung.

Bruce later acknowledged that he'd been wary of a live album in part because he just didn't know what had gone onto the live tapes they'd been making for the past decade, usually when near the sophisticated remote recording facilities of New York and Los Angeles. "I didn't understand that the band had played really well over the years," he said. "I mean, I knew we'd been doing something right, but I didn't know exactly what. And I wasn't so sure I wanted to find out. It seemed things were going well, and I was kinda superstitious about it."

Landau *had* listened to those tapes, and he knew that the band was playing well (if not always impeccably) straight through. And once Bruce listened, he agreed: "I'd never really heard the band until I heard the tapes," he said, sounding a little like someone who'd just heard his first E Street Band concert. "When I heard the band on the tapes, it gave me a whole new insight as to what it sounded like and what we had been doing over a ten-year period. And mainly, they were just doing their job really well. Like Danny—on the record, he's incredible.

"I was never completely satisfied with any of the recorded versions of things that we did—certainly not before *The River*. I never felt the band learned to play in the studio before *The River*. On 'Badlands' or 'Darkness,' the live versions are the way that stuff was supposed to sound. And we couldn't have ever got that in the studio, even if we·had been playing well—because the audience allows you to attack something with a lot more intensity, and if you did it the same in the studio, it would sound overdone or oversung.

"So the surprise when we listened to all the tapes was that we could just mix 'em and put 'em out. Even when the playing wasn't at what you'd call a technically high level, the enthusiasm was so crazy that it kinda lifted the whole thing. Like, listen to 'Rosalita.' 'Rosalita' is so funny, there's so many strange parts, but people were playing so hard and so intensely and so happily, that the whole thing just kinda takes off."

Making the decision for a live album proved quick and easy; deciding what shape that record would take was a bit more complicated.

"Once I heard the sequence tape, the question became, Are we going to make one record or two records? One record wouldn't be enough; two records felt limiting," Bruce said. But from the beginning, Landau's concept was that the live album was worth doing precisely because it didn't have to be a condensation of Bruce's show, it didn't have to be drawn entirely from the *Born in the U.S.A.* tour or exclusively from any single tour.

Columbia Records was eager for a live Springsteen album; they'd happily issue an expansive (and expensive) multidisc set. The advent of compact discs, which could accommodate more than seventy minutes of music per disc, made multi-hour recordings more practical and even more desirable. And the CD technology could be tested—even given a public boost—by the most recent live tapes (from 1984 and 1985), which were digitally recorded.

Most important, once Bruce and Jon came upon the idea of doing a record that wouldn't be a live album or a greatest hits album so much as it would be the *next Bruce Springsteen album,* the issue resolved itself: This album would be as long as necessary to tell the story, and since the story was an epic, that might be real long.

Still, Bruce Springsteen was cautious as man and artist, and he moved slowly. At first, he and Landau spent some hours together just listening to tapes. A key moment came when Jon dredged up the tape of "Thunder Road" from Bruce's show at the Roxy (a Los Angeles club) during the *Born to Run* tour in 1975.

"Bruce and I were sitting one day that December [1985] and just playing cassettes and starting to get into the process of making that record," Landau said. "We put it on and one of us said, 'Well, if we ever did do a live album and it was a retrospective, *that's* what should open it.' And from that point on that's always been the song that opened the album. Looking back, that was probably the first thing we knew about this album. If it existed, it was gonna start with this version of this song. And I think that that was almost a handle for Bruce to get into the album, because that already established the idea that we could make a live album that would just be a creative endeavor. Because that was a creative decision."

For Bruce, "Thunder Road" was also the key to understanding the record's historical reach. "That kinda opened the thing up to take in the time span, 'cause we knew we wanted to use that version. And if we're gonna use that and 'War,' what's the matter with all the stuff in between?"

That Roxy version of "Thunder Road" was remarkable at the time by virtue of Bruce's simple audacity in opening the show with such a radical revision of one of his best-known numbers. As the opening track of *Born to Run*, "Thunder Road" was presented in full-band grandeur, a sweeping statement of romantic questing on a broadly mythic American landscape, from the opening reference to Roy Orbison to the final declamatory "This is a town fulla losers/And I'm pullin' outta here to win." But when the *Born to Run* tour began, Bruce wasn't playing the song with the full band. Instead, he came out and did it as the first number of the night, standing stock still at the microphone, guitar slung behind his back, accompanied only by Roy Bittan on piano and Danny Federici playing electric glockenspiel. The result was a tender and vulnerable recasting that transformed a promise into a plea. By situating this revision at the very beginning of his shows, at a time when his image was just being locked in, Bruce suggested a more open, less monolithic vision of both self and show. You felt that between the time he'd recorded the song and began performing it, Springsteen had outgrown its conceits without letting go of its hopes.

In fact, the origins of the rearrangement were more prosaic. Bruce remembered that "the band just couldn't seem to get a handle on the arrangement."

Landau remembered why. "When we cut the track, Bruce wasn't singing," Jon said. "And where he sings, 'Tonight we'll be free, all the promises will be broken,' he intended the music to go on for an extra line so those words would float more gracefully into that spot. But when we cut the track he forgot about that, so it's just the length it would normally be, musically. So when you listen on *Born to Run* (and it would never bother anybody at all), he sings it right up against the limit of the music.

"But when he went to perform the song, he hadn't figured out how to do that little piece of business with the band the correct way. So he did it with the piano. And when you listen on that

1975 version, he puts in that extension that he always wanted to have."

So pragmatism produced poetry. But after a while, when the memory of what he'd wanted to do was eclipsed by what he *had* done, Bruce went back to the arrangement on the album.

It wasn't memories that Bruce Springsteen was seeking—and finding. It was a decade of "Growin' Up," to give it the name of the song in which he first spoke clearly about the relationship between early days and adulthood.

Springsteen and Landau had access to about thirty professionally recorded shows, far fewer than the number that had been bootlegged. But those shows were more than sufficient to their purpose, and anyway, they couldn't have used any less technically sophisticated material and maintained the necessary sound quality. In the end, the digital tapes from the *Born in the U.S.A.* concerts set an extraordinary standard for everything else. This meant that some memorable moments simply weren't available. For instance, the concert rendition of "Racing in the Streets," preceded by and concluded with Bruce's narration, didn't make the record because it had never been professionally recorded.

And while they didn't stint themselves in terms of quantity of songs or time, it wasn't just the warhorse concert staples they sought, either. As Bruce put it, they were looking for the songs "before they were institutionalized," while their meanings were still fermenting.

Around Christmas 1985 Jon Landau sent Chuck Plotkin a rough assemblage of what became the live album's first side: the piano-and-glockenspiel "Thunder Road," a frothing "Adam Raised a Cain" that began with shouts and feedback akin to the MC5, and a pair of songs from Bruce's first two albums, "Spirit in the Night" and "4th of July Asbury Park (Sandy)," in sleek late Seventies/early Eighties arrangements. Plotkin was scheduled to rejoin the team in New York the first week in January. (He knew nothing about the project, because Bruce and Jon hadn't yet discussed their intentions with him.) Then Bruce's plans changed. He decided to meet with Plotkin in Los Angeles instead, so Landau decided to send Plotkin a little homework.

Landau put the tape together from low-fi cassettes on his

home dubbing deck, and Plotkin described what arrived in Los Angeles as "a third-generation cassette copy of lousy rough mixes. There was as much noise as there was music."

Plotkin's response was accordingly confused and disdainful. "I mean, 'Thunder Road' is like . . . *'Thunder Road!'* This is some historical document? Bruce makes records, he doesn't make historical documents. I said, 'Jon, I don't know about this.' " Landau was annoyed but sent more tapes: whole shows instead of just selections.

Plotkin later realized that he'd succumbed to one of the inherent difficulties of working with Landau and Springsteen. The ideas the two men concocted between themselves were rarely fully articulated to anyone else.

But Plotkin finally began listening with an open ear. The first thing he reviewed was the 1978 tape from the Roxy, recorded in the same club as "Thunder Road" but three years later. Plotkin had been among the 500 patrons at the original '78 show. "And when I got done with it, I just said, 'Oh yeah. Jon's right.' "

By the time Springsteen himself arrived in Los Angeles, a couple of days after the benefit for the Freehold 3M workers, Plotkin had done his homework. "I've done a lot of work with him, and I can jump in quickly and catch up very fast. And hey, listen, I love that 'Thunder Road.' "

They spent the next two months sitting together, assessing a stockpile of shows that, with a bit of research by engineer Toby Scott, grew to fifty or sixty, a total of about 200 hours of music. They had reached an apotheosis of the process Plotkin described as the essence of Bruce Springsteen's record-making: "You listen to the music. The music speaks to you. If you listen to it, it speaks to you. Whatever you *think* you're doing doesn't make any difference—it's what you *are* in fact doing. And if you listen hard enough, you can hear what you're doing; you can hear what you've done."

Except in this case it wasn't just the essence of the process—it *was* the process. The songs were written; the performances were done. The job was picking which songs and which takes and deciding the order in which they'd best be heard.

"We just tried to pick the best takes," Bruce recalled.

"Charley's real good at knowing when you have the best take of something. He hears the way something moves and what's going on on the bottom. He's the kind of guy who hears something and sees a diagram of everything that's going on. I don't hear that at all. For the most part, I listen to it the way a kid would listen to it. I never listen to the bottom or this or that; I just listen to it, from the very beginning.

"Charley sees through the whole thing really quickly, and he can tell you pretty quickly. He can just tell when something feels right, is moving right and also has the heart and soul, which is ultimately what we based the choices on. Like 'Born in the U.S.A.,' which is the rawest one we had that held together, the wildest one we had."

Picking the takes took only two or three weeks. Given such a huge body of material, it could have been a fearsome task for a pair of perfectionists, but Plotkin makes it sound like a cruise.

"It was the easiest thing in the world. Once we got into it and you could see what was shaping up, Bruce and I spent about six hours a day, five days a week, essentially trying to come up with the right songs to use, come up with little segments of sequences, and to come up with the right takes of the songs.

"It was an enormous amount of work and it was easy as hell. First of all, we didn't do it in a studio. We just went to Bruce's house. The two of us tend to have fun together. I don't have the same kind of responsibilities that Jon has for his career, and I don't have some of the same roles that Jon has in his life. And the two of us have a good time. We just listen to music. And if you're listening to music, even when it's his music, it's fun.

"There were days when he was on and I was a little under, and there were days when I was on and he was a little under. And there were days when I thought, 'What am I doin' here? He can be doing this himself; he doesn't need my help.' And there were days when I thought, 'My God, he wants me to choose all these things. He's just sort of sitting here to make sure I do my work.' It was the entire range of those kinds of things."

When they'd picked takes of between forty and fifty songs, Jon Landau flew to Los Angeles, and they set to work on sequencing, a much more delicate process. Gradually the live album revealed itself by a process of elimination, as a sculpture will sometimes reveal itself to an artist who knows just how to view a chunk of stone. Chip by chip, bit by bit, they fit it together.

"Sequencing was real important, because that was how we were setting up the story to be told," said Bruce. They chose the right takes of as many songs as seemed fitting. But sequencing this album was also a matter of narrowing it down, putting the right songs in the right order to reflect the personal and musical evolution of an entire decade. They didn't want to make a record of curios, so the rarity of a song counted for nothing and, when the chips were down, neither did any individual song's everyday power. For instance, "Badlands," Bruce's original post–"Born to Run" anthem, was the last song added to the sequence, and then not until the following summer.

Everyone endured some frustrations, including Bruce. "In the end, there's no 'Glory Days,' which is one of my favorite songs. Like hey, I got my complaint, too," he said, referring to the moans of fans disgruntled by the lack of this or that selection. "I would've liked to put that on, and I tried to the bitter end, and I just couldn't fit it on."

They'd decided to shoot for a five-record set, which would be the equivalent of five vinyl discs or three cassettes or compact discs, similar to Bob Dylan's retrospective *Biograph*, issued in early 1986. "There could have been twelve sides as easily as ten," Plotkin said. "At fourteen sides, you're into a different thing. But there were some close calls. There was at least one side of close calls—I think probably two sides of close calls.

"For instance, there's a solo version of 'No Surrender.' Bruce said, 'I don't think we have room for it.' I said, 'Bruce, this solo version of "No Surrender" has literally saved me from depression and self-contempt on more days than I choose to tell you about— just from putting it on and listening to it.' It's a beautiful, highly particular, and stirring version of a song that basically just gets lost in the shuffle on [*Born in the U.S.A.*]. That's what the album had to have; it has to have things that you only got to find out about because of the show." ("No Surrender" made the record.)

They weren't trying to recreate a concert but, as Plotkin

pointed out, what they came up with is about the same length as a concert, and the sides actually take a shape resembling segments of shows and they're paced accordingly. As the central criterion of selection, they wanted versions that were *alive*—"either the most alive or alive in a very particular way," as Plotkin said. "That is, nothing got on the record because the song needed to be on the record. We came close to not putting 'Born to Run' on the album. We were cruising into the end of the sequencing without an acceptable take of 'Born to Run.' "

The reason was simple: They had comparatively few workable takes of any given song, and there was no way to get more. "Born to Run" was a special problem. "That was a song that for a long time we didn't know how to play," Bruce admitted. "It was hard to sing and hard to play." In the end they used a rendition from the Giants Stadium shows of August 1985, more than eleven years after they'd begun performing it. "I was so happy when I put that version of it on, because I *never* thought we were gonna have a good live version of that song on tape."

"Badlands" was another such problem. In fact, that song might not have made the lineup at all if the version recorded November 4, 1980—the night after Ronald Reagan's first election as President—hadn't turned up late in the game.

In general, they followed the chronology in which the songs were composed, though not always the sequence in which they were performed. For instance, "Sandy," which crops up on Side One and has a "club" feel, is actually from the arena tour of 1980.

To increase the sense of continuity, they relied heavily on certain shows in each period: the 1978 Roxy date for the club and theater years, the 1980 New Year's concerts at Nassau Coliseum for the arena material, the second night of the Los Angeles Coliseum shows for the stadium tour. Other shows also cropped up, notably those from the inaugural Meadowlands stand in 1981 and the Jersey shows of 1984 and 1985. The continuity was further enhanced because the original playing was for keeps. "There were no vocal overdubs, no resinging anything, no replaying anything, unless something was actually broken or a channel wasn't on or something like that," Bruce said.

The record's key transitions came at the beginning of Side Four, as the show entered its arena phase, and at the top of Side Seven, when the full-scale stadium show kicked in. (Although the six-sided cassette and CD versions probably outsold the LP, everyone refers to the record in terms of its breakdown into ten album sides, a convenience born from tradition.)

But they weren't sticklers about chronology for its own sake. The transition to arenas comes with "Hungry Heart," even though none of the material from *Darkness on the Edge of Town* has yet been heard. But the choice is correct—"Hungry Heart" is thrilling before you hear a note of music, because the crowd sounds impossibly big and wild. The lead-in to the stadium shows is both more subtle (because the rock material is prefaced by a trilogy of *Nebraska* songs, themselves prefaced by "This Land Is Your Land" from 1980) and more stunning (because "Born in the U.S.A." emerges in such a mighty roar). At the end, arena and stadium performances are again mingled in order to fit the larger plan.

Bruce's raps presented another sort of problem. However fascinating they might have been in the heat of a moment, spoken passages can be deadening on record, because generally they survive repetition less well than music. On the other hand, Bruce's story-telling at its best was exquisite and integral. For example, in the sequence running from "Born in the U.S.A." to "War," what Bruce says determines the meaning of the music he plays. Again, the task was to sculpt the mass of material, carving the structure they wanted to show. So Bruce's spoken interlude in "Growin' Up" made the record because it foreshadowed future developments, while a moving introduction to "Independence Day" wound up on the cutting room floor because it wasn't as necessary to the overall tale. In other places they managed to edit with remarkable effectiveness pieces that were originally heavily visual: "Fire," with its extended mugging with Clarence Clemons, was snipped to the bone and yet retained its sense of humor.

In general, the idea was that this was a *record,* and that meant it had to reward the casual listener as well as the one who paid close attention—you had to be able to simply sit back and listen. When it was finally released, the live album was criticized for wandering away from the point after "War," but, as Bruce pointed out, that was part of the concept, too.

"It's just a break in the action. The whole point is, there's times when you have to take the record as a whole. And at that point, you're not gonna put 'Jungleland' in there. You need songs for what they're *not* saying right then. You gotta bring it back down to everyday life. Life goes on, man, life rolls on," he said. "The whole idea of the record was that you could put on any side at any time, that it would be a record that would contain a certain group of ideas but that those ideas were not necessary—it was just a rock record, it was just like a rock and roll record. Dance to it, listen to it, do whatever you wanna do with it. That was the point of the thing, you know.

"From the very beginning that was how we wanted to present the thing, you know. And this came up in the sequencing a lot. When we began to sequence the thing, if we began to construct it too intellectually or too conceptually—too superficially conceptually—it started to sound like, 'What are you trying to do?' The whole point was, it had to roll. And in the end, that's what made it what it was. So after 'War,' we're rolling a little bit, you know. It's gotta keep going, and it's gotta scale back down.

"We wanted the record to rock, and one of the most important things we were trying to do with the record, we were tellin' a story. There's a story bein' told here. And the record had to have its internal logic. It wasn't a greatest hits album; there were certain songs we knew we would like on. But nothing was sacred; anything could've been left out if it really and truly wasn't gonna work."

If anything made assembling the live set truly difficult, it was this dual purpose: trying to capture accurately the spirit of the moment on which the concerts were built, while building a retrospective that would document the periods of Bruce's career and his growth as man and artist—his transition from aspiring young singer-songwriter fumbling in the dark to adult confidence in the full spotlight of rock and roll stardom. The result was an unusual set of choices, a hybrid of expectations and necessities, neither a catalog of obscurities to replace the bootlegs nor a simple concert documentary.

"The thing is that you don't actually know what's coming, even if you know what's coming," said Plotkin, referring to both the actual Springsteen concert experience and what he helped shape from it. "You may have heard the songs; you may know what it's like to sit there and have that experience. But it's a slightly different experience each night. The stuff isn't canned. He tells stories; the stories are a little different each time. I've heard stories for the seventh time that I thought I knew, and you'll see this funny expression on his face and you realize that he's remembering some detail of that story that he didn't remember before *that moment*. And you realize that there is a live thing taking place. That it's not simply some guy getting up and repeating a series of songs—that it is a live celebration, in that moment, in real time. And that's what you have to try to get this album to catch."

They caught more than their share of moments. But what was just as startling was the sense of continuity that the live album demonstrated. In introducing "Growin' Up" in 1978, Springsteen relied upon almost the same experience that he later developed for the introduction to "The River" at the Los Angeles Coliseum. (Just as, for instance, his 1981 raps about his history book became the RFK Stadium introduction to "My Hometown," which evolved into the "War" intro.) The same kind of development was expressed in his songwriting, as the characters of "Thunder Road" and "Backstreets" became those of "Darkness on the Edge of Town," and those in turn became the forebears of the folks in "Born in the U.S.A.," "Bobby Jean," and "My Hometown."

Certainly his themes hadn't changed much, although, of course, his way of looking at them had altered drastically. But from "Backstreets" to "Racing in the Street" to "Bobby Jean," and from "Sandy" to "Two Hearts" to "Reason to Believe" and "I'm on Fire," the quest and the pain and the triumph all evolved from the same stem.

■

Throughout 1986 Bruce Springsteen's legend continued to expand, even without any public activity. In 1985 year-end media polls ranging from trade magazines to television shows, he scooped up dozens of awards (although he won no Grammies). He was named *Rolling Stone* Artist of the Year for the second straight year, outpolling runner-up Phil Collins three to one, and won best male singer, songwriter, and live performer as well.

In the end, though, Springsteen's omnipresence had little to do with that sort of thing. He'd become a reference point in American popular culture, even though he remained intensely private, as uninterested as ever in the conventional mechanisms of creating and sustaining celebrity. He made no talk show appearances or cable television specials, ignored every one of the dozens of movie offers that flooded Landau's office, went out to dinner in out-of-the-way places that never hit the gossip columns, never did interviews—didn't even have a press agent—and was rarely if ever troubled by paparazzi. Somehow, this homespun life-style only stirred the juices of exploitation in others to a froth.

Perhaps the first indication of this was the song parody written by Cheech and Chong: "Born in East L.A.," a good single and an even better video about the consequences of being born brown in America. In the Cheech and Chong version, the Immigration and Naturalization Service deports the singer, born in the Chicano ghetto of East Los Angeles, "back" to Mexico because he "doesn't look American" and confuses Ronald Reagan with John Wayne. He then has to fight his way home from Tijuana ("Now I know what it means to be born to run," he sings against a mariachi version of Roy Bittan's synth riff), a home he recognizes by the glow of the golden arches. The video, which wreaks havoc both with the imagery of the original song and with the bejeaned iconography of Springsteen the pop idol, is a fabulous act of guerrilla rock criticism.

Ironically, in satirizing and vulgarizing Springsteen's original song, Cheech and Chong tapped into its darkest heart. The song hit the *Billboard* chart just as the *Born in the U.S.A.* tour was ending, and though it missed the Top Forty, it prefigured the coming commercial exploitation of Springsteen's imagery. As Bill Lane of the J. Walter Thompson advertising agency predicted during the summer of 1985, the coming trend in advertising would be "the Springsteen heartland of America approach."

"Just wait until you hear how many Bruce Springsteen sound-alike songs are on commercials this fall," Lane predicted. "I can feel in my bones that we're on our way to Boss Land." And he was right. The Safeway grocery chain, AM-PM convenience stores, Stroh's and Miller beer, and dozens of local ads all picked up on the superficial details of Springsteen, *Born in the U.S.A.*, or both.

Of course, not every "made in America" commercial was a Springsteen exploitation. Ronald Reagan's virtual deification, the new cold war spirit, and the impending celebration of the Statue of Liberty restoration all helped turn the concept into a trend. Nevertheless, Springsteen was still at the center of the phenomenon. As Joan Neary, the New York jingle producer who made Chrysler's "The Pride Is Back" commercials, pointed out, "Now 'all-American' commercials are all over the place. But if you think about it, about the only 'American' commercials I recall *before* 'Born in the U.S.A.' were those union commercials—you know: all those people standing around singing 'Look for the union label'—which were really kind of corny."

Neary had good reason to know, for as she told Jimmy Magahern of the Phoenix (Arizona) *New Times*, she and partner Marc Blatte (composer of the Four Tops hit "When She Was My Girl") wrote "The Pride Is Back" as a deliberate knock-off of "Born in the U.S.A." Indeed, they were hired only after Chrysler had found Springsteen himself to be unapproachable.

Chrysler had been so eager to obtain Springsteen's endorsement that they made an initial offer estimated to be worth $12 million for his services—to sing and show his face in a sixty-second commercial. According to one advertising industry source, Chrysler was so certain that this enormous offer would land Springsteen that they actually had written and begun production on a "Born in the U.S.A." ad campaign. The auto manufacturer and its ad reps were confident not so much because the money was so lucrative as because *Rolling Stone* had identified Chrysler chairman Lee Iacocca as "the Bruce Springsteen of business," while Iacocca had projected himself—through his autobiographical best-seller, *Iacocca*—as a kind of folk hero of capitalism. The mass media had cheerfully contributed to sustaining that bit of hype.

"Actually, the reason they thought he *might* do the commercial in the first place was because Chrysler was such a real American success story," Neary told Magahern. "A story of a company coming back from the grave—from practically going down the tubes, with all those people in danger of losing their jobs—that just came up incredibly under Lee Iacocca's leadership. And we all know that Springsteen's *all for* the working man—he's all for people working and having jobs. And there are a lot of people working now making Chrysler cars who were very nearly in the unemployment lines. So in that respect, we did kinda think that Springsteen might be interested in working specifically for Chrysler, as opposed to, say, a cola company or something. But as it turned out, he wasn't even into doing that."

Apparently Springsteen, along with the rest of America, was supposed to ignore the fact that Lee Iacocca's "leadership" consisted of several billion dollars of government loans; that Iacocca tried to welsh when it came time to pay off those loans; and that Chrysler's success was built on the backs of concessions by the members of the United Automobile Workers union, who continued to work for the lowest wages in the American automobile industry for more than a year after Lee Iacocca's salary had risen from a dollar a year to several million.

But chances are, Bruce Springsteen never had to confront such ugly facts. His distaste for doing commercials or endorsements remained total. If Landau ever brought up the offer with him, it could only have been as a joke: "Guess how much money we turned down today?" (Of course, other companies had weighed in with similarly hefty bids.)

For those who had to endure the "Pride Is Back" jingle through the next six months of prime time TV, the laughs were less enduring. Sung by Kenny Rogers and Sandy Farina (management clients of U.S.A. for Africa's Ken Kragen), the song was abrasively memorable. (Ironically, the Plymouth minivans being pushed via the ads weren't "born in America" in the jingoist sense the song intended anyway; they were assembled in Canada.)

"We knew from the start that Chrysler really wanted 'Born in the U.S.A.' " Neary said. "So obviously we didn't want to go way in the opposite direction. But it doesn't specifically *sound* like

'Born in the U.S.A,' either. There's a certain bell sound in there that's definitely Springsteen. And, of course, the hook line—'The pride is back, born in America'—is pretty similar. But the commercial didn't really copy his song. It's just got the *spirit* of his music."

Actually, as Neary knew, the jingle violated that spirit. "Even though what came across most in 'Born in the U.S.A.' was the chorus, we do realize that the lyrics of that song were more critical of America—all that Vietnam veteran stuff and all," she told Magahern. "The lyrics weren't as positive as 'The pride is back, born in America.' So from that angle, I don't know. But I think 'Pride' just makes a statement the way that 'Born in the U.S.A.' did. It's like, the pride in our country was gone for a long time, and now it's back, you know?"

The reaction of the advertising industry and the record industry was nearly as blithe. "The Pride Is Back" won an *Advertising Age* award for best "original" music; the jingle was publicly credited by Chrysler as one of the big reasons for its boost in '86 sales. And RCA released Kenny Rogers' secularized version of the song as a single. (It wasn't a hit.)

As part of a trend of increased usage of rock music in commercials, often songs that played on sentimental themes without mentioning products, "The Pride Is Back" was nothing special. But it was an indication of how deeply Springsteen's image had penetrated into contemporary American mythology that he could be exploited in the same way that the telephone company abused children's guilt about being out of touch with their parents.

It wasn't only corporations and ad agencies who wanted a piece of the Springsteen myth and were willing to settle for mimicry. Ads for *American Ninja*, a summer '85 exploitation flick, knocked off the *Born in the U.S.A.* album cover; a drive-in–level loser called *No Surrender* and several others featured huge flag backdrops or behinds encased in faded Levis.

One movie did benefit from Bruce's actual contribution, although it wasn't released until 1987. While in Los Angeles for the final shows of the tour, Bruce took director Paul Schrader out to dinner, apologized for swiping the title of his *Born in the U.S.A.* script, and offered to provide a title song if Schrader still wanted to go ahead with the story. Schrader did, and Bruce sent along "Just Around the Corner to the Light of Day," a song from the band sessions the summer after *Nebraska*. Schrader made the film, *Light of Day* (Bruce's title was marquee-proof), in late 1986, starring Michael J. Fox and Joan Jett.

So whether he wanted to or not, Bruce Springsteen stayed in the spotlight. Ironically, though, no one guessed what he was really doing until he'd been at work on the live album for many months. One measure of the mass success of *Born in the U.S.A.*, after the crisis surrounding *Nebraska*, was the extraordinary degree to which Bruce had managed to maintain his privacy. And in the case of the live album, for which so many had various expectations, it was a good thing he did. Even without additional weeks of anticipatory speculation, it proved hard enough to get people to hear the album for what it was, rather than for what it could or should or might have been.

■

In the end, making the live album went more smoothly than any other Springsteen album project. By March Springsteen, Landau, and Plotkin had arrived at a sequence that was altered only slightly in the final release.

Beginning in June and continuing through October, Clearmountain mixed close to fifty songs at Right Track studio in New York. Forty of these wound up on the album, with a few—"Merry Christmas Baby," "Incident on 57th Street," "For You"—reserved as B sides for anticipated singles off the album.

The digital recordings of the stadium material gave Bob Clearmountain a very tough standard to live up to when mixing the analog recordings from the earlier years, but he was up to the task. As Bruce remarked, Clearmountain managed to circumvent the artist's mercurial sense of production values by "taking that and putting it on automatic pilot."

Clearmountain's confident expertise with the technical details freed the production team to work on the big picture. It must have been clear soon after they began that the live album would be more than just the next step in the sequence of albums that began with *Born to Run*. It would be a culmination—not only a recapitulation but the closing of the door on one story as the next began to unfold.

What made the live set a distinctive part of the album series to date was its continuity and its narrative quality. "I guess what I was always interested in was doing a *body* of work—albums that would relate to and play off of each other," Bruce had told Kurt Loder in his *Rolling Stone* interview. "And I was always concerned with doin' *albums* instead of, like, collections of songs. . . . I was very concerned about gettin' a group of characters and followin' them through their lives a little bit."

The live material took the measure of how well he'd done. Like its brethren, the album told a tale—not a simple or necessarily obvious one, but a story nevertheless. The album had no title until very late, and the name eventually selected was the most neutral possible: *Bruce Springsteen and the E Street Band Live/1975–1985*. But that was just a feint. At heart this album was the latest in a series through which a rock star and his cast of characters struggled from innocence to maturity.

The exact nature of the underlying story is best revealed via this question: How do you get from the innocent glory of "Thunder Road," as performed at the Roxy in 1975 before an audience of perhaps 500, to the harrowing rampage that runs from "Born in the U.S.A." to "War," sung in the same city ten years later before an audience of 100,000? Posing that question, with all its internal and external implications, unlocks *Bruce Springsteen and the E Street Band Live*, adding dimensions that few rock albums—let alone live albums or retrospectives—have ever possessed.

Because the live album was a five-record boxed set, it was frequently compared to Dylan's *Biograph*, whose five discs spanned the length of a twenty-five-year career. That album had sold comparatively well—more than 200,000 copies—and it probably did help inspire Springsteen and Landau. But the album that *Live* really resembles most is Neil Young's *Decade*, a three-record set from 1976 programmed and annotated by Young himself with an eye toward making a case for his artistic development and achievements. (*Biograph* was put together without Dylan, and it includes many minor rarities at the expense of some of his core material and greatest performances.)

As Bruce looked over the music he'd made in the previous decade, he found himself, like Young, recapitulating the entire journey of his passage from childhood dreams of rock and roll glory to grappling with the real thing as an adult. It was an intensely personal story but, at its broadest, it was also the rock and roll archetype come to life and brought up to date. The album did *not* conform to rock and roll mythology; these descendants of Johnny B. Goode grew up, and the ending of their story was collected not chaotic, open rather than closed, nurturing rather than wasteful.

By the time he released each of his preceding albums, Bruce had invariably come to understand the implications of what he'd done, but rarely much before then. This time the music's secrets revealed themselves to him more rapidly; that was one reason the assembly could proceed so swiftly. That only made sense: He was gathering up old friends, not creating new ones. But as these familiar faces shifted themselves into position, Bruce found them telling a new version of their stories.

"The record opens with 'Thunder Road,' and as I've said before, when the *Born to Run* album came out, the record was so tied in with who I was, I felt like, hey, I felt like I was born," Springsteen said in early 1987. "I felt like it was a birthday. I know that's why those words are in the title. *Born*—why is that word there? That's there because it's real. And"—he began to laugh at his own presumption—"that's probably why the word *run* is there—that's real, too.

"And that 'Thunder Road' is the birth song; it's the panorama, the scene and the characters, setting the situation. So that was why, from the very beginning, we knew that that was gonna start the live album.

"Then you get 'Adam Raised a Cain'; we wanted a gut punch right after that, just so you'd be ready for what was gonna happen. And then you get to 'Spirit in the Night,' which is kinda the cast of characters—friends. It's a real localized situation. Then you get 'Sandy.' That's the guy and he's on the boardwalk, and I guess that was me then, when I was still around Asbury. And there's the girl.

"That first side, that's the whole idea: Here it is. This is the beginning of the whole trip that's about to take place. All those people. Some of 'em are gonna go, some of 'em are gonna stay, some of 'em are gonna make that trip, some of 'em aren't gonna make it. And let's see what happens.

"And then you flip the thing over. 'Paradise by the "C" '—the Clarence instrumental—that's bar band music, that's who we are. And that's real important. That sets the tone. That's what we were doing in those clubs—we were blowin' the roof off with that kinda stuff. People were dancin' and goin' crazy and havin' a great time.

"And then you get that 'Growin' Up.' That's sort of a little bit of a statement of purpose. Sort of. And then there's the rest of that—'Saint in the City,' 'Backstreets,' 'Rosalita,' and 'Raise Your Hand.' 'Rosalita' was funny because, even though it came before 'Born to Run,' the guy gets the girl—or he's trying to get the girl. And he's got the record deal, and he's trying to get away. And if he gets all these things, he thinks everything's gonna be *great*. And I guess that was kind of . . . *That happened*, I guess.

"Then the 'Hungry Heart' side with all those songs from *The River*, which is funny, because that side felt right there even if it was a little out of chronological order . . . and I think felt right because the next thing you hear, you hear that big crowd. Right after 'Rosalita,' you get 'Raise Your Hand,' and that's the idea: You want it and then, Bang! You got it.

"And the rest of that side is kind of 'Two Hearts' and 'Cadillac Ranch' and 'You Can Look but You Better Not Touch.' And now the underside starts to kinda sneak in there; you start to pick up a little undercurrent there."

That undercurrent motivated Bruce's best songs from *Darkness on the Edge of Town* to *Born in the U.S.A.*, from "Badlands" to "Reason to Believe" to "Dancing in the Dark"—that is, from the confidence of youth to a crisis of faith to the realization that you overcome only when you keep moving. Like all journeys to experience, it began with questions that seemed simple: Why me? What about everybody else? What next?

"At some point I said to myself—and I know this is one of the things that caused me a lot of distress—I said, Well okay, what if I am the guy in 'Born to Run,' with the bike and the girl, shooting down the road," Bruce said. "But when you get out there a little ways, there's not that much traffic. And you can't see the people in the cars next to you; all the windows are tinted. And all of a sudden you're out there, but where is everybody? So I guess I kinda thought, Well, all right, you know; so maybe I get to do these things, but what about everybody else?

"And that didn't come from a real selfless motivation or some idea to do good. Because I understood that it was a self-preservation question. I realized that you will *die* out there, simple as that. I understood that underneath this illusion of freedom was an oppressiveness that would kill me. And that where maybe I was different was that I knew it.

"So when I got in that situation, I felt tremendously threatened, and I did not know why. It was totally instinctive. Matter of fact, I don't think I really knew why until not that long ago. But initially, when I was twenty-five, it was just instinctive—I felt threatened, I felt in danger. And it was funny because those were the exact opposite responses that people generally have. But I didn't know why I was havin' 'em; I was just havin' 'em.

"So initially, I wanted to just reject the whole thing—'This is bad; all this is bad'—as people have done before. I think you look at some of the older rock and rollers, they've chosen to reject it and their opposite choice was to move to religious fundamentalism. But I got so alienated from religion when I was younger that there was no way that that was ever gonna be an alternative, in that sense, for me. I just could never see it.

"I think when I got in that spot, I really did feel—and not in a paranoid fashion—attacked on the essence of who I felt that I was. So at that point I realized that, unattached from community, it was impossible to find any meaning. And if you can't find any meaning, you will go insane and you will either kill yourself or somebody will do the job for you, either by doping you or one thing or another.

"I began to question from that moment on the values and the ideas that I set out and believed in on that *Born to Run* record: friendship, hope, belief in a better day. I questioned all of these things. And so *Darkness on the Edge of Town* was basically saying, You get out there and you turn around and you come back because that's just the beginning. That's the real beginning.

"I got out there—hey, the wind's whipping through your hair, you feel real good, you're the guy with the gold guitar or whatever, and all of a sudden you feel that sense of *dread* that is overwhelming everything you do. It's like that great scene in *The Last Picture Show* where the guy hits the brakes and turns around. The *Darkness* record was a confrontation record: 'Badlands,' 'Adam Raised a Cain,' 'Racing in the Street'—all those people, all those faces, you gotta look at 'em all. Right through to 'Darkness on the Edge of Town'—that was a whole other beginning.

"Now, you strip a whole bunch of things away from the thing, and you lose a lot of your illusions and a lot of, I suppose, your romantic dreams. And you decide . . . you make a particular decision. And that is a decision, I believe, that saves your life— your real life, your internal life, your emotional life, your essential life. Because you can live on, and a lotta people do; there's all sorts of people livin' on out there, you know. But I knew—and this ties right in with the discussion I had with Jon about *Born in the U.S.A.*—that the reason I began to do what I did was for connection. I desperately needed connection. I couldn't get it; I wanted it.

"And that's why the guitar was my lifeline. That was my connection with other people, more than anything else. Because other things will not sustain you. Maybe for a while you'll be distracted and have some fun, but in the end, your real life, you'll die, you will really die. And then once that happens, I believe there's only a certain amount of time before the physical thing catches up to you.

"So you've got that situation, where I turn around—on the live record, that's where 'Badlands' fits. Then you're there—from 'Badlands' through to 'War' really. But from 'Badlands' through to 'Reason to Believe,' that's kind of an investigation of that place."

Springsteen began to question not only the values he'd found in rock and roll but whether rock and roll itself, which offered the most romantic illusion of heroic Yankee individualism imaginable, was worth the effort. It all came back to the questions he'd asked himself as he put together *Born in the U.S.A.*

"Is making the Loud Noise worth it?" is how he put it in the winter of '87. "That's a question that I feel like I'm constantly asking myself, and the only answer I come up with is, Well, you don't know unless you try.

"I think that when I did the *Nebraska* record, obviously I was in a deepening process of questioning those values that were set out on *Born to Run*. I did the *Darkness on the Edge of Town* thing, and with *The River* thing I allowed some light to come in, part of the time. I had to—had to. In a funny way, I felt that I didn't have the center, so what I had to do was I had to get left and right, in hope that it would create some sort of center—or some sense of center. That probably wasn't embodied in any one given song or something, and that was the juggling that I had to do on that record."

So the same Bruce Springsteen who had sung "I'm pullin' outta here to win" at the beginning of *Born to Run* found himself opening *Nebraska* by imagining someone being hurled into a "great void." But that wasn't all.

"Here's where this thing breaks down all the social type barriers that we put up in society. That void that you feel in that situation is the same one you can feel breathin' down your neck when you got that sun behind you, drivin' down the road; you got the girl, got that guitar. It's the same, for some reason. Because of that isolation. There are guys who come home from the factory, sit in front of that TV with a sixpack of beer, that are as isolated as the *Nebraska* record, if not more so."

It's the spectre of that void that sends men down to the river when their dreams fall through or their marriages crumble or the plant closes and leaves them not just without a paycheck but empty of purpose. And rich men or poor, when they've stared long enough into that void, they make a leap. They may jump into the abyss of doubt or across a chasm of faith, but they leap.

Having reached that desperate place himself, Bruce Springsteen pushed forward, not because he rejected the hopelessness he found, but because he accepted it. "That was the subject of the *Nebraska* record," he said. "And it's the central thing at this moment in our band; we're kinda locked in with this thing. That was just the idea of the band, from the very beginning, from the minute when I touched the guitar for the first time. That was what moved me, what motivated me. And that's why as you follow the way the whole thing has developed, the moment after *Nebraska* and before *Born in the U.S.A.* is where I'm having this exact conversation with Jon . . . about these things. These are what the records are about.

"When you're in the live record, you run up to 'Reason to Believe' and at that point—well, that was the bottom. I would hope not to be in that particular place ever again. It was a thing where all my ideas might have been working musically but they were failing me personally.

"I always feel like I was lucky. I got to a point where all my answers—rock and roll answers—were running out. All the old things stopped working—as they should've and as they have to, and as time and the world and the way it is demands and dictates, in order for you to go on. They run dry, not as a joyous thing in and of itself, but as some sort of shelter for your inability to take your place in the world, whatever that may be. That's when either you recognize that that's happening or you don't and you continue with your trappings and your ceremony, whatever *that* may be, and slowly you just get strangled to death and you die. You just die."

It was at this point that Bruce Springsteen did a remarkable thing. Rather than surrendering to the "trappings and ceremony" of show biz rite or retreating into a cocoon of protective "artistic independence" (as Young and Dylan had done), he reached out, opening himself in a way that very few public figures have ever done. He found a response as powerful as any public figure has ever known and learned to live with it. Was he another Elvis? Of course not. He didn't start something; he helped put it on the road to completion. But Bruce Springsteen had finally become like Elvis in another way. He used popular music to change himself and the slice of history he could affect. And rather than dying, he lived more whole than before.

Bruce Springsteen had finally circumvented—or rather, defused—the trap depicted by the Band's Robbie Robertson:

> See the man with the stage fright
> Just standin' up there, givin' all his might

And he got caught in the spotlight
But when we get to the end, you wanna start all
over again

Springsteen escaped this Sisyphean fate by ignoring the advice given in "Stage Fright": "You can make it in your disguise/ Just never show the fear that's in your eyes." On the contrary, he'd taken the risk of turning the glare of his personal terrors full upon his audience and, what was most startling, found that many recognized them as their own.

When they did, Bruce Springsteen crossed the line between idol and hero as defined by the art critic John Berger: "The function of the hero in art is to inspire the reader or spectator to continue in the same spirit from where he, the hero, leaves off. He must release the spectator's potentiality, for potentiality is the historical force behind nobility. And to do this the hero must be typical of the characters and class who at that time only need to be made aware of their heroic potentiality in order to be able to make their society juster and nobler. . . . The function of the idol is the exact opposite to that of the hero. The idol is self-sufficient; the hero never is. The idol is so superficially desirable, spectacular, witty, happy, that he or she merely supplies a context for fantasy and therefore, instead of inspiring, lulls. The idol is based on the *appearance* of perfection, but never on the striving towards it."

But what Springsteen achieved also confounded Berger, because he'd done it through the mechanism of popular culture, mediated by one of the country's largest industrial corporations. Like most good leftists, Berger believes that culture to be bankrupt; like any pragmatic member of the working class, Bruce Springsteen worked with the tools that came to hand.

If Springsteen proved able to restore a sense of center to rock and roll without entirely dulling that idiom's status as the cutting edge of popular culture, it was not only because he'd dared expose to a mass audience what seemed to be his least conventional thoughts and feelings but also because he'd done that while risking the inconveniences and dangers of genuine mass popularity. It would have profited him not at all to gain the pink Cadillac and lose his own soul, but it would have served him equally poorly to have hardened his heart against the public from which he sprang. In that regard, his success was genuinely antibohemian, because it sprang not from a refusal to participate in social conventions, but from a refusal to be excluded from them.

For its first five sides, then, *Bruce Springsteen and the E Street Band Live/1975–1985* defines a dream and chronicles its dissolution and the ways that dawning realizations transform the dreamer. Its final four are concerned with how you live with what's left. The transition is expressed on Side Six, which runs from "This Land Is Your Land" to "Reason to Believe," a leap every bit as long as it looks. Introducing Woody Guthrie's greatest hit, Springsteen acknowledges that Guthrie wrote in anger, but when Bruce sings the song it's about dreams and visions. What's emphasized isn't the grandeur of the landscapes or the mockery society makes of them, it's the voices that call out at the end of each verse, promising something better.

"Nebraska" and "Johnny 99" are songs about people who cannot hear those voices, the consequence of which is a death sentence. But "Reason to Believe" is something worse: a requiem for those who have heard the voices, pursued them to the end, and then discovered that they were lying. It's about the greatest menace that lurks in the darkness on the edge of town, about the compulsion to leap into the river and be swept downstream, about the temptation to run and keep on running, not toward freedom but away from the facts. Springsteen defines the song precisely: "That was the bottom."

"But at the end of *Nebraska*—it's kind of ironic—I wrote another song with the word *born* in it, which is really weird," Springsteen observed. "And from that point on, the answer to 'Reason to Believe' was 'Born in the U.S.A.'—I guess either record, but particularly the live version. That's the answer to it. That's the only answer that I can perceive. And that connects back to 'Badlands,' you know. And that was the moment that I felt I'd gotten things in a little healthier perspective, and that I stopped—I didn't stop using my job; I stopped abusing my job, which I felt part of me had been doing. In the end, I just understood a lot more about what it takes to get by.

"No, it ain't gonna save you; you gotta save yourself. And you're gonna need a lotta help."

The rest of the record—and, it is not entirely unreasonable to imagine, the rest of Bruce Springsteen's work—is about giving that help and, just as important, receiving it. It begins with "Born in the U.S.A.," with that singer "born down in a dead man's town," but at the end, standing in the shadows of a prison, the singer has made a choice: He will run, and keep on running, but he will never *fail* to look back. He will always remember what's been done to him—and his friend at Khe Sanh, that woman he loved in Saigon, and the Viet Cong—and those memories will shape his future, no matter where it leads. In order to be "a cool rockin' daddy in the U.S.A.," you have to go beyond hearing the voices Woody Guthrie wrote about; you have to try to answer them back—you have to join them. And that is exactly what "Seeds," "The River," and "War" do.

"The 'Born in the U.S.A.' side, that's everything I know—at the moment, or at that time," Springsteen said with a short laugh. "And I know Jon felt that the opening section of 'The River' was the real center of the record. It moves out in all directions. The band on that night, the thirtieth of September 1985, they were great that night. They just played better than other nights. And it was a thing where just intensity and the forward thrust of the music was the best it's ever been."

Springsteen knew exactly what he was doing in the live show when he didn't stop for a reaction after "War." He compared his sense of what to do with Alfred Hitchcock's *Vertigo*—the entire film leads up to James Stewart stepping out onto a ledge, a shot that lasts less than ten seconds and is almost immediately followed by the picture's end. Springsteen calls what he learned from watching this "the integrity of the moment," which, he adds, "is a lesson I can use, because I'll be excessive. I've got the energy and I'll crank on forever. But you get to a point, you gotta have the confidence not to do that. You need confidence to do less and let it be more."

At the end of the album version of "War," the cheers are quickly faded out, and the record moves with barely a pause into "Darlington County" and "Working on the Highway," the most modest of the *Born in the U.S.A.* songs and the most embedded in the workaday world. But as life goes on, what might be missed is that it doesn't end with the "Born in the U.S.A." to "War" sequence. It carries the story onward, forward, and since that means eschewing melodrama, what's left is a finish that's as oddly muted as the start.

Yet it would be a mistake to think the story's over. It couldn't be, not as long as Bruce Springsteen's juices still flow. Even when anthems like "The Promised Land" and "No Surrender" crop up in the aftermath of "War," they are cooled down, taken in stride, without a hint of finality.

Ending the album proved one of the most difficult aspects of making it. Bruce knew that he didn't want to finish with the rock and roll medleys that always concluded his shows. But knowing what he didn't want only emphasized the magnitude of the question: So how do you end the record?

"The first time we played it through the way it was, I wasn't sure. And then we played it again and it started to really sync in—'cause 'Born to Run' tops the tenth side and you go all the way back to 'Thunder Road.' And it restates the central question.

"And the central question of 'Born to Run' is really 'I wanna know if love is real.' That's the question of that song. We go from there; we go to 'No Surrender,' a modern-day reaffirmation and restatement of all those things in the present tense. Then we get to 'Tenth Avenue'; believe it or not, that kinda connects back up to 'Spirit in the Night.' That's the cast of characters and friends; it's the band. And hey, that's what we did, you know."

At one point the plan was to end the album right there. The song told the band's story and it was modest. "We didn't want to end it with something big," Bruce said. It was Jon Landau—arguing for the softer noise for once—who suggested that a love song would be more appropriate. And although "Jersey Girl" had already been issued (as the B side of the "Cover Me" single in 1984), although it was one of only three songs in the set that Bruce didn't write, although it was obscure and quiet and ended the record somewhat mysteriously, it still felt like the right ending.

"That's the same guy that's on the boardwalk in 'Sandy,' back in the same place," Bruce said. "The same guy in 'Rosalita'—you know, he got that Jersey girl. I guess I wanted the record to feel like the middle of summer—real soft moonlight, you're takin' a real slow ride in that convertible, and you're back in that place where you began. You got somebody beside you and you feel good, and you've been through all those things.

"When I listened to that song, I'd always see myself ridin' through Asbury. There'd be people I know a little bit on the corner, and we'd just drive by. I guess that you feel in some way you're changed forever. But you also have all those connections, so you feel really at home.

"The most important thing, though, is that the question gets thrown back at 'Born to Run.' 'I wanna know if love is real.' And the answer is yes."

The live album project remained almost perfectly secret. Not even the band was in on it until there was already a preliminary sequence; CBS Records executives didn't find out until midsummer. They were given just enough notice to arrange pressing plant time, gather the huge stockpile of materials—vinyl, paper, cardboard for the boxes—and work out the logistics of distributing a five-record set that they projected would sell well over a million copies.

Columbia Records chiefs Walter Yetnikoff and Al Teller were not only willing but eager to release a massive Springsteen live set. Manufacturing the sets on such short notice would prove enormously disruptive to the company's day-to-day business, but the profit potential from a live Springsteen album was so great that the temporary chaos was worthwhile. Besides, *Live* sounded so good and was so much easier to play on compact disc that it had the potential to inaugurate a CD boom equivalent to the boom in stereo sales prompted by the Beatles' *Sgt. Pepper's Lonely Hearts Club Band*.

CBS laid plans for a worldwide promotional blitz as big as that for *Born in the U.S.A.* The label sent stores a full-color, four-page "marketing overview" that read, in part: "All told, *Bruce Springsteen and the E Street Band Live/1975–1985* represents the definitive performance package from the ultimate American rock and roll performer. As a result, you can count on it being *the* biggest holiday gift of 1986 as well as the major release throughout 1987."

Manufacturing, particularly of the CD, was problematic because it threatened to outstrip the capacity of the industry to produce so many albums, cassettes, and discs that fast. No other five-record set in record industry history had sold more than a quarter of a million copies (*Biograph* and RCA's eight-disc *Elvis Aron Presley* both sold in that neighborhood). But CBS planned to manufacture more than 2 million copies of *Bruce Springsteen and the E Street Band Live/1975–1985* and stockpiled materials for several hundred thousand more.

As it turned out, that was barely enough, since the company got initial orders for more than 1.5 million sets, 500,000 more than advance orders for *Born in the U.S.A.*, which was, after all, much cheaper for stores to buy. (Wholesale price for each cassette or LP box was about $18; for the CD, around $28. Estimates were that *Live* grossed $50 million out of the gate.) For three weeks in October CBS reserved its only American CD pressing plant exclusively for pressing the Springsteen box; the 300,000 CD sets they pressed virtually sold out by the end of the set's first week of release, and no new CD pressings could be produced until January 1987. CBS had to order a million pounds of paper and hire extra trucks because only 16,000 Springsteen sets could be loaded on one tractor trailer, compared to 100,000 units of a single album. At the Carrollton, Georgia, LP pressing plant, the boxes alone filled a space equal to five football fields.

Security around the project remained tight. Even when the album was officially announced on September 11, 1986, Columbia's release kept information to an absolute minimum: the album's title and that it would contain forty tracks on five LPs or three cassettes or CDs and be accompanied by a thirty-six page booklet. Because the mixes weren't yet complete and Bruce and art director Sandra Choron were still putting together the cover and the booklet, not even a specific release date could be stated, although dealers were told that the label was shooting for November 10, just in the nick of time to cash in on holiday gift buying.

The Springsteen/Landau style was to maintain as much secrecy about their doings as possible, but this time the motivation was much more than a desire to maintain control. As Chuck Plotkin told *Rolling Stone*'s Michael Goldberg, "Someone hears Bruce is doing a live record. Is there any way for it not to be disappointing, really, given the level of expectation that one has to have? Yet the only thing I can tell you for sure: The damn thing is *not* disappointing."

Record retailers almost drooled at the prospect of a live Springsteen set. Russ Solomon, owner of the Tower Records chain, called it "this year's Beatles album," referring to the Beatles' practice of releasing their albums just before Christmas. Jim Thompson of the Record Bar chain (the same company that had predicted that *Born in the U.S.A.* would be outsold by the Jacksons' *Victory*) went even further: "It'll definitely be *the* hit of the Eighties," he told *USA Today*.

He wasn't alone in that thinking. "Bruce sold ten million albums last time," said Lew Garrett of the 187-store Camelot Music chain. "How many people out there will feel they *have* to get this set? He must have a core of at least two million people that will crave it. If you look at it realistically in terms of dollars, it's a big buy. But you've got to think it's one of those items you can't afford to run out of." *Billboard* reported that the Springsteen live anthology was "on its way to generating the biggest dollar-volume preorders of any album in history."

Meanwhile, Springsteen and Choron were struggling with the album's graphic presentation. The original cover concept as well as the initial idea for the accompanying booklet had both been scrapped. Bruce's first idea for a cover shot was a picture taken by Eric Meola in the Utah desert, a reverse of the *Nebraska* shot: A car approaches out of the dust on two-lane blacktop. (The picture had been taken as a possible cover for *Darkness on the Edge of Town* and was used for the sheet music of "Badlands" in 1978.) The shot is powerfully evocative, but in the end Choron and Springsteen both felt that it was too restrictive—it would make the live album feel too connected to the *Nebraska* period. Bruce wanted something more open and inviting. The darker elements of the songs and music were there for the taking; he wasn't about to force them on anybody. Neal Preston's live photograph seemed much more inviting and, therefore, fitting.

The booklet presented similar problems. It seemed right that the box should contain some kind of program, and the obvious approach was to follow the *Biograph* model. It was also conceivable that Bruce might want to comment on why certain songs were chosen or how they added up. But in the end, he didn't want to do that; again, the implications were there for the listener to find or ignore. After all, if it hadn't been necessary to explain *Nebraska*, it surely wasn't necessary to explain the live record. The brief handwritten note Bruce wrote for the book's inside front cover was stuck in only at the last minute, when he realized that there were a few simple things that did need saying.

The other approach to creating a booklet was to make it a pictorial history of the E Street Band, similar to the first *Born in the U.S.A.* tour program. Choron spent months gathering together thousands of photos from every era of the band's career, even reaching into Bruce's private photo collection. But as they worked through the summer, both she and Bruce realized that the best choice would be pictures that were specific and personal, pictures that would offset the lyrics, which appeared in the same order as on the album. So the booklet opened with Bruce at the piano, proceeded through bearded shots from the *Born to Run* days, showed him diving into the crowd during "Spirit in the Night," on the boardwalk for "Sandy," and looking as greaser tough as Vincent Spano in *Baby It's you* for "Saint in the City." As on the album, by the time the pictures got to "Darkness on the Edge of Town," they'd taken on more ominous colorations, then opened up with depictions of Americana for "This Land Is Your Land" to "Born in the U.S.A." before scaling back down with shots of Bruce and the E Streeters. Particularly moving was a two-page spread showing Bruce's old Randolph Street neighborhood in Freehold flanked by the lyrics to "My Hometown" and "Born to Run."

Hitting on the concept and then finding the right photos took weeks, a process not dissimilar to the way Springsteen made albums. And as always, at the end, Bruce had one final good idea that cinched it. He took out a solo shot of himself that accompanied "The River" and added a picture of his father, looking just like John Garfield, with his sister Virginia and Bruce himself at age five.

◼

Bruce didn't have his nose continually to the grindstone of the record-making machinery. He spent part of September in Paris, where Julianne was costarring with Treat Williams in *Sweet Lies*, a film directed by Natalie Delon. He was home by the end of the month, though, in time for a performance of *Lady Beth* at the Stone Pony on September 28. The Los Angeles–based troupe was on a six-city national tour that Springsteen had partially funded. Bruce spoke for about five minutes during the second set discussion period, talking about the idea that "a plant owes a responsibility to a community," a particularly appropriate sentiment since Stanley Fischer had helped organize the Asbury Park performance and many of the Freehold 3M workers were in the audience.

Springsteen had to get back to New York both to finish work on the album and in order to prepare an acoustic set for an October 8 benefit he'd agreed to do in California. Neil Young and his wife, Pegi, were staging the benefit at the Shoreline Amphitheatre in Mountain View, near their home, to raise funds for The Bridge, a San Francisco–based program that would make available vocal computers for severely handicapped children who otherwise had no way of speaking. (The Youngs have two children with that problem.) Bruce finished the album mixing on October 5 and the next morning flew to San Francisco, where he spent the weekend with his parents, who lived not far from Mountain View themselves.

Shoreline Amphitheatre holds 17,000, which would have been ludicrously inadequate for a show with the E Street Band. But on his own—even with support acts including Young, Don Henley, Tom Petty, Robin Williams, and Nils Lofgren—the facility was manageable, although the tickets sold out instantly, of course.

There was a certain irony to the benefit. It was Young's night, but it was unquestionably Springsteen who sold the tickets. The alliance between Springsteen and Young proved that music was thicker than politics: Neil Young was an ardent supporter of

Ronald Reagan. Moreover, Young was raising funds for a program that couldn't get federal education funds because his
President's "free market" policies had all but eliminated them.

That was barely relevant at this point. The night opened with
Pegi Young introducing ten-year-old Alan Forderer, who typed a
message into the computer on his lap, which then rang out over
the p.a. system: "Talking computers are neat . . . It makes you
feel like one of the gang. I'll be glad when other kids like me have
talking computers, too."

Neil Young opened the show, but for his second song,
"Helpless," he brought out "my friend Bruce" to sing harmonies,
which Bruce did even though they were far out of his range.
Springsteen, dressed in black jeans and sweatshirt, came and
went to thunderous applause, matched only by the rousing
ovation for Young's erstwhile sidekicks David Crosby (just out of
jail), Stephen Stills, and Graham Nash. CSNY sang Young's
"Only Love Can Break Your Heart" and an amazingly powerful
"Ohio" (with Crosby dominating) to close his set and put hefty
musical chips on the table.

The rules of the benefit were that each performer could bring
as many sidemen as he wished but that all the instrumentation
had to be acoustic. So Nils Lofgren performed by himself
(including a great solo on "Keith Don't Go" and a rendition of
Bruce's "Man at the Top"), while Don Henley, a harmony expert
from his years with the Eagles, sang with J. D. Souther, ex-Eagle
Timothy B. Schmit, and southern California all-'rounder Danny
Kootch. Tom Petty also came on solo, which, he confessed, he'd
never done before, and acquitted himself well. He was followed
by a hilarious verbal blitzkreig from Williams, which left the
crowd roaring and raring for Bruce. Bruce stepped to the mike
with no band behind him and without so much as a harmonica in
his hand. He took a deep breath and began to rap out the lyrics to
"You Can Look but You Better Not Touch," which turned into an
arm-waving acappella boogaloo somehow reminiscent of North
Beach poetry readings of the Fifties. It was a deliberately
eccentric performance, reminiscent of the kind of willfully odd
music that defined recent Neil Young albums, and it set up a
performance that oscillated between the brilliant and the weird.

From this near-naked beginning, Springsteen built up his music sequentially. For his second number, he pulled up a chair and strummed a red-trimmed acoustic guitar. "This is a song about a snake that comes around to eat its own tail," he said, and began a version of "Born in the U.S.A." unlike anything heard before. He sang it slow and with an odd meter, banging out the downbeats by stomping his feet on a tambourine, which gave the song the accents of classic country blues—it was "Born in the U.S.A." as Skip James or Son House might have done it. The result was ravishing and as integral to the song as "You Can Look" had seemed artificial.

Bruce seemed to feel edgy or maybe just strange. "Big Man, where are ya when I need ya?" he rasped after "Born in the U.S.A.," and yet that song proved he could mesmerize without a band. Having proved the point, he brought out his sidemen, Lofgren on acoustic guitar and Danny Federici on his original instrument, accordion. Bruce sang "Seeds," with the same introduction he'd used during the tour but pared down to something like a talking blues, and then, adding a harp rack, he lurched into the story that usually introduced "Open All Night," but which now became "Darlington County."

Confronted with momentary technical confusion, he pointed to Federici: "Danny, 'Lady of Spain.' " Federici began the song in an instant; after a chorus or eighty, Bruce cut him off with a curt "Thanks" and sat back down. He told a story about his father and began "Mansion on the Hill," his tone and rhythms again closer to speech than song. More technical glitches, then Danny's accordion solo on "Satin Doll" led into "Fire."

Bruce had now built the show into something all his own. However purposeful it may have been, he'd built from the most basic element of music—the human voice—to a point where you could feel the need for a band: "Ummm . . . rock and roll, huh?" he said. "I dunno. I can't get too excited."

Bruce sang the first half of "Fire" sitting down, then paused at the spot where he usually faced off with Clarence Clemons. "No," he said, as if to himself, "I gotta stay calm—this is acoustic." From the wings Jim McDuffie appeared and took his chair away, leaving him no choice but to stay on his feet and do his best to rock the house—which he did pretty well. By the time "Fire" was finished, the entire crowd was on its feet and hollering. Bruce let the music flow right into a beautiful arrangement of "Dancing in the Dark," which somehow managed to retain the size and dynamics of the original.

"Glory Days" followed, but that didn't work as well. By now it felt like Springsteen was having too much fun at the expense of the acoustic idea. He'd been onstage the better part of an hour, and he'd avoided the bulk of the songs most likely to benefit from acoustic treatment—material like "The River," "Highway Patrol- man," and "Used Cars." As long as he was offering something different and just as good, if not better, his mockery made sense. But with "Glory Days" Bruce seemed simply to be longing for a band to work with, and that seemed to play into this audience's simplest expectations of him: He was playing the hard rockin' fool.

But that impression was partly dispelled by "Follow That Dream," the first song he did that seemed to have a direct connection to The Bridge. When that was done, he called out, "Where's those old-timers?" and Crosby, Stills, Nash, and Young joined him for a ragged but gorgeous "Hungry Heart." After that everybody got into the act and the show closed, inevitably, with Nash's "Teach Your Children."

It was hard to discern just what Bruce's Bridge benefit performance meant. Was it just an oddity, a chance for him to be as weird for one night as Young, one of the contemporary artists he most admired? Or was it an omen, an exploration of a musical approach he'd pursue in the future? Chances are, Springsteen himself couldn't have told you for sure.

■

A few days after the Bridge benefit, Bruce flew back to Paris to stay with Julianne in a Left Bank apartment while she continued work on *Sweet Lies*. Matty DiLea, the same friend who'd driven with him to California in 1982, also came along. Bruce wasn't nearly as recognizable in Paris as he was in New York or Los Angeles, and it was a good chance to get out and stretch.

The first week in November, Huey Lewis and the News

played Paris, and Bruce went along to the show. Backstage, Lewis and another visitor, Bob Geldof, razzed Springsteen about the frenzied anticipation over the live set. Both had new albums out, but everything was being swallowed in Bruce's wake. At the end of the show Bruce and Geldof joined Lewis to sing the Robert Parker soul hit "Barefootin'."

On Monday, November 10, Bruce got up early and went to DeGaulle Airport with DiLea. They boarded the Air France Concorde for JFK, where they landed around nine A.M., then got into a car and drove into the city.

They couldn't have imagined what they were walking into. It was the live album's release date and record stores all over the United States were madhouses. Columbia had released an eight-song sampler, led by "War," to radio stations the previous Friday, and those tracks dominated national airplay throughout the weekend, which further piqued anticipation for the live set. As *Boston Phoenix* music editor Milo Miles wrote, to lead in to what was easily the most perceptive review the live set received, "Many visions of stardom fueled Bruce Springsteen in his adolescence, but he surely never imagined that someday local and network crews would flock to record stores to film lines of fans waiting to buy his latest album. *Born in the U.S.A.* became news as it was scooting toward the 10-million sales mark and Springsteen was bringing down stadiums across the country. *Live/1975–85* (Columbia) was born news on November 10."

Record stores were poised to do land office business. There had been some concern at CBS about the album's selling price, but competition was so avid that many stores sold it for only a few cents more than it cost them: Tower Records offered the LP and cassette for $19.95; Record World's $24.88 price was more typical. Both were cheap.

When the stores opened that morning, many already faced lines. "We're selling them as fast as we can get them out of the box," Don Bergentry, manager of Sam Goody's Rockefeller Center store, told the *New York Times*. "This is the biggest thing I have ever seen in records." In Times Square, Disc-o-mat sold 500 of its 1,000 sets between ten A.M. and two thirty P.M. By one P.M. the Sam Goody's in the Monmouth Mall was completely sold out of the live set.

But this was no regional success story. "Nobody has seen anything like this since the madness when Elvis died," said Hays Carlock, purchasing manager of Music City Record Distributors in Nashville. "It's the craziest I've seen it since then. I wish I had a pressing plant." Record Bar owner Barrie Bergman called the entire week "the wildest I've seen in twenty-five years in the business. There wasn't this kind of money involved with the Beatles' albums," and Bergman's chain operated in the Southeast, one of Bruce's weakest markets.

Billboard reported the next Monday that most retail outlets sold out their entire initial shipments the first day. California's Music Plus chain ordered 22,000 sets; by close of business on the tenth, they'd reordered another 15,000. There were shots on the television news of customers walking out with stacks of boxes; some reportedly bought the CDs even though they didn't yet own compact disc players. By the end of the first day, Columbia had 300,000 reorders for all three configurations.

Nor was Bossmania confined to the United States. The album was expected to be the biggest-selling international record of 1986 in Japan, with an initial pressing of 150,000 and the anticipation that CBS/Sony could double that figure before the end of 1986. The goal seemed easily attainable when, only a week after release, twenty front office employees had to be transferred to a factory to box albums by hand. In England, *Live* became "the biggest CBS money grosser ever in terms of prerelease orders," according to Paul Burger of CBS International. Sweden surpassed England in advance orders, and out-of-the-chute sales were also strong in Norway, France, and West Germany. A consignment of 10,000 box sets on its way from Holland to Italy was hijacked. Burger estimated that *Live* would be the biggest CD package ever issued in Europe. "Our prediction is that 250,000 CD box sets will be sold in Europe alone," he said. By the end of the year the box set was Number One in the United States and Canada; Top Ten in England, West Germany, Australia, and Italy, and on the "Pan-European" chart.

But if America wasn't the only site of triumph for *Bruce Springsteen and the E Street Band Live/1975–1985*, it was the principal one. Saturation airplay ensured that. "It's Here: All-Bruce Radio," headlined *Billboard* the next week, and the facts backed up the hype. Some stations were airing all forty of the album's tracks; the *Album Network* tipsheet reported that of 1184 new playlist additions at its reporting stations, fully *half* were from the Springsteen album. Boston's leading music station, WBCN, said it was playing at least two cuts an hour; in Los Angeles KLOS program director Tom Kelly said, "We'll probably hold off to about ten cuts pretty soon." As Kid Leo, the veteran Bossmaniac who programmed Cleveland's WMMS, put it, "To call this a big deal is kind of badmouthing the event."

All this held up for several weeks. Over Thanksgiving weekend, Dallas stores reported that *Live* outsold the Number Two album (Bruce Hornsby's debut) by three to one. Radio stations tapered off their airplay, but when "War" was issued as the first single it was immediately added to almost eighty percent of the Top Forty (CHR) playlists in the country. Supported by an agonizingly powerful video directed by Arthur Rosato, which added a fictionalized intro and epilogue and interwove Bruce's rap with footage from Vietnam and Central America before letting the music speak for itself, "War" soon became Springsteen's eighth straight Top Ten hit.

Bruce Springsteen and the E Street Band Live/1975–1985 would become only the third album in the past three years to debut in *Billboard's* Top Ten. (The others also featured Springsteen: *Born in the U.S.A.* and *We Are the World*.) But something even more stunning happened: The album debuted on the chart at Number One, something that had happened with only three previous albums in history: Stevie Wonder's 1976 *Songs in the Key of Life* and two 1975 Elton John albums, *Captain Fantastic and the Brown Dirt Cowboy* and *Rock of the Westies*.

In the face of all this, the rich got richer. By the end of 1986 *Bruce Springsteen and the E Street Band Live/1975–1985* had sold about 3.5 million sets. *Time* estimated gross revenues at more than $450 million and guessed that Bruce's royalties were over $7.5 million for the first *week* of live set sales. Wild figures were tossed around, with people guessing that *Live* might sell as many units as *Born in the U.S.A.* Given the price barrier, that seemed pretty unlikely—not that the guaranteed reality of 4 to 5 million units sold was just your everyday hit record.

Bruce wasn't going to tour in support of the live box. He

posed for the cover of *Rolling Stone,* where the readers voted him
Artist of the Year for the third consecutive time, but he did no
accompanying interview, although he did do a television interview with the BBC's Hepworth for Europe. *Live* would spawn
more singles—"Fire," the second, was even accompanied by a
strange and funny video from the Bridge benefit—but it was out
there on its own now.

Bruce Springsteen was not. When MTV ran a Thanksgiving
weekend contest in which fifty CD boxes were given away (along
with the players to go with them), entrants had to call an AT&T
900 number. Knowing how Bruce might feel about that, MTV
proposed donating its end of the fifty cents per call to an
organization specified by Springsteen. He chose Chris Sprowal's
Committee for Dignity and Fairness for the Homeless, which
subsequently received more than $25,000, enabling the National
Union for the Homeless to organize in several additional cities
during a cruelly cold winter. Tour or no tour, Bruce Springsteen
still meant what he'd said to his Philadelphia fans: "The ideas
that I sing about in my songs these people put into action in real
life. Fifteen percent of the population in this country lives below
the poverty line, and for no good reason. It's gotten so we just
accept this as a fact of life—that some people are poor and will
stay poor—and that's not right."

Yet in some ways Bruce remained the loner. On his day of
maximum celebrity, with *Bruce Springsteen and the E Street Band
Live/1975–1985* as ubiquitous a presence as any record since
Abbey Road, Springsteen stepped off the most famous plane on
the planet, at the most famous airport in the world, and not one
paparazzo snapped his picture.

When Bruce reached Manhattan, he went up to Jon Landau's
office, expecting to pick up his copies of the album. They hadn't
arrived yet. So he went out for his first cheeseburger in a couple
of weeks, then took in a movie. In the midst of the mania, he was
able to walk public streets undisturbed.

Was it too much to think that he'd really beaten the system?
Not at all. Just as long as you understood that he hadn't done it
alone.

21 GLORY DAYS

Springsteen's idea of what a rock concert should be is fairly simple—it should be Christmas, something anticipated, slow-coming, cherished and festive.

—JOYCE MILLMAN

You can feel the show beginning to complete itself. Most nights that means careening through a veritable history of rock and roll—some basic Springsteen originals, a little Creedence, and a lot of rhythm and blues. All the numbers are present in their proper order tonight: "Bobby Jean" and "Ramrod," "Travellin' Band" and the inevitable medley of "Twist and Shout" and "Do You Love Me." But the feeling is different. There's no rush; it's as if the band and crowd are conspiring to set a pace that will keep this show on the brink of becoming a complete madhouse without ever letting it end.

The entire stadium is bathed in light now, enough light to televise a football game, and if you had binoculars and the inclination, you could count the smiles and the tears as parting looms inexorably closer. Warding off any unwanted sobriety is that perfect fool up on the stage. He's dancing in the light, wearing a blue cap backwards and a little boy grin, chasing his own tail now that he's brought this massive crowd as close together as it could possibly be. The step and the smile express many things, but not the thought that this night is the end of something. At most, Bruce Springsteen's bright face seems to promise, what's coming is only a pause in the action.

So it makes sense that, as the rhythm and blues medley dies down, he turns 'round and shouts to the band, "Hey, guys, I think we forgot one." The entire E Street Band and Jon Landau look at Bruce blankly; he's winging it now. But when he grinds out the opening chord of "Glory Days," they burst into grins and a moment later, when they pick up the signature sound of the song, so does the entire crowd.

They take the song at an almost ambling pace, as if they've just started playing and have all the time and energy in the world. Reaching the final chorus, Bruce begins to toy with the terrors of aging, as he always does. "I can hear that clock tickin' away," he shouts. "It says, 'Boss, you're thirty—thirty-one—thirty-two—thirty-three—thirty-four—thirty-five—thirty-six!" Reaching his actual age, he groans and flails even harder at his Fender.

But then his face brightens again and he looks to Clarence Clemons, standing at his right. "Big Man," he hollers, shaking his fist. "We're adults, man!"

"Right on," says the Big Man.

"We're *adults!*"

"Right on."

"Right on," says Bruce quite happily. "Let's dance."

SELECTED
BIBLIOGRAPHY

Articles

Alexander, Randy. "Springsteen Shows 'Em Who's the Boss in Philly." *Trenton Times*, 8/15/85.

——————. "Bruce's Kingdom Expands." *Trenton Times*, 8/16–18/85.

Arthur Baker interview. *Musician*.

Bailey, Brad. "Scalping the Boss: Transient Army Formed to Await Today's Sales of Springsteen Tickets." *Dallas Morning News*, 8/29/85.

Barol, Bill. "He's on Fire." *Newsweek*, 8/5/85.

Berman, Marshall. "Blowin' Away the Lies." *Village Voice*, 12/9/86.

Bernstein, Fred, Todd Gold and Dirk Mathison. "Bruce Bids Bye-Bye to His Bachelor Days." *People*, 5/27/85.

Bernstein, Margaret. "The Boss Gives Bonus: 5 Volumes of Live Music." *USA Today*, 9/11/86.

Blau, Eleanor. "Throngs Line Up Early for Springsteen Album." *New York Times*, 11/11/86.

"BOSSY! Springsteen Minders Fight Airport 'Mob.' " *Sun* (Sydney), 3/19/86.

Bradley, Bill. "He's New Jersey and He Is Ours." *USA Today*, 8/5/85.

Bream, Jon. "Bruce Springsteen: Rock & Roll Glory Days!" *Creem*, 1/85.

Breskin, David, and Cheryl McCall. "There Comes a Time When We Heed a Certain Call: United in a Song of Hope, America's Greatest Pop Stars Raise Their Voices to Help America's Hungry." *Life*, 4/85.

Brogan, Daniel. "The Boss Report." *Chicago Tribune*, 8/9/85.

Cara, Holly. "Gary U.S. Bonds Makes a Good Investment." *Goldmine*, 8/81.

Carson, Tom. "Nice Guy Finishes First." *Los Angeles Weekly*, 10/11–17/85.

Castro, Janice. "The Boss's Thunder Road to Riches." *Time*, 12/15/86.

Chollet, Laurence. "Rock's Voice of Responsibility." *Sunday Record* (New Jersey), 1/13/85.

Christgau, Robert. "Working the Crowd." *Village Voice*, 8/21/84.

──────────. "The Rise of the Corporate Single." *Village Voice*, 2/19/85.

Clerk, Carol. "Bruced Ego." *Melody Maker*, 7/13/85.

Clines, Francis X. "President Heaps Praise on Voters in the Northeast; Jersey and Conn Stops Show Buoyancy." *New York Times*, 9/20/84.

Cocks, Jay. "Against the American Grain." *Time*, 11/15/82.

──────────. " 'Round the World: A Boss Boom." *Time*, 8/26/85.

──────────. "There's Magic in the Night." *Time*, 11/10/86.

Collins, Marion. "Freehold's Claim to Fame." *New York Daily News*, 8/12/85.

──────────. "Old Friends, Mixed Feelings." *New York Daily News*, 8/12/85.

──────────. "He's Wealthy but He Doesn't Flaunt It." *New York Daily News*, 8/14/85.

──────────. "The House That Bruce Built." *New York Daily News*, 8/14/86.

──────────. "The Boss's Wife." *New York Daily News*, 8/11/85.

Connelly, Christopher. "Bruce Ends US Tour." *Rolling Stone*.

Cook, Richard. "Of E Street and Flip Side." *New Musical Express*, 6/15/85.

Corn, David. "The Boss' Other America." *In These Times* 9/28–10/1/85.

Dalton, Joseph. "My Hometown." *Rolling Stone*.

Delaney, Ted, and Ann Schrader. "Sunday Show Put Off; Boss Fans Cry 'Wimp.' " *Denver Post*, 9/23/85.

Devine, Jill. "Food Bank Receives $10,000 Gift from Rock Star Bruce Springsteen." *Pittsburgh Press*.

Diamond, Randy, and James Harney. " 'Hometown' Jobs Target of The Boss." *New York Daily News*, 12/5/85.

Doerschuk, Bob. "Roy Bittan: Rocking America with the Boss." *Keyboard*, 12/86.

Dowd, Maureen. "Why Are All the Politicians Watching Rock Video?" *New York Times*, 4/?/85.

Flanagan, Bill. "Hitting the High Hard One." *Musician*, 11/84.

──────────. "Nils Lofgren: Second That Emotion." *Musician*.

──────────. Review of *Bruce Springsteen & the E Street Band Live/1975– 1985*. *Musician*, 1/87.

Flippo, Chet. "Blue Collar Troubadour." *People*, 9/3/84.

──────────. "Bruce Springsteen, A Rock 'n' Roll Evangelist for Our Times Crusades for Patriotism and Puritanism of a Different Stripe." *Musician*, 11/84.

Fouratt, Jim. "Rock 'n' Ron—The President Moves on the Music." *Village Voice*, 10/30/84.

Freeman, Kim. "It's Here: All-Bruce Radio." *Billboard*, 11/22/86.

Fricke, David. "Bruce Looks Down the Long Road." *Rolling Stone*, 1/15/87.

Friedlich, Jim. "The Business of Bruce Booming for S.F. Firm." *San Francisco Chronicle*, 9/20/85.

Fusilli, Jim. "The Selling of Bruce Springsteen." *Wall Street Journal*, 7/2/84.

Gill, Andy, and Gavin Martin. "Marathon Man." *New Musical Express*, 6/15/85.

Gilmore, Mikal. "Springsteen's Neb: One from the Heartland." *Los Angeles Herald Examiner*, 9/24/82.

——————. "Springsteen on Life in the U.S.A." *Los Angeles Herald Examiner*, 6/1/84.

——————. "Star Spangled Rock 'n' Roll." *Los Angeles Herald Examiner*, 9/25/84.

——————. "Springsteen's Glory Days: Bruce Carries on His Rock 'n' Roll Mission in Los Angeles." *Los Angeles Herald Examiner*, 10/27/84.

——————. "Bruce Stages a Family Reunion." *Los Angeles Herald Examiner*, 8/7/85.

——————. "Springsteen's Born to Run, but His Tour Is Ending." *Los Angeles Herald Examiner*, 9/27/85.

——————. "Bruce's Goodbye." *Los Angeles Herald Examiner*, 10/?/85.

Gold, Todd. "Rock's Finest Hour." *People*, 5/25/85.

Goldberg, Michael. "USA for Africa: Record Could Raise Millions for Hungry. *Rolling Stone*, 3/14/85.

——————. "The Springsteen Christmas." *Rolling Stone*, 12/4/86.

——————. "Bruce Boosts Bridge Benefit." *Rolling Stone*, 11/20/86.

Golz, Earl, and Steven Edwards. "Bruce Springsteen's Hometown Keeps on Singing His Praises: Friends & Workers Back Rock Star's Stand Against Closing of Plant." *The Star* (tabloid), 12/24/85.

Goodman, Fred. "No Let Up in Columbia's Springsteen Push." *Billboard*, 7/6/85.

——————. "Bruce Springs Out of the Box." *Billboard*, 11/22/86.

Grein, Paul. "Plotkin in Springsteen's Shadow." *Billboard*, 8/4/84.

——————. "Bruce Does It: 'Live' Album Debuts at No. 1." *Billboard*, 11/29/86.

Hankin, Craig, and Ebersberger. "Max Weinberg: Q&A." *City Paper* (Baltimore), 9/7/84.

Harrington, Richard. "Bruuuuce! 'Live' and at His Best." *Washington Post*, 11/10/86.

Heilman, Elizabeth. "Jersey Jewel." *Town & Country*, 7/86.

Hilburn, Robert. "Steve Van Zandt Moves Out of Springsteen's Shadow." *Los Angeles Times Calendar*, 11/24/85.

——————. "Springsteen Wedding Is 'Private.' " *Los Angeles Times*, 5/14/85.

Hill, Dave. "History Man." *City Limits*, 6/28/–7/4/85.

Hinckley, David. "Hail to the Boss in D.C." *New York Daily News*, 8/6/85.

——————. "Glory Days." *New York Daily News*, 8/7/85.

——————. "Non-Glory Days." *New York Daily News*, 8/12/85.

——————. "Pizza & Privacy." *New York Daily News*, 8/14/85.

——————. "Why Now?" *New York Daily News*, 8/11/85.

Holden, Stephen. "Springsteen Scans the American Dream." *New York Times*.

——————. "Springsteen's 'Live/1975–1985' Is Loaded with History." *New York Times*, 11/9/86.

Hull, Robert. "Truth Justice and Fun: Springsteen's America." *Unicorn Times* (Virginia).

Isler, Scott. "Damaged Hands." *Musician*.

Japenga, Ann. "Ex-Steelworkers to Test Mettle as Playwrights." *Los Angeles Times*, 11/8/84.

——————. "Springsteen Pays a Visit to Union Hall." *Los Angeles Times*, 11/8/84.

King, Wayne. " 'It's a Real Human Experience': Bruce Springsteen and the Greatest Show on Earth." *Record*, 11/84.

" 'Lady Beth' Celebrates Worker." *Unifier* (NRFAC) No. 4, 12/86.

Levin, Eric. "The '57 Chevy of Rock 'n' Roll." *People*.

List, S. K. "Setting the Standard." *Ithaca Times*, 9/20–26/84.

——————. "Springsteen: Nobody Wins Unless Everybody Wins." *Ithaca Times*, 1/31–2/6/85.

Loder, Kurt. "The Rolling Stone Interview: Bruce Springsteen." *Rolling Stone*, 12/6/84.

——————. "Jingo Bells." *Rolling Stone Yearbook*, 1985.

——————. "Bruce!" *Rolling Stone*, 2/28/85.

——————, and Michael Goldberg. "Inside the USA for Africa Session." *Rolling Stone*, 3/28/85.

MacCambridge, Michael. "Springsteen Expected to Sell Through Roof, Despite High Price." *Variety*, 10/1/86.

McGee, David. "Little Steven on Main Street, U.S.A." *Record*, 9/84.

McLeese, Don. "Boss in D.C.: By Performing Before Huge Crowd, Springsteen Risks Losing Intimacy with Fans." *Chicago Sun-Times*, 8/7/85.

——————. "The Bruce Springsteen Interviews." *International Musician and Recording World*.

Magahern, Jimmy. "The Boss of Madison Avenue." *New Times* (Phoenix), 5/21/86.

Marcus, Greil. "Born in the USA" (*Nebraska* review). *New West*, 11/82.

——————. "Speaker to Speaker" column. *ArtForum*, 11/85.

——————. "Speaker to Speaker" column. *ArtForum*, 12/85.

——————. "In Your Heart You Know He's Right." *ArtForum*.

Martin, Gavin. "Bruce Digs Deep in Durham." *New Musical Express*, 6/22/85.

——————. "He Can Do Magic!" *New Musical Express*.

Miles, Milo. "Bossograph." *Boston Phoenix*, 11/18/86.

——————. "The Return of the Native: BS Brings It All Back Home." *Boston Phoenix*, 6/12/84.

——————. "Tour De Force: Sometimes More Is Less." *Boston Phoenix*, 9/3/85.

Mikesell, Tim. "Rock's Patriotic Prophet." *City Newspaper* (Rochester, New York), 10/4/84.

Miller, Jim. "The Wizards of Sound: The Secret Behind Many Musical Hits Is the Producer." *Newsweek*, 9/10/84.

Millman, Joyce. "Springsteen Comes to Your Hometown." *Boston Phoenix*, 9/11/84.

Mitchell, Jann. "The Woman Who Got Springsteen." *The Oregonian* (Portland, Oregon), 5/14/85.

Morris, Chris. "Glory Days, Glory Nights." *Los Angeles Reader*, 10/4/85.

Nelson, Paul. "Let Us Now Praise Famous Men" (review of *The River*). *Rolling Stone*, 12/11/80.

Nelson, Paul. "Bruce Springsteen's Nebraska." *Musician*.

Newfield, Jack. "Springsteen: A Spark Starting a Fire." *Voice*, 9/24/85.

————. "Stallone vs. Springsteen." *Playboy*, 4/85.

————. "Bruce Springsteen: Man with a Message." *ASCAP in Action*, spring 1986.

Obrecht, Jas, with Jeff Gay. "Nils Lofgren: A Cult Favorite Reaches Millions with Bruce Springsteen." *Guitar Player*, 12/85.

Palmer, Robert. "Bruce Springsteen Fashions a Compelling, Austere Message." *New York Times*, 9/26/82.

Pareles, Jon. "Bruce Springsteen's Mass Appeal." *New York Times*, 8/18/85.

Perry, Steve. (article) *In These Times*, 11/27–12/10/85.

————. (article) *Minnesota Daily*, 1/31–2/5/86.

————. "Rave On." *Buzz* (Minneapolis), 12/10/86.

Podhoretz, Norman. "The Boss Isn't a Reagan Rocker." News-America Syndicate (ran in *Los Angeles Times*, 8/29/85; *New York Post*, 8/27/85).

Pollock, Bruce. "Bruce Springsteen: Born to Run . . . Four More Years." *Guitar*, 12/84.

Pond, Steve. Review of *Nebraska*. *Rolling Stone*.

————. "Bruce's Live LP Battles Great Expectations." *Los Angeles Times Calendar*, 11/9/86.

"The Rambo of Rock and Roll." *Chicago Tribune* (editorial), 8/9/85.

Rea, Steven. "Springsteen Phone-In to Benefit Homeless." *Philadelphia Inquirer*, 11/14/86.

Richardson, Derk. (article) *After Dark, Bay Guardian*, 10/9/85.

Rizzo, Frank. "Greetings from Asbury Park—Born and Bred in Jersey: The Boss's Beginnings." *Hartford Courant*, 9/6/84.

Rose, Cynthia. "Banking on Food: Springsteen Inspires Donations of Time, Money." *Dallas Morning News*, 11/20/85.

————. "Old Glory Days." *New Musical Express*, 10/5/85.

Russell, Lisa. "Little Steven (Van Zandt) Says Goodbye to the Boss." *People*.

Santelli, Robert. "The Rise and Fall of the Asbury Park Music Empire." *Goldmine*, 10/81.

————. "Steve Van Zandt AKA Little Steven." *Goldmine*, 2/83.

Santoro, Gene. "Max Weinberg: The Boss's Backbeat." *Downbeat*, 7/86.

Schipper, Henry. "Springsteen Fever Seizes Dealers as His New Live Set Hits Street." *Variety*, 11/12/86.

Scoppa, Bud, and Don Perretta. "Nils Lofgren: Boss Guitarist Bounces from Cultville to E Street." *Music Connection*, 9/30–10/13/85.

Schruers, Fred. "The Boss Is Back." *Rolling Stone*, 11/27/80.

Sexton, Adam. "Bruce Springsteen: His Back Pages." *Boston Phoenix*, 4/1/86.

Silberman, Jeff, and Bill Forman. "Springsteen Fights for America's Hometowns." *BAM*, 11/16/84.

Simmons, Russ. "Houston Radio Station Has Springsteen Fans Going." *Performance*, 12/28/84.

Smith, Russell. "Bruce Comes Through." *Dallas Morning News*, 9/17/85.

Sonnenschein, Allan. "The Big Man." *Penthouse*, 6/86.

"Springsteen Calls Sun City Song Great Rock Record." Reuters wire story, 10/24/85.

"Springsteen Demand Jams D.C. Phone Lines; Concert Sells Out Fast." *Variety*, 7/24/85.

"Springsteen's New Album Born to Sell Out Quickly." *Wall Street Journal*, 11/11/86.

Strother, Shelby. "Springsteen: A Guy Who Comes to Play." *Detroit News*, 9/5/85.

Sumrall, Harry. "Young Has a Few Friends Over to Play." *San Jose Mercury News*, 10/9/86.

Suzy. "Bruce Will 'I Do' Again." *New York Daily News*, 5/15/85.

Swartley, Ariel. "The Loneliness of the Long-Distance Driver." *Boston Phoenix*, ca. 1982.

Takiff, Jonathan. "Springsteen in Studio While World Wonders." Knight-Ridder News Service, 9/11/86.

Tucker, Ken. Review. *Philadelphia Inquirer*, 11/7/85.

——————. "Springsteen: Beyond the Music, A Challenge to Better the USA." *Philadelphia Inquirer*, 8/16/85.

——————. "Live Offering by the Boss Arrives Today." *Philadelphia Inquirer*, 11/10/86.

"Wedding Bells for 'The Boss.' " *Chicago Sun-Times* (editorial), 5/16/85.

Will, George. "A Yankee-Doodle Springsteen." *New York Daily News*, 9/13/84.

Wolcott, James. "The Hagiography of Bruce Springsteen." *Vanity Fair*, 12/85.

Zuckerman, Steve. "The E Street Band Warms Up—and Heats Up Asbury Park." *Rock*.

Magazines

Backstreets #8

Backstreets #9

Backstreets, Vol. 3, #2 (summer 1984)

Backstreets, Vol. 4, #1 (spring 1985)

Backstreets, Vol. 4, #2

Backstreets, Vol. 4, #3

Backstreets, spring 1986

Backstreets, #19 (winter 1987)

Bruceness: The E Street Press #1, 9/81
Bruceness: The E Street Press #2, 6/83
Candy's Room #2 (winter/spring 1981)
Candy's Room #3 (summer/autumn 1981)
The Fever #1 (September 1981)
The Fever #2 (May 1982)
The Fever #3 (spring 1983)
The Fever #4 (April 1984)
Point Blank, September 1980
Point Blank #3 (spring 1981)
Point Blank #4 (undated, circa 9/81)
Reason to Believe #1 (undated, circa spring 1986) (France)
Rock Scene Spotlights Bruce Springsteen
StarBlitz 11—Unofficially Springsteen (United Kingdom)
Thunder Road #6–7 (undated final issue—double)
Voice of America #1 (December 1985)

Books

Gambaccini, Peter. *Bruce Springsteen*. Perigee/Delilah, 1979, 1985.

Hilburn, Robert. *Springsteen*. Rolling Stone Press/Scribner's, 1985.

Humphries, Patrick, and Chris Hunt. *Springsteen: Blinded by the Light*. Plexus (London), 1985.

Kamin, Philip, and Peter Goddard. *Springsteen Live*. Beaufort, 1984.

Lynch, Kate. *Springsteen: No Surrender*. Proteus, 1984.

Meyer, Marianne. *Bruce Springsteen*. Ballantine, 1984.

Montana, Tony. *The Bruce Springsteen Bootleg Bible*. Montana Production, 1985.

St. Pierre, Roger. *Bruce Springsteen: An Independent Story in Words and Pictures*. Anabas Look Book Series (UK), 1985.

Slaughter, Mike. *Bruce Springsteen, An American Classic*. Proteus/Cherry Lane, 1984.

Sweeting, Adam. *Springsteen: Visions of America*. Holborn Group (London), 1985.

INDEX